THE PROGRESS OF
WORLD-WIDE MISSIONS

Rev. ROBERT H. GLOVER, M.D., F.R.G.S.

THE PROGRESS OF
WORLD-WIDE MISSIONS

BY

Rev. ROBERT HALL GLOVER, M.D., F.R.G.S.

Missionary in China for Eighteen Years; Foreign Missions
Secretary for Eight Years; Director of Missionary
Course in the Moody Bible Institute of Chicago
for Five Years; Now Home Director for
North America of the China Inland
Mission

INTRODUCTION BY
DELAVAN L. PIERSON
EDITOR OF *The Missionary Review of the World*

FOURTH EDITION WITH MAPS

HARPER & BROTHERS PUBLISHERS
NEW YORK   LONDON

THE PROGRESS OF WORLD-WIDE MISSIONS
— B —
PRINTED IN THE UNITED STATES OF AMERICA

"The night lies dark upon the earth, and *we* have light;
So many have to grope their way, and *we* have sight;
One path is theirs and ours—of sin and care,
But *we* are borne along, and *they* their burden bear;
Footsore, heart-weary, faint *they* on the way,
Mute in their sorrow, while *we* kneel and pray;
Glad are *they* of a stone on which to rest,
While *we* lie pillowed on the Father's breast.

"Father, why is it that these millions roam,
And *guess* that that is Home, and urge their way?
Is it enough to keep the door ajar,
In hope that some may see the gleam afar,
And guess that that is Home, and urge their way
To reach it, haply, somehow and some day?
May not *I* go, and lend them of *my* light?
May not *mine* eyes be unto them for sight?
May not the brother-love *Thy* love portray?
And news of Home make Home less far away?"

—Rev. R. Wright Hay

BY WAY OF INTRODUCTION

The story of the world-wide progress of Christian missions is more wonderful than are tales of Oriental magic. It is almost unbelievable that a little group of obscure men and women, belonging to a small and subject people in an insignificant land on the shore of the Mediterranean, could, without military forces, prestige, money or elaborate organization, grow until they have enlisted in their ranks one-third of the earth's population. It is still more wonderful that this little band were the followers of a despised, rejected and condemned Leader, who left with them only the inspiration of His life and teachings, the command to go and to preach His message and the promise of His power and presence.

The story of the carrying out of this commission includes the exploration of unknown and hostile territory, the mastery of thousands of strange languages and dialects, the conversion of many primitive and savage peoples, the building of hospitals for the ministry of healing for both body and soul, the establishment of thousands of schools in all quarters of the globe for the education of mind and heart, and the development of natural resources and of industries for the temporal welfare of men. This is the story of a victorious conflict against slavery, superstition, idolatry, drunkenness and all forms of personal and social sins; the story of the marvelous metamorphosis of individuals from savagery to sainthood, and the transformation of whole communities from a menace into a blessing to mankind.

All material and human forces have been commandeered and made to contribute to these results, but the work has been accomplished, not through physical might or human intelligence and energy, but by the spiritual power given to the messengers of the crucified and risen Redeemer. It is no wonder, therefore, that even a brief study of "The Progress of World-wide Missions" should be full of fascination as a record of God's work in the world. This study suggests many inviting by-paths for further investigation.

Few men are better qualified to record this history of Christian missions than is the author of the present volume. Dr. Glover has an international background. He was born and educated in Canada; has lived much of his life in the United States; was, for eighteen years, a missionary in China; traveled over one hundred thousand miles in foreign lands visiting missions in Japan, Korea, the Philippines, Indo-China, India, Africa, the Near East and Latin America. He has had experience both as a home and a foreign missionary, as a missionary executive, teacher and lecturer, so that he has obtained both a theoretical and practical understanding of missions and their problems. His medical and theological training have combined to give him a comprehensive knowledge of God as revealed in nature, in history and in the Bible.

As might be expected, Dr. Glover has given us a valuable compendium of Christian missions, packed full of interesting and important information which might have been expanded into a series of volumes. But there is here much more than a skeleton of dry bones. There is human flesh and blood and the Divine Spirit that gives life and power. The book reveals an intelligent and confident faith in the authority of the Scriptures and in the efficacy of the salvation provided by Jesus Christ, the Eternal Son of God.

Those who read and study this volume will find here missionary history recorded and interpreted as "His Story," and will be inspired with a desire to have a larger part in helping to carry out the program of God for the redemption of mankind.

DELAVAN L. PIERSON.

PREFACE

The author did not set out to write a book. The present volume has grown out of outline studies prepared for his own classes in Missions. He has yielded to the repeated requests of his students, and of others who shared the studies in pamphlet form, that they might be made more widely available in permanent book form.

The volume makes no pretense of furnishing a complete account of Christian Missions. It merely attempts to sketch in simple outline the development and extension of the missionary enterprise from apostolic times to the present day, with emphasis upon some of the events and characters of outstanding importance and inspiration. It is designed primarily as a textbook for use in institutions and mission study groups, where the object sought is some familiarity with the missionary enterprise in general, without particular reference to any one section of the Church. But it has been the author's aim to give to the book a popular rather than a technical tone, as to its subject matter and style, and thus to make it adaptable and interesting to the individual reader as well.

Book references at the foot of the page and a condensed Bibliography at the end of the book are given to facilitate further research. Questions for review are appended to each chapter, and outline maps are inserted to aid the student in following the geographical expansion of Missions as traced in the successive chapters.

The question of the place statistics should occupy has caused some perplexity, because of the desire on the one hand to satisfy those who seek concrete and detailed information, and the fear on the other hand of making the book heavy with a lot of dry figures and tables. The aim has been to strike a happy medium in this matter.

A uniform summary of mission statistics at the end of each chapter was at first planned, but this was later felt to be unsatisfactory because of the fact that the statistics available for the different fields are far from uniform, whether in their classification, their date or their interpretation. The latest complete figures, contained in *World Statistics of Christian Missions,* published in 1916, are already in many instances far from accurate because of the marked development of the work as well as the drastic world changes which have taken place since they were compiled.

In the case of such fields as India, China and Japan, which publish Year Books of their own, brief up-to-date statistical summaries have been given, but in other cases, like Africa and Latin America, where many separate fields are involved, this has been found impracticable.

General figures such as areas, populations, etc., are based upon the latest edition of the *Statesman's Year Book* (1923), except where data from more direct sources may have been available. Round numbers have frequently been substituted for exact ones as being easier to remember.

As regards the geographical scope of the book, obviously some limits have had to be imposed. No attempt, therefore, has been made to deal with the great field for evangelical missions in European countries to-day, nor yet with the work among Indians, immigrants and other special classes in the United States and Canada. The Arctic regions, comprising Alaska, Hudson Bay, Labrador and Greenland, have been omitted because these areas have been already largely evangelized, and the task which remains within them is in the hands of the home churches of America and Denmark. For the same reason Australia and New Zealand have not been included in the chapter on Oceania, since the evangelization of the diminishing remnants of the aborigines of Australia and the Maoris of New Zealand is now being cared for by the various churches of those lands. All the above areas and constituencies fall more properly under the head of Home Missions, and together they furnish ample material for a separate volume.

It is hardly necessary to state that much of the material incorporated in the present volume has been drawn from other books, of which the number consulted must have reached to many hundreds. Wherever quotations have been made acknowledgment is given in footnotes.

The author's heartfelt thanks are due in particular, and are here tendered, to two esteemed friends—to Mr. Delavan L. Pierson, Editor of *The Missionary Review of the World*, who has painstakingly read through the manuscript, made corrections and given valuable counsel, and to Rev. J. E. Jaderquist of New York, who by his sympathy, suggestions and practical help in a number of ways has contributed no little to the task of preparing the volume for publication.

If the Lord may be pleased to use this book in some measure to deepen missionary conviction and quicken the pulse of missionary effort, in this strategic hour of unprecedented missionary opportunity combined with vast missionary need still existing, the author will be profoundly grateful.

ROBERT H. GLOVER.

Chicago, February, 1924.

PREFACE TO FOURTH EDITION

Since the first publication of this book in 1924, two revised editions have been prepared and issued, in 1925 and 1931 respectively, in order to keep abreast of the developments and changes which have taken place in the missionary world. For some time now inquiries have been coming in as to the prospect of a fresh revision, these being more especially from some of the many Bible institutes, seminaries, and other educational institutions where the book has been adopted as a text. The author has been keenly conscious of the desirability of once more bringing the volume up to date, for in an enterprise of such vitality as Christian Missions an interval of even a few years inevitably witnesses substantial growth and expansion, while at the same time the march of world events brings external changes of many kinds which have their practical bearing upon the work of missions.

But while the need for a new edition of the book has been fully recognized, and the desire to produce it has not been wanting, the problem has been how to accomplish the matter. There was first of all the difficulty of finding time for such a task in the midst of other and pressing duties which seemed to claim all of one's time and strength, so that what has now been effected in the way of revision has meant overtime labor and no little strain.

But an even more serious difficulty has been the abnormal and uncertain world conditions prevailing during the past two or three years, which have intimately affected missionary operations and outlook in a number of fields, and have made it practically impossible to appraise the present situation or forecast future conditions of work accurately. One would naturally desire, for instance, to revise or supplement the sections of the book dealing with such fields as Abyssinia, China, and Japan, in the light of what has been transpiring in those countries, but the situation is yet much too uncertain to do so with any safety or satisfaction. While the present highly strained relations among the European powers persist, threatening the possibility of the outbreak of another world war at any moment, and while the cruel Sino-Japanese conflict continues, with its tremendous consequences to the nations of the Far East, and also its vital bearing upon relations between those nations and the western lands from which the missionary forces laboring within them have come, it will readily be seen that to venture beyond the actual record to date of mission activities in the fields involved would be inopportune and profitless. The facts already recorded in this volume remain true, but what must yet be added no one can at present presume to say.

This last remark applies no less to the closing chapter of the book, entitled *The Present Missionary Outlook*. Serious thought has been given as to whether it should be rewritten, or altered so as to include reference to the present distressing events and conditions in the world which are causing such grave concern, and which obviously have a vital relation to the present work and future prospects of missions. But the conclusion reached was that this would be venturing too far at present, and that the wiser course is to let the chapter remain as it stands, expressing as it does certain broad facts and features which are still true and pertinent, and leaving anything more until the present international situation resolves itself into some more definite shape.

Accordingly the author has felt constrained to confine the present revision of the book to such new facts and figures as represent the progress of mission work in the various fields from the date of the last revision (1931) down to the present, aside from any discussion of present international happenings and relations. These fresh facts and figures as related to the last eight years of mission work throughout the world are in themselves of no small import, for perhaps no eight-year period in missions has ever seen more marked development in the work in hand or greater advance afield than this period can record.

Fortunately fresh compilations of missionary facts and figures are available just now, particularly through the publication by the International Missionary Council in 1938 of a new and comprehensive volume entitled *Interpretative Statistical Survey of the World Mission of the Christian Church,* and also the various reports and findings of the last World Conference on missions held at Madras, India, in December last. With these valuable sources of latest information to draw from, as well as much other up-to-date material which has been consulted, the entire text has been thoroughly scrutinized, a large number of statistical changes have been made, and many paragraphs—at a few points whole pages—have been rewritten in keeping with new events and developments that have taken place.

It has been gratifying to find in this latest Survey of missions just mentioned additional statistical summaries for Africa as a whole, as well as the several main divisions of Latin America, for such figures have been lacking in previous surveys. These new summaries have been inserted, and also (on p. 371) an added table giving the ratio of missionaries to population in the different major mission fields.

Careful attention has been given to the revision of the bibliography, and some eighty of the most valuable recent missionary books have been added, while a much smaller number of older titles has been dropped. The list of reference books has thus been appreciably enlarged and enriched.

The author would again express grateful appreciation of the generous help given by Miss Hollis W. Hering, M.A., Librarian of the Missionary Research Library, New York City, in the examination and selection of the new books as well as in checking statistics and other data.

For the continued acceptance this volume finds with Christian institutions and mission study groups, as well as with individual readers, and for the extension of its ministry to such lands as Korea, China, and France through translations for which permission has been asked and heartily granted, the author gives humble thanks to God. That it may still contribute in some small way to carrying out more effectively and speedily our Lord's will and command for the world's complete evangelization shall be his constant prayer.

R. H. G.

Philadelphia, August, 1939.

CONTENTS

PART I: Rise and Development

CONTENTS

MAPS

PERIODS OF CHRISTIAN MISSIONS

For convenience of study the history of Christian Missions may be divided into the following periods:—

I. Period of Apostolic Missions. 1st Century.
   From the Ascension of Christ to the Death of John (33-100).

II. Period of Early Church Missions. 2nd and 3rd Centuries.
    From the Death of John to Constantine (100-313).

III. Period of Early European Missions. 4th to 8th Centuries.
    From Constantine to Charlemagne (313-800).

IV. Period of the Middle Ages. 9th to 15th Centuries.
    From Charlemagne to Luther (800-1517).

V. Period of the Reformation. 16th and 17th Centuries.
    From Luther to the Halle Missionaries (1517-1650).

VI. Period of the Early Missionary Societies. 18th Century.
    From the Halle Missionaries to Carey (1650-1792).

VII. Period of Modern Missions. 19th and 20th Centuries.
    From Carey to the Present Day (1792-   ).

PART I: Rise and Development

THE PROGRESS OF WORLD-WIDE MISSIONS

CHAPTER I

INTRODUCTORY

Christian Missions Defined.

To the question "What is meant by 'Christian Missions'?" various answers might be given. The following definition is quoted as being at once simple and clear:

"Christian Missions" is the Proclamation of the Gospel to the Unconverted Everywhere According to the Command of Christ.

"Missions" comes from the Latin *mitto*—"I send." A missionary is therefore a "sent one." "Apostle," from the Greek *apostello*—"I send," is a synonym for missionary, and the latter and more familiar word may be substituted for the former throughout the New Testament without altering the sense. For example, the fifth book of the New Testament may be called "The Acts of the Missionaries." The term "missions" implies three essential factors, viz., a sender, one sent, one to whom sent.

Jesus Himself was the great missionary. He constantly spoke of Himself as the Messenger sent by the Father to a lost world. And He said, "As my Father hath sent me, even so send I you" (John 20:21).

The missionary does not go or speak at his own initiative, but as the commissioned agent of the One who sent him. And the more absolutely he represents Him, and the more intelligently and faithfully he conveys His message, the more perfectly does he fulfill his missionary calling.

"Proclamation" carries the idea of publicity and also of authority. The missionary's message is no private or com-

monplace matter to be whispered in the ear, but an official declaration of supreme authority and universal import, to be sounded forth in clarion notes. The missionary is to "cry aloud and spare not."

"Gospel" means "good tidings." The very name "gospel" indicates its missionary nature, for "tidings" can be tidings only to those who are ignorant of them, and they can be "good" tidings only to those who hear them. It is therefore the very essence of the gospel (good tidings) that it be proclaimed to all men.

"Unconverted" means "not turned to"—Christ, and hence signifies a lost condition. Cf. Ezek. 33 : 11—"Turn ye, turn ye; for why will ye die?" The term embraces equally those who through wilfulness reject the gospel, those who through indifference neglect it, and those who through ignorance do not know it—that is, *all men everywhere*. The terms "home" and "foreign," commonly applied to missions, are not scriptural, they are merely human terms of convenience. "Unconverted" men are lost—in America, Africa or Asia alike. Whether the sinner is such through inexcusable wilfulness or through unfortunate ignorance, his condition is alike one of peril, and his only hope is in turning to Christ.

"According to the Command of Christ." The missionary enterprise rests upon His command and commission for its authority. Christ did not merely express a wish or offer a suggestion. He gave an order, clear, explicit, peremptory —"GO YE into all the world and preach the gospel to every creature." Such is His final, most imperative, most inclusive command, and it is binding upon His followers everywhere and for all time.

Missionary Motives.

Having defined Christian Missions, it naturally follows to consider what have been and what should still be the principal motives to missionary effort. What considerations mainly prompted the first apostles, the early church, and the long succession of noble men and women who all through the ensuing years have toiled and sacrificed and hazarded their lives in the missionary enterprise? And what are the motives that should actuate Christians to-day to similar service and sacrifice?

These motives may be divided into two classes :—

1. *Motives Based upon External Facts,* or, *Motives which Spring from a Consideration of the Condition of the Heathen.*

(a) *Their Temporal Condition.* Even on mere philanthropic grounds the needs and claims of missionary lands have always been, and still are, tremendous. Their dire poverty, wretched homes, unremitting toil, gross intellectual ignorance, unrelieved physical sufferings, and the utter absence of a thousand features which brighten and bless the homes and communities of Christian lands—all this is a mute and pathetic appeal for help.

(b) *Their Moral Condition.* Heathen lands reek with filthy and degrading habits, abominable practices, unmentionable cruelties and crimes, and every form of moral corruption freely tolerated and indulged. Slavery, witchcraft, caste, polygamy and the like furnish notorious illustrations of these things. They call insistently for correction.

(c) *Their Spiritual Condition.* This constitutes a paramount claim, far outweighing the previous two. The heathen are not only temporally unfortunate and morally depraved; they are also spiritually lost, for they are wicked and wilful sinners. They are not living up to the light of their own consciences, indeed few of them profess to be.

Scripture describes the heathen as "having their understanding darkened, being alienated from the life of God" (Eph. 4:17-19); "enemies (of God) by wicked works" (Col. 1:21); "children of disobedience" (Eph. 2:2; 5:6); "children of wrath" (Eph. 2:3); "without Christ, having no hope, and without God in the world" (Eph. 2:12).

Scripture likewise unfolds God's mode of dealing with all men on the sin question. It declares that "the wages of sin is death" (Rom. 6:23); that "the wicked shall be turned into hell, and all the nations that forget God" (Psa. 9:17); that "the fearful, and the unbelieving, and the abominable, and murderers, and whoremongers, and sorcerers, and idolaters, and all liars, shall have their part in the lake which burneth with fire and brimstone" (Rev. 21:8); that the only hope of escape is through Christ, for "neither is there salvation in any other" (Acts 4:12).

The basis of God's judicial dealing with all classes of

mankind is most clearly set forth in the Epistle to the Romans. In Chapter I, directly following the Apostle's great statement of missionary obligation and the power of the gospel (vv. 14-17), we find a terrific indictment of the heathen world and an appalling picture of its spiritual wickedness and moral filthiness. The heathen are declared to be without excuse as to their idolatrous rites and abominable practices, because of the measure of light which God has given them, even apart from the gospel, through nature and conscience (vv. 19, 20). In Chapter II the cases of the self-righteous Gentile moralist and Jewish legalist are taken up, and their guilt is shown to be aggravated by reason of their added light and privilege. The absolute fairness of God's judgment of all men, whether the heathen under conscience, the Jew under law, or the hearer of the gospel under grace, is made clear (vv. 6, 12, 14, 15). In Chapter III the argument leads on to a final verdict of guilt against the whole human race (vv. 2, 9-12), culminating with the words, "that every mouth may be stopped, and all the world may become guilty before God" (v. 19).

The world's guilt and need thus established, the Apostle thereupon proceeds at once to introduce God's great plan of salvation through faith in Jesus Christ. When Chapter X is reached, a clear and beautiful summary is given of the equality before God of Jew and Gentile, and of His abounding grace toward all alike, so that "whosoever shall call upon the name of the Lord shall be saved" (vv. 12, 13). But immediately afterwards come those convicting words: *"How* then shall they call on him in whom they have not believed? and how shall they believe in him of whom they have not heard? and *how* shall they hear without a preacher? and *how* shall they preach, except they be sent?" (vv. 14, 15). *How? How? How? How?*—unanswerable questions these, constituting one of the most convincing arguments for missions! What solemn responsibility do they lay upon all those who hold the only remedy for the condemning sin of the heathen world!

Acts 10:34-35 is sometimes cited as proof that the heathen can be saved without the gospel. But the very incident with which the text is connected defeats any such argument. For Cornelius was "accepted" of God only as an approved candidate for fuller light, and it was through the gospel message preached by Peter that he and his family were finally saved.[1]

2. *Motives Based upon Internal Experience, or, Motives which Spring from a Consideration of Jesus Christ and Our Relation to Him.*

(a) *Loyalty*—the loyalty of servants to their master, of soldiers to their captain, of subjects to their sovereign. And this not in a mere slavish or legal sense, but with whole-hearted allegiance and a supreme desire for the exaltation of Christ. This motive was uppermost in the apostles and the early church. Jesus Christ, who claimed to be the Son of God and the Saviour of men, had been despised and rejected, shamefully treated and crucified as a condemned criminal. His claims must be vindicated, His honor defended, the beauty and holiness of His character and the divinity of His person and work displayed. He must be recognized, be accepted, be loved and enthroned in the hearts of men as Saviour and Lord. To this end all their preaching and efforts were directed (Acts 2:22-24, 32, 36; 3:6, 13-16; 4:10-12, 26-30).

This should be no less potent a missionary motive to-day, for Jesus Christ is still despised and hated both by multitudes in nominally Christian lands and by millions under the sway of Satan and his wicked spirits in heathen lands. Having made complete atonement for sin, Christ "sat down on the right hand of God, from henceforth expecting till his enemies be made his footstool." How long His expectation has remained unfulfilled! Much is rightly said of the boon that the Lord's Coming will be to Christians and to all suffering humanity, as well as to "the whole creation which groaneth and travaileth in pain." But all too little is said or thought of what it will mean to Himself, who so long has waited to "see of the travail of his soul and be satisfied." Loyalty to Christ, then, and a jealous passion for His exaltation, should be the first compelling motive of missions.

[1] Limits of space forbid fuller discussion here of this solemn subject, but those who experience difficulty in reconciling the condemnation of the heathen with divine justice and love will find a most helpful treatment of the subject in Dr. Dennis' "Foreign Missions After a Century," pp. 202-214.

(b) *Gratitude*—for His infinite grace and countless blessings received. Why was I not a heathen, a deluded idolater or demon worshiper? Why was I born in a gospel-lighted land, with Christian parents and churches and an open Bible, and countless uplifting influences? Is there any *inherent* difference between me and a poor pagan in Africa or India? No, the difference is all due to the grace of God. All I am and all I have I owe to Him. And unless I am a base ingrate, I shall measure my responsibility to less favored souls by my own blessings and privileges in Christ. Remembering that in the sovereign arrangement of God the positions of the heathen and myself might have been interchanged, I should resolve to do as much for them as I should wish and expect them to do for me if they were where I am and I where they are.

(c) *Love*—for Him who died for us, and His love within us for all for whom He died. This is the supreme motive. It embraces loyalty and gratitude, but transcends them both. It is God's own and only motive. "God so LOVED the world that he gave his only begotten Son." "Christ LOVED the church and gave Himself for it." "Hereby perceive we the LOVE OF GOD, because he laid down his life for us; and *we ought to lay down our lives for the brethren.*" "If ye LOVE me, ye will keep my commandments." "LOVEST thou me? Feed my sheep." Love does not merely regard the command, but cherishes the wish behind it. Love is not measured and calculating, but reckless, prodigal. It counts no service too long, no sacrifice too great. Such love has burned like a holy fire in the hearts of missionaries of all ages.

"To Thee, O Lord, I offer myself, my wife, my children, and all that I possess."—RAYMOND LULL.

"I have one passion; it is He and He alone."—ZINZENDORF.

"I wanted to wear out my life in His service, for His glory. I rejoiced in my necessity of self-denial. I cared not where or how I lived or what hardships I went through, so that I could but gain souls for Christ."—DAVID BRAINERD.

Only divine love filling the heart and pervading the life is equal to the tests and demands of true missionary service to-day.

The Missionary Idea in the Old Testament.

It should not be overlooked that while Christian Missions properly begin only with the New Testament, yet the missionary idea is found all through the Old Testament. The Bible from cover to cover is a missionary book. From the very beginning God revealed His plan and purpose as a world-wide one. He said to Adam, "Be fruitful, and multiply and *replenish the earth*" (Gen. 1:28), indicating a world-wide design for Adam's race. The same charge, identically, was repeated when the race was given a new start under Noah (Gen. 9:1). *Diffusion* was God's thought. Strange indeed, then, yet true, that the history of men, God's creatures, has been one long persistent effort, either ignorantly or wilfully, to evade or thwart this purpose.

As early as Genesis IV we detect this in the worldly family of Cain, who "builded a city and called it after the name of his son." Then in Gen. 11:1-9 we find a people not aiming, as God would have them, to reach the ends of the earth, but saying, "Go to now, let us build *us* a city and a tower whose top may reach unto heaven, and let us make *us* a name *lest* we be scattered abroad upon the face of the whole earth." The very thing God wanted was the thing they set to work explicitly to defeat. And more than this. For already it was God's purpose, although not yet revealed, to make the human race a means to the exaltation of His Son, that *His* name should be "above every name, that at the name of Jesus every knee should bow—" (Phil. 2:9-11). But *they* said, "Let us make *us* a name." Does not this same spirit of self-love and self-glory still dominate the nations of the world, even those that are nominally Christian, whose chief ambition and whose strenuous effort is not to bring about the universal kingdom of Christ, but rather their own dominion and glory? And so God had to interpose, confound their language and upset their ambitious plans. We read, "So the Lord scattered them abroad from thence *upon the face of the whole earth;* and they left off to build the city."

Next, God chose Abraham and the Jewish people, not to lavish upon them an exclusive love, but with the world-wide purpose, expressed in His own words, that "in thee shall *all the families of the earth* be blessed" (Gen. 12:3; also repeated to Abraham, 22: 17, 18; to Isaac, 26: 2-4; and to Jacob, 28: 12-14). But the Jews stumbled at the divine purpose and selfishly misappropriated His blessings to themselves. Consequently God had to lay that nation aside for the time as a failure.

Suggestions of the world-wide reach of God's plan of grace and striking examples of missionary spirit and effort are not wanting all through the Old Testament. Abraham begins the long procession of missionaries which has covered four thousand years of time. His divine call (Gen. 12: 1) still furnishes a worthy model for that of every modern missionary, while his later discharge of active missionary functions in relation to the raid of Chedorlaomer (Gen. 14: 1-16) and sinful heathen Sodom (Gen. 18: 22-33) are fine examples of love and zeal.

Joseph was indeed a God-sent missionary to Egypt and the adjoining countries of his day.

Esther is another beautiful missionary type. Identified by nature with a condemned race, but elevated by grace to a place of royal favor, she rightly interprets her position of privilege as meant not for her own selfish gratification, but as a God-given opportunity to help her afflicted people. And so, with noble self-renunciation and courage she flings herself into the breach, and at the risk of her own life rescues a whole nation from impending doom.

The story of Jonah is a fine illustration of God's concern for the heathen, and His patience in leading them to repentance. It also gives us an example of a runaway missionary —an example which it is to be feared has been followed all too often since. Yet Jonah was finally a successful missionary, as the results proved.

The missionary aim and spirit pervade such Psalms as the 2nd, 67th, 72nd and others, and the same world-wide outlook is to be found throughout the prophets, even where the central message relates to Israel. (Compare such passages as Isa. 45: 22; 52: 10; 55: 5; 56: 6, 7; Jer. 16: 19; Zech. 9: 10; Mal. 1: 11.) Some of the messages of Isaiah and Amos reached out beyond Israel, while Jeremiah's main "burden" was concerning the Gentiles. The Jews of the Captivity and the Dispersion, headed by the royal Daniel himself, were theistic missionaries to the East, as well as

Southern Europe and Northern Africa, down to the time of
Christ.

Beautifully suggestive of the breadth of God's sovereign
grace is His placing of Rahab and Ruth, both originally
heathen women, in the covenant line of which Christ came.
The same spirit breathes in the prayer with which Solomon,
the type of Christ in His glorious coming kingdom, dedicated the temple, making request on behalf of "a stranger
that is not of thy people Israel, when he shall come out of
a far country for thy name's sake." "Hear thou in heaven,
thy dwelling place, and do according to all that the stranger
calleth to thee for; that *all peoples of the earth* shall know
thy name to fear thee" (1 Kings 8: 41, 43). And the divine
response was, "I have heard thy prayer and thy supplica-
tion that thou hast made before me" (1 Kings 9: 3).

By such landmarks is God's missionary design distinctly
traceable throughout the Old Testament.

QUESTIONS

1. Give a satisfactory definition of Christian Missions.
2. What is the significance of the words "missions," "proclamation," "gospel" and "unconverted" in this definition?
3. Into what two classes may missionary motives be divided?
4. Give three motives under each of these two heads.
5. Give Scripture texts and teaching upon the spiritual condition
of the heathen and God's dealing with them.
6. Trace God's world-wide plan through the Old Testament—
e.g., in Genesis, the Psalms, and the Prophets.
7. Mention five prominent missionary characters in the Old
Testament.

CHAPTER II

PERIOD OF APOSTOLIC MISSIONS

FROM THE ASCENSION OF CHRIST TO THE DEATH OF JOHN (33-100)

Christian Missions, in the strict sense of the term, began with the return of the disciples to Jerusalem from the Mount of Ascension. But the earthly ministry of Jesus is by common consent included in the Apostolic Period, as being not only in itself preëminently missionary but also fundamental to the whole subject and enterprise.

Excellent books, such as Latham's "Pastor Pastorum" and Bruce's "Training of the Twelve," have traced in the course which Christ's earthly life and labors took the distinctive design of schooling His disciples for their future work. And it is but an easy step farther to conceive of His aim as reaching out beyond the narrow circle of His immediate followers to the larger company of His appointed laborers in every succeeding age. For these His life constitutes not only an abiding inspiration but, as well, a permanent model of service. The same may consistently be said of the record of the apostles, inasmuch as it is continually reiterated that they were filled and controlled by the Holy Spirit in their utterances, counsels and operations. God evidently intended the inspired record of the first generation of missionary activity to be a sample for every succeeding one. Without therefore disparaging the cry in some quarters for more books on the science of missions, and while fully recognizing the value of collations of opinion and experience, is it not still true that altogether the best, the safest, the most practical textbook on missionary principles and practice for all time is the New Testament? This applies even to methods as well, since in their broad scope they also remain

30

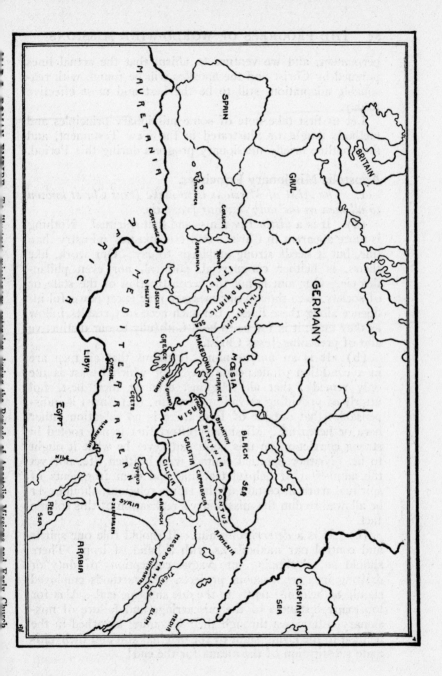

permanent, and we venture to affirm that the actual lines
pursued by Christ and the apostles will be found, with reasonable adaptation, still to be the best and most effective
to-day.

Let us first take note of some missionary principles and
methods taught or illustrated in the New Testament, and
then outline briefly missionary progress during this Period.

Apostolic Missionary Principles.

1.   *The AIM of Missions is to make Jesus Christ known
to all men as the only Saviour from sin.*

(a)   It is a *distinctive* aim—and that spiritual. Nothing
is more apparent in Christ's and His apostles' ministry than
this, but it needs strong emphasis to-day. Our work, like
theirs, is neither commercial, political, nor even philanthropic. Our aim is not the reconstruction of the state or
of society, even though our message may exert powerful influence along these lines. Let such accessory results follow
as they may; it is for us to hold faithfully to our distinctive
aim of preaching Jesus Christ.

(b)   It is an *unique* aim. It claims that all men are
in a condition of desperate need, for which Christ is the
only remedy; that all religions, even at their best, fail
utterly of providing salvation from sin; that Christ is indispensable; that outside of Him there is no salvation either
here or hereafter. Missionary effort that is not rooted in
strong conviction on this point can never be what it ought
to be. Neither habitual contact with heathen life, nor yet
the admission of helpful teaching and even fragments of
spiritual truth in certain of the ethnic religions, should ever
be allowed to dim the missionary's realization of this solemn
fact.

(c)   It is a *determining* aim. It should rule our spirits
and control our methods as with a hand of iron. There
should be no slipping into vague conceptions of duty or
drifting into promiscuous projects. All methods employed
should be held insistently to the one supreme end. Alas for
too many instances of the miscarriage and failure of missionary enterprises through their becoming absorbed in the
method to the losing sight of the original aim and their ultimate substitution of the means for the end!

2. *The POLICY of Missions is the widest diffusion, in contrast to any narrower delimitation.*

This is everywhere apparent in our Lord's ministry, both in precept and in practice. "The field is the world," "Go ye into all the world," "to all nations," "to every creature," "unto the uttermost part of the earth"—such are His own words. His personal example was no less emphatic. Witness His constant movements from place to place, His journeys from one extreme of Palestine to the other, His three distinct circuits throughout Galilee, His visits to Samaria and the coasts of Tyre and Sidon. When a Sabbath's strenuous work in Capernaum had created for Him an unique opportunity, His deliberate words to His disciples are, "Let us go into the next towns that I may preach there also, for therefore came I forth." He sends out first the twelve and later the seventy, two by two, "into every city and place, whither he himself would come." In despised Samaria He bids His exclusive Jewish disciples lift up their eyes and behold their spiritual harvest field. In the parable of the Good Samaritan He strikes a blow at provincialism by interpreting the term "neighbor" to mean the man who needs help, whoever or wherever he be. He makes the miracle of feeding the five thousand a missionary parable in itself, directing an equal and impartial distribution of bread to near and far alike, until "they were *all* filled."

The same policy is repeatedly illustrated in the Acts. The first Pentecost after Christ's death sees representatives of a dozen or more countries gathered providentially at Jerusalem to hear "every man in his own tongue" the new gospel message. A little later God uses persecution to scatter abroad the tardy church so that they "went everywhere preaching the Word." Philip is divinely called away from the Samaria revival to minister to the Ethiopian eunuch and thus extend the witness of the gospel into Africa. Bigoted Peter is despatched to Gentile Cornelius at Cæsarea, with results as vital to himself and the other apostles as to Cornelius. Antioch displaces Jerusalem as the Christian center because of its more liberal spirit and wider outreach. The conservative Jewish leaders give place to Paul, the apostle to the Gentiles, and the real foreign missionary movement is launched. Even after this, God has to correct the persistent tendency to narrower vision and effort by halting Paul in his second missionary tour of Asia Minor. A man of Macedonia beckons him to regions yet untouched, and God turns the tide of evangelization westward into Europe, the cradle of modern civilization. Paul himself, in a career that knows no parallel in missionary annals, eventually reaches Italy and even Spain.

Is it not incumbent upon the church at home and missionaries abroad to examine their policy of work as to whether it squares with the New Testament in insisting on giving precedence to direct and aggressive evangelism and pressing ever onward and outward to "the regions beyond" so long as there remain anywhere areas and populations still wholly unevangelized? There will always be the excuse of much to do nearer home and apparently too few to do it. Yet this cannot alter the fact of the irreparable loss to those left wholly destitute, nor yet the fact that an impartial and undelayed offer of salvation to all men is the Divine command. The terms of our Lord's commission make the first great task of the church to be *the evangelization of all men* rather than the conversion of any one favored section or the education of any one preferred class.

3. *The RESPONSIBILITY of Missions rests upon every member of Christ.*

The command "GO YE" did not exhaust itself upon the little group that first heard it from the lips of their risen Lord, but is authoritatively repeated whenever and wherever a new company of believers is formed.

The Apostolic Age furnishes a fine example on this point. We read of the Christians in Jerusalem that "they were ALL scattered abroad, except the Apostles; therefore they went everywhere preaching the Word." Of the Thessalonian converts it is said that "from them sounded forth the Word of God not only in Macedonia and Achaia, but also in every place," so that the Apostles "needed not to speak anything." As to missionary giving, the Macedonian churches in deep poverty "abounded unto the riches of their liberality." With such conditions, little wonder that the work moved forward and results were what they were.

It is quite true that the *leadership* was invested then, as now, in a distinctive class, divinely called and qualified by

special spiritual gifts. But these official workers exercised
their true function not by monopolizing the work, but by
leading and "perfecting the saints (the entire church) unto
the work of ministering" (Eph. 4: 11, 12 R. V.). It was a
time preëminently of individual effort, of general consecration to the task of proclaiming the gospel. Some one aptly
terms it the "Laymen's Missionary Movement of the First
Century." "Of missionaries in the modern sense of the
term there were few; of those who devoted their full time
and strength to the work of preaching there were few; but
of those who made their trade, their profession, their every-
day occupation, of whatever sort, the means of extending
their faith, there was a multitude." [1]

No principle is of more vital importance to-day, whether
to the church at home or on the mission field. The success
or failure of world evangelization is wrapped up in it, for
as long as the spread of the gospel in any land depends solely
upon a corps of official workers, however efficient and
earnest, the outlook is hopeless. The only hope lies in
response to the truth—"every Christian a missionary."

Apostolic Missionary Methods.

Principles are fundamental; methods grow out of them by
a natural process. If we have been guided to a right selection of principles these will be productive of fruitful suggestion as to proper methods. Space forbids more than the
briefest mention of methods employed in New Testament
times. The student can readily and profitably develop for
himself the points cited.

1. *Oral Preaching*—the supreme method for all time.
"He ordained twelve . . . that he might send them forth
to preach" (Mk. 3: 14). "They went forth and *preached
everywhere*" (Mk. 16: 20). "It pleased God by the *foolish-
ness of preaching* to save them which believed" (1 Cor.
1: 21). Is there not a significance in the fact that the Holy
Spirit at Pentecost assumed the form of tongues, as be-
tokening the part that preaching was to play in the Church
Age? The direct and immediate result of Spirit-indited
preaching was 3,000 souls saved that day and 5,000 more

---

[1] "The Missionary Enterprise," p. 14.

a little later. (See also Acts 5:42; 8:4, 5, 35, 40; 13:5; 28:31; 1 Tim. 2:7; 2 Tim. 1:11; 4:2; 1 Cor. 1:17.)

There is need for a revival of *the preaching idea,* and for a deeper sense of the glory and dignity of simple gospel preaching. Would that God would give to every mission field, from among her own sons, preachers like Wesley, and Whitefield, and Spurgeon and Moody—great-souled, impassioned, convincing—and through them show forth the true power of preaching!

Where shall we preach? From Christ's day to ours this question has given little difficulty wherever and whenever the true evangelistic spirit has been present. Jesus Himself preached in the Jewish synagogue, on the mountain side, by the Lake of Galilee, at Samaria's well. The apostles preached in the temple and synagogue, in house, marketplace, amphitheater, the courts of prisons and the audience hall of a Roman governor. Later evangelists and missionaries have preached in English barns and meadows, in Welsh mines and workshops, in American theaters and city slums, in Chinese teashops and temple squares, in Indian bazaars and at Tibetan fairs, in accustomed and unaccustomed places —in a word, everywhere.

Especially would we emphasize *open-air preaching,* a method adopted by Jesus and valuable not only for His own time and conditions, but for every age and land. It is a bad sign when any church abandons it, no matter how good its chapel equipment may be.

2. *Strategic Centers.* Such centers as Jerusalem, Capernaum, Antioch, Ephesus, Corinth and Rome stand out far too plainly in New Testament Missions for us to escape the lesson of the importance of similar centers to-day, with their vast populations and powerful radiating influences.

3. *Itineration.* Witness Jesus' successive Galilean circuits and Paul's missionary tours. Such work still demands its full share of attention along with the centers, and must be systematic and sustained to yield the full results. It has two ends in view: (a) the proclaiming of the gospel to the unsaved, and (b) the visitation of groups of converts for teaching and oversight (Cf. Acts 8:14, 25; 11:22-26; 15:36).

4. *Personal Work and Social Intercourse.* Looking again at the Master's ministry, one has only to think of Nicodemus, the woman at Sychar's well, Zacchæus, the rich young ruler, the wedding feast at Cana, Simon the Pharisee's dinner, and the home at Bethany, to be impressed with the prominent place these methods hold in missions. (See also Acts 10:24; 16:13-15; 18:2, 3, 26; 28:23, 30, 31.) Nowhere do conditions and customs lend themselves more happily to such measures than on the mission fields to-day. But these social opportunities need to be seized and held faithfully to the spiritual ends in view, or they may easily become profitless and even a snare.

5. *Literature and Letter-Writing.* What are the four Gospels but written accounts of the gospel message designed to supplement verbal preaching when the wide extension of the field of missionary operations required such added means? What were the New Testament Epistles originally but letters from missionaries to mission churches and individual converts at a distance? These records took permanent form as the New Testament Scriptures and led the way to the vast output of printed Scriptures, and later on of tracts and other literature as well, which constitute so effective and indispensable a factor in the missionary enterprise to-day. Nor would it be easy to estimate the value of the ministry of personal letter-writing on the part of the missionary as a means of help and blessing, both to believers and unbelievers.

6. *Training of Native Workers.* John the Baptist began such work. Our Lord made it His own greatest ministry, as we have already seen. Paul selected and trained younger men, notably Timothy and Titus, and urged them in turn to do the same (2 Tim. 2:2). This is to be regarded as the crowning missionary method, inasmuch as the missionary's true aim should not be to make himself indispensable, but rather the very reverse, by raising up native agents to take his place. The missionary who successfully does this may be said to work by multiplication instead of mere addition. It should be noted, too, that our Lord's method as a trainer was to maintain the closest connection between class studies and the actual work. Didactic instruction should always be interspersed liberally with practice in chapel

preaching, personal work and itineration, and preferably
under the leadership of the teacher himself.

Apostolic Missionary Progress.

The authentic record of missionary progress during this
Period is to be found in the New Testament itself, to which
record secular history adds its corroborative testimony.

1. *Extent of Propagation.*   The countries mentioned in
Acts as represented by the company assembled in Jerusalem
on the occasion of the first Pentecost after Christ's ascension
indicate something of the extensity of gospel witness-bear-
ing even thus early in the Period.   We read of "Parthians
and Medes, and Elamites, and the dwellers in Mesopotamia,
and in Judæa, and Cappadocia, in Pontus, and Asia, Phrygia,
and Pamphylia, in Egypt, and in the parts of Libya about
Cyrene, and strangers of Rome, Jews and proselytes, Cretes
and Arabians" (Acts 2:9-11).   A glance at the map shows
the territory here mentioned to include the entire area now
known as the Near East, from Persia on the east to the
Mediterranean on the west and Arabia and Egypt on the
south, with the addition of Rome far to the west in Europe.

Other passages attest the extension of the field of mission-
ary operations still farther, for we read of Barnabas of
Cyprus (Acts 4:36), Nicolas of Antioch (Acts 6:5), the
Ethiopian eunuch (Acts 8:27), and Ananias of Damascus
(Acts 9:2, 10).

Then we have the record in Acts of the missionary activities of Peter in Judea and Philip in Samaria, and the much
more extensive journeys of the Apostle Paul.   These journeys are summed up by Paul himself in Romans 15:19
in one comprehensive statement—"from Jerusalem, and
round about unto Illyricum," which makes them cover Palestine, Syria, Asia Minor, Greece, Macedonia and the territory on the eastern shore of the Adriatic Sea.   Subsequently
this great missionary's career extended to Italy, and there
is good reason to believe that he even lived to see the fulfillment of his desire to visit Spain, at the western confines
of Europe (Rom. 15:24).   Some authorities take 1 Peter
5:13 as evidence that the Apostle Peter labored at Babylon
in Mesopotamia.

So wonderfully effective was the missionary propaganda

of this brief Period that before the death of the Apostles churches had been planted in all influential centers of Asia Minor and Greece, and in Rome itself, and few parts of the vast Roman Empire had not at least heard of the new faith. "By the end of the first century Christ had been preached from Babylon to Spain (3,000 miles), from Alexandria to Rome, by a Greek-speaking Church. It was a *witnessing* church. The word 'witness' occurs in the New Testament 175 times."

The great centers of missionary propagation during this Period were, in turn, Jerusalem, Antioch, Ephesus and Alexandria. The greatest missionary was the Apostle Paul. The first Christian martyr was Stephen.

2. *Number of Converts.* Not only the extent of propagation, but also the results achieved must be taken into account in appraising missionary work. While the New Testament furnishes no complete numerical summary of the missionary results of this Period, it bears abundant testimony to the fruitful character of the work done. Acts 2 : 41 tells of 3,000 souls being won to Christ on the day of Pentecost, and Acts 4 : 4 tells of 5,000 more very soon afterwards. The subsequent chapters of Acts make frequent mention of other conversions, and the repeated use of the word "multitudes" is evidence of large accessions to the church. (Cf. Acts 5 : 14; 6 : 1, 7; 8 : 6, 12; 10 : 44, 48; 11 : 21, 24; 12 : 24 et al.)

The various epistles of the New Testament were written to organized congregations of Christians scattered over the wide area above outlined. On the basis of all the data available it has been estimated that by the close of the Apostolic Period the total number of Christian disciples had reached half a million.

3. *Quality of Converts.* This is another important feature which enters into the appraisal of missionary results. The Book of Acts and the New Testament Epistles throw clear light upon the character of the Christian converts and churches of the Apostolic Age. On the one hand, they bear witness to the mighty power of the Holy Spirit upon individuals and assemblies, to the varied gifts and graces of the Spirit in exercise among them, to keen discernment of spiritual truth, to fervent praying, sacrificial giving and

heroic enduring of persecution for Christ's sake. On the other hand, they reveal moral weaknesses and lapses into sin, doctrinal errors and subtle heresies, painful discord and schism among the brethren.

All this goes to show the admixture of true and false professors, robust and feeble Christians in the missionary churches from the very beginning. The Holy Spirit has given a faithful record of both the bright and the dark side of the early Church, for the comfort and encouragement of missionaries in later times.

QUESTIONS

1. Divide Christian Missions into seven Periods, giving dates.
2. What missionary features were illustrated in Jesus' personal ministry and teaching?
3. What is the true aim of Missions, according to the New Testament?
4. What is the true policy of Missions as to breadth of operations, according to the New Testament?
5. How is this policy illustrated (a) in the Gospels, (b) in the Acts?
6. Upon whom does missionary responsibility rest?
7. Give instances of how the New Testament Church met this responsibility.
8. Mention six prominent missionary methods in the New Testament.
9. Name six prominent missionary centers during the Apostolic Period.
10. Indicate the geographical scope of missionary operations during this Period.
11. What do we gather from the New Testament record as to (a) the number, (b) the quality of the Christian converts during this Period?

CHAPTER III

PERIOD OF EARLY CHURCH MISSIONS

FROM THE DEATH OF JOHN TO CONSTANTINE (100-313)

While the first century of Missions must ever stand in a class by itself because of the personal life and ministry of our blessed Master and His immediate disciples as its very center and inspiration, yet, when due allowance has been made for this unique fact, it may be said that the general lines and features of the work during this earliest period continued largely unchanged throughout the two centuries which followed, which we have designated The Period of the Early Church. Among the features to be noted are :—

Extension.

It would be erroneous to draw the conclusion from the Acts and other New Testament references to missionary operations of the time that only the few apostles and others mentioned had an active share in the extension of the gospel. Mark tells us that "they went forth and preached everywhere," and Luke says that "they that were scattered abroad went everywhere preaching the word." The record of the Acts serves merely as a sample. We have already noted the wide scope of the gospel testimony in the Apostolic Period as indicated by the list of countries represented in Jerusalem at Pentecost. Persia, Arabia, Mesopotamia, Asia Minor, Greece, Italy, Egypt and other parts of North Africa all received the message. Nor should we conclude that this first Pentecost was the only one from which seeds were scattered into many distant parts to spring up and bear fruit.

The Period following the death of the apostles was not one of great leaders so much as of many leaders. The whole church was imbued with the spirit of witnessing, and in the course of ordinary social intercourse, travel and commerce, rather than by any extensive organized movement, the gospel spread far and wide, and little companies of believers sprang up in many lands.

From Ephesus the work extended through Asia Minor, and the seven Churches mentioned in the Apocalypse were established and became self-supporting and self-propagating. The well-known letter of Pliny, Governor of Pontus in Asia Minor, to the Emperor Trajan bears impressive testimony to both the number and the character of Christians in that province. Connected with Syria during this Period are such famous names as *Ignatius,* the writer of epistles and martyr under Trajan, *Justin Martyr,* the philosopher, *Eusebius,* the early Church historian, and a little later, *Jerome,* the great scholar who produced the Latin version of the Scriptures called the Vulgate.

In Egypt and North Africa Christianity became strongly entrenched in such centers as Alexandria and Carthage, and there is a touching story of its introduction into the court of the queen of Abyssinia by two young Tyrian captives, and the beginning therefrom of the Abyssinian Church which even Mohammedanism failed to overcome.

Whatever of truth there may be in the tradition that Thaddeus and Peter became missionaries to Persia, certain it is that at Edessa, the modern Urfa, there was a strong Christian community in the middle of the second century, and that the king, Abgar, himself became a zealous Christian and is claimed by the Armenians as their first leader in the faith. There are notices of churches in Arabia in the early part of the third century. It is authentic history that *Pantænus* of Alexandria went to India about A.D. 190, in response to messengers sent with an appeal for Christian teachers, and that he found Christians there who possessed a Hebrew Gospel of St. Matthew. Just after the close of this Period there existed there about three hundred and fifty flourishing churches.

Athens and Corinth early became strong Christian centers in Greece, while Tacitus, the Roman historian, records that multitudes of Christians abode in Rome. From that city they spread northward through Italy into Gaul, where such noted men as *Irenæus* and *Pothinus,* friends and disciples of Polycarp, the disciple of John, introduced Christianity among the Franks and founded churches in Lyons, Vienne and Paris. Others crossed the Rhine to the Germanic tribes, and some went even to the British Isles.

Clement and Irenæus, in the first and second centuries respectively, speak of the evangelization of Spain. In the middle of the third century Cyprian of North Africa addresses a letter to a church in Spain, and so great was the advance there that a gathering of nineteen bishops in A.D. 306 is mentioned.

Missionary Centers.

Jerusalem, Antioch, Ephesus, Alexandria and Carthage were successively, along with Rome, the great missionary centers of the first three centuries.

Jerusalem, ever to be remembered as the starting point of world-wide missions, retained its broad missionary character only a short time, and then became merely the center of the Church of the Circumcision, with the Apostle James as its first Bishop.

Antioch, much more cosmopolitan, soon succeeded Jerusalem as the home base of missions, from which Paul started on his three missionary tours. It became the patriarchate of all the East till eclipsed by Constantinople, and shed its light far and wide over Asia. It sent missionaries overland through Persia to India and even remote China, and promised to conquer Central and Eastern Asia for Christ till overwhelmed by Saracen and Tartar. Antioch, once a city of half a million, is now a mere squalid village.

Ephesus won distinction as a missionary center through the successive labors of Paul and John. In the fifth century a council was held there to settle a bitter theological controversy led by rival archbishops, Cyril of Alexandria and Nestorius of Constantinople, the result of which was that Nestorius became an exile and founded the Nestorian church, which for five centuries was notable for its missionary zeal and its devoted and successful efforts throughout Asia.

Alexandria in turn eclipsed the cities already mentioned, and became the intellectual center of the world and the most aggressive and influential center of Christendom, with *Carthage* as a second great center in Africa. They produced the ablest teachers and writers of this Period, the best known being *Clement, Origen, Tertullian, Cyprian* and *Augustine*. Specially worthy of mention here is the great *Catechumens' School of Pantænus* in Alexandria, which served the combined purpose of the defense of the orthodox faith against current heresy and of a training school for missionaries—the first of its kind—who went forth not only into northwestern and eastern Africa, but also to Arabia, India and Ceylon. Pantænus himself, its president, as already noted, went to India about A.D. 180-190.

Growth and Influence.

The following quotations will serve to impress the fact of the remarkable progress of the gospel during this Period, and of the widespread and profound influence exerted by its devoted adherents.

"There is no people, Greek or Barbarian, or any other race, by whatsoever appellation or manner they may be distinguished, however ignorant of art and agriculture, whether they dwell in tents or wander about in covered wagons, among whom prayers and thanksgivings are not offered, in the name of the crucified Jesus, to the Father and creator of all things."—*Justin Martyr* (103-165).

"We are but of yesterday, and yet we already fill your cities, islands, camps, your palace, senate, and forum. We have left you only your temples."—*Tertullian* (160-240).

"In all Greece and in all barbarous races within our world, there are tens of thousands who have left their national laws and customary gods for the law of Moses and the Word of Jesus Christ; though to adhere to that Law is to incur the hatred of idolaters and to have embraced that Word is to incur the risk of death as well. And considering how, in a few years and with no great store of teachers, in spite of the attacks which have cost us life and property, the preaching of that Word has found its way into every part of the world, so that Greeks and Barbarians, wise and unwise, adhere to the religion of Jesus—doubtless it is a work greater than any work of man."—*Origen* (185-251).

"There flourished at that time many successors of the apostles, who reared the edifice on the foundations which they laid, continuing the work of preaching the gospel, and scattering abundantly over the whole earth the wholesome seed of the heavenly kingdom. For a very large number of disciples, carried away by fervent love of the truth, which the divine Word had revealed to them, fulfilled the command of the Saviour to divide their goods among the poor. Then, taking leave of their country, they filled the office of evangelists, coveting eagerly to preach Christ and to carry the glad tidings of God to those who had not heard the word of faith. And after laying the foundations of the faith in some remote and barbarous countries, establishing pastors among them and confiding to them the care of those young settlements, without stopping longer they hastened on to other nations, attended by the grace and virtue of God."— *Eusebius* (266-340).

Accurate statements as to the actual number of Christians at the close of this Period are obviously impossible. Estimates by various authorities range from one-tenth to one-twentieth of the entire population of the Roman Empire. In A.D. 240, when Gregory Thaumaturgus went as Bishop to Neo-Cæsarea, chief town of Pontus, he found there only seventeen Christians, and when he left in A.D. 265, he left only seventeen heathen.

About the same time Cornelius, Bishop of Rome, gives the number of Roman Christians as fifty thousand, or one-twentieth of the total population of a million.

"By the opening of the fourth century Christian Missions had so covered the then known world, that when Constantine came to the throne, he found Christianity if not numerically, at least intellectually and morally, so potent a factor that it must be considered and deferred to. It could not be ignored."[1]

Persecutions.

From the time of the first martyr, Stephen, the early Christian Church was destined to suffer persecution as it faced the mighty political power of Rome, the whole moral force of the most immoral and vicious age the world has known, and the barbarous cruelties of heathen nations to which it carried the gospel.

Rome, at first inclined to regard the Christians as harm-

[1] "The Missionary Enterprise," p. 20.

less fanatics, soon changed her attitude, and despite their loyalty and exemplary conduct treated them with suspicion and dislike. As the new cult grew and spread rapidly the rulers became alarmed lest it should weaken the imperial grasp upon great provinces. Prohibition of the faith and persecution of those who embraced it set in and became more and more severe. So unpopular were Christians that for centuries parts of Rome were undermined to form catacombs, where Christians held their meetings in days of persecution, and where the bodies of the dead were laid away. Hundreds of thousands of martyrs sealed their testimony with their blood, among the earlier and most noted of whom were Paul, Ignatius, Polycarp and Justin Martyr.

Ten distinct persecutions are usually recognized, ranging at intervals from A.D. 64, under Nero, to A.D. 303, under Diocletian. The first of these, planned and carried out by the inhuman monster Nero, serves as a sample of all. To cover up his own crime of having wantonly set fire to the city of Rome, and escape the fury of the populace, Nero deliberately charged the Christians with the crime. The following sentences are taken from a full and vivid description of the horrible orgy by the historian Tacitus :—

"First those were seized who confessed they were Christians; next, on their information, a vast multitude were convicted, not so much on the charge of burning the city as of hating the human race. And in their deaths they were also made the subject of sport, for they were covered with the hides of wild beasts, and worried to death by dogs, or nailed to crosses, or set fire to, and when day declined, were burned to serve for nocturnal lights. Nero offered his own gardens for that spectacle, and exhibited a Circensian game, indiscriminately mingling with the common people in the habit of a charioteer."

In the catacombs of St. Sebastian in Rome rest the bodies of 174,000 martyrs, nor were these by any means all who loved their Master even unto death. Needless to say, all such efforts to quench the vital spark of divine truth, far from succeeding, only fanned it into a flame and scattered it the more widely. The blood of the martyrs proved then, as it has proved ever since, to be the seed of the Church.

QUESTIONS

1. Give the name and dates of the Second Period of Christian Missions.

2. Indicate the extent of the spread of the gospel during this Period—(a) in Asia, (b) in Europe, (c) in Africa.

3. Name the six most prominent missionary centers of the Period, in the order of their development as such.

4. What famous theological controversy took place at Ephesus in the 5th century, and what effect did it exert upon missionary extension?

5. Give the names of five prominent Christian teachers or writers of this Period in Africa.

6. Where, and by whom, was the first great missionary training school founded?

7. What great writers attest the growth and influence of Christianity during this Period, and what is the general nature of their testimony?

8. How many distinct Roman persecutions against Christians are usually cited, and over what years did they extend?

9. Name the Roman Emperor who instigated the first great persecution, and give some idea of its character.

CHAPTER IV

PERIOD OF EARLY EUROPEAN MISSIONS

FROM CONSTANTINE TO CHARLEMAGNE (313-800)

The Church at Home and Missionary Effort Abroad.
Constantine's professed conversion on the eve of his becoming Emperor of Rome was the beginning of a mighty change in the outward standing of the Christian Church and also in its inward character. The story is well known of his seeing a wonderful cross in the sky with the words *"In hoc signo vince!"* (By this sign conquer!). At once adopting the cross as his standard, he led his armies on to victory and then, in his famous Edict of 313, proclaimed Christianity the State religion. Viewed from without this seemed a glorious triumph for the faith, and it is true that it meant new safety of profession and liberty to preach. But in reality it wrought grievous injury to the true cause of Christ through the influx into the Church of a great mass of heathenism. The foes which had previously threatened the Church from without now began to attack it from within. Purity of faith and simplicity of worship gradually were lost and spiritual declension set in. Missionary zeal and activity at once began to wane. The Church leaders were compelled to divert their energies from propagating the gospel to defending the faith. "From a purely missionary point of view, it began the system of compromise with error —of nationalism instead of individualism in conversion— which in the East made the Church an easy prey to Mohammedanism, and in the West produced Jesuit Missions." [1]

From A.D. 328, when Constantine removed the capital from Rome to Byzantium (now Constantinople), the history of the Church, like that of the Empire, was divided into Eastern and Western. The *Eastern Church* became engrossed in theological controversies, to the sad loss of its

---

[1] "Short History of Christian Missions," p. 57.

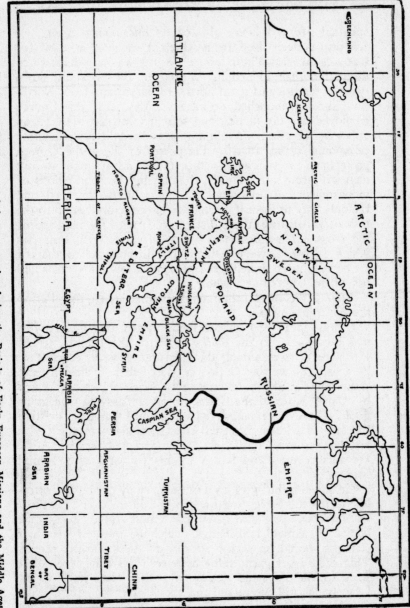

MAP II: OLD WORLD: To illustrate missionary extension during the Periods of Early European Missions and the Middle Ages (Chapters IV and V)

spiritual life and hence also of its missionary vision. It fell into a deep sleep from which it was not aroused for many centuries. The *Western Church* was less disposed to discussion than to action. Moreover, the sweeping down upon its territory of great hordes of barbarians from Northern Europe compelled attention. Alas, that the Church employed worldly tactics, and sought to attract these pagan tribes by the glitter of religious paraphernalia and elaborate ceremonial rather than by the power of the gospel. As a protest and reaction against this state of affairs many devout men withdrew into solitude, thus laying the foundations of monasticism. A few, more discerning of the real need, and the only way to meet it, heroically gave themselves up to the task of penetrating these distant wilds with the message of the cross. The missionary work of the several centuries which follow, however, stands out in contrast to that of the early Church in being the effort of a few individuals and not of the Church as a whole.

Among the most prominent missionaries of this Period are the following:—

Ulfilas (311-388), whose name means "the little wolf," was the apostle to the *Goths* north of the Danube River. His parents were among the Christian captives carried off by a band of warlike Goths on one of their incursions into Asia Minor. When about twenty years old he was taken by Alaric, King of the Goths, on an embassy to Constantinople, where he remained ten years and became a Christian scholar. He then returned as a missionary to the Goths and labored until the whole nation accepted the new faith. He was revered and hailed by his converts as a second Moses.

He added to his work as a missionary by giving the letterless Goths the Bible, to do which he had to invent for them an alphabet. He translated the whole Bible, except the books of Samuel and Kings, which he omitted lest their contents should prove too stirring to these warlike people. This Bible is of great value because of its being the oldest form of the Teutonic speech, and more than half of the Gospels is still preserved in the University of Upsala, Sweden. It is known as the "silver Bible" because of its being written in silver letters on a purple ground.

Martin, Bishop of Tours (316-396), was the pioneer missionary of *Gaul* (France) after the Franks and other northern tribes had invaded this region, where Christianity had earlier been brought by Irenæus and others. Martin was a soldier, and adopted military methods which would be strange and inconsistent in our day. From Tours as a center he led his army of monks through the land, destroying idol temples and groves and proclaiming the gospel. He is still held as the patron saint of France.

Patrick (396-493), the first great missionary to *Ireland*, and its immortal patron saint, was, contrary to common repute, not an Irishman but a Scotchman. As a boy he was carried captive from his Christian father's home near the present Glasgow, and sold as a slave to a chieftain in North Ireland, who used him to herd his sheep. There he reflected on his early teaching, and, like the prodigal son, "came to himself." Later he escaped, was retaken, and again escaped. He spent some time in one of the monastic schools of France, and then returning to his father's home he had a night vision like Paul, and heard voices from the Irish coast crying, "We beseech thee, child of God, come and again walk among us." Unheeding the entreaties of his parents and friends, he set out for Ireland, where he spent more than a third of a century in widespread and vigorous evangelism. He was undaunted by the opposition of the pagan chieftains of the Druids. Everywhere he gathered the people about him in the open field and preached Christ to them. His burning zeal and deep sincerity, coupled with a kindly gentleness of manner, completely won the hearts of the peasants and nobility alike. He planted hundreds of churches and baptized thousands of converts. He also founded monastic schools, which became centers of learning and devotion, and whose influence was felt throughout the Middle Ages and to distant parts of the world.

Altogether Patrick imparted a stronger impulse than any other man to Medieval Missions. A mass of grotesque and unreliable legends clings about his name. It is significant that despite the claims of the Roman Catholic Church upon St. Patrick, his message and methods were more distinctly those of Protestantism than were those of his contemporaries. He had no connection with the Pope, his grandfather was a married priest, and in the reliable accounts of his career there is no reference to such Romish practices as auricular confession, extreme unction, or the worship of Mary.

Columba (521-596). It was fitting that Ireland, indebted for her evangelization to a Scotchman, should in return give to *Scotland* her apostle. Columba was of royal birth, liberal gifts and high education. He was distinguished for his piety and zeal, and like Patrick was a man of constant prayer. After founding several monastic communities in Ireland, he crossed the Irish Channel with twelve companions in 563, and on the small Island of Iona, the most famous center of the Druid superstition, established a center which became one of the most noted missionary schools in history. Not only were all North Scotland and the adjacent Hebrides, Orkney and Shetland Islands evangelized by Columba and his immediate followers, but "for two centuries or more Iona was the place in all the world whence the greatest amount of evangelistic influence went forth, and on which, therefore, the greatest amount of blessing from on high rested." [2]

Augustine (505?-605) was the great missionary pioneer to *England*. Gregory the Great, while an abbot, saw three Anglo-Saxon youths exposed for sale in the market at Rome. Attracted by their fair complexion and hair, he asked of what race they were, and when told they were Angles, he wittily replied "Not 'Angles' but 'angels.'" He desired to go to England as a missionary, but was not permitted by the Pope. When later he himself became Pope he despatched Augustine with forty Benedictine monks. Hearing tales of the savagery of the Saxons, Augustine at first, like Jonah, turned back. But sternly ordered forward by Gregory the company landed at Kent. They were kindly received by King Ethelbert, who already had some knowledge of the truth through his Frankish wife, Bertha, herself a Christian. Within a year Ethelbert was baptized, and soon after, in accord with the times, his parliament adopted the faith and in a single day ten thousand of his people were immersed. Canterbury Cathedral was founded and Augustine became its first Archbishop.

2 "Medieval Missions," pp. 50, 51.

Columbanus (543-615), a scholarly Irish monk, whose heart became fired with missionary zeal, set out with twelve companions for Germany. Landing in *Burgundy,* he won the disfavor of the king by his simple austerity and fearless censure of evil living, and pressed onward beyond the Rhine, even reaching the wild Suevi, ancestors of the modern *Swiss.* Like Martin of Tours he waged war against paganism with fiery zeal, smashing idols and burning temples and establishing monasteries in their place. His last effort was to establish work in Italy. He succeeded in founding a monastery across the Alps at Bobbio, where he soon died at an advanced age.

Willibrord (657-739), an Englishman educated and deeply influenced by the Irish Church, was the first missionary to *Holland* and *Denmark.* He faced great pioneer hardships in a rough land and among wild people, but battled on courageously against much opposition, and though finally rejected, he planted the gospel among a people destined centuries later to be among the boldest defenders of the Christian faith.

Boniface (680-755), the great missionary of Central Europe, was the apostle especially of *Germany.* He was of noble birth and fine scholarship, but roused by the tales of Willibrord's sufferings, he turned his back upon attractive prospects at home and set out for Holland to join that then aged missionary. Later, declining to succeed Willibrord as Bishop of Utrecht, he pressed on into Hessia and Saxony. He found among the Germanic tribes a chaotic condition of paganism interwoven with some Christian ideas received from earlier Roman, and perhaps also Irish, missionaries. With heroic courage he undertook perilous pioneer journeys in many directions. On one occasion, finding that many of his converts had returned to their old Thor-worship, he seized an axe and in the presence of thousands of enraged heathen and trembling half-Christians cut down a sacred oak of Thor. When the mighty tree crashed to the ground and Boniface was not, as they expected, stricken by a bolt from heaven, the people shouted his praise and came in thousands to be baptized.

During twenty years he is said actually to have baptized one hundred thousand converts, though this statement is likely an exaggeration. He was as great an organizer as an evangelist, founded monasteries, schools, and even convents, and welded together these raw heathen into a strong church, although it must be admitted that his methods were not above question, judged by present standards. In his old age Boniface yearned over the land of his first love and returned to Holland. On the shores of the Zuyder Zee, at the age of seventy-five, pillowing his head upon a volume of the Gospels, he received the death stroke at the hands of the pagan ancestors of the Dutch and became a martyr for Christ. His disciple, Gregory of Utrecht, founded there the great missionary college of the time—a fitting memorial of Boniface.

The Rise and Spread of Mohammedanism.

While the gospel was thus being carried to the countries of Western Europe, there suddenly arose in the East a new religion, destined to have a vital bearing upon world evangelization as one of its most powerful antagonists. This was Mohammedanism. Its founder, *Mohammed,* was born in Mecca about A.D. 570. His early life was passed in obscurity, but his marriage at the age of twenty-eight to a wealthy widow, Kadijah, freed him from temporal cares and afforded him leisure for contemplation. He had opportunity to observe not only the degraded paganism of the Arabs, but also Judaism and Christianity, both of which had entered Arabia and were all too sadly tainted in doctrine and enervated in spiritual power. When about forty years of age Mohammed began to have "visions." His own temperament, together with the persuasions of his wife, who was ambitious for his advancement, led him to interpret these as revelations from God and a call to take up the task of a spiritual reformer. He began to preach, his message being that "there is one God and Mohammed is His Prophet." He called his doctrine *Islam*—meaning resignation to the divine will.

Believers slowly gathered round him, but his claims for himself, as well as his bitter opposition to idolatry, aroused the rulers and townsfolk of Mecca, and in A.D. 622 he was forced to flee for his life to Medina. From this flight, known as the *Hegira,* the Mohammedan calendar is dated.

His career soon changed from that of a mere preacher to that of a political leader and warrior. At first his aims seemed to be confined to exterminating idolatry from his own land of Arabia, but his signal military successes at the head of a small band of followers whetted his ambition. He came to aspire to be the leader of a fierce worldwide crusade against idolatry, and to restore the pure religion which had been revealed by God to the prophets, of which he claimed to be the last and greatest. Meeting with opposition from the Jews, on whose support he had counted, he became fired with a bitter hatred toward them. There was in him a strange mingling of lofty devotion to the will of God and of craft and cruelty in carrying out his own ambitions.

His biographers differ widely in their estimates of his character. Some earlier writers extol him as a virtuous man, a pure patriot, and a sincere philanthropist. Later ones swing to the opposite extreme and brand him as a monster of iniquity. Rejecting both of these extreme views one author says, "He was an Oriental, and became an Oriental potentate. He had the Oriental idea that the privilege of a potentate included indulgence in sensuality. He was not only an Asiatic, but an Arab, an Ishmaelite, nurtured in the faith that his hand must be against every man, strength against strength, stratagem against stratagem, force and fraud against fraud and force. That he believed throughout in his own divine commission no judicious biographer maintains. That he was earnest and honest in his desire to put a stop to the profanities and corruptions of Asiatic heathenism I think should be frankly admitted." [3]

His Arabian armies were possessed by a wild fanaticism and a thirst for plunder and conquest. The prophet's injunction to them was to exterminate all heathen and apostates, and to offer to Jews and Christians the choice of the Koran, tribute or death. The Eastern provinces of the Roman Empire fell an easy prey before their furious advance. Syria, Mesopotamia, Persia, Asia Minor, Egypt and North Africa, with their great cities, all fell into the hands of the Moslems. They even swept westward through Europe, and in eight years completed the conquest of Spain. From there they crossed the Pyrenees into Southern Gaul,

[3] "Medieval Missions," p. 164.

and the Mohammedan power threatened to encircle Christendom and wipe out the Christian Church.   Such a calamity
was averted by the crushing defeat dealt the Moslem army
by *Charles Martel* and his Frankish soldiers in A.D. 732 at
Tours.   The tide was stemmed and Europe saved from
being overrun by the Arab hordes.   The terrible blight of
Islam remained, however, and steadily extended over the
Levant, North Africa, and Western Asia including Persia.

The doctrines and rites of Mohammedanism are to be
found in the *Koran,* which professes to be a divine revelation to the prophet and is accepted by his followers as the
Word of God.   Somewhat smaller than the New Testament
in size, it is a strange jumble of facts and fables, laws and
legends, full of historical errors and superstitions, and is
unintelligible without a commentary.   While the Moslem
doctrine of God is a monotheism, its deity, far from being
the loving and beneficent God of the Christian Bible, is an
unfeeling despot, infinitely removed from His creatures, and
with no mediator between.   It depicts a hell of fearful tor-
ments and a heaven of grossest sensual delights.   It sanctions slavery, polygamy, and the degradation of woman.   Its
only real philosophy is a blind fatalism, which has stamped
itself upon every Moslem country and subject and paralyzed
all progress.   Its prayers are merely the "vain repetitions"
of a formula, its fastings are a farce, its almsgivings are
but a pittance.   Its pilgrimages to Mecca constitute a strong
bond of union among its widely scattered adherents.

As to the bearing of the religion of Islam upon Christian
Missions, past or present, we cannot do better than quote
the following words written by Sir William Muir, and
which express not only our own personal conviction, but
that also, we believe, of the body of evangelical missionaries at large:

"They labor under a miserable delusion who suppose that Mohammedanism paves the way for a purer faith.   No system could
have been devised with more consummate skill for shutting out
the nations over which it has sway from the Christian faith; for
there is in it just so much truth—truth borrowed from previous
Revelations, yet cast in another mold—as to divert attention from
the need of more.   *Idolatrous* Arabia (judging from the analogy
of other nations) might have been aroused to spiritual life, and the
adoption of the faith of Jesus; while *Mohammedan* Arabia is, to

the human eye, sealed against the divine influences of the gospel. Many a flourishing land in Africa and in Asia, which once rejoiced in the light and liberty of Christianity, is now crushed and over-spread by darkness gross and barbarous. It is as if their day of grace had come and gone, and there remained to them 'No more sacrifice for sins.' That a brighter morn will yet dawn on these countries we may not doubt; but the history of the past, and the condition of the present, is not the less true and sad. The sword of Mohammed, and the Koran, are the most stubborn enemies of Civilization, Liberty, and Truth which the world has yet known."

QUESTIONS

1. Give the name and dates of the Third Period of Christian Missions.

2. What Emperor made Christianity the State religion of Rome, and in what year?

3. How did this action affect the standing and character of the Church?

4. Compare the character of missionary activity in the Third Period with that of the First and Second Periods.

5. Name the pioneer missionary to each of the following peoples, and give a brief description of his work: Goths, Franks, Irish, Scotch, English, Swiss, Dutch, Germans.

6. Name the founder of the Moslem religion, give the date of his birth and flight, and briefly describe his career.

7. Indicate the scope of the spread of Mohammedanism during this Period.

8. Where, when, and by whom was the onsweep of this religion in Europe checked?

9. How do the doctrines and rites of Islam compare with those of Christianity?

10. What has been the prevailing effect of the Moslem propaganda upon the lands which it has dominated, and what is its bearing upon Christian missionary work?

11. Describe the doctrines and rites of Mohammedanism, and compare that religion with Christianity in essential points.

CHAPTER V

PERIOD OF THE MIDDLE AGES

FROM CHARLEMAGNE TO LUTHER (800-1517)

The features of this Period to be noted as bearing upon the course of Missions may be summed up under three heads: 1. Direct Missionary Operations. 2. The Crusades. 3. The Monastic Orders.

Direct Missionary Operations.

The succession of pioneer efforts to evangelize the countries of Northern Europe, which we have already noted in the previous Period extended into the earlier portion of this Period. Among the leaders and movements deserving mention were the following:—

Ansgar (800?-865). A monk of Corvey, a French convent, he was sent back to *Denmark* by the Emperor Louis the Pious, along with King Harold, who had been converted to Christianity. It was a mission of danger that called for a heroic spirit. He opened a Christian school in Denmark, but its success was limited by the unfriendly attitude of the people. Later he made two visits to *Sweden,* on the first of which his ship and all his belongings were seized by pirates. He established his center at Hamburg, on the border between Denmark and Germany, from which convenient point he paid visits in turn to Denmark and Sweden. An attack by heathen Danes, however, completely destroyed his church, school and library, and his work suffered many vicissitudes. But he was a man of piety, courage and prayer, and finally succeeded in breaking down the opposition of King Olaf of Sweden, and even of King Horic of Denmark, the bitterest foe of Christianity. Freedom for Christian worship and the building of churches followed, and thus the way of the gospel was prepared in both of these northern kingdoms, where Ansgar is now venerated as "the ideal missionary" and the Apostle of the North.

Norway, Iceland and Greenland. Norway received Christianity from England in the tenth century. Three valiant and patriotic Norman princes—Hakon and the two Olafs—tried to introduce it by force, and their zeal and violent measures for the extermination of the worship of Odin and Thor were worthy of Mohammed himself. The final triumph came when the sacred image of Thor fell in fragments under the blows of a Christian soldier, and out of it crept a multitude of mice, snakes and lizards.

Iceland was colonized in the ninth and tenth centuries by noble families of Norsemen, who took with them their gods Odin and Thor. An Icelander, having been converted in Saxony, took home with him a priest who endeavored to start a mission there in 981, but after seven years he was banished. The precious seed, however, had been planted. King Olaf of Norway himself continued to send missionaries, and finally paganism was completely stamped out and Iceland won to Christianity.

Greenland was in turn evangelized from Iceland, the main instrument being *Lief the Lucky,* son of the Norseman, Eric the Red, the reputed colonizer of Greenland. On his voyage Lief is said to have been driven south by storms and to have landed on the coast of New England four hundred years before Columbus made his voyage of discovery.

Otto, Bishop of Bamberg. Otto carried the gospel in the twelfth century to the *Pomeranians,* who had come under the sway of Poland. In contrast to the first missionaries, who were men of shabby dress and ascetic habits, he went in great episcopal pomp, supported by the King of Poland, and attended by a richly robed retinue whose splendor profoundly impressed this pleasure-loving people. But more than this, Otto's many Christ-like deeds and his spirit of unselfish devotion won their hearts. Thousands accepted baptism, Slavic idols and temples were destroyed and finally, after thirty years, their most famous idol of gigantic size, whose worship was supported by taxes, war spoils and votive offerings, was dethroned in its temple on the island of Rügen and committed to the flames.

Cyril and Methodius (815?-885). These two brothers,

who were Greek priests, were sent from Constantinople to the *Bulgarians* in response to a call from a Bulgarian prince whose sister had been converted while a captive on the Bosphorus. Cyril was a philosopher and Methodius an artist. The interesting story is recorded of the conversion of Bogoris, the savage King of the Bulgarians, by the drawing by Methodius of the Scene of the Last Judgment upon the wall of the palace. The king led his subjects in being baptized and Christianity was established. From Bulgaria these brother-missionaries extended their labors into *Moravia* and *Bohemia,* and thus their good work became prophetic of that later brotherhood known by the name Moravian, which became one of the foremost agencies in carrying the gospel to the very confines of the heathen world.

In addition to their evangelistic work, Cyril and Methodius did for the Slavs what Ulfilas had done for the Goths, by reducing their language to writing and translating the Bible and Liturgy into Slavonian. The language of this Bible is to-day to the Russian what Gothic is to the German. A far-reaching effect of this provision of the written character has been to bind the Slavic peoples together, and thus raise an impassable barrier between them and Latin Christianity.

Conversion of the Russians. A century later the Eastern Slavs were turned in a body to Christianity, after the fashion of the early Franks and English, by the baptism of King Vladimir in 988. A princess of his house, Olga, had been led into the Christian faith by a visit to Constantinople in 955 and had been baptized. Vladimir, her grandson, was a thorough pagan, but after investigating through envoys the various religions—Christian, Jewish and Moslem—he finally became Christian, and cemented his profession of the new faith by marriage with the sister of the Greek Emperor. This marriage laid the foundation for Russia's claim to the inheritance of the Byzantine Empire.

(One more missionary name belonging to this Period remains to be mentioned and his career sketched, and that the greatest of all—Raymond Lull. But the account of his life much more appropriately follows that of the Crusades, not merely from the standpoint of the order of events, but even

more because of the bearing of the Crusades and Lull's
career upon each other.)

The Crusades.

The remarkable series of expeditions known as the Crusades, termed by some the "missions militant" of the Church,
cannot, strictly speaking, be regarded as a missionary movement, but so great and widespread were the influences
exerted by them, directly or indirectly, upon the religious,
intellectual and social life of the whole civilized world that
they cannot be passed by without mention.

Seven Crusades are usually reckoned, occurring at intervals between 1095 and 1272. Their immediate object
was to avenge the oppression and cruelties practised by the
fanatical Moslems against the Christians of Syria and particularly the pilgrims to Jerusalem, and to deliver the Holy
Land from the power of Islam. Peter the Hermit, an
enthusiast, was sent by Pope Urban II through Northern
Italy and France to preach a Crusade. Urban himself lent
his strong influence to the movement. At the close of a
memorable speech of his the whole assembly, swept by a
tide of emotion, cried out as one man *"Deus Vult"* ("God
wills it"), and this expression became the war-cry of the
advancing hosts. A flame of fanatical zeal spread over all
Western Christendom. King and subject, noble and peas-
ant, clergy and laity, old and young, saint and sinner became
bound together under the spell of this new inspiration, and
willingly sacrificing home, possessions and even life, flung
themselves into the holy war.

Their motives differed widely. Every passion of the
human heart was appealed to by the Pope. Penitents were
promised absolution from all sins; debtors were made im-
mune from the hand of the law; those who died in action
were assured of eternal blessedness and reward. Love of
adventure, desire for military renown, and even greed for
loot all had their place along with religious zeal as incentives
to spur on these promiscuous multitudes, which numbered
many hundreds of thousands.

Among the more important leaders, besides Pope Urban
and Peter the Hermit, were Godfrey of Bouillon, Bernard

of Clairvaux, King Louis VII of France, Emperor Conrad
III of Germany and Richard "the lion-hearted" of England.
The sufferings and losses sustained by the Crusaders were
terrible indeed.   Many succumbed to the hardships of the
journey, others perished in shipwrecks, while vast numbers
fell in battle or were taken captive by their Saracen foes.
The military successes won were few and short-lived.   True,
Constantinople, Nice and Antioch were in turn occupied, and
Jerusalem was captured in 1099 by Godfrey, who was
elected its Christian King.   But the repeated attacks of surrounding Moslems upon Palestine could not long be withstood, and finally in 1187 the Holy City itself was retaken,
to remain ever since, until 1917, in Mohammedan hands.

As time went on the religious fervor which had at first
dominated the Crusades cooled, worldly motives prevailed,
political and religious rivalries sprang up among the various
leaders, and failure to realize the ends hoped for at length
led to the abandonment of the enterprise.   But if the immediate objects of the Crusades were not achieved, yet the
effects were manifold and far-reaching.   The following may
be mentioned:—

1. A better acquaintance and understanding came about
between the people of the West and East.   The old spirit
of prejudice and even hatred, which had prevailed in the
West toward the East, and notably toward all Moslems, gave
way to a larger spirit of appreciation and sympathy—a
change distinctly favorable to missionary progress.

2. The Crusaders came in contact with the older and
more advanced civilizations of the Greeks and Saracens, and
Eastern arts, sciences and inventions were introduced into
Europe.

3. Commerce, especially maritime, greatly expanded,
bringing new wealth to Europe and causing great cities to
spring up.   Along with these changes, the fact also that so
many nobles impoverished themselves in preparation for the
Crusades tended to an equalizing of the social classes.

4. The closer relations into which the Crusades brought
laymen with the clergy served to give to the former a truer
knowledge of the latter.   Much of the traditional spirit of
veneration for the papal court and clergy was lost and
freedom of opinion fostered—a change which became a real

factor in preparing the way for the Reformation of a century later.

5. While, as already remarked, the Crusades were not in any true sense a missionary movement, yet they did contribute to the spread of Christianity in regions where it was little known. Also, while their aims and efforts were for the punishment and overthrow of the Moslems, rather than their Christianization, yet there were a few souls in that age who in contrast to the prevailing spirit showed a genuine concern for the spiritual welfare of Mohammedans, and set on foot the earliest plans for missionary work among them. Such, for example, was Peter the Venerable, Abbot of Clugny in France, who studied the Moslem creed with sympathy and prepared translations of the Scriptures and other works with a view to influencing them.

But the one whose name will forever stand out in this connection with incomparable luster is Raymond Lull, the first and still the greatest missionary to the Moslems. After the Crusades had proved a failure, it was he who inaugurated the gospel method of conquering the false faith. He seemed to be raised up by God to prove by his example what the Crusades might have become, and might have done for the world, had they fought for the Cross with spiritual instead of carnal weapons, and approached the Saracens with the Word of Truth rather than with force of arms.

Raymond Lull (1235-1315) was born of a noble Spanish family, on the Island of Majorca. His father took part in one of the Crusades. The story of Lull's life reads like a romance. He was a brilliant student, a skilled musician, and a gay courtier. In the midst of a profligate career he was arrested by a vision of Christ on the Cross, experienced an agony of repentance, and then, turning his back on all his former life and associates, gave himself up in full consecration to Christ and to preparations and plans for the conversion of the Saracens. Convinced of the need of a thorough knowledge of the language of any people for a successful approach to them, he himself mastered Arabic and used his wealth in seeking to establish schools in which others might study various languages and fit themselves for missionary work.

In vain, however, did he appeal to both Church and State

for help, and at length, failing to induce others to join him, he went alone to the fanatical Moslem center of Tunis, North Africa. There he was so successful in his arguments with the Moslem doctors that he was thrown into prison and shortly afterwards sent from the country. Returning a second time to Africa, he was again imprisoned, though the Moslems spared his life in recognition of his splendid courage. When a third time he persisted in going to Africa in spite of threats against his life, he was set upon while preaching at Bugia and was stoned to death at the age of eighty. "In an age of violence he was the apostle of heavenly love. Let this motto from his own great book be adopted by all of his true successors. *'He who loves not, lives not; he who lives by the Life cannot die.'* " [1]

"He is the one connecting link in Missions between the apostles of Northern Europe and the leaders who, following the Reformation, carried the Gospel to every part of the rapidly increasing world." [2]

The Monastic Orders.

Christian monasticism (a word signifying the "lonely" life) had its rise in Egypt in the third century, when Paul the Hermit and other Christians withdrew into the desert to avoid the Decian persecution.

During the Period after Constantine made Christianity the State religion the monastic movement grew apace. Devout men, grieved and disgusted by the formalism and corruption of the Church and the shocking moral evils of the age, but lacking courage or conviction actively to oppose these things, retired to lonely retreats with the idea of preserving their own sanctity. Some went to fanatical lengths of asceticism in their unnatural life of solitude and idleness, and became a prey to the very evils and excesses which they had sought to escape. Others, more moderate, formed themselves into cloisters or communities, supporting themselves by various industries, and extending hospitality to strangers and help to the poor. And not a few of these communities became centers of missionary training and propagation. "Monachism on its good side was the missionary organiza-

---

[1] "Short History of Christian Missions," p. 108.
[2] "The Missionary Enterprise," p. 33.

tion through which Christendom worked up to Wycliffe, Huss and Luther." [3]   Such centers were Iona in Scotland and those founded by Martin in France, Patrick in Ireland and Boniface in Germany.   In fact all the missionary pioneers cited in this and the preceding Periods were monks and monastic leaders.

Later, mainly during this Medieval Period, there sprang up the various monastic sects which have since become so famous as constituting the Missionary Orders of the Church of Rome.   The most prominent of these are:—

The Benedictines.   This sect was the earliest in the West and was founded by *Benedict of Nursia* (480-543), who was regarded as the ideal monk.   His great monastery was at Monte Cassino, near Naples, but the order rapidly extended so that at one time there are said to have been as many as thirty-seven thousand monasteries, the majority in France, though not a few also in Italy, Sicily, Spain and other countries.   They promoted education and literature during those intellectually sterile centuries, and thus while not actually missionary they contributed materially to the development of religious life and Christian civilization.   Because of their long black gown and cowl they were sometimes called "Black Monks."

The Franciscans.   This sect owed its existence to *Francis of Assisi* (1182-1226).   He was the son of a rich merchant, and, like Lull, was suddenly converted from a life of sin and pleasure and devoted himself to preaching repentance and caring for the sick.   He drew to himself a band of followers whom he called "Fratres Minores" ("Little Brothers"), otherwise known from their garb as "Gray Friars." Francis took upon himself and imposed upon them the threefold vow of celibacy, poverty and obedience, and sent them out, two by two, to preach in several countries, observing literally Christ's injunction to take neither shoes, scrip nor staves.

Francis himself took part in one of the Crusades, evidently with a genuine purpose for the evangelization of the Saracens.   In Egypt, where a price was upon every Christian's head, he fearlessly marched alone into the Moslem army and approached the Sultan with the words, "I am not

[3] "Short History of Christian Missions," p. 146.

sent of man, but of God, to shew thee the way of salvation."
So touched was the Sultan's heart by this display of zeal
and courage that he dismissed Francis with honor, allowed
him to preach the gospel to the Moslems, and even manifested some spiritual concern himself.

The Franciscan order produced some of the great the-
ologians of the Period. It has sent out more missionaries
than any other Roman Catholic sect except the Jesuits, and
is still an active force along these lines. The mention of
Monte Corvino and other Franciscan missionaries to China
and the Far East, who belonged to this Period, is reserved
for a later section.

The Dominicans. This order was founded by a Spanish
priest named *Dominic* (1170-1221) about the same time
as the Franciscans. Its members were called Preaching
Friars, and it spread rapidly as a theological and missionary
body within the Roman Church. Aside from their far-
reaching missionary efforts the Dominicans became notorious mainly as being the agents of the Pope in carrying
on a relentless and bloody campaign with the object of
uprooting the Albigenses of Southern France and other
sects who because of their determined resistance of the
claims of the Roman Catholic priesthood and the abuses
of the Papacy were branded as heretics. Thus began the
inhuman Inquisition, which will forever remain an indelible
stain upon Rome.

The Jesuits. By far the most renowned of all the monastic orders is that known as the Jesuits, or the Society of
Jesus. It was founded by *Ignatius Loyola* (1491-1556), a
Spaniard of noble birth, together with several others of
like mind, among whom was *Francis Xavier,* destined to become the greatest of Jesuit missionaries. Their initial object was to devote their lives to the care of Christians and
the conversion of Saracens in the Holy Land, but the organization soon extended its aims and became the greatest of
all Roman Catholic foreign missionary agencies.

To the three vows of the other orders was added a fourth
vow, by which every Jesuit bound himself to go in unques-
tioning obedience to any part of the world and to undertake any task at the command of his superior. The binding
nature of this Jesuit vow, the secret machinations of the

Society, and its persistent ambition for both ecclesiastical
and political power have brought it into frequent conflict
with Church and State.

As a missionary society its operations extended principally to India, China, Japan, the Philippine Islands, Africa,
South America, Mexico, California and Canada.   Two
strong institutions of missionary training, established at
Rome and heavily endowed by rich patrons of the Society,
have supplied most of its missionaries.   In 1893 their number was 2,500, according to the Society's latest report published to that date.   The account of Xavier's missionary
career belongs to the next Period.   A few other early
Roman Catholic missionaries of prominence will be mentioned later on in the discussion of different mission fields.

QUESTIONS

1. Give the name and dates of the Fourth Period of Christian
Missions.

2. Give an account of the beginning of missionary work in the
following countries: Denmark, Sweden, Norway, Iceland, Greenland, Pomerania, Bulgaria, Moravia, Bohemia, Russia.

3. What were the Crusades?   When did they occur?   How
many are recorded?

4. Mention the prominent Crusade leaders, and also some of
the motives which actuated the Crusaders.

5. To what extent, if any, were the Crusades successful in
attaining their direct object?

6. Mention five important effects of the Crusades.

7. Sketch briefly the career of the earliest and greatest missionary to the Moslems.

8. What is meant by the term "monasticism," and when and
where did the system take its rise?

9. Name the well-known Monastic Orders, giving the founder's
name and the main features of each.

10. Name the greatest Jesuit missionary, and the main fields of
Jesuit missionary operations.

CHAPTER VI

PERIOD OF THE REFORMATION

FROM LUTHER TO THE HALLE MISSIONARIES (1517-1650)

Relation of the Reformation to Missions.

Mighty as were the changes wrought, and far-reaching as were the influences exerted, by the Reformation, it is to be borne in mind that that movement was not missionary in its character. It was a battle against ecclesiastical abuses, moral corruption and veritable heathenism within existing Christendom; and so absorbed were the Reformers with the struggle for freedom from the Papacy, and with the task also of establishing new communities in the faith and developing the church life of these, that the needs of the outside world were forgotten. Indeed, there is all too abundant evidence that most of the leaders of the Reformation, including *Luther, Melancthon, Calvin, Zwingli* and *Knox,* seem to have had no serious sense of responsibility for direct missionary efforts in behalf of heathen or Moslem. Despite their clear conceptions and statements of the fundamental doctrines of evangelical faith, they showed a remarkable ignorance of the scope of the divine plan and of Christian duty in relation to the gospel. Great mission fields lay round about them, especially in North Africa and Western Asia, while large communities of Jews were scattered among them. Yet for these they did nothing and apparently cared nothing.

"Hence we have the remarkable spectacle for many years of a live Protestant Church without mission interest, while the church which had been left because it lacked life was carrying on extensive missions in the Orient, and a little later in America." [1]

Indirectly, the Reformation was perhaps responsible for this effort on the part of the Latin Church, inasmuch as it

[1] "Via Christi," p. 161.

was the loss of so much territory in the Old World that
stirred up the papal power to seek fresh conquests in the
New.

"Having been themselves emancipated from the superstitions and
slavery of a false doctrine and a harsh ecclesiastical government,
it would be thought most natural that the reformers and those who
followed them should promptly turn their attention to spreading
these glad tidings among non-Christian peoples, but here a strange
anomaly is found in the fact that there has been hardly any period
in the entire history of the Christian Church so destitute of any
concerted effort to spread the gospel in heathen lands than just this
period of the Reformation." [2]

At the same time it must be recognized that by the Reformation new and better foundations were laid for greater
work which was to follow.   There was an insistent call for
a return to the teachings of the Bible, and the Bible plainly
taught the duty of the evangelization of the world.   Moreover, the Reformers applied themselves to the task of translating the whole Bible into the principal European languages.

"The vernacular Bible became a missionary book to Christendom
itself; and when Christians had mastered it somewhat during two
centuries they began to send it to the rest of the world, with missionaries to translate and to preach it." [3]

It was a slow process, and it took no little time, to
restore the sense of personal responsibility for the salvation
of non-Christians which has always been an underlying
principle of missionary activity, but which during ten or
more centuries of doctrinal corruption and spiritual darkness had practically disappeared.   But here and there noble
souls arose to lead the way in discerning and responding to
this long-lost-sight-of Christian duty.

Active Missionary Efforts.
Up to the Reformation the missionary work of the Christian Church was undivided, but from the Reformation onward it became separated into two very distinct, and often-
times antagonistic forces—Roman Catholicism and Protes-

2 "Outlines of Missionary History," p. 53.
3 "Short History of Christian Missions," p. 122.

tantism. It is scarcely necessary to say that the scope of
this course of study does not extend, in the main, beyond
the missionary work of the evangelical section of the Christian Church known by the name Protestant. The false
doctrines, unscrupulous methods, and questionable results
of Roman Catholic missions, with the addition not infre-
quently of shocking immoralities and grievous scandals connected with them, forbid their recognition in the same class
with Protestant missionary work. It will be essential, however, to the completeness of the outline of Christian missionary effort in most of the great mission fields to mention
Roman Catholic operations, as in many instances antedating
Protestant efforts. And it is to be acknowledged that, despite the condemnable features of Papal propaganda just
referred to, the lives and labors of some of its missionaries,
particularly the early pioneers, have displayed a spirit of
self-sacrificing devotion, fortitude and zeal that compels
appreciation and admiration. Foremost among such is one
who belonged to the Reformation Period and who must
ever be ranked among the greatest characters of missionary
annals. This was:

Francis Xavier (1506-1552). Xavier was the disciple
and associate of Loyola, founder of the Jesuits, and com-
menced the great foreign missionary work of that order.
In 1540 he was sent by the Pope to Goa, the Portuguese
colony on the west coast of Hindustan, and thence shortly
to the pearl fisheries extending from Cape Comorin to
Madras along the east coast. Later he labored at Travan-
core, where he baptized thousands of natives. After three
years in Southern India his restless spirit impelled him onward to the Malay Peninsula and adjoining islands, where
he spent another three years. There he came in contact with
a young Japanese, an escaped murderer, whom he made a
convert; and learning through him of the Japanese nation
Xavier's soul became fired with zeal to visit and evangelize
Japan. With this Japanese convert, Hanjiro, as his guide
the great missionary landed in Japan in 1549.

The picture is drawn of him "trudging bare-footed,
carrying his box containing everything necessary for cele-
brating the Holy Sacrament up and down the hills of Kioto
or along the shore of Oita, calling the nation that alternately

gave him welcome and rebuff, and which he termed 'the delight of my soul.' " His journeys in Japan occupied two and a half years, and although unable to speak the language and laboring under other great disadvantages he claimed and baptized many thousands of converts.

His latest efforts, after revisiting Goa, were to enter China, but they were unavailing, and in 1552 he died of fever on the little island of Sancian (St. John), off the southeast coast of China. His despairing cry, *"O rock! rock! when wilt thou open to my Master?"*, uttered as he faced the impassable wall of Chinese exclusion, has found an echo in the hearts of many hundreds of later missionaries, whose fervent prayers and faithful labors, along with Xavier's, have been God's instrumentality in breaching the wall and forcing open the door into the greatest nation of the world.

In Francis Xavier perhaps more strikingly than in any other Romish missionary have we an example of that strange and paradoxical combination of depth of genuine love and devotion to Christ and holy passion for souls along with doctrines woefully unsound and policies of work utterly unworthy.

In attempting to sum up his character and career we cannot do better than to quote from Dr. Arthur T. Pierson's rarely fine appreciation of Xavier, expressed in his inimitable style. Referring to him as the Romish Apostle to the Indies, Dr. Pierson writes:

"He was misguided, no doubt; but no other life, since Paul's, has shewn such ardor and fervor, such absorbing zeal for the greater glory of God, such self-forgetting, self-denying passion for the souls of men, as that of the young Saint of Navarre, whose withered relics are still adored in the Church of Bom Jesus at Goa.

"To the doctrine of free grace, unconsciously imbibed in boyhood, he owed his genuine experience of faith in Christ, his strong hold upon Him, and the inspiration of an unselfish purpose. To his Papal and Jesuit training we trace that admixture of confidence in outward rites and good works which alloyed and vitiated his otherwise superb service. To sprinkle holy water in baptism, to recite the creed and a few prayers, limited his methods and measured his success. His preaching practically knew nothing of the purging away of sin by intelligent faith in the atoning blood. He said, *'feci christianos'*—'I make Christians'; and it is not strange if the disciples he made often shocked their 'maker' by glaring vices and flagrant sins.

"He mastered no Oriental language, and was often without an interpreter. . . . His was the gospel of sacraments and ceremonies, preached in mute action, but with what lofty enthusiasm! To baptize a new-born babe would save a soul; to mumble a few prayers would deliver from purgatory; and so he went on with wild passion for numbers, carrying the counting of converts to the last extreme of error and absurdity. It was the lasting warning against that mechanical theory which gauges the success of missions by numerical results. . . .

"Yet, notwithstanding all these drawbacks, this Jesuit fanatic puts to shame all who read the story of his life, by the utter self-abnegation he exhibited. . . . The man who could cheerfully forsake the paths of indulgence and scholarship for one perpetual pilgrimage amid the sickening sights and stifling air of Oriental heathenism; who could on God's altar lay himself, with his brilliant mind and prospects of preferment, with youth, wealth, worldly ambition, all tempting him to self-seeking—and know only the glory of God—such a man cannot be simply set aside as a fool or a fanatic." [4]

During a brief but intense missionary career of only ten years this remarkable man is said to have planted the cross "in fifty-two different kingdoms, preached through nine thousand miles of territory, and baptized over one million persons."

"In visions of the night when he saw the world conquered for Christ, he would spring up shouting, 'Yet more, O my God, yet more!' and his whole life was a commentary on his own motto: *'Ad Majorem Dei Gloriam'* ('To the greater glory of God')." [5]

Of missionary efforts on the part of the Reformation church there is sadly little to record. It is true that, following out the ideas advanced by Calvin and others of the reform leaders as to the duty of extending the gospel into non-Christian lands resting with the State rather than the Church, some Protestant governments, notably those of Geneva and Holland, and later England also, did make attempts to found Christian colonies in heathen lands. In the charters granted to both the Dutch and the English East India Companies it was stipulated that measures should be taken for the planting of the Church and the conversion of the heathen, and chaplains were sent out for this purpose with the early colonizing and trading expeditions to the Far

[4] "The New Acts of the Apostles," pp. 67, 68.
[5] *Ibid.,* p. 69.

East and the New World. But mission interests were always secondary to colonial interests, and whenever the two clashed mission work had to yield.

Weird interest attaches to an expedition of French Huguenots sent to Brazil by Calvin and Coligny, but which ended disastrously through the treachery of its leader Villegagnon.

But the truth is that neither the new church itself, nor yet its leaders, were ready for a missionary movement, and it was not until the middle of the seventeenth century that the agitations and efforts of the few individuals who were ahead of their times in discerning the church's true mission in the world gathered sufficient momentum to set in motion missionary plans once more.

QUESTIONS

1. Give the name and dates of the Fifth Period of Christian Missions.
2. Describe the attitude of the Reformation leaders toward missions, and the bearing of that upheaval, directly or indirectly, upon the missionary enterprise.
3. Give an account of the greatest of all Roman Catholic missionaries.
4. What efforts were put forth along missionary lines by Protestantism during this Period, and with what success?

Chapter VII

PERIOD OF THE EARLY MISSIONARY SOCIETIES

FROM THE HALLE MISSIONARIES TO CAREY (1650-1792)

The roots of modern missions reach back to the Reformation in the very real sense that a revival of apostolic faith was the necessary precursor of a revival of apostolic life and work. Yet, as already remarked, the Reform leaders, and the Reformation church as a whole, were for at least a full century almost completely devoid of missionary spirit or effort. Indeed, the Reformation movement ran into a serious new danger from its rigid preoccupation with matters of doctrine alone. As Dr. George Smith expresses it, the seeds of controversy sown by Lutheran orthodoxy began to bear a harvest which would have been fatal to the spirituality of the church but for the Pietist Movement, which by example and preaching gradually aroused the church to a deeper spiritual life and, as a natural consequence, to renewed missionary zeal and action.

"Here and there one man was reached and roused, his eyes opening to the fact that millions were dying without the gospel; his ears opening to the cry of want and woe which, like the moan and sob of waves on the seashore, tells of storm and wreck. Now and then a man went forth, while as yet the church as a whole seemed locked in icy indifference and insensibility." [1]

It remains to trace the course of this stream from its fountainhead of quickened spiritual life and missionary conviction, through the rivulet stage of feeble individual effort, until, fed from every side, it steadily grows into a river which has continued to flow on and out, with ever deepening current and widening reach, unto the ends of the earth.

[1] "The New Acts of the Apostles," p. 74.

The subject matter of this Period does not call for any particular classification. It will suffice to sketch briefly in order the individuals and groups who were the most prominent factors in leading the way to the formation of the early missionary societies which were, in turn, forerunners of the greater and more highly organized missionary enterprise of the Modern Period.

Von Welz, the Missionary Agitator.

To this Austrian baron, singular as the fact is, belongs the credit of sounding, about 1664, the first general and vigorous missionary appeal to the church. He was the first of that succession of godly pioneers of this Period who, to use Dr. Pierson's words, "formed the mold in which modern missions took shape." In a series of three pamphlets he boldly set forth the missionary duty of the church, and called for the formation of an association for the extension of the gospel among the heathen, and for the establishment of a college to train missionaries. He put the following three searching questions before the slumbering conscience of the church: (1) "Is it right that we, evangelical Christians, hold the gospel for ourselves alone, and do not seek to spread it?" (2) "Is it right that in all places we have so many students of theology, and do not induce them to labor elsewhere in the spiritual vineyard of Jesus Christ?" (3) "Is it right that we spend so much on all sorts of dress, delicacies in eating and drinking, etc., but have hitherto thought of no means for the spread of the gospel?"

His manifesto was an anticipation of Carey's epoch-making "Inquiry into the Obligation of Christians" more than a century later, and it met with a similar or even worse reception. It is a commentary upon the religious condition of the times that one of the leading and best men among the clergy met Von Welz's appeal by a bitter rebuke, denouncing him as a dreamer, fanatic, hypocrite and heretic, and arguing that it was absurd, even wicked, to cast the pearls of the gospel before the dogs of heathen.

Meeting thus with rebuff and ridicule, and failing to move others to action, Von Welz heroically resolved to be true to his own convictions. He proceeded to Holland, was there ordained by a poor priest as "an apostle to the Gentiles," and taking with him 36,000 marks set sail for *Dutch Guiana.* There he soon fell victim to an inhospitable climate and bad conditions and filled a martyr missionary's grave. But in vain? A thousand times, no! He was a corn of wheat which, cast into the ground to die, brought forth abundant and abiding fruit. "Such men are God's agitators, sent to marshal the conscience of the church, to mold the law of its life and the methods of its work in conformity with His Word and will." [2]

The Pietist Leaders and Training School.

The emphasis laid by the Reformation leaders upon justification by faith, vital as was that doctrine, was at the expense of the equally vital truth of sanctification, and a trend toward moral degeneration in the new church set in. The Pietist Movement, led by *Philip Spener* (1635-1705), who was called "the German Wesley," and his even more distinguished follower, *August Francke* (1663-1727), was a revolt against barren orthodoxy and dead formalism, and an earnest effort to raise the standards of Christian life. Spener's bold protest against wickedness in high places naturally called forth bitter opposition. Nevertheless the revival movement sowed seed in some hearts which eventually bore a great harvest. It led to founding, in 1698, of the *University of Halle,* which became a center of the strongest missionary influence and the birthplace of the first organized foreign missionary effort.

The Danish-Halle Mission to India.

This was the first foreign mission to be the direct product of Reformed Christianity. It was brought about through the influence of Dr. Lütkens, a chaplain of the Danish court and the bosom friend of Francke. He laid before King Friedrich IV of Denmark the duty of providing Christian education for the people of the Danish colonies. The good king cordially responded with both sympathy and financial help. Lütkens proceeded to found at Copenhagen a College for the preparation of missionaries, but in the meantime secured through Francke at Halle the first two missionaries for the project.

2 "The New Acts of the Apostles," p. 76.

These were *Bartholomew Ziegenbalg* and *Henry Plüt-schau,* who, sent forth in November, 1705, reached *Tranquebar,* 150 miles south of Madras, on the east coast of India, only in July, 1706. Touching on their way at the Cape they saw the pitiable condition of the Hottentots under the blighting rule of the Dutch, and it was the appeal sent home by these two men that moved the Moravians to undertake the first mission to South Africa.

Upon their arrival in India they at once encountered severe trials and difficulties. Strangely and sadly enough, the greatest of these came not, as might have been expected, from the heathen, but from the Danish authorities. In spite of the fact that the mission had the sanction and support of the King of Denmark, the Danish East India Company dared to send to the Danish Governor at Tranquebar, by the same ship on which Ziegenbalg and Plütschau sailed, secret instructions to block their way by every possible means, and that official obeyed his instructions with a will.

Picture, then, these first two Protestant missionaries to tread the soil of India standing unsheltered on the shore the first night after they landed, left by the Governor to shift for themselves. Being finally allowed to occupy a house upon the city wall, close by the heathen quarters, with dauntless courage they began to study the Tamil language within six days of their arrival, at first sitting down with the native children and writing in the sand with their fingers. Such remarkable progress did Ziegenbalg make that in eight months he could talk fluently in Tamil, and in his third year he completed the first translation of the New Testament into any of the native languages of India.

On the 12th of May, 1707, ten months after their arrival, they publicly baptized five adult heathen slaves of Danish masters, and a few months later nine Hindoos, as the first-fruits of their labors. Next year Ziegenbalg made his first preaching tour into the kingdom of Tanjore. The publication at home of his letters to his former instructors, Lange and Francke, and particularly his accounts of friendly conferences held by him with the Brahmans, aroused widespread interest in Europe. One result was that help, financial and otherwise, was given to the mission by two English Societies, one "for Promoting Christian Knowledge" formed in 1699, the other "for the Propagation of the Gospel" in 1701. Both of these originally had colonial rather than foreign missionary work in view.

Ill health took Plütschau from the field in 1711. Ziegenbalg continued his labors arduously, though weakened as a result of hardships endured, for which the cruel treatment of the Danish Governor was in part responsible. In 1719, at the early age of thirty-six, and after twelve short but momentous years of foreign service, this noble pioneer passed from earthly toil and suffering to heavenly rest and reward. The following word picture of his deathbed is given by Dr. Pierson:—

"When about to depart, so intense was the glory that smote him, that he suddenly put his hands to his eyes, exclaiming, 'How is it so bright, as if the sun shone full in my face!' Soon after, he asked that his favorite hymn might be sung, 'Jesus, my confidence,' and on the wings of sacred song he took his flight, leaving behind over three hundred and fifty converts, catechumens and pupils, a missionary seminary and a Tamil lexicon, but best of all the Tamil Bible." [3]

Who can estimate the worth to God of such lives, in relation to His purpose of grace toward a great land like India, comprising one-fifth of the entire living human family and all in unrelieved heathenism? But such lives belong not alone to one land, however great. They are a priceless benediction and heritage to Christians of every land and age. And may that benediction and heritage be made secure to those who read these lines, through the yielding of their hearts to be freshly filled with that divine love and grace which alone inspired those saintly men to the sacrifice they endured and the service they rendered!

Still another name connected with this same mission and also Halle University stands out with deserved prominence and claims mention here. It is that of *Christian Frederic Schwartz* (1726-1798), whom Dr. Pierson calls "the founder of the native Christian church in India." It was while a pupil under Francke at Halle that his missionary interest was first awakened by seeing the Bible in strange Tamil characters, as it was being put through the press for the Tranquebar Mission; although long before this his godly

[3] "The New Acts of the Apostles," p. 80.

mother, dying in his infancy, dedicated her child, as did Hannah, to the Lord for His peculiar service.

Schwartz' missionary career in India, which began in 1750 and lasted forty-eight years, was as remarkable as it was long. Coupled with singular piety and the zeal of love were extraordinary linguistic gifts and a magnetic force of character that won all hearts and held their unbounded confidence. He mastered not only Tamil but also Persian, Hindustani, English and Hindoo-Portuguese, and versed himself in Hindustani literature and mythology, thereby extending his ministry and influence beyond the masses to the greatest Mohammedan princes, the educated Brahmans and the various European classes. He preached everywhere and incessantly, covering the whole eastern coast and opening many chapels and schools.

In addition to such direct missionary work, "on account of his perfect integrity, fluency in the language and knowledge of public affairs, he became the chief medium of communication between the native princes and the British Government. So loved and trusted was he on both sides that, when the fiercest enmity prevailed between a native province and the government, 'Father Schwartz' was at liberty to go in either camp at his will." [4]

A striking instance of this was afforded when an insurrection was raised by Hyder Ali, a Mohammedan. Schwartz was the only man through whom that proud tyrant would consent to treat with the British. "Send me the Christian; he will not deceive me," he demanded. All unsought, this humble missionary wielded the power of a foreign ambassador as well as of a magistrate within the native state. Nor did these high honors or offices affect in the least his essential missionary spirit or ministry. To the end he lived in the most unassuming and frugal manner, uniformly refused the princely gifts repeatedly pressed upon him in return for valued services rendered, and even declined to accept a large legacy left him by a military officer.

His career was indeed unique and remarkable. When at last he died, in 1798, noble monuments were erected to his memory by the native prince of Tanjore and the East India Company, while a granite tablet was placed by the foreigners

4 "Via Christi," p. 205.

in his chapel.   But a more precious and abiding monument than all of these is the rare record of fruitful service to multitudes and the fragrant memory of a life that magnified Christ his Master before men.

Perhaps no closing testimony to this great missionary could be more impressive than the following:—At his funeral

"the Rajah's heir, Serjofee, could not be kept, even by Hindu custom, from taking his place as a chief mourner; and three years later, at his own cost, built him a superb marble monument, executed by Flaxman. The epitaph he himself wrote, the first English verse ever known to be written by a native Hindu:

'Firm wast Thou, humble and wise,
Honest and pure, free from disguise;
Father of orphans, the widow's support;
Comfort in sorrow of every sort.
To the benighted, dispenser of light,
Doing, and pointing to that which is right.
Blessing to princes, to people, to me,
May I, my Father, be worthy of Thee,
Wisheth and prayeth thy Sarabojee.' " [5]

Hans Egede, the Apostle to Greenland.

Turning from the hot tropics to the frozen polar regions, we have another example of one who was called and thrust out by God to carry the gospel to that inhospitable clime. The story of Hans Egede (1686-1758) and his equally heroic wife, Elizabeth, and their mission to Greenland is full of impressive features.   Egede was educated at Copenhagen College and had settled in a pastorate in Norway when he heard the tale of the early colonizing and evangelizing work under Lief the Lucky in Greenland, and of the misfortunes through which communications with that remote region had been broken off, with the result that after nearly three centuries of neglect the poor inhabitants had relapsed into heathenism.   His impression at the time was that these people were the descendants of the old Norsemen colonists and hence in a double sense his brethren. His heart was strangely moved and he could not shake off the conviction that God was calling him to Greenland.   His proposal to go met with strong opposition from both his wife and his parish, which it took several years to overcome.

[5] "The New Acts of the Apostles," p. 93.

Meanwhile God wrought a deeper conviction and preparation in Egede's own heart, and then so completely changed his wife's attitude that she became perhaps the stronger of the two.

In 1721 they set sail from Bergen with a company of forty-six persons, to find at the end of their perilous voyage not the Norwegian descendants they looked for, but instead a race of dwarfed and stupid Eskimos. The outlook was most discouraging, but they threw themselves undaunted into the hard task, learning the unwritten language and framing new words where necessary for the expression of the new ideas which they brought. They suffered the severest hardships, their support from home became more and more reduced and uncertain, and finally the new Danish king recalled the European colonists.

But the heroic Egedes persuaded a few to remain with them, and through many fresh trials and vicissitudes they succeeded in laying the foundation of the modern colony of Christian Eskimos, of which Godt-haab (good hope) is the capital. During an awful scourge of smallpox, which decimated the people, Egede and his wife were veritable angels of life in their devoted ministry to both the bodies and the souls of the dying Eskimos. They were the sole means of bringing salvation to hundreds of precious souls. An unique and impressive feature of Egede's missionary work was that in a time of deep distress of soul because of the stolid apathy of the people he asked and received from God, as a token of the divine presence and power, the supernatural gift of healing, and exercised it in scores of cases.

Zinzendorf and the Moravians.

It was from the Pietist Movement that the Moravian Church received its missionary call. The sect now generally called Moravian is among themselves known as the United Brethren. Zinzendorf was not its founder, but rather its reviver and the progenitor of its missionary work. The sect itself dates back to the pre-Reformation period, when, in 1467, the persecuted Bohemian followers of John Huss, with certain Waldenses and Moravians, joined together under the name *Unitas Fratrum* (United Brotherhood).

Bitterly persecuted though they were by their enemies they numbered 400 churches when the Reformation awoke. Later, in the seventeenth century, they again suffered at the hands of the Jesuits and were well nigh exterminated. In 1722, Christian David, a humble but zealous convert from Romanism, gathered together the remnant and led them into Saxony, where in a most providential way they came upon one of the estates of Count Zinzendorf. That good Christian nobleman gave them refuge and land, and a settlement was built called *Herrnhut* ("the Lord's Watch"), which to this day remains the center and headquarters of the Moravian Church.

Count von Zinzendorf (1700-1760) himself was grandson of an Austrian nobleman who for conscience' sake gave up all his estates. Young Zinzendorf was brought up by a godly grandmother and aunt, who were Pietists, and almost from infancy he evinced spiritual traits of rare depth. He was first educated as a boy under Francke at Halle, afterwards at the University of Wittenberg, where he was noted for his fervent spiritual character. Although later exposed to the strongest temptations in the way of worldly allurements and honors at Paris and Dresden he withstood them all, and finally he felt constrained, against the wishes of his guardian and friends, to resign the high position he had been given at Dresden and to devote his life wholly to evangelistic work.

His chosen life-motto was, *"I have one passion; it is He, and He alone."* At the marriage altar he and his young bride, also of noble birth, covenanted together and with the Lord to renounce their rank and to devote all their property as well as themselves to the service of Christ. In 1727 he became the spiritual superintendent of the Herrnhut colony, and in 1737 was ordained Bishop of the Moravian Church.

Meanwhile an incident occurred which exerted a deep and lasting influence upon Zinzendorf, and through him turned the tide of the whole Moravian movement in a missionary direction. It was in 1731 that the Count was called upon to represent the Saxon court at the coronation in Copenhagen of Christian VI. of Denmark. While there he saw two Eskimos who had been baptized by Hans Egede, and learned with deep regret of the decision to give up the mission in Greenland. His attendants also met a negro, Anthony, who told them of the cruel lot of the slaves in the Danish West Indian colonies. Zinzendorf's sympathies were profoundly stirred, as in turn were those of the Brotherhood when he narrated to them the incidents upon his return home. It was promptly resolved to take up the work in Greenland, while two devoted men were found and almost immediately sent out to St. Thomas in the West Indies. Thus in God's own simple but wonderful way began the renowned foreign missionary work of the Moravians, which rapidly extended farther to Central and South America, Labrador, the Indians of the United States and Alaska, to South Africa and Australia, and even to the snow-bound passes of the Himalayan mountains on the remote borders of Tibet.

Some of their missionary efforts seem not to have been fully successful, and, measured by the size of their work or the number of converts in any particular field, their undertakings may perhaps appear to some minds to have fallen short of the most satisfactory results. Notwithstanding, the Moravians have set and maintained a standard of missionary devotion never yet approached by any other church body.

They began in 1732 by sending out two missionaries. During the next 150 years they sent out 2,170 to various foreign fields. Their report for 1930 showed 136 main stations occupied, 366 missionaries (including 113 native missionaries), and 2,242 other native helpers. There were upwards of 75,000 baptized Christians, and more than 37,000 pupils in day schools.

While the Protestant churches at large are sending, at the very highest estimate, one member in two or three thousand, the Moravian Church sends *one in every ninety-two*. They furnish the unique spectacle of having three times as many members in their foreign missions as in their home churches.

Such a report on the part of a community so weak in numbers and in wealth constitutes one of the marvels of modern missions. Without a doubt it is traceable in large measure to the mighty spiritual impulse imparted by that remarkable man, who as their leader set before them an example of such unqualified consecration of every talent, faculty and resource he possessed to the Christ whom he adored. The Brotherhood caught and perpetuated the spirit of their leader. Their seal is a lamb on a crimson ground, with the cross of resurrection and a banner of triumph, with the motto: *"Vicit agnus noster, eum sequamur"* ("Our Lamb has conquered; let us follow Him"). They have presented to the church of Christ a splendid object lesson of the great fundamental missionary principles as taught in the Scriptures. They have recognized themselves in debt to the world as trustees of the gospel, and have been taught frugality of habits, readiness to sacrifice, and prompt obedience to the call of God to go anywhere, and with an emphasis upon the worst and hardest of fields as having the first claim. And no missionaries of the cross have been bolder as pioneers, more patient or persistent under difficulties, more heroic in suffering, or more entirely devoted to Christ and the soul needs of men than those of the Moravian Brotherhood.

Missions to North American Indians.

High-handed policy on the part of English sovereigns, and in particular religious intolerance, led to an ever-increasing stream of emigration to America, beginning early in the seventeenth century. The first company of these Puritans, known ever since in history as *"the Pilgrim Fathers,"* sailed in the *Mayflower* in 1620, and landed at New Plymouth on the Massachusetts coast. While the dominating motive of these new colonists was religious freedom for themselves rather than the carrying of the gospel to others, yet the fact of their religious character and of the price they had paid for their convictions naturally prompted to efforts in behalf of the Indians around them, and it is claimed that the various accounts sent back to England of the extension of the gospel among the red men contributed much to the interest aroused in the new continent.

Among those who devoted themselves to the spiritual needs of the Indians mention here can be made of only a few of the most prominent.

Roger Williams (1606-1683), the founder of Rhode

Island, while filling a pastoral charge among the whites devoted his best energy to working among the Indians. He learned their language, published a helpful Indian-English handbook, and was for forty years the staunch friend of the tribesmen, laboring for their material and spiritual welfare and frequently standing boldly in defense of their rights against the aggressions of the white man.

John Eliot (1604-1690) occupies the first place in the list, because of the great length and signal value of his service, and has been called the Apostle to the North American Indians. A distinguished student at Cambridge and a master of the original languages of the Scriptures, young Eliot himself traced his conversion and deepest spiritual blessing to the holy influences of the home of Thomas Hooker, the Puritan exile, under whom he was for a time a teacher and whom he followed to the New World in 1630.

Eliot began work as a minister at Roxbury, Mass., but his heart was soon drawn out intensely toward the Indians, and taking up the study of the language of the Pequot tribe of Iroquois Indians he gave the remaining fifty-eight years of his life to the work of their evangelization. In 1646, in the wigwam of one of the chiefs, he preached the first sermon ever known in their language. It proved a memorable service indeed, for the spirit of religious inquiry began to burn, and from that starting point souls in ever-increasing numbers came under conviction of sin and were saved. He threw himself unreservedly into the work with all his splendid gifts and energies, fearlessly facing perils and cheerfully bearing privations for Christ's sake. He naturally incurred the bitter hatred and opposition of the Indian priests, and plots were laid against his life, but in vain. As the influence of his preaching spread farther and farther afield his labors grew both in intensity and in variety. He became in turn evangelist, pastor, teacher, statesman, translator and trainer of a native ministry.

Facing the great difficulty of maintaining proper standards of Christian living among his converts in their old heathen setting, he gathered them together and organized a number of centers which became known as "Praying Towns," the first of which was at Natick, near Boston. "Here the Christian Indian could go to a church where an Indian pastor preached, and to a school where an Indian teacher taught, and could live a Christian life free from the persecutions of the heathen Indians about them. The Indians who came to this town made a covenant as follows: 'The grace of Christ helping us, we do give ourselves and our children to God to be His people. He shall rule over us in all our affairs, not only in our religion and the affairs of the church, but also in all our works and affairs of this world.' " [6]

By 1671 Eliot had gathered some 3,600 converted Indians into fourteen settlements. But perhaps an even greater legacy which he left behind him consisted of twenty-four carefully trained native preachers, and the "Moheecan Bible," a complete translation of the Word of God into Indian, which he effected during the years 1661-1663—*the first Bible ever printed in America*. The fact that that famous Bible has no longer one living reader in no way takes from the value of Eliot's gifted and consecrated labor upon it. But it does constitute a lasting monument to the shameful and indefensible treatment by which Eliot's Christian community and the Indians in general were basely destroyed before the insatiate greed and unscrupulous measures of the "civilized" white settlers, whose acts of violence were too often unrestrained and even condoned by those in authority. The National period of the government's relation to the Indian has been fitly called a "century of dishonor," and must always remain a disgraceful stain upon the pages of American history.

Even in Eliot's day there were not a few among his own countrymen who "not content to withhold aid, pitilessly pelted him with the hail of ridicule, or hurled at him the mud clods of aspersion." Yet long before his death his work had compelled recognition in Britain. "It was largely because of the interest excited in England by Eliot's work that 'the Society for the Propagation of the Gospel in New England' was organized in England (1649), one hundred and forty-eight years before the Society inspired by William Carey. Its work, with a largely increased scope, was later taken over by 'the Society for the Propagation of the Gospel in Foreign Parts' (1701)." [7]

[6] "Winners of the World," p. 90.
[7] "Two Thousand Years Before Carey," p. 409.

In addition to the translation of the Bible, Eliot produced several valuable original works in the Indian language, and it was at the end of his Indian Grammar that he appended his famous motto, so fittingly applicable to all true missions: *"Prayer and pains, through faith in Jesus Christ, will do anything."*

The Mayhews. The record of this family, like that of the well-known Scudder family later in India, is unique in that the missionary spirit was carried down through five consecutive generations, their continuous service extending for one hundred and sixty years. Thomas Mayhew, Sr., an English merchant, in 1641 became the Crown patentee of the Islands now known as Martha's Vineyard, Nantucket and the Elizabeth Isles, off the coast of Massachusetts, and the Governor of the colony which was formed thereon. His son was pastor of the Colonists' Church, but soon took up work for the native tribes living on the islands. With deep devotion the five generations of Mayhews undertook and accomplished the evangelization of these Indians, some thousands of whom became Christians and were organized into churches. Zechariah Mayhew, of the fifth generation, continued his work as pastor to the tribes until his death in 1806.

David Brainerd (1718-1747), under the auspices of the Scottish Propagation Society, began work among the Indians near Stockbridge, Mass., on the Hudson River, but his main field of labor was among the aborigines of the Delaware River region. His missionary career was a brief one of only three or four years. Then, broken down by the hardships and exposures to which he had unfalteringly subjected himself in his long and perilous journeys and self-sacrificing labors for the Indians, he died of consumption at the home of his warm friend, Jonathan Edwards, the famous preacher. But his short life of twenty-nine years has left behind it an influence seldom equaled in its powerful effect upon others. The memory of David Brainerd has been cherished by the most spiritual of each succeeding generation of Christians, and to-day is still as fresh and fragrant as ever—not because of his work but because of the rare depth of his spiritual life and his saintliness of character. Like Enoch, he walked with God, and the memoirs left of his inner life of communion and prayer lead the reader into the very "holiest of all."

It was Brainerd's holy life that influenced Henry Martyn to become a missionary and was a prime factor in William Carey's inspiration. Carey in turn moved Adoniram Judson. And so we trace the spiritual lineage from step to step —Huss, Wycliffe, Francke, Zinzendorf, the Wesleys and Whitefield, Brainerd, Edwards, Carey, Judson, and ever onward in the true apostolic succession of spiritual grace and power and world-wide ministry.

Roman Catholic Efforts. Mention may be made of Roman Catholic missions of this Period to the Indians of the United States and Canada, but particularly Quebec. These missions were happily of a distinctly higher order than those carried on in South and Central America. The Franciscans began work among the Hurons near Quebec in 1615, followed by the Jesuits among the Iroquois south of Montreal in 1669. Among the names of these early laborers stand such as *Brebœuf, Marquette, La Salle* and others—hardy pioneers who penetrated the forests and braved the greatest hardships without a murmur. Not a few fell victims to the passions of the cruel savages; others gave their strength and life for their Indian converts. The work of these worthy men is commemorated by beautiful paintings of the scenes of their labors still to be seen in the Roman Catholic Cathedral of St. James in Montreal. The bitter wars which followed between the French and English sadly interfered with this work, and finally most of the missions disappeared entirely.

QUESTIONS

1. Give the name and dates of the Sixth Period of Christian Missions.

2. (a) Who first sought to arouse the Reformed church to missionary effort, and with what success? (b) What course did he afterwards personally pursue?

3. What was the Pietist Movement? Who were its leaders? What missionary training school did they establish?

4. Name the first foreign missionary enterprise of Reformed Christianity, and give a brief account of the work of its three most prominent missionaries.

5. Give an account of the mission among the Eskimos of Greenland during this Period.

6. Sketch the career of the great leader of the sect first known as Unitas Fratrum.

7. Mention the outstanding feature of the Moravian Church, and indicate in general the location and results of its missionary work.

8. What valuable lessons bearing upon Missions has the Moravian Church taught by its example?

9. Give the names of four leading early missionaries to the North American Indians, and sketch the work of the most noted of these.

10. Give an account of Roman Catholic missions to the Indians of Quebec.

PART II: World-wide Extension

CHAPTER VIII

PERIOD OF MODERN MISSIONS

FROM CAREY TO THE PRESENT DAY (1792—)

The foregoing records bring us to the dawn of the modern missionary era, which by common consent and for substantial reasons is said to have begun with Carey. "The gathering at Kettering marks the beginning of the associate organization, which has been at the basis of the most successful missionary enterprises. Individual responsibility and mutual action took the place of the pure individualism of the apostolic and medieval ages, the ecclesiastical order of Roman Catholicism, and the State missions of the early Protestant era." [1]

Preparatory Forces.

Changes in the world at large as well as within the church now witnessed that a new epoch had been reached. Geographically, a new hemisphere had been discovered, while knowledge of the old had vastly increased. Commercial and colonizing schemes had brought the ends of the earth into new contact. The great East India Companies, Dutch and English, had—without intention or desire, it is true—paved the way for the missionary by making travel to, and residence in, eastern countries more practicable and safe. New inventions and scientific discoveries began to contribute their help. But a far greater factor still was what is known as the *Renaissance,* which had freed the intellectual and religious world from the tyranny and blight of medieval systems and traditions. On every hand there was the awakening of new life.

The developments in the religious world were by no means the least notable. The effects of the Reformation

[1] "The Missionary Enterprise," p. 66.

and Pietist movements have already been traced. It must be confessed that rationalism had brought evangelical religion to a low ebb in Germany and Holland, and formalism was sadly in evidence in the Established Church of England. But meanwhile the evangelistic movement under the Wesleys and Whitefield had begun, and the visit of John Wesley to America and his later contact with Zinzendorf and the Moravian center at Herrnhut exerted a distinct missionary influence upon the great leaders of Methodism.

Last of all to be mentioned, but surely not least in effect, was a marked revival of prayer for the heathen world among the more spiritual Christians of the Old and the New Worlds. Robert Millar, of Paisley, published in 1723 a "History of the Propagation of Christianity, and the Overthrow of Heathenism," in which he powerfully urged prayer as the first of nine means for the conversion of the heathen. The effect was great. Similar appeals by other leaders followed at intervals. In 1744, as a result of a refreshing revival, a call was issued widely for a sustained concert of prayer "that God's kingdom may come," and in 1746 a memorial was sent to America inviting all Christians there to unite in the same petition. It met with a hearty response from Jonathan Edwards, and a sermon by him which followed was one of the influences that stirred the heart of William Carey. To this new volume of prayer, the fruit of spiritual revival, are to be traced the beginnings of the modern missionary enterprise.

"The Father of Modern Missions."

William Carey has been justly called "the father of modern missions." His career constituted an epoch indeed. It brought about a veritable revolution in missionary planning and thinking. Hitherto missionary undertakings had been mere isolated and spasmodic efforts on the part of individuals or little groups, while the mass of the churches, ministers and members alike, remained utterly indifferent and apathetic toward the condition of the pagan world. It was through Carey that there came an outburst of general missionary zeal and effort such as had not been since the days of the apostles, inaugurating a new era of united, organized, and systematic operations which have continued without abatement and with ever-widening reach and increasing force to the present day.

More than one missionary writer refers to the year 1792 as *"annus mirabilis,"* the famous date from which missionary annals are to be reckoned backward and forward. Dr. D. L. Leonard places this year along with 44 A.D., when the Holy Ghost said, "Separate me Barnabas and Saul for the work whereunto I have called them," and 53 A.D., when by a vision Paul was bidden to lay the foundations of the gospel in Europe. He adds: "We may speak of the 'Carey epoch' with every whit as much propriety as of the Luther Reformation. We may as fitly term him the apostle of Modern Missions as Paul the apostle to the Gentiles, or Augustine apostle to the Britons, or Boniface apostle to the Germans." [2]

The decided change in the character and scope of the missionary enterprise from this point onward calls for a change in the manner of setting forth the facts. Hitherto the point of vision has been Christendom, as we have sought to trace the development of conviction and zeal for the world's evangelization within the home churches, and the outreach of efforts in behalf of the heathen. Now we must transfer the point of vision to heathendom itself, and present in order the general facts and features of the different missionary lands and the beginnings and progress of gospel work within them. The facts connected with the ushering in of this new Period make our natural starting point to be India.

QUESTIONS

1. Give the name and opening date of the Seventh Period of Christian Missions.

2. What different factors helped to prepare the way for the modern missionary era?

3. Who is known as the "Father of Modern Missions," and why?

4. What difference of aspect did Missions assume from the beginning of the Modern Period?

2 "A Hundred Years of Missions," p. 71

CHAPTER IX

INDIA

AREA, 1,600,000 SQUARE MILES.*   POPULATION, 343,500,000*

I. General Features.

The Land. India, including Ceylon and Burma, extends
from Afghanistan on the west to Siam on the east, a distance of over 2,000 miles; from the Himalayas on the
north to Cape Comorin on the south, a distance almost as
great. Its area is six-tenths that of the United States, or
as large as that portion of the United States east of the
Rocky Mountains. It is a great peninsula, triangular in
shape, and divided physically into three distinct sections,
the mountainous Himalayan region in the north, the fertile
river plains of the Ganges, Indus and Brahmaputra in the
center, and the plateau known as the Deccan in the south,
girt about by the Vindhya mountains on the north and the
Eastern and Western Ghauts on either side.

India thus possesses every variety of climate, soil and
product, presenting the widest extremes of heat and cold,
and wet and dry atmosphere. The greater portion of the
country is hot, and therefore trying for Europeans.

Resources. Of natural resources India has a vast and
varied store. Her agricultural products are enormous, including rice, wheat, cereals, cotton, jute, sugar-cane, tea and
coffee. Her forests still cover large areas and yield a variety of valuable woods. Her manufactures of cotton, fine
textiles—chiefly silks, muslins, shawls and rugs—and metal
wares are extensive.

The People. India's population is equal to that of North
and South America and Africa combined. Only two per
cent. of the people live in cities of 10,000 or over, the remainder in small towns and innumerable villages.

* These figures include Ceylon, which is a separate crown colony, with a
population of 5,300,000.

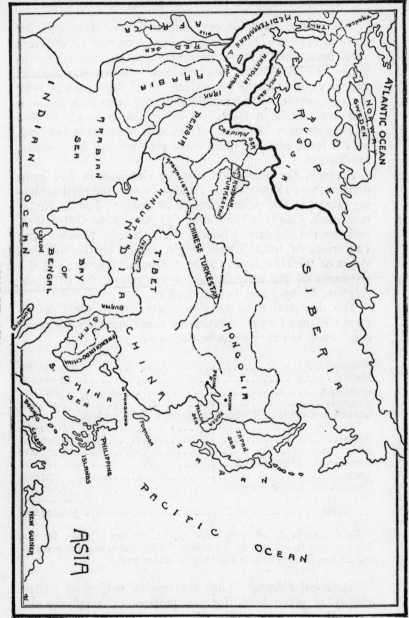

MAP III: ASIA

We cannot speak of one Indian nation or people, for there is not such, but rather a conglomeration of different races presenting every variety of color, physiognomy, language, social custom and religion. Some 200 distinct languages and dialects are spoken, 33 of them each by over 300,000 people. Illiteracy abounds, only one male in seven and one female in thirty-five being able to read, so that of persons over five years of age only about nine per cent. of the total, and not quite three per cent. of the females, are literate.

Racially, the population may be classified in five main divisions:—(1) Aryans or Hindus proper, the predominating race; (2) Dravidians (known as Telugus, Tamils, Kanarese, etc.), mainly in the south; (3) Aboriginal Hill Tribes, such as the Santals, Khonds, Bhils, Khols, Karens, etc.; (4) tribes of Indo-Chinese origin, chiefly on the southern slopes of the Himalayas and in Assam and Burma; (5) descendants of the early Mohammedan conquerors of Arab, Afghan, Mongol and Persian origin.

The distribution by religion, according to the Government Census of 1931, substituting round numbers for more exact ones, as easier to memorize, is:—

Hindus	239,000,000
Moslems	79,000,000
Buddhists	13,000,000
Animists	8,300,000
Christians (including Protestants, Roman Catholics and Syrians)	6,300,000
Sikhs	4,300,000
Jains	1,200,000
Zoroastrians (Parsees)	110,000
Jews	24,000
Unclassified Minor Religions	2,900,000
Total	354,134,000

On this basis out of every 1,000 natives 677 are Hindus, 221 are Moslems, 40 Buddhists, 23 Animists, 18 Christians, and the remaining 21 are divided among the various minor sects.

Historical Résumé. Only the briefest outline of Indian history is given here, for the purpose of supplying the connection between India and the outside world. For unknown centuries before the Christian Era, as well as later, invasion and conquest have been the lot of almost every generation. The attacks sometimes came from the sea, but mostly through the famous Khyber Pass on the northwest frontier. A long series of assaults by Moslems, Afghans, and Tartars began in 644 A.D. and continued through seven or eight centuries, always attended by ruthless pillage and slaughter. In the sixteenth century *Akbar* founded the great *Mogul Empire,* whose fatal decline began a century later.

The first Europeans to reach India were the Portuguese, in about 1500. Their sole object was trade, and they established their center at Goa on the west coast. The Danish East India Company founded settlements in 1616 at Tranquebar and Serampore. The Dutch soon followed, dispossessed the Portuguese of Ceylon in 1651, and opened a factory above Calcutta on the Hoogly.

England's first contact with Indian soil began in 1614, through the *British East India Company,* which soon after established trading posts at Madras, Calcutta and Bombay. Although at first purely a commercial concern, this Company was destined by a combination of forces gradually to gain possession of large territories and to assume civil authority. Ultimately a series of struggles ensued between this powerful Company and its Dutch, Portuguese and French rivals, of whom the French East India Company had become the most formidable. The last blow was struck in 1761, resulting in capitulation by the French and leaving British influence supreme.

Even more serious was the conflict between the Company in its politico-commercial capacity and the native Indian rulers, who with their armies bitterly contended for their sovereign rights and dealt treacherously with the encroaching foreigner. Little by little the British Government was drawn into the situation, not at first with any design of conquest, but compelled by moral obligations to see treaty rights respected and defend its subjects from Hindu treachery and barbarities. In revenge for the horrid tragedy of the Black Hole of Calcutta, in 1757, Britain seized the whole of Bengal, and thereupon began the building of a new British Indian Empire. The climax came a century later through the memorable Sepoy mutiny of 1857, which marked the passing of the East India Company and the open assumption by the English Crown, in 1858, of political control. Finally, on January 1st, 1877, Queen Victoria was proclaimed Empress of India. Two-fifths of India's territory and more than one-fifth of its population still remains semi-independent as native states, though subject to Britain's oversight and ultimate authority.

The attitude of the East India Company toward missions was anything but favorable, and its treatment of Carey, Judson and others was a sore trial to them and a disgrace to civilization. Yet none the less is it true that unintentionally this enterprise proved of great service to the missionary cause and an important factor in its development. Under British rule all native religions are allowed freedom of exercise, but Christianity is recognized as the religion of the Government and its propagation a legitimate enterprise.

II. Missionary Work.

Early Efforts. Mention has already been made of the earliest recorded efforts by *Pantænus* (p. 44) of early Roman Catholic Missions under *Francis Xavier* (pp. 70-72) and of the devoted and fruitful labors of *Ziegenbalg, Plütschau* and *Schwartz,* all of the Danish-Halle Mission (pp. 76-80), who hold the distinction of being the first Protestant missionaries to India.

William Carey (1793-1834).[1] This Nestor of Modern Missions was born of poor parents in a village of Northamptonshire, England, in 1761. As a boy he evinced a taste for learning, and was a diligent pupil of the village school. At the age of fourteen William was apprenticed to a shoemaker at Hackleton. Brought up as a Churchman, he early experienced a real change of heart, joined the humble Baptist Church, and at eighteen began to preach. To supplement his meager support as a pastor he continued his work as a cobbler. Resolved to fit himself for higher service, he utilized every available moment for classical study and wide reading, and by dogged perseverance, per-

---

[1] The dates following names of missionaries, hereafter given, are those of their missionary service.

haps even more than by brilliancy of intellect, he mastered Latin, Greek, Hebrew, French and Dutch, and gained a good knowledge of Botany and Zoölogy.

A copy of Cook's "Voyages around the World," which fell into his hands, made a deep impression upon him, leading his thoughts and sympathies out to distant lands, and a profound conviction laid hold upon him of the greater duty and task of the church to carry the gospel to the heathen world. Before him in his cobbler's stall hung a large map of the world, with such statistics and other information written upon it as he was able to collect respecting every country.

At a ministerial meeting in Nottingham, when invited by the moderator to suggest a subject for discussion, young Carey proposed "The duty of Christians to attempt the spread of the gospel among heathen nations." As revealing something of the weight of cold indifference and even stubborn opposition to missions which Carey had to overcome single-handed, the venerable moderator rose and in an agitated voice said: "Young man, sit down. When God pleases to convert the heathen, He will do it without your aid or mine." Soon after this Carey published "An Enquiry into the Obligation of Christians to use means for the Conversion of the Heathen," which still holds high rank among missionary treatises.

But May 31st, 1792, is the date which will always remain memorable as the birthday of the new world-wide era of missions, for on that day Carey preached his famous sermon from Isaiah 54: 2, 3, giving out the great missionary maxims, *"Expect great things from God," "Attempt great things for God."* So profound was the impression made that soon afterwards, at *Kettering,* a company of twelve ministers formed the first *Baptist Missionary Society,* subscribing for its expenses £13. 2s. 6d. ($65.62). Carey offered himself as the first missionary, and after overcoming further severe opposition and tests of faith, and being refused passage in an English ship because of the hostility of the East India Company to missionary work, he finally, with his wife and a companion, sailed in June, 1793, in a Danish vessel, and five months later landed at Calcutta. His parting message to the friends at home was terse and impressive. "Yonder in India," said he, "is a gold mine. I will descend and dig, but you at home must hold the ropes."

Carey's first years in India were years of severe trial, the opposition of the civil authorities, the ill health of his family, and financial need being added to the many formidable difficulties of a pioneer missionary career in that early period. But with heroic courage and a firm faith in God he faced and overcame them all. For five years he supported himself as superintendent of an indigo factory, while mastering several languages, holding daily religious services for the factory employees, itinerating among the villages and working at the translation of the Scriptures.

In 1799 he was joined by *Marshman* and *Ward,* the three forming the famous "Serampore Triad." Together they laid strong foundations for subsequent missionary activities by establishing schools, colleges and printing presses, in addition to their evangelistic and pastoral work. Later, Carey's rare linguistic gifts were recognized by the Governor General, who invited him to accept the post of teacher of Bengali, Marathi and Sanskrit in the new Fort William College at Calcutta. With the liberal salary of £1500 received for this service Carey supported himself and his two colleagues on a frugal scale, devoting the larger portion to the promotion of his beloved work.

Carey's monumental work was that of translator and author. By himself or under his supervision translations of the Scriptures, in whole or in part, were made in no fewer than 35 languages or dialects. In addition to these he compiled and published grammars in the Sanskrit, Bengali, Marathi, Telugu and Sikh languages, and dictionaries in Bengali and Marathi, besides editing numerous works in both English and the native languages. The magnitude of his literary accomplishments is truly astonishing, and well earned for him the title of "The Wycliffe of the East."

Withal, he believed in preaching, practised his belief uncompromisingly everywhere, and labored constantly for the conversion of individuals. He also threw his whole force and influence into efforts to abolish degrading and inhuman heathen practices, and was largely the means of securing the passage, in 1801, of a law prohibiting the throwing of children into the Ganges in sacrifice, and of another law, in 1829, abolishing the horrid "suttee" rite of burning widows on the funeral pyres of their husbands.

It was when Dr. Carey had corrected the last sheet of the eighth edition of the Bengali New Testament, in 1832, that he uttered the words: "My work is done. I have nothing more to do but to wait the will of God." He did not relinquish his labors, however, until he was compelled to take to his couch. On the ninth of June, 1834, the aged saint and veteran apostle entered into rest, having given to India forty-one years of priceless service, and leaving the whole Christian Church and heathen world his permanent debtors.

Following closely upon Carey and his colleagues we have several other great missionary pioneers of India, who call for mention not only on the ground of their personal merits, but even more because of the representative character of their work. Each was, so to speak, a mold after which some one of the various lines of approved missionary policy and activity for the future was shaped.

Henry Martyn (1806-1812). Born in southern England in 1781, this "saint and scholar" distinguished himself as a student at Cambridge, and expected to follow the legal profession. But out of a deepened spiritual experience, due in large measure to reading David Brainerd's life, he was impelled to dedicate himself to God for missionary service. He applied to the newly formed Society of the Church of England to be sent to India, but since, under the rule of the East India Company, this was impossible, he accepted a chaplaincy as the only means to his end in view.

Landing in Calcutta in 1806, he enjoyed a brief season of fellowship with Dr. Carey and his co-laborers, and this connection proved a providential link in the chain of God's leading, by which Martyn's rare literary gifts were applied to the work of translation. While faithfully performing his chaplain's duties in several successive military posts, his spirit reached out to a wider ministry of preaching, holding discussions and opening schools among Hindus and Mohammedans; but particularly did he devote himself to the study of Arabic and Persian, as well as to Hindustani and Sanskrit. By arrangement with the Serampore missionaries the Persian translation of the New Testament was committed to Mr. Martyn. The heat of the Indian plains proved too severe a test to his delicate constitution, a change became imperative, and an ocean voyage was recommended. This plan was taken advantage of by this devoted servant of God to attempt to verify the accuracy and utility of his Persian version of the New Testament by a visit to Arabia and Persia for intercourse with learned natives of these lands.

In January, 1811, he sailed from Calcutta, and touching at Bombay and Muscat, reached Persia in May, when the heat was at its height. The remainder of the pathetic but thrilling story cannot be told in detail—Martyn's long desert marches, attended by bitter hardships; his loneliness of spirit; the completion and revision of his Persian translation amid physical weakness and suffering; his work of witnessing to the many Mullahs and students who sought him out. He prepared two beautiful gift copies of the Persian New Testament for the Shah of Persia and his son, but before the volumes could be presented, Martyn's growing ill health compelled him to start for Constantinople with the hope of reaching England. The long and desperately hard journey overland proved too much for his frail body, and after enduring the most acute suffering he breathed his last on October 16th, 1812, at Tocat in Armenia, where his remains still lie buried.

Two days after his arrival in India, Henry Martyn had written: "Now let me burn out for God," and no words could more fitly express the spirit and record of that life "whose devotion, fervid zeal, and deep spirituality have led as many to become missionaries as David Brainerd's flaming life." [2]

Alexander Duff (1829-1863). This hardy Scotchman and great missionary was a pioneer in two senses, as being the first missionary of the Church of Scotland to India, and as leading the way to higher educational missions in that land. Dr. Pierson ranks him with Carey and Livingstone as "one of the great missionary triad of the new age."

[2] "India and Christian Opportunity," p. 167.

Reaching Calcutta in 1830, at the age of 24, after a memorable voyage on which he twice suffered shipwreck, Duff threw himself energetically into his appointed task. He began a new chapter in Indian missions by introducing the policy of making English rather than the vernacular the medium of higher education, and also by insisting upon giving the Bible an essential place in the daily school curriculum. His plan was novel, and it was greeted with mistrust by missionary leaders and with opposition by Indian Brahmans. But the aged Carey gave him his approval and sympathy, and the friendship of an educated and enlightened Brahman of great influence, Rammohun Roy by name, proved a timely help.

With unflinching courage the young missionary educator opened his school, and on the very first day faced the issue by bidding his pupils repeat after him the Lord's Prayer in Bengali, and then putting into the hands of each one a copy of the Gospels and calling upon a pupil to read. An ominous silence ensued, after which one of the number said: "This is the Christian Master. We are not Christians. How then can we read it?" Whereupon Ram Mohan Roy, who was present, quietly rose and replied: "Christians have read the Hindu Shasters and have not become Hindus. I have read the whole Bible, and you know that I am not a Christian. Read the book and judge for yourselves." The day was won, and the school became so popular that increased accommodation was soon necessary and many had to be turned away. Duff followed up his advantage by arranging a course of lectures for educated men on natural and revealed religion. These lectures aroused great excitement and no little antagonism, but a spirit of inquiry was awakened, and Duff was rewarded by seeing a number of gifted men renounce Hinduism and accept Christ. Some of these later became prominent in the gospel ministry.

Ill health twice compelled Dr. Duff to return home, in 1834 and 1849, but the loss to India was perhaps more than compensated by the missionary impulse he imparted to the home churches, not only of Great Britain, but also of the United States, which he toured in 1854. Dr. A. T. Pierson calls him "the most eloquent missionary orator of the century," and writes: "He made the very pulse of missions to beat quicker, shaping missionary effort and moving hundreds to *go*, as well as tens of thousands to *give* . . . and gave such impetus to work in other lands as no man since has ever equaled." [3]

Dr. Duff's home church conferred upon him high degrees and honors, and after failing health required his taking final leave of India he accepted, in 1863, a Missionary Professorship, in which position he delivered lectures each winter in the colleges of Aberdeen, Edinburgh and Glasgow. By this and every other means, until death removed him in 1878, he labored to strengthen and extend the cause of missions, on whose altar his own gifts and powers had been unreservedly laid.

Reginald Heber (1822-1826). This early missionary of the Church of England became the second Bishop of Calcutta. His career was cut short by death, but his name will ever be remembered and honored in connection with his immortal missionary and devotional hymns. The best known of these are: "From Greenland's Icy Mountains," "The Son of God Goes Forth to War," and "Holy, Holy, Holy, Lord God Almighty." He "united the zeal and piety of the Christian with the accomplishments of the scholar and the gentleman. Few men have ever won in equal measure the general esteem of society in India." [4]

Early British Societies. In addition to the Societies represented by the distinguished pioneers already mentioned—the *English Baptist,* the *Church of Scotland,* and the *Church Missionary Society*—other British Societies also early entered the field, whose work has played an important part in Indian missions. The most prominent of these are the *London Missionary Society,* which first occupied South India in 1804, and the *Wesleyan Missionary Society,* which opened work in Ceylon in 1813.

Genesis of American Missions. Samuel J. Mills may be termed the counterpart in America of William Carey in England, and the now famous *"Haystack Prayermeeting"*

---

[3] "The New Acts of the Apostles," pp. 130, 132.
[4] "Lux Christi," p. 146.

at Williamstown, Mass., was the birthplace of Modern American Missions, just as the Kettering assembly was of English Missions.

The story is too familiar to require recounting in detail of how Mills, in whose soul the missionary passion had begun to burn from the very hour of his conversion, gathered around him at Williams College a little company of kindred spirits—James Richards, Francis Robbins, Harvey Loomis, Gordon Hall, Luther Rice, and Byron Green—now known as *"the Haystack group,"* to pray, ponder, and plan for some mission to the heathen. Later, at Andover Seminary, three others—Adoniram Judson, Samuel Newell and Samuel Nott—joined the infant Society, and it was directly due to the prayers and efforts of this consecrated company that, in 1810, the *American Board of Commissioners for Foreign Missions* came into being as the first Society of its kind on this side of the Atlantic.

On the 19th of February, 1812, Messrs. Judson and Newell, with their wives, embarked for India, followed only nine days later by Gordon Hall, Luther Rice and Mr. and Mrs. Nott, for the same field.

Adoniram Judson (1812-1850). In the above list of noble missionary names Judson's stands to-day by far the most prominent, and we single him out for particular mention as a representative of American pioneers to India, but more than this, as the God-chosen apostle of Burma.

During his voyage to India Judson's views of baptism were radically changed, and this fact providentially led to the formation of the *American Baptist Missionary Union,* in 1814. He arrived in Calcutta only to be ordered out by the despotic and gospel-hating East India Company. His efforts to be allowed to labor at Madras proving in vain, as the only resort he took passage in a vessel for Burma and landed at Rangoon in July, 1813. Thus did the opposition of man but work out God's higher purpose, as subsequent events proved. "Judson was forbidden by the Spirit to enter India because God would have him in Burma. There, among its wild tribes, was a people prepared for the Lord. The Karens had for centuries nourished the tradition of white teachers ere long to appear among them, bringing the

Book of God. When such a teacher came, they gave ready ear to his message." [5]

It has been said of the Karen Mission that "in intensity of interest and measure of success it has scarcely been equaled by any other in modern times." "When Judson died, hundreds of baptized Burmans and Karens were sleeping in Jesus, and over 7,000 survived in 63 churches, under oversight of 163 missionaries, native pastors and helpers. Judson had finished his Bible translation, compiled a Burmese dictionary, and laid the basis of Christian character deep down in the Burman heart." [6]

But these results were not achieved without the keenest suffering in addition to arduous toil. When war broke out in 1824 between Burma and England, Judson, suspected of being a spy, was thrown into prison. The story of his confinement and the brutal treatment and physical agony he endured for nearly two years in filthy native jails, and of the heroic devotion of his gifted and consecrated first wife, *Ann Hasseltine Judson,* who labored to support him and effect his release, is among the most heart-moving of missionary anecdotes.

It was during the tedious early period of waiting in vain for permission to begin active preaching work, and while occupied with language study and translating the Scriptures, the awful powers of dominant Buddhism among the Burmans and gross devil-worship among the Karens meanwhile mockingly challenging his faith, that Judson was asked as to the outlook, and replied: "It is as bright as the promises of God." Such words, under such circumstances, are a fitting commentary upon this great missionary's character and service. Dr. Geo. Smith calls him "the greatest of all American missionaries," and continues: "Adoniram Judson is surpassed by no missionary since the apostle Paul in self-devotion and scholarship, in labors and perils, in saintliness and humility, in the result of his toils on the future of an empire and its multitudinous peoples." [7]

In the Baptist meeting-house at Malden, Mass., is a simple memorial tablet with the following inscription:

---

[5] "The Holy Spirit in Missions," p. 92.
[6] "The New Acts of the Apostles," pp. 109, 110.
[7] Quoted in "India and Christian Opportunity," p. 173.

In Memoriam.
Rev. Adoniram Judson
Born August 9, 1788
Died April 12, 1850
Malden, His Birthplace
The Ocean, His Sepulchre;
Converted Burmans and the Burman Bible
His Monument,
His Record is on High.

John Scudder, M.D. (1819-1855). To this man belongs the honor of being the first medical missionary to India. Picking up Gordon Hall's tract entitled "The Conversion of the World," the heart of the young physician of New York City was stirred, and in 1819 he sailed for India under the American Board. Later the *Reformed Church in America*, of which he was a member, organized its own separate work on the field. Dr. Scudder labored in Ceylon and afterwards established a work of great value at Madras.

"No stronger, more versatile, or more successful missionary pioneer ever evangelized a people as healer, preacher, teacher, and translator, in season and out of season. He lived in praying and working till, although he knew it not, he realized his ambition even in this world, 'to be one of the inner circle around Jesus.' There was not a town in southeastern India which had not heard the gospel from his lips, while his descendants worked by his side and took up his mantle." [8]   Not only did Dr. and Mrs. Scudder's whole family follow their parents' example of devoting their lives to missionary service, but also their children's children after them, and now the fourth generation of this illustrious family is in preparation to take up the work.

Later Societies. It is obviously impossible to attempt here to enumerate the many Societies and agencies which since the first quarter of last century have entered the India field. During the second quarter (1826-1850) thirteen Societies began work, during the third quarter (1851-1875) twenty-four others, and during the fourth quarter (1876-1900) some fifty more.

In addition to the earlier Societies already referred to, others which stand out prominently because of their strong staff of workers and large native Christian community are

[8] "Conversion of India." pp. 164, 165.

the *American Presbyterian,* which began work in 1834, and the *American Methodist Episcopal,* whose worthy pioneer, *Dr. William Butler,* arrived in 1856, and connected with which are also the well-known names of *Bishops William Taylor* and *James M. Thoburn.* Prominent among several Societies from Continental Europe are the *Basel Mission* (1834), the *Evangelical Lutheran* (1841), and *Gossner's Society* (1845). The World War struck a sad blow to these Missions through the necessary withdrawal of their German missionaries from British territory. Every possible effort was made by the British and American Societies of similar church order to care for the mission churches and activities thus left without oversight. Yet in spite of this the work has suffered a severe setback.

Among the largest of a number of non-denominational Societies are the *Christian and Missionary Alliance* (1889) and the *Ceylon and India General Mission* (1893). The former has a force of about fifty missionaries, occupying seventeen stations in the central part of India. The latter has its field in South India and Ceylon, with sixteen stations and thirty-five missionaries.

Mass Movements. The work of the Baptist Mission among the outcaste Telugus of Madras furnishes one of the most wonderful instances of the miracle-working power of God in modern missions. The unfruitfulness of that field during some thirty years of labor had won for it the name of *"The Lone Star Mission,"* and a decision was all but reached at home to discontinue the work. But the divine restraint was felt, *Dr.* and *Mrs. Clough* were sent out, and soon there began a mighty revival which swept a multitude of souls into the kingdom. In a single day at *Ongole,* during 1878, 2,222 were baptized, and 8,000 within six weeks, and the church there became the largest in the world. Nor did this latter-day Pentecost soon pass, but continued on with no permanent abatement, so that the report of the Mission for 1937 showed 382 organized Telugu churches, with a membership of more than 110,000.

A similar movement has more recently taken place among the Sweeper caste in North India, where many thousands of converts have been received by the Methodist Episcopal Church alone.

It is recognized that such mass movements are not without their serious resultant problems. Unworthy motives are usually to be found on the part of some in seasons of what may be termed "wholesale conversions"; others are apt to get wrong or superficial ideas of what Christianity really is; others again mistake Christian liberty for license and are tempted to lay aside courtesy for their neighbors and due respect for their superiors. These and other dangers call for much prayer and watchfulness, and for careful Bible instruction and discipline. Alas, too often the missionary staff is painfully insufficient for the added strain.

Policies and Methods. The early missionaries, following Carey's lead, gave themselves to preaching to the masses in bazaars, temples and fairs, in mission hall and bungalow, and in systematic village tours, at the same time supplementing such evangelistic work with translation, publication and school work. In general, most Missions adopt the policy of uniting these various methods.

Some Societies, notably the Scotch, have laid special emphasis upon higher educational work, and large colleges are carried on at Calcutta, Madras, Bombay and other main centers. Others, like the Basel Mission, have emphasized industrial work, the need and opportunity for which, as well as for orphanages, grew largely out of successive years of dire famine and plague, as well as from caste difficulties.

Medical missions have always been given an important place, although owing to the aid of this kind provided by the British Government there has not been the same necessity for them as in China and Africa. Yet they have been much used in opening new fields, and particularly has the female physician unlocked many a door closed to all others, and ministered untold relief to the suffering bodies, as well as salvation to the souls, of multitudes of India's poor secluded women. It was America that took the lead in this form of service, and the first medical woman missionary was *Clara Swain, M.D.,* sent out by the Methodist Episcopal Mission in 1869.

One line of medical work deserving of special mention is that for the unfortunate lepers, of whom India has so many. Leper asylums were early established by several

Societies, and in 1874 a *Mission to Lepers* was organized in England by *Mr. Wellesley C. Bailey,* which is doing a most worthy work.

Bible, tract and Christian literature work has been strongly developed by the special Societies existing for that purpose, and such work is universally recognized as an invaluable part of the missionary enterprise.

Since 1889, when the first *Y.M.C.A.* Secretary went to Madras, the work of that organization has steadily developed into a strong and fruitful factor, especially in reaching the great student body numbering at least 200,000, in 16 universities, 340 colleges and several thousand other high grade institutions of technical training.

Special Work for Women. Such work is deserving of separate mention in any mission field, but the more so in India because of the peculiar seclusion of India's women and the peculiarly distressing conditions attending their life by reason of customs such as child-marriage, the position of widows, and formerly the *suttee.* The wives of the earliest missionaries—*Mrs. Marshman, Mrs. Sarah* (Boardman) *Judson* and others—began direct work for women. *Miss M. A. Cooke,* sent out by the Church Missionary Society in 1820, was the first single woman missionary to India and opened many schools for girls.

Zenana work, which consists of visiting the secluded inmates of Hindu and Mohammedan homes, especially among the more well-to-do, occupies a large place in evangelism for women. "In this close, heart-to-heart encounter the Christian missionary learns the needs and sorrows of India's oppressed wives and mothers. Here, in the very deepest heart of it, absolutely closed to men missionaries, the family life in all its multiform misery can be reached with the healing and purifying touch of Christianity." [9]

There are estimated to be 40,000,000 women in zenanas, and 50,000 zenanas are now open to the visits of missionary women. The number of child-widows, whose lot is pitiable in the extreme, is 27,000,000, and of these 281,000 are under fifteen years of age. In connection with the vile rites of Hinduism, 288 in every 10,000 of the population

9 "Lux Christi," p. 203.

are said to be consigned as dancing-girls or priestesses to a life of prostitution in the temples.

Educational work of every stage, from kindergarten and primary school up to college and Bible-training school, now includes females. The higher education of girls and young women was brought about only after long struggles against native prejudices. The first *Christian College for Women,* not only in India but in all Asia, was established at Lucknow, in 1886, by *Miss Isabella Thoburn* of the Methodist Episcopal Mission. This was followed in 1890 by another at *Palmacotta,* in South India, under the Church Missionary Society. Government colleges were also opened to women in 1870, and during the first thirty years over 1,300 women passed the entrance examination.

A few examples will serve to show something of the readiness and ability of Indian women to respond to these higher privileges. *Miss Lilavati Singh, B.A.,* a young Hindu lady professor in Lucknow College, made such an impression by her address at the Ecumenical Conference of 1900, in New York, that the late President Harrison remarked: "If I had given a million dollars to foreign missions, I should count it wisely invested if it led only to the conversion of that one woman."

Mrs. Sorabji, the wife of one of the first Christian converts from among the Parsees, together with her daughters, has justly won distinction by her splendid work of conducting vernacular schools of a high order, and vitalized by a true Christian tone, for the various native races.

But the best known and most worthy of all is *Pandita Ramabai,* universally acknowledged to be the most distinguished woman in India, native or foreign. Her education was so thorough and her intellectual ability so great that the highest title possible for a native woman was conferred upon her. Forsaking idolatry she turned to Christ, and then consecrated herself with a love and devotion truly wonderful to the emancipation of child-wives and child-widows from their terrible bondage. In the famines and pestilences of 1897 and later years her ministry expanded far beyond her original design, as she threw herself into the desperate situation and rescued thousands of girls and women from death, destitution and the base designs of wicked men. Never will the writer forget the privilege he enjoyed of being the guest of this remarkable woman in her great Christian settlement known as *"Mukti"* (salvation), and addressing her "family" of many hundred sweet-faced little child-widows. Her schools, orphanage and rescue home have witnessed some wonderful outpourings of the Holy Spirit and the conversion of great numbers of souls.

After more than thirty years of prodigious labor, this great "scholar, saint and servant," as one of her biographers designates her, fell asleep in Jesus on the 5th of April, 1922. Her death was noted in both the secular and the religious press the world around, and a host of her friends of every race deeply mourn her loss. But she "being dead yet speaketh" through thousands of lives touched and changed by her direct ministry, and other thousands inspired by her noble example.

Opposing Forces. Among the many which could be mentioned we must pass over the majority, as being more or less common to all heathen lands, and refer only to three which bear in a peculiar way upon India.

(a) *Caste.* This hoary system of rigid division of society into innumerable cliques holds the Hindu nation in a mighty thraldom and is beyond question the most potent enemy of missionary work. It permeates every phase of daily life with its vitiating poison. It promotes physical degeneracy by restricting the circle in which marriage is permitted, engenders bitter class hatred, and obstructs intellectual progress by its dictum that only the Brahmans are fit to read or teach. As bearing directly upon missions, it is responsible for these two grave evils among others: "First, it threatens every person inclined to become a Christian with losses and sufferings of the most grievous character; and secondly, it segregates the new convert and puts him in a position where he can have little or no influence over his former friends." [10]

(b) *Hinduism.* This religion of three-fourths of the people of India actually boasts 330,000,000 gods and goddesses. Originating in Brahmanism, it has long since degenerated into a huge system of demonology.

After many years of experience in China and some con-

[10] "India and Christian Opportunity," p. 22.

tact with a number of other mission lands, the writer feels bound to say that nowhere else has he seen heathen religion sunken to such unspeakable depths of vileness and impurity. Krishna, one of the most popular Hindu deities, is reputed to have had 16,100 wives and is the very incarnation of sensual lust. The religious rites and temple carvings to be seen in Benares, the sacred city of the Hindus, are so abominable that any description of them is out of the question. Hindu religion is utterly divorced from morality. The Hindu believes that a religious motive justifies every immorality, however gross. Indeed, lust has been deliberately deified, and the whole system of Hindu worship reeks with the filthiest sensual suggestions and is an active force for the corruption of morals.

A well-known lecturer who cannot be charged with prejudice or pro-missionary sentiment writes on his visit to India: "India is so much worse than any one can describe it; the people are so much more vile than can be imagined; the forms of vice are all so disgusting! If you will consider that for generations, every power that wicked imaginations can devise has been used to develop the lowest passions of both men and women, when the most widely worshiped god is the mere personification of the most debasing of sins, you can imagine the condition of things." [11]

(c) *Modern Cults.* Various attempts have been made of later years by educated Hindus to effect a reform of Hinduism. Recognizing its weakness and corrupt practices, but unwilling wholly to renounce it and turn to Christianity, these men have sought to effect an amalgamation of Christian ideas with the old Hindu Vedas, and to form a sort of composite or eclectic religion. Thus various *Somajes* have sprung up—such as the *Brahmo Samaj, Arya Samaj,* and others—which, while progressive in spirit and aiming at social reform, are strongly rationalistic and pantheistic in their tendencies. These mere "half-way houses between Hinduism and Christianity" cannot be regarded as helpful, any more than can Islam with its boasted monotheism. They include no mention of Christ in their creed, refuse to acknowledge Him as Saviour, and are at heart and in actual operation foes of the gospel. By their attractive

11 "Lux Christi," p. 114.

philosophies and reform propaganda they exercise a powerful influence over the student body, and thus must be classed among the serious opposing forces to missionary work.

Under the heading of anti-Christian education, such a high authority as the late Dr. S. H. Kellogg writes: "Than the Arya Samaj, Christianity has no more deadly enemy in India. In its active and unceasing hostility to all missionary effort, it can only be compared with Islam." [12]

The Unfinished Task. After nearly 150 years of continuous work since Carey's arrival, India has still much land to be possessed for Christ. To quote from the World Missionary Conference Report: "Quite apart from those fields in which the present missionary staff is insufficient for the accomplishment of the work begun in them, there are vast districts still unoccupied, or not effectively occupied. . . . Large portions of the United Provinces, Eastern Bengal, Chota Nagpur, the Central Provinces and the Central Indian Agency are absolutely undermanned. Two generations have passed away since Missions began work in some of these sections, yet scarcely one-third of the population have had the gospel made known to them." [13]

A careful survey made in 1921 showed that of the 493 districts into which India may be divided (with an average area greater than Delaware and Rhode Island combined), 185 districts had no resident missionary, 113 were very inadequately occupied, and only 195 were fairly well occupied.

From one of the latest reports we quote the following: "India with 14 missionaries to 1,000,000 population is relatively poorly occupied. A number of areas consisting of 2,000,000, 3,000,000, and 5,000,000 people have no missionaries. The occupation of the Frontier States is still only nominal. Nearly 500 Indian States have no missionary occupation, and in many cases their rulers refuse all permission to enter. Missionaries reside in 1,110 centers, a disproportionately large number of which are urban. Out of the 683,740 towns and villages in India and Ceylon, the tables show 21,933 organized and unorganized groups of Christians, and it is estimated that there may be Christians residing in 50,000 towns and villages altogether. The actual

[12] *The Missionary Review of the World,* December, 1899, p. 885.
[13] *Report of World Missionary Conference, Edinburgh,* Vol. 1, p. 159.

areas and groups of India urgently calling for evangelization are the densely populated districts of the United Provinces, Bihar and Orissa, and Bengal, the Himalayan States, the 8,000,000 aboriginals and the 52,000,000 of the depressed classes, many of whom if not reached within the next ten years may well drift into Hinduism or Islam." [14]

New Political Situation. Great as have been the claims of India and grave her missionary problems at any time, recent political developments have added a new and serious factor to the situation. The defeat of Turkey by the Allies and the threatened dismemberment of that foremost Moslem Power were taken advantage of by shrewd Mohammedan propagandists to stir up the religious feelings of the great Moslem population of India, and for a time ominous rumblings threatened an outbreak of violence.

But even more serious has been the persistent agitation of the Indian Nationalist party against British rule. Despite the liberal attitude of the British Government in adopting legislation granting an increased measure of self-government to its Indian subjects, the radical wing of the Nationalists refused to be satisfied and became loud in their demands for complete home-rule. Revolutionary mass meetings were held, inflammatory speeches delivered and literature circulated, and under the name of the "Non-coöperation Movement" a boycott of English courts, schools and merchandise was started.

For a time the situation was very grave, and much anxiety was felt for the safety of Europeans in India, including the missionaries. But the Government faced conditions with a cool head and a firm hand, and at the most critical moment its prompt action in arresting and imprisoning *"Mahatma"* *Gandhi,* the popular leader of non-coöperation and the idol of the people, had the salutary effect of putting a stop to public demonstrations and restoring order. Indian affairs have resumed normalcy and the outlook seems more hopeful.

It is indeed a cause for thanksgiving that throughout this period of social unrest and political uncertainty mission work has gone forward without interruption or slackened pace. On the contrary, missionaries in many parts testify to increased interest in the gospel, larger sales of Christian

[14] *Statistical Survey of the World Mission* (1938), p. 266.

literature and greater numbers of inquirers and converts. Surely the good hand of God is to be seen in thus preserving the open door for missions and prospering the work of His servants in troublous times like these.

India's Appeal. "No country needs the gospel more than India. With all her antagonistic faiths, her superstitions, her idolatry and in some quarters her intolerance, India cannot make real progress or attain to the heights of her deserved destiny unless she has become unified under Christ. The political situation makes the need more urgent. Under the liberal British administration, education has become widespread and the machinery of modern civilization is to be found everywhere. One result has been an embryonic spirit of democracy and a desire for self-government. To this desire Great Britain is acceding as rapidly as conditions warrant. Every year sees the Indian in possession of greater political power. Some day India will be a great self-governing unit. If the unit be Christian the world will be the gainer; if not Christian, the world will be the loser. Missionaries in India render the whole world a glorious service." [15]

Statistical Summary. The following figures for Protestant Missions in India and Ceylon are from the *Statistical Survey of the World Mission* (1938).

Societies at work	165
Foreign missionary staff	5,478
Residence stations	1,197
Native workers	50,152
Organized churches and other groups	21,933
Communicants	1,067,143

NOTE: The total Protestant Indian Christian community is estimated at approximately 2,700,000.

QUESTIONS

1. Give the area and population of India, and describe its physical features, climate and resources.

2. Divide India's population into its main constituent groups (a) racially, (b) religiously, giving approximate numbers.

3. Describe briefly the course of events in India leading up to complete British control, giving main dates and names involved.

4. Give an account of the birth of Modern Missions (a) in England, (b) in America, with dates.

[15] From article in *The Missionary Review of the World*, April, 1922.

5. Name those who composed the "Serampore Triad," and sketch the career of the most prominent one.

6. Name the three most prominent India missionaries following after Carey, and state the outstanding feature of the work of each.

7. Give an account of the career of the "Apostle of Burma."

8. Name five of the most prominent British Societies laboring in India, four American, three Continental, and two non-denominational Societies, and give date when each entered the field.

9. Identify the "Lone Star Mission," and give a brief account of its earlier and later history.

10. What special forms of mission work exist in India for particularly needy classes.

11. Name and give date of arrival of (a) first male medical missionary, (b) first female medical missionary, (c) first single lady missionary.

12. Give names and brief accounts of three prominent Christian women of India.

13. Cite three of the chief opposing forces to Christian Missions in India.

14. To what extent is India's evangelization still incomplete?

15. Describe the latest political situation in India, and the events leading up to it.

16. Give latest statistical summary of Protestant Missions in India.

CHAPTER X

SOUTHEASTERN ASIA

Under this heading may be grouped several countries which together occupy a large area, peninsular in shape, in the southeastern corner of Asia, between India and China. These countries are Farther India (comprising Assam and Burma), Siam, the Malay Peninsula, and French Indo-China.

While world events have brought other missionary lands into prominent notice and discussion, nothing seems to have occurred in late years to call special attention to this group of countries. For this reason the story of missionary effort and achievement within them, although in some respects of an unique character, is less familiar in general than the record of work in other fields.

ASSAM

Assam has now the status of a province of India proper, and forms a connecting link between that land on its extreme northeastern frontier and Burma. Its population (9,250,000) includes the Assamese people, who have mostly become Hindus, some of them Mohammedans, and several wild hill tribes who are still pagan demon-worshipers. Yet it is among these more primitive people that the gospel has had its greatest success, and accounts are given of some wonderful conversions in recent years, and of scenes that recall the Welsh revival.

The chief agencies are the *American* and *British Baptists, Welsh Calvinistic Methodists, Society for the Propagation of the Gospel* and *North East India General Mission.*

BURMA

Area and Divisions. This northeasternmost part of Britain's vast Indian Empire now consists of *Lower Burma,*

Upper Burma and the *Shan States*. Its total area exceeds 260,000 square miles and is thus somewhat smaller than Texas or about twice the size of the British Isles. Lower Burma has been British since 1826, but Upper Burma only since 1885, when the outrageous crimes of the notorious King Thibaw compelled Britain to intervene, overthrow this bloody tyrant and establish humane and righteous rule.

The People. The population is over 14,600,000. About four-fifths are Burmans, who are Mongolian in race and supposed originally to have migrated from the borders of Tibet. In character they are indolent, self-satisfied and fond of pleasure. In religion they are Buddhists. Burma is called "the land of Buddhism and pagodas." The pagodas are the shrines of the Buddhists and are found everywhere and in almost countless numbers. The lofty Shwe Dagon pagoda at Rangoon, covered with gold plate at a cost of a million dollars, is one of the most famous shrines in the world.

The remaining one-fifth of the population is made up of various tribes—the Karens, Shans, Chins, Kachins and others—living mostly in the hills. These tribespeople are mainly descendants of migrations from western China many centuries ago. They are lower than the Burmans in civilization and are demon-worshipers in religion.

In addition to the native races, there are many Chinese and East Indian residents, particularly in Rangoon and the few other large centers. The Chinese number 150,000 and, as elsewhere, by their proverbial industry and thrift they have secured the bulk of the business of the whole country.

Karen Tradition. Special interest attaches to the Karens from the missionary viewpoint. A simple-minded people numbering about 1,200,000, they suffered cruel treatment at the hands of the Burmans prior to the coming of the British. They cherished certain old traditions which, strangely enough, seem to point to some earlier knowledge of the biblical narrative, and which gave them a vague expectancy of some kind of deliverance and blessing that would come to them through white teachers from the West. They were thus remarkably prepared for the coming of the missionary, gave heed to his message, and from the beginning evinced a spiritual receptivity which has few parallels in missionary annals.

Missions. The oldest and largest missionary work in Burma is that of the *Northern Baptists* of America, dating back to 1813. The story of the noble *Adoniram Judson,* who laid the foundations of this work amidst great suffering and trial, has already been outlined in the previous chapter. Burma was the first, and for considerable time the only, foreign mission field of this Board. It has been given a strong staff of workers and liberal support and has yielded one of the richest harvests of all Baptist Missions.

It has now more than 1,600 churches, with 143,000 members, and its schools give instruction to 40,000 pupils.

By far the greatest results have been among the Karens. The transformation wrought by the gospel among these formerly despised and degraded people is one of the outstanding miracles of modern missions. Fully eighty per cent. of the hundreds of Karen churches and schools are now entirely self-supporting, and they have sent their own missionaries among other tribes of Burma and the Karens of Siam.

The other main agencies at work are the *Society for the Propagation of the Gospel, Methodist Episcopal* and *Wesleyan Methodist Societies* and the *Salvation Army.*

Missionary work is carried on along all usual lines. There are a number of missionary educational institutions of high grade, and Rangoon has two large colleges and a Mission Press.

SIAM

Area, 200,000 *square miles. Population,* 14,500,000.

The Land. Siam lies between Burma on the north and west, French Indo-China on the east and the Malay States on the south, with a long coast line on the Gulf of Siam and the Indian Ocean. In area it is about equal to Spain or four times the size of New York State. It is mountainous in the north and south, while its central part is an alluvial plain. It is tropical in climate and products, with a rich soil and vast and valuable forests.

The People. The population of Siam is far from homogeneous. The natives belong to the Tai race, who came originally from China. The Siamese proper are one of three subdivisions of the Tai. They live in southern Siam and are the dominating element in the land. The other subdivisions are called Eastern and Western Shan (or Tai). Then come the Laos, of whom there are well over a million in northern Siam. The Chinese constitute a third important class, even more numerous than the Laos and are to be found all over the country. They are the strongest and wealthiest element in Siam, and almost completely control the trade of the kingdom. Their free intermarriage with the Siamese has had the effect of improving the quality of the latter race.

In addition to these main racial elements the population includes many natives of the adjacent countries—Malays, Cambodians, Annamese, Karens, etc.

Advanced Conditions. Although the Siamese, like the Burmans, are inclined to be indolent and easy-going, Siam is next to Japan the most advanced country in Asia. It possesses excellent roads, modern postal, telegraph and police systems, well-equipped schools and many other features of Western civilization. Bangkok, the capital, has its trolley cars, electric lighting system, automobiles and up-to-date manufacturing plants.

Such advancement is to be traced to the enlightenment which came to the late monarch, *King Chulalongkorn,* while still the Crown Prince, through the influence of the early missionaries and his subsequent travels in Europe. When later he became king he introduced a program of reforms which revolutionized material conditions and government affairs. Yet the morals of the country have not been correspondingly affected; polygamy and concubinage with their train of social evils are commonly practised, and other imported vices have taken strong hold upon the land.

Missions. Attention was first drawn to Siam by visits from early missionaries to the Chinese, nearly a century ago, in the hope of securing an entrance to China from that quarter. The *American Congregationalists* and *Baptists* responded to an earnest appeal sent home by these workers to occupy Siam. Both these Societies began work, but a series of misfortunes compelled them to withdraw before any assured results had been achieved. The *American Pres-byterians* (North) soon followed and by 1847 had com-menced permanent work.

The early years were filled with hardship and trial, owing mainly to the bitter opposition of the anti-foreign king and Buddhist priests. The missionaries were prevented from renting or buying property, were on one occasion ordered out of their premises to find shelter as best they could, their few native converts were fiercely persecuted and their helpers imprisoned. But when the prospect seemed hope-less the hostile king suddenly died, the enlightened and friendly prince succeeded to the throne and all was changed. Since then the missionaries have enjoyed the marked favor of the government and their work has had unhindered course. Some of them were placed in charge of royal hos-pitals and given official position. Several lady missionaries were invited to teach the women of the royal household.

The Southern Field. Mission work was for some years confined to southern Siam, where in spite of the friendliness which developed on the part of the people of all ranks the results in actual converts have not been large. Languid in-difference due to physical and mental sloth, the influence of strongly entrenched Buddhism and the prejudicial example of Roman Catholicism, which entered from the adjacent French territory, have all been serious hindrances. Never-theless there have been some true and notable conversions among both Siamese and Chinese, and the social results of missionary effort in this field have been unusually great.

The Northern Field. Work in northern Siam among the Laos began only in 1867. In this region results came more quickly and have been much larger than in the south. At the very beginning an able and influential Buddhist scholar was wonderfully converted. Others followed, the work at-tracted attention, persecution broke out, and two noble Christians were cruelly murdered. But God overruled this sad event for good, the hostile governor died, a "Procla-mation of Religious Liberty to the Laos" was issued and persecution ceased. Since then the work has steadily de-veloped and has extended even beyond the borders of Siam into French and Chinese territory.

Apart from the publication and circulation of the Scriptures through the *American Bible Society,* missionary work in Siam is mainly in the hands of the *Presbyterian Mission,* which now has 10 stations, a staff of 70 foreign and 415 native workers, several hospitals and schools of higher grade, and a large Mission Press. Of the 8,700 Christians in Siam 8,100 are now members of the "Church of Christ in Siam."

Neglected Eastern Siam. The present missionary force is far too small for the task of evangelizing this country. Its entire eastern section, with one-half the whole population, has no missionary and is still practically untouched by the gospel.

Larger Region of the Tai Race. Mention has already been made of the Tai race as the original stock from which most of the people of Siam have come, but the present distribution of this great race extends over a wide region 400,000 square miles in area, comprising not only northern Siam, but also the Shan States of Burma, the Laos frontier of French Indo-China and a section of the southwestern provinces of China.

The Tai are a primitive race, as ancient as the Chinese and resembling them a good deal in appearance. Most authorities seem to regard them as of Mongolian origin, although some think them more akin to the Aryans of India. Known in general as the Tai (meaning "free") race, they are in certain sections also called the Shan and the Lao people. Until touched by missionaries in northern Siam they were almost lost to the knowledge of the world. Yet recent and reliable estimates place their total number at between sixteen and twenty millions. To *Dr. W. Clifton Dodd* of the North Siam Presbyterian Mission, who labored for these people with a consuming zeal until his death in 1919, belongs largely the credit of establishing missionary contact with the Tai in their remote interior habitat. The beginnings of work among them have been signally blessed and some thousands have already turned from their "demons" to the Lord. But the vast field as a whole has barely been touched, and the present handful of missionaries needs to be multiplied many times over if this long neglected but promising race is ever to be properly evangelized.

MALAY PENINSULA

This long, finger-like peninsula, extending southward almost to the equator, forms the extreme southeastern tip of the continent of Asia. It comprises the British crown colony known as the Straits Settlements at the southern end, the Federated Malay States under British protection, and five other States adjoining Siam in the north, four of which were formerly tributaries of Siam, but were ceded to Britain in 1909.

The total population of the peninsula is about 5,000,000, divided among Malays, Chinese (native born and immigrants), Tamils from India, and aboriginal tribes, besides a rapidly increasing number of Europeans and Americans. The diversity of races and languages constitutes a serious difficulty in the way of missionary work.

In the Straits Settlements several Societies are at work. The *American Methodist Episcopal Mission* has large schools at Singapore and Penang, where thousands have received Christian education. It has also an extensive publishing plant at Singapore. Its church members number 9,300. The *Society for the Propagation of the Gospel* has about the same number, and the *English Presbyterians* and the *Brethren* have a few hundred each. Missionary effort even in this most accessible area is far from adequate, and is mostly confined to the Chinese and Tamil immigrants. Almost nothing is attempted in behalf of the Malays, who are the most numerous and are almost all Mohammedans.

As to the other sections of the peninsula, comprising almost three-fourths of the total population, the situation is even worse, for missionary effort is feeble and straggling. On the east coast are many diverse tribes of degraded aborigines, living away in the jungles, who have scarcely been touched, while the northern states adjacent to Siam are devoid of missionaries.

It is a shameful fact that within this peninsula, every part of it under the control, directly or indirectly, of a so-called Christian nation, there are at least 2,000,000 souls for whose spiritual enlightenment and conversion absolutely nothing has yet been done. Meanwhile the soul-blighting religion of Islam is becoming a more and more pervasive force throughout the peninsula.

FRENCH INDO-CHINA

Area, 285,000 *square miles.   Population,* 23,850,000.

The Land. This last section of Southeastern Asia lies to the east of Siam, bordering on the China Sea and touching China on the north.   In size one-fourth larger than France, this territory came piece by piece into the possession of that Power, and in 1898 was united under the name of French Indo-China.   Politically, it consists of five States: the Colony of *Cochin China* and the Protectorates of *Annam, Tonking, Cambodia* and *Laos.*

Physically, it consists of two parts: vast alluvial plains in the east and south, drained by two large rivers; and heavily wooded mountains in the interior to the north and west.   The soil of the plains is rich and produces one of the world's greatest rice crops, besides other grains, cereals, fruits and spices.   The mountains yield valuable minerals. The climate is hot and trying to Europeans.

The People. The inhabitants, aside from some 33,000 Europeans, are mainly Annamese, who occupy the fertile plains; Cambodians, who are more akin to the people of India; and aboriginal tribes known as Mois, Thais, Tchams, etc., who have been driven back for the most part into the mountainous interior.

The Annamese are an extremely ancient people, descended from a tribe belonging to the Mongolian race, which between 2,000 and 3,000 years before the Christian era occupied the southern part of China as well as the territory now known as Tonking.   For more than 1,000 years (B.C. 111- A.D. 968) they were ruled by a Chinese dynasty, and thus became strongly influenced by Chinese civilization.   The literary and moral code of Confucius gave definite shape to Annamese thought and religion, with results distinctly seen even at this late date, for the prevailing religion of the Annamese is a Chinese mixture of Confucianism, Buddhism and Taoism, with the worship of ancestors and genii as the dominant feature.

Besides the native races, there is a large Chinese population in the main cities and towns. As in all adjacent lands, the Chinese merchants with their keen business sense and enterprise have captured most of the big business of the country, including the large export trade in rice. They are amongst the most well-to-do and highly respected citizens.

French Influence. The French Government has given much attention to its Far Eastern possession, and the visitor from the West is surprised to find such cities as Saigon, Haiphong and Hanoi thoroughly Europeanized, with broad, well-paved streets, beautiful parks and boulevards and handsome buildings. Some 2,000 miles of railroad and three times that length of automobile roads provide excellent transportation throughout a large portion of the country.

In sad contrast to these material improvements are the spiritual and moral conditions, for Indo-China is still a benighted heathen land. It is true that Roman Catholicism has been disseminated to some extent and boasts not a few churches and converts. But, as the writer can testify from a personal visit, investigation finds it to be a superficial thing of form, tolerating all the old superstitions and vices and giving no new spiritual possession to its converts. And it is painful to add that the morals of the natives have been made worse, rather than better, through contact with civilization, because of the shocking example and enticement of many European residents and visitors of the baser sort.

Missions. Owing to the historic attitude of France, as a Roman Catholic Power, toward Protestantism, this extensive country with its vast population has had to be classed, up to a few years ago, among the totally unoccupied fields. With the exception of two *Swiss Brethren* missionaries in the remote interior of Laos, near the Siam border, and one colporteur of the *British and Foreign Bible Society,* Protestant missionaries were barred from Indo-China.

Only in 1911, following the severance of Church-State relations in France, was the *Christian and Missionary Alliance* able to effect an entrance from its adjacent field in South China. The first foothold was secured in Tourane, on the coast of Annam. From that beginning the work has gradually extended, not without difficulties, and until recently under hampering official restrictions. In answer to sustained prayer the French and Annamese Governments have now authorized the preaching of the gospel in Annam and Tonkin, and it is hoped that the same privilege will soon be granted in Cambodia. Work is carried on in all of the five States of Indo-China and has even extended over into Eastern Siam. Twenty stations and 146 outstations are occupied by 68 missionaries and 191 native workers.

In this new and neglected field there is already a native church of 11,000 members, which has become largely self-supporting and is nobly measuring up in the assumption of responsibility for the evangelization of the whole land. The church offerings in 1938 exceeded U. S. $11,400. The main Annamese Bible School has 112 students, while a beginning of Bible School work has been made among several of the tribes and in eastern Siam.

The arduous task of translating the entire Bible into the Annamese language has been completed, and the Mission Press at Hanoi is printing and circulating large numbers of Christian tracts and books in addition to the Scriptures. The total output in 1938 was over 18,550 pages in Annamese and English, and printing has now been begun in three of the Tribal languages.

French Indo-China still remains one of the least evangelized and most needy mission fields in the world.

QUESTIONS

1. Name the countries comprising Southeastern Asia, and give the location, size, population, different racial elements and dominant religions of each.

2. Name the main missionary agencies at work in each of these countries.

3. Give some account of the work of the largest Mission in (a) Burma, (b) Siam, (c) French Indo-China.

4. Among what section of the population has missionary success been greatest in (a) Burma, (b) Siam?

5. Describe present material, political and moral conditions in Siam, and their bearing upon mission work.

6. (a) Locate and describe the Tai people. (b) How numerous are they? (c) What mission work has been done among them?

7. Give the political divisions of French Indo-China, and sketch briefly its history.

8. Indicate the sections of Southeastern Asia wholly or largely unevangelized, and approximate number of people unreached.

Chapter XI

CHINA

AREA, 4,000,000 SQUARE MILES. POPULATION, 429,000,000

I. General Features.

Area and Divisions. The Chinese Republic consists of 24 provinces, these being the original 18 provinces of old "China proper," besides Sinkiang (Chinese Turkistan) and 5 new provinces—Chahar, Suiyuan, Ningsia, Chinghai, and Sikang—carved out of the borders of Mongolia on the north and Tibet on the west. Nominally Mongolia and Tibet also belong to China, but of recent years her actual control over them has become less and less. Since 1932 Manchuria has been lost to China and claims independence under the name of Manchukuo, but is really a mere puppet of Japan. China's 24 provinces have an area of over 2,900,000 square miles, or about the same as the United States. If Mongolia and Tibet are added, the total area of the Republic is 4,000,-000 square miles, or more than the entire continent of Europe.

Physical Features. Covering the full extent, in latitude, of the north temperate zone, China presents a wide variety of altitude, soil and climate. It has 2,000 miles of coastline, abounds in mountain ranges, and is traversed by many great rivers and a perfect network of smaller streams and artificial canals. The Yangtse River is 60 miles wide at its mouth, and is navigable by large ocean steamers for 700 miles, and by smaller vessels, designed to overcome the rapids, for 1,100 miles farther. China offers every variety of landscape—broad, level plains, rolling hills, loess deposits, lofty mountains, and the sublime Yangtse gorges.

Resources. China's resources of every kind are practically inexhaustible. There are said to be 600,000,000 acres of arable soil. In minerals probably no other country in the world can compare with China. Coal areas alone are estimated at 200,000 square miles—twenty-five times the size of Wales, and rich deposits of iron alongside of the coal make a combination well known to be the basis of modern industry and material wealth.

Population. The lack of any reliable census has made computations largely a matter of guess work. Published estimates have ranged all the way from 250,000,000 to 485,000,000. The estimate of the Ministry of the Interior in 1936 for China proper (or the 24 provinces) was 422,-707,868. The addition of Mongolia and Tibet, on the same basis of estimate, would raise this to 428,507,548, while if Manchuria were included the total population would be 463,-845,548.

It is a solemn fact to reflect upon that fully one-fourth of the entire human family live in China. The density of population varies greatly in the different provinces, from 872 to the square mile in Kiangsu to 48 in Kansu. The Eighteen Provinces and Manchuria together comprise much less than one-half the total area of the Republic, and yet contain more than thirty-nine-fortieths of the population.

Antiquity. China, otherwise called the Middle Kingdom, the Flowery Kingdom, the Celestial Empire, and the land of Sinim (Isa. 49: 12), is the oldest of existing nations. Its legendary history goes back to about thirty centuries before the Christian era, and its true historical period is conceded by Western scholars to date from 2000 or 2200 B.C.—in other words, 1,500 years before the founding of Rome, 700 years before the Exodus, 300 years before the call of Abraham. Think of a people that can boast a national history of forty centuries, during which their language, institutions, arts, government and religion have all continued on lines clearly formulated at that remote period! Think of a nation which has seen the rise and wane and final extinction of the greatest world empires of history—Assyria, Babylon, Greece and Rome—and yet lives on, the same compact race, unimpaired in vitality and even increasing steadily in numbers!

Qualities and Achievements. Among the indisputable marks of a worthy and venerable civilization of which the Chinese can boast are their elaborate system of patriarchal government; their remarkable written language and literature; their world-famed discoveries, such as the mariner's compass, gunpowder, and the art of block-printing; their unique manufactures of silks, porcelain, lacquerware, etc.; and their vast store of valuable empirical knowledge along every line. The present Chinese are physically strong, possess great powers of endurance and adaptability, are proverbially industrious, patient, frugal, and, as a rule, peaceloving. Their great drawback has been that, as true disciples of their illustrious sage, Confucius, their faces have been turned backward in a worship of the immeasurable past. For long centuries this characteristic effectively blocked the way to all advancement. With a spirit of intense conservatism they stubbornly resisted any change and fought the importation of foreign ideas, until a series of startling events and providences within the past twenty-five years has wrought undreamed-of changes, forced the nation from her age-long seclusion, and launched a new China upon the stage of international affairs.

Religions. It is usually stated that there are three chief religions in China—Confucianism, Taoism, and Buddhism. This does not mean, however, as might be inferred, that the people are divided into three different sects each with its separate faith. Most of the Chinese profess all three religions, and practise one or other as occasion prompts them.

Confucianism, derived from the teachings of the great Chinese philosopher, Confucius, who lived in the 6th century B.C., is, strictly speaking, not so much a religion as a system of political and social ethics. The instructions of Confucius are confined to the duties and relations of society and the State. While he mentioned the Supreme Ruler, under the term "heaven," he gave no clear account of such a being, did not define man's duties toward him, and was silent regarding a future life. Yet the system embodies the worship of nature and of departed spirits, ancestors in particular. "Thus sanctioned by the sage, ancestral worship has remained the heart and soul of Chinese religion." [1]

Confucius himself is an object of special worship, all cities being provided with temples in his honor. The Mandarins perform official worship to the sage twice a year. No images or priests are connected with this worship, and Confucianism in theory is opposed to idolatry. Yet in popular practice the worship of idols, as well as nature worship (the

[5] "The Uplift of China," p. 92.

deities of the hills, the rivers, the wind, the rain, etc.), goes on along with ancestral worship, all enjoying together the official sanction of the State.

Taoism claims as its founder Lao-tse, a great philosopher born fifty years before Confucius, but the system has long since departed from the theories of its reputed founder, and is to-day grossly materialistic and full of all kinds of grotesque superstition. It has brought the Chinese into bondage to innumerable demons and evil spirits, and is responsible for a great variety of absurd beliefs and harmful practices.

Buddhism was imported into China from India in 67 A.D. by the Emperor Ming Ti, who was dissatisfied with the materialistic trend oi Confucianism and Taoism, and welcomed a religion which by its doctrines of the transmigration of souls and future punishment professed to shed some light upon the fate of the dead. It met with much opposition, and even to-day "its position is that of an officially proscribed, though actually tolerated, heresy." [2] Yet it has gained general recognition and a multitude of followers, and has filled China with its temples and shrines.

Both the Taoist and Buddhist priests are for the most part lazy, ignorant, vicious parasites on society, actuated only by mercenary motives and despised by the people, who regard them as indispensable evils.

There are also scattered through China, mainly in the western provinces, *Mohammedans,* estimated at from five to ten millions in number. They are much less zealous in their religious practices than the Moslems of India and the Near East, but maintain their forms of faith, abstain rigidly from eating pork, and do not intermarry with the Chinese. They are, as a rule, stronger in their resistance of Christianity than any other of the religious sects, and thus far very few have become Christians.

II. Missionary Work.

The Nestorians. The earliest known introduction of the Christian faith into China was by the Nestorians, who early in the sixth century came overland from the west, resolutely pushing their way across vast deserts and lofty mountains. These Syrian priests appear to have been kindly re-

[2] "The Uplift of China," p. 105.

ceived by the Emperor, and to have made a large number of disciples. Strange indeed is it that after being propagated for some eight centuries the Nestorian faith lost its influence to the extent that every trace of the movement disappeared and its very existence in the Empire was forgotten. Only in 1625 was a buried marble tablet discovered by accident in Sian Fu, province of Shensi, bearing the date 781 A.D., and recording in Chinese and Syriac characters the arrival of the missionaries and the success of their work. This famous *Nestorian Tablet* is still on exhibit in the city of Sian.

Early Romanist Efforts. An Italian monk, *John de Monte Corvino,* reached China by the overland route from India about 1294. Like the Nestorians, he was well received by the Mongol Emperor, the great Kublai Khan, and his work was at least outwardly very successful. A church was built and an orphan asylum conducted at Peking, thousands were baptized, and the New Testament and Psalms were translated into Chinese. But in 1368 the Mongol dynasty gave place to the Ming dynasty, and the new rulers viewed the "foreign religion" with disfavor. A period of bitter persecution broke out, and a blank of nearly 200 years followed in the history of Christianity in China.

Later Romanist Activities. Next came the effort of the great Jesuit missionary, *Francis Xavier,* to enter China— an effort cut short by his death in 1552. The actual entrance was effected by the distinguished monk, *Matteo Ricci,* and a companion, who were sent from Macao in 1580 and traveled through the country disguised as Buddhist priests. After encountering many trials and difficulties, the labors of these men and their successors met with pronounced success, churches were built and Christian communities formed. The priests' scientific knowledge won for them no little prestige and favor at Peking. But then the inherent proclivity of Romanism to internal dissension and political intrigue asserted itself. Bitter disputes arose among the various orders —Jesuits, Franciscans and Dominicans—with respect to the consistency of Christians practising Confucian rites. Their persistent meddling in political affairs, moreover, was strongly resented by the Chinese authorities. The result was a growing disfavor, and in the early eighteenth century outbreaks of violent persecution all but annihilated the Roman Catholic Church in China. At last, in 1724, Christianity was proscribed by edict and the missionaries were banished from the Empire.

Protestant Missions. Protestant missionary work began with Morrison's arrival in 1807, and may be divided into the following periods:

(1) 1807-1842—to the Opium War.
(2) 1842-1860—to the Treaty of Tientsin.
(3) 1860-1895—to the Chino-Japanese War.
(4) 1895-1911—to the Chinese Revolution.
(5) 1911-   —to the present.

FIRST PERIOD (1807-1842)

Robert Morrison (1807-1834),[3] the noble Protestant missionary pioneer to the Chinese nation, was sent out by the *London Missionary Society* in 1807. Like Carey, he was of humble parentage and occupation—a shoe-last maker—and acquired a good education and several languages by dint of persevering application. Like Carey, too, he was refused passage by the East India Company, so reached Canton *via* the United States in an American ship. His famous retort to a sneering question put to him by a shipowner in New York reveals something of the Christian character of the young pioneer. "So then, Mr. Morrison, you really expect to make an impression on the idolatry of the great Chinese Empire?" asked the skeptic. Quickly and with emphasis came the reply, "No, sir, but I expect God will."

None but a man prepared by God would have been equal to the task Morrison faced. He was unwelcome alike to the Chinese, the East India Company, and the Jesuit missionaries at Macao. Trials and discouragements thickly beset him; he met with opposition at every turn. At first he dwelt in a room of an American warehouse in Canton, dressed in Chinese garb, and was obliged to conceal himself indoors while pressing his task of Chinese language study. Soon he was compelled to withdraw to Macao, a coast port 90 miles south, which had been in the possession

[3] The dates after names of missionaries are those of their missionary service.

of Portugal since 1557. At the end of two years his linguistic attainments won for him the position of translator for the East India Company. God's hand was unmistakably in this, for it not only provided Morrison with a liberal salary, but, what was far more, it secured him the safest and perhaps the only means of remaining in China.

In addition to his official duties he applied himself assiduously to the task of thoroughly mastering the language and translating the Scriptures, while also embracing the limited opportunities presented to him for evangelistic work. In 1813 the translation of the New Testament was completed, and that of the entire Bible in 1818, with some help from Dr. Milne. Besides the Bible, Morrison ultimately published more than a score of different works, including a Chinese grammar and his monumental dictionary of six volumes and 4,500 pages. In 1814, after seven long years of patient toil, he baptized in Macao Tsai A-ko, the first known Chinese Christian convert. In 1824 Morrison visited England and was received with honor by the churches and also by the King. He returned to China in 1826 and died there in 1834.

"The missionary life of Dr. Morrison covered but twenty-seven years, yet in view of the circumstances and the difficulties of the time, his achievements are almost incredible. Although his actual converts were less than a dozen, and although he was excluded from all but a corner of the land to which he devoted his life, yet by his literary labors he laid the foundations for all future work, and by giving the Chinese the Christian Scriptures in their own language he captured a commanding position in the very heart of the land to be possessed. 'By the Chinese Bible,' he said himself, 'when dead, I shall yet speak.' " [4]

William Milne, Morrison's first associate, arrived in 1813. He attempted to join him in Macao, but was compelled to withdraw, and finally settled at Malacca. There he established an Anglo-Chinese college and a printing press. He was joined in 1816 by *Walter Medhurst*, and together these two pioneers, undaunted by the fact of being denied residence in China, carried on in Malacca, Batavia and other points in Malaysia and the Dutch East Indies, to which many

[4] "The Uplift of China," p. 141.

Chinese had emigrated, a vigorous work of preaching, teaching, translation and publication, the influence of which was mightily felt within the Empire itself, despite the best efforts of her rulers to counteract it.

Dr. Karl Gutzlaff, of the *Netherlands Missionary Society,* deserves mention along with the above named trio of the London Missionary Society as an able and effective pioneer of this early period. Despite the rigid prohibitions of the Chinese Government against missionaries and Christian literature, Gutzlaff contrived, as surgeon or interpreter, to make several voyages in trading vessels up and down the coast. Stoned by angry mobs, hounded by the police, haled before the mandarins, he yet succeeded in distributing large quantities of Scripture portions and tracts, and the accounts of his adventures stirred up new interest at home in Chinese missions.

American Pioneers. The earliest American missionaries to China were *Rev. E. C. Bridgman* and *Rev. David Abeel,* sent out by the *American Board* in 1829. Bridgman's most valuable contribution to Chinese missions was his literary works. His name ranks high among Bible translators and revisers. He began the publication of the *Chinese Repository,* a storehouse of valuable information about China, which continued to be issued for twenty years.

In 1833 *Dr. S. Wells Williams* joined the little group as missionary printer, but was destined to distinction later on as sinologue, historian and diplomat. His "Middle Kingdom" is still the standard authority on the Chinese Empire.

Dr. Peter Parker was the first medical missionary to China, sent out by the *American Board* in 1834. He established a hospital at Canton, which lays just claim to being the first institution in heathen lands with distinctive aims of its kind. It has had a marvelous career under the direction of a long line of distinguished missionary physicians, and still continues its beneficent work of healing to many thousands annually. Dr. Parker was singularly successful in overcoming by his skill the animosity of the Chinese, and has been said to have "opened China at the point of the lancet." In no mission field has medical work met with a more imperative call of need, or found a vaster field of service; in none has such work been more signally used in disarming bitter prejudice, in opening the door for the gospel, and thus in ministering healing to sinful souls as well as to diseased bodies.

Second Period (1842-1860)

This period dates from the end of the Opium War in 1842 to the ratification of the Treaty of Tientsin in 1860, at the close of what is known as the "Arrow War." Some knowledge of the course of development of political and commercial relations between China and other nations during these early years is essential to a proper appreciation of the conditions attending the efforts of pioneers in introducing missionary work.

The immediate occasion of the *Opium War* was the attempt of British vessels to import a consignment of Indian opium at Canton. This act of forcing upon China a destructive drug which has proved her greatest national curse and the ruin of countless millions of her people, body and soul, can never in itself be justly defended, but must be regarded as an indelible blot upon the fair name of Britain. Yet it must be recognized that opium was not the real *cause,* but only the *occasion* of the war. The true cause lay in the conceited arrogance of the Chinese Government, its utter contempt for treaty obligations entered into, the outrageous restrictions placed upon commerce, and the insulting and intolerable treatment of foreigners. The war clearly had to come, but it is ever to be regretted that an unrighteous and indefensible incident was the occasion of it.

God, however, turned the unhappy event to China's spiritual blessing, for by the *Treaty of Nanking* the five ports of Canton, Amoy, Fuchow, Ningpo and Shanghai were opened to foreign residence and trade, and Hongkong was ceded to Great Britain. At once there followed an inrush of missionary forces and activities such as has probably never been paralleled in any other land in the same time. In addition to the London Missionary Society (1807), the American Board (1830), and the Protestant Episcopal Church of America (1835), which were already on the ground, or, more properly speaking, waiting at the doors, other Societies entered the field in the following order:—

1842. American Baptist Missionary Union
      American Presbyterian Mission
      American Reformed Church Mission
1843. American Southern Baptist Mission
1844. Church Missionary Society
1846. Basel Missionary Society
1847. American Methodist Episcopal Mission
      English Presbyterian Mission
      Rhenish Mission
1848. American Southern Methodist Mission
1852. English Wesleyan Missionary Society
1859. English Baptist Missionary Society

Not a few memorable names occur in the list of the missionaries of this period. Among the best known are *Dr. Legge,* whose translation of the Chinese Classics, and commentary thereupon, have become famous; *Drs. Lockhart, Hobson* and *Kerr,* medical pioneers; *Dr. Wm. Ashmore,* best remembered as a staunch champion of the principle of a self-supporting and self-propagating native church; *Rev. Wm. C. Burns,* translator of Bunyan's "Pilgrim's Progress" and many helpful hymns, whose saintly character as well as distinctive methods of getting close to the Chinese exerted a powerful influence.

A few sentences may well be quoted from Dr. A. H. Smith's general summary of the above two periods of Protestant Missions in China. Referring to the missionary movement in military terms, he writes: "To this Christian invasion there was almost everywhere opposed on the part of the Chinese a steady and a powerful resistance. . . . The missionaries were everywhere watched, suspected, despised, insulted, and, as opportunity offered, plundered. They were denied a spot for the sole of their foot to rest upon, were repeatedly driven out only to return again, and when at last a habitation or a chapel had been laboriously secured, it was perhaps torn down, and the weary process had to be begun anew. It is not strange that amid insanitary surroundings, with unwholesome food, and incessant anxieties and toils, many men and women utterly broke down. Out of a total of 214 male missionaries previous to 1860, 44 had died. . . . The foundations of all the subsequent mission work in China were by them laid deep, and strong, and well. The average missionary life of this handful of men was but seven years, and but one attained to forty years. But in view of the Bible translations and repeated revisions, 'commentaries on the Scripture written, grammars and dictionaries of the language prepared, tracts printed, converts made, churches formed, native preachers employed, Christian schools organized,' the way hewn out of obstinate rock, and China in spite of the Chinese themselves opened, it was impossible for those then living not to exclaim in devout thanksgiving and praise, 'What hath God wrought?' . . . Let us learn from the records of the past how vast are the results which God can accomplish with but a handful of human laborers, and from a contemplation of the yet greater task remaining, what a trumpet-call is sounding for men and women of like spirit with those who have gone before to enter into and complete their labors." [5]

THIRD PERIOD (1860-1895)

The Opium War had not after all settled the matters at issue between China and foreign nations, and the ground had all to be wearily gone over again. Another war broke out in 1856, known as the *"Arrow War."* Canton was captured by the British and French, treaties were made at Tientsin in 1858, only to be set at nought by China, and it was only in 1860, when Peking was taken by a foreign force, that the treaties were finally ratified. The *Treaty of Tientsin* stipulated that ten more cities should be opened to trade and the whole Empire opened to missionaries, and that Christian converts should be free from persecution.

As a result of this second "opening of China" there was at once an exodus of missionaries from the few centers already occupied to the new treaty ports, and efforts soon followed to penetrate the interior. But despite all treaties signed, and promises made, by China's rulers, the actual opening up of China, whether to missionary work or to foreign intercourse, was destined to be in the teeth of bitter opposition from the authorities and frequent anti-foreign uprisings of the people, throughout this entire period and

[5] "The Uplift of China," pp. 151-153.

even beyond it. Missionary progress up to the very end of the nineteenth century was punctuated by insult, riot and bloodshed.

Serious outbreaks occurred in 1870 at Tientsin and Hankow, when over a score of foreigners were brutally killed and much property was destroyed. Another virulent anti-foreign demonstration took the form of vile anti-Christian placards and pamphlets issued from the capital of Hunan province in 1890. These were followed by riots in the Yangtse valley and the murder of missionaries in Hupeh province in 1891 and 1893. In 1895 took place the memorable Kucheng massacre in Fukien province, when ten members of the Church Missionary Society were murdered. In all, 26 Protestant martyrs are recorded previous to the Boxer massacre of 1900, while many Roman Catholics and other foreigners suffered a like fate.

Tai Ping Rebellion (1850-1865). This great event calls for notice both on account of its tremendous effect in shaking the Empire to its very foundations, and because of the relation it bore to the missionary propaganda in its origin. Its leader was a southern Chinese named Hung Siu Ch'uan, who was given some Christian tracts by Liang A-fa, a convert of Morrison. Professing to have adopted Christianity, he entered upon a vigorous crusade against the three evils of idolatry, opium, and the Manchu dynasty. At first the movement was a religious one, with commendable and hopeful features. But success turned the leader's head, and he became a political aspirant, at the same time making for himself blasphemous claims of partnership with God and Jesus Christ.

The Taipings swept like a scourge over the most fertile provinces, pillaging and murdering everywhere, captured Nanking, the southern capital, and even threatened Peking. It was only with the help of European officers that the Government finally crushed the rebels, the most conspicuous part being played by the noble Christian soldier, *General Charles G. Gordon,* and his "Ever-Victorious Army." It is estimated that in that awful struggle of 15 years 20,000,000 lives were lost.

The Great Famine (1877-1878). This terrible affliction, which befell the northern provinces of Shantung, Honan

and Shansi, took a toll of over 10,000,000 human lives.
But it also proved an occasion for the display of the true
character and aims of the missionaries. Large sums of
money were subscribed by foreigners in China and abroad,
and a staff of missionaries administered effective relief to
the distressed districts. This practical exhibition of Christian sympathy and help proved the golden key to unlock
many a hitherto closed door to missionary service in inland
China.

Some Prominent Missionaries. Among the many worthy
names connected with this third period only a few can be
mentioned:

Dr. Griffith John (1855-1912), of the London Missionary
Society, was the pioneer worker at Hankow, where for half
a century he remained the central missionary figure. He
was a fearless itinerant and an indefatigable preacher, and
the great number of splendid gospel tracts which came from
his pen have carried conviction to multitudes, and made Dr.
John's name a beloved household word all over China.

Dr. W. A. P. Martin (1850-1916) was noted as a Christian educator and writer. His best known work, entitled
"Evidences of Christianity," became a missionary classic
and had an enormous circulation. He was signally honored
by the Chinese Government in being made President of
several high Government institutions, including the Imperial
University at Peking.

James Gilmour (1870-1891), known as "Gilmour of
Mongolia," labored heroically for the wild, roving Mongols of that vast, elevated northern plain. He cheerfully
endured hardships and privation, spending long periods
afield among them, sharing their black skin tents and un-
palatable food, and suffering the rigor of their bitterly cold
winters, as he relieved their sick bodies and ministered the
gospel to their dark souls steeped in the superstitions and
vices of a degraded Lamaism.

Others of this period were *Dr. J. L. Nevius* (1854-1893),
strong in his advocacy of missionary methods making for a
self-propagating native church; *Dr. Ernest Faber* (1865-
1899), one of the ablest and most voluminous writers in
Chinese, whose books exerted a deep and lasting influence;
Rev. David Hill (1865-1896), of the Wesleyan Mission at

Hankow, saintly in character and rich in good works, who during his relief work in the great famine of 1877-78 first influenced Mr. Hsi, afterwards a distinguished pastor of the China Inland Mission; *Bishop Moule* (1858-1918), of the Church Mission at Hangchow; *Dr. A. H. Smith* (1872-), easily the foremost among a host of missionary book writers on China, and still in active service; *Dr. Y. J. Allen* (1860-1907), and *Dr. Timothy Richard* (1869-1919), able contributors to Chinese Christian literature; *Dr. J. C. Gibson* (1874-1919) of Swatow, one of the two Chairmen of the great China Centenary Conference in 1907; *Rev. F. W. Baller* (1873-1922), of the China Inland Mission, whose Chinese dictionary, language primer and other textbooks have assisted hundreds of missionaries in acquiring Chinese. But a host of other missionary leaders of almost or quite equal prominence with these could be mentioned.

China Inland Mission (1865). One outstanding figure of this period we have reserved for separate mention in connection with the Society of which he was the founder. This is *Rev. J. Hudson Taylor* (1853-1905), whom God chose and prepared for a part of unique importance in the task of evangelizing the millions of China. Mr. Taylor first went to China in 1853. His early intimate relations with Rev. Wm. Burns exercised a strong influence upon his life and subsequent service. Compelled soon to return home because of ill-health, he became overwhelmed with the thought of the spiritual needs of the vast interior of China, still scarcely touched with the gospel. Before long he became convicted that God was calling him to undertake a forward movement in this direction. The result was the formation in 1865 of the China Inland Mission, and in the following year Hudson Taylor with a party of fifteen sailed for China to begin that work.

The China Inland Mission was the first, and is still the largest, of a number of missionary movements to which the name "faith mission" has been applied, because of their principle of making no direct solicitation of funds for their work. The workers are guaranteed no fixed salary, but trust the Lord to supply their needs through the voluntary offerings of His people in answer to prayer. This Mission is international and interdenominational, candidates from different countries and various evangelical sects all working together harmoniously. The missionaries include laymen as well as ordained ministers, and both single and married women receive official appointment as well as men, and together constitute more than half of the missionary staff.

The policy of the work is strongly evangelistic, the great objective being the widest possible witnessing of the gospel to those who have never heard it, to the end that all may have the opportunity of salvation, and that the task of worldwide evangelization committed by Christ to His Church may speedily be completed in preparation for the Lord's return.

The whole history of this Mission has been attended by the rich blessing of God. *Mr. D. E. Hoste* succeeded Dr. Taylor as its General Director, holding office from 1903 to 1935. Its work has extended into the remotest parts of China, and its report for 1938 shows 377 stations, 2,453 outstations, 1,363 missionaries and 4,403 native workers. Since the commencement of the work 190,550 converts have been baptized. Besides being the largest of the many Missions working in China, the China Inland Mission stands out before the whole world as one of the strongest witnesses to the faithfulness of God in supplying the needs of so great a company of His workers these many years, in answer to simple faith and prayer.

Christian and Missionary Alliance (1888). This Society, patterned largely after the China Inland Mission in its principles and practice, had a worthy share in the pioneer work of several of the last provinces of China to be entered with the gospel. It now has in China 26 main stations in seven provinces, and a force of about 94 missionaries.

Fourth Period (1895-1911)

Chino-Japanese War (1894-1895). This war broke out over a dispute between China and Japan regarding their respective rights in Korea. Within a few months the Chinese troops were everywhere defeated, the Chinese navy destroyed, several important ports captured, and Manchuria occupied. China's defeat at the hands of a small nation like Japan was a keen humiliation, and rudely awakened her more thoughtful leaders to the first realization of her national impotence. The conviction grew upon them that drastic reforms must be carried out and modern institutions and methods no longer scouted but adopted, if China was not to be hopelessly doomed. Thereupon began a bitter struggle between the progressive and reactionary parties in Chinese officialdom, in which struggle the young Emperor, Kuang Hsu, openly aligned himself with the reformers, while his aunt, the notorious Empress Dowager, as strongly sided with the opposing faction. By a skilful stroke of diplomacy the Empress Dowager and her party gained the upper hand, the Emperor was made virtually a prisoner, and the newly initiated program of reform was suddenly laid in the dust.

Boxer Uprising (1900). The triumph of the Empress Dowager and the reactionary party at Peking swiftly culminated in the memorable Boxer uprising of 1900. Numerous points of friction with foreign governments and with foreigners in China, and growing alarm at the steady gain of foreign ideas and influence within the Empire, united to precipitate a crisis. An elaborate plot was hatched to murder or drive out every "foreign devil" and to stamp out every seed of hated foreign-ism from the country. The blow fell most heavily upon the missionaries, because of their being scattered far in the interior in every part of the realm. Volumes have been written of the fearful sufferings endured by the missionary body and the native church, especially in the north, but the full story can never be told. Altogether 189 Protestant missionaries and their children were put to a cruel death. The two Missions which lost most heavily were the China Inland Mission, with 79 martyrs, and the Christian and Missionary Alliance, with 36. How many Chinese Christians suffered martyrdom will never be accurately known, but the number certainly reaches into thousands. Many of these Christians refused the offer of life at the price of renouncing allegiance to the Saviour, calmly laid their heads upon the block and sealed their testimony in their blood. Such a record will ever constitute an enriching heritage to the Church of Christ in China and the whole world.

The extent of damage done to foreign property and interests may be seen in the fact that the foreign Powers imposed upon China an indemnity of $333,000,000 in gold.

As to the effect upon missions, never did a storm-cloud more truly have a silver lining.   Never did a malicious blow of Satan hurled against the Church of the living God more signally fail of its object and rebound to his own hurt.   Once again was it demonstrated that "the blood of the martyrs is the seed of the Church."   The Boxer uprising not only put missionary work upon a safer basis, through the new conditions insisted upon by the great Powers, but it imparted to the movement the mightiest spiritual impetus up to that time. A comparison of figures shows that the direct results of the work during the first decade after 1900 far exceeded those of the entire preceding century.

FIFTH PERIOD (1911 TO THE PRESENT)

Chinese Revolution. The Revolution which broke out with startling suddenness on October 9th, 1911, was the final outburst of smoldering fires of discontent which had existed under the surface for years.   While the precipitating cause of the outbreak was a dispute between the provinces and the central government over the control of railways, yet the real cause lay far deeper, in the misrule, injustice, and tyranny of the hated alien Manchu government.   Elaborate revolutionary preparations had been made in secret. In an incredibly short time the Imperial forces were defeated, the revolutionists were in control, the baby Emperor and Prince Regent were forced to abdicate, and the whole world stood aghast at the spectacle of the oldest despotic monarchy suddenly turned into the youngest republic.

This Revolution was in no sense anti-foreign.   Indeed, some of its leaders had been pupils in mission schools or otherwise in touch with missionary propaganda, and it may be said that far as that propaganda was, and always is, from advocating political revolution, yet the great ideas of righteousness, justice, and liberty, which Christianity inculcates, had begun to exercise their inevitable influence in China, as they earlier had done in Western lands, so that many who were not prepared to give their personal allegiance to Christ were nevertheless made impatient of conditions to which they formerly submitted with feelings either of indifference or of helplessness.   From this viewpoint Christian Missions may be regarded a. having been the *efficient* cause of the Chinese Revolution.

Of the earliest leaders in the new order—*Sun Yat-Sen, Yuan Shih-Kai, Li Yuan-heng* and others—we cannot speak, nor yet in any detail of the subsequent fortunes of the young republic. Its path has been strewn with difficulties arising from conflicting ambitions among political leaders and parties and also the fact that the masses of the Chinese are yet far from ready for the exercise of democratic functions.

Later Political Developments. The lack of any outstanding leader to unite the different factions and put into effect a strong, constructive government policy and program has cost China a prolonged period of painful disruption and distress. The country gradually fell into the grip of ambitious warlords who have vied one with another for ascendancy and have exposed the populace to the wanton acts of their unrestrained soldiery. Lawless elements, moreover, seized the opportunity afforded by this disordered state of affairs to commit depredations, until the entire country became overrun by armed bands of desperate brigands who have inflicted untold cruelties, sufferings and losses upon the people. The normal processes of trade and industry have been well-nigh paralyzed, and the nation has been heading toward destruction.

Ultimately the desultory civil strife resolved itself into a long-drawn struggle between two factions, the progressive Nationalists of the south, led by the young *Marshal Chiang Kai-shek,* and the reactionary northern party under the Manchurian war-lord *Chang Tso-lin.* After a series of advances the Nationalists finally overthrew the northern forces at Peking in 1928, and the nation was nominally unified under a Nationalist Government, with the capital removed from Peking to Nanking.

Spread of Communism. Meanwhile a new and sinister factor was introduced into the situation in the form of Communism from Russia. The Red leaders in Moscow shrewdly contrived to ally themselves with China's Nationalists, and by loaning them money and sending them civil and military advisors succeeded in practically "bolshevising" China's nationalism. Not until Moscow had sown widespread the pernicious seed of Red radicalism did the Chinese Government leaders become aware of the deception which had been practiced upon them, and although they then promptly repudiated Communism and banished its unscrupulous Russian emissaries from the realm, they are still engaged in a desperate struggle to uproot this evil force, which has become strongly entrenched and is attempting to subvert all rightful authority and gain control of China's central provinces.

A Grave Missionary Crisis and Its Sequel. The Communist agitators in China made foreigners and Christians their special target, and stirred up the soldiery and student body to acts of insult and injury against them. This line of things climaxed in the "Nanking Incident" of 1927, when a sudden and fierce attack was made upon the foreign and Christian communities at Nanking. The Western Governments became alarmed and at once ordered their nationals to withdraw from the interior. This meant the compulsory evacuation of most of the missionaries and the temporary suspension of their work. It was a dark hour and, humanly speaking, a dark outlook, and many feared that the end of foreign missionary effort in China had come. But the tide soon turned, reaction set in, and in less than a year the door began to swing open for the missionaries' return. The unfeignedly warm welcome accorded them everywhere, by Chinese Christians and non-Christians alike, proved conclusively that the anti-foreign and anti-Christian agitation had been artificial, the subtle work of Red propagandists. While many missionary institutions have remained closed or passed into the hands of Chinese, a new and larger opportunity confronts the evangelistic missionary, and multitudes are showing greater response to the gospel than before. This had led to an aggressive forward movement of evangelism by the *China Inland Mission* into hitherto unworked areas, and the sending out from home of substantial reënforcements. The union Chinese Christian body known as the *Church of Christ in China* has also launched a five-year evangelistic campaign. In these and other ways God has turned the untoward events of the last few years to the furtherance of His cause in China, despite the severe sufferings and losses which for the time have befallen many missionaries and Chinese Christians.

A New Epoch Begun. The *National Christian Conference,* held at Shanghai in May, 1922, marked an epoch in the Christian movement in China of even greater import than the Centenary Conference of Protestant Missions in 1907.

The significance lay not in the large attendance, even though 1,100 delegates were present representing every branch of missionary work and every section of China. It lay rather in the fact that this was the first Christian Conference to which the Chinese came as delegated representatives of their own communions, and on an equal standing with the missionary delegates. The leadership of the Conference, from the presiding officer down to the chairman of the least sub-committee, was in Chinese hands. The Conference created a *National Christian Council,* composed of Chinese and foreigners in equal numbers, for the task of guiding and coördinating the Christian forces within the republic.

Chinese Christian Leaders of To-day. The mention of a few names among so many that are eligible may be regarded as invidious. Yet most persons familiar with China will agree as to the unique character of the few here selected, and their influential relation, albeit along different lines, to the Christian movement in China to-day. Among the best known are *Dr. Cheng Ching-yi,* the able chairman of the National Christian Conference of 1922 and moderator of the Church of Christ in China; *Marshal Feng Yü-hsiang,* powerful military leader; *General Chang Tsï-chiang,* cabinet member in the National Government and head of its bureau for opium suppression; *Dr. C. T. Wang,* Minister of State for Foreign Affairs; *Dr. Chang Po-ling,* noted educationalist; *David Yui,* national Y.M.C.A. executive; and *Ting Li-mei* and *Leland Wong,* recognized leaders in the field of sound and aggressive evangelism.

Mention should here be made of the fact that the President of the Nationalist Government, *Chiang Kai-shek,* recently made public confession of Christ in baptism, and that a majority of his cabinet members are professing Christians.

Changed Conditions. The world has probably never seen another national transformation so gigantic, so complete, so far-reaching, within so short a time. The old China of even twenty years ago is no more, and a new China has taken its place. New politics, new transportation, new commerce and industry, new education, new social and moral ideas, new dress and customs—all this and much more. The queue discarded, opium prohibited, footbinding condemned, even

idols destroyed and temples turned into schools—surely all
this is cheering indeed! But over against such hopeful features are new and grave menaces—the curse of foreign rum,
cigarettes, harlotry, atheistic books, foul movies, and other
moral evils and baneful influences which are pouring in, even
faster than the gospel, through the new "open door." Nor
dare we conclude that any or all of the improved material
conditions necessarily bring China a whit nearer spiritual
renovation. China's root difficulty is sin, the only remedy
for which is the salvation provided in Christ the Saviour.

Unoccupied Territory. With due appreciation of all that
a century of missionary work has accomplished, the evangelization of this great land is yet very far from completion.

The consideration of the vast dependencies of Mongolia,
Chinese Turkistan and Tibet is left for the chapter on Unoccupied Fields. But even as regards China proper, the proportions of the unfinished task are startling. Of the 34 counties of Heilungkiang, the northern province of Manchuria,
with 6,000,000 of a population, 25 counties are wholly unoccupied. Of China's original 18 provinces, one-quarter of the
total area is still unclaimed as the field of any Mission, while
many parts of the remaining three-fourths are yet unworked.

The latest statistics put the number of resident missionary
centers at 1,112, yet the *Hsien,* or officially recognized, cities
alone number 2,000 or more. It has to be remembered also
that three-fourths of the people of China live in the rural
districts, while two-thirds of the foreign missionary forces
and one-third of the Chinese workers are located in cities
with populations of 50,000 or over. When all the facts are
put together it is found that nearly one-half of China proper
is still out of reach of the gospel.

Moreover, there are specially neglected *classes* as well as
areas, such as six million aboriginal tribesmen in the southwest, one or two million boat people in the south, and some
ten million Moslems, largely in the northwest, for whom
comparatively little has yet been done.

Conclusion. From every viewpoint the unmet missionary
need is overwhelming and the task remaining is gigantic.
The whole situation is a supreme challenge which demands
fresh vision, determination and coöperation on the part of
the missionary body and the Chinese church.

Statistical Summary. The following are the latest figures for Protestant Missions as furnished by *Interpretative Statistical Survey of the World Mission of the Christian Church* (1938):

Societies at work	157
Foreign missionary staff	5,747
Residence stations	1,112
Native workers	29,964
Organized churches and other groups	12,726
Communicants	536,089

QUESTIONS

1. Give the area, divisions, and population of China, and compare its size with some Western countries.
2. State some of its physical features and resources.
3. How long has China existed as a nation? Mention some of her high qualities and past achievements.
4. Describe briefly the main religions of China.
5. Outline missionary efforts previous to Protestant Missions.
6. Divide Protestant Missions in China into its main Periods.
7. Give an account of the first Protestant missionary to China.
8. Mention seven other missionaries of the First Period.
9. Sketch the events connected with the opening of China to foreign trade and missionary work, giving names and dates of wars and treaties involved.
10. Name at least ten Societies and five missionaries of the Second Period.
11. Sketch the Tai Ping Rebellion and the great famine of 1877-78.
12. Give brief accounts of ten missionaries of the Third Period.
13. State the distinctive features of the China Inland Mission.
14. Describe the Chino-Japanese War, citing its cause and effect.
15. State the causes and results of the Boxer uprising.
16. Give the number of Protestant martyrs before and during 1900.
17. Describe the causes and course of the Chinese Revolution.
18. Trace the events leading up to the present political régime.
19. Describe the rise and development of Communism in China.
20. Give a brief account of the National Christian Conference of 1922, and indicate its bearing upon the future of the Christian movement in China.
21. Name eight prominent Chinese Christian leaders of to-day.
22. Cite some of the changed conditions prevailing in the New China as affecting missionary work.
23. Indicate the portions of China still unevangelized.

CHAPTER XII

JAPAN

AREA, 176,000 SQUARE MILES.[1]   POPULATION, 75,000,000 [1]

I. General Features.

Location and Size. Japan, otherwise known as Nippon, or the Sunrise Kingdom, is an island empire lying in crescentic shape off the northeast coast of Asia, close to Korea and China. It consists of four main islands, besides Formosa, which was ceded to Japan in 1895, at the close of the war with China. These islands form a chain over two thousand miles long, but averaging only one hundred miles in width. If placed on the east coast of the United States they would extend from Maine to Cuba, with Tokyo, the capital, lying off Cape Hatteras. The total land area, including Formosa, is more than that of California, or equal to the British Isles with Belgium, Holland and Denmark thrown in.

The Empire also includes a large number of small islands, estimated at 3,000 to 4,000, of which 548 have a circumference of one *ri* (2.44 miles) or over. The Kurile Islands and Japanese Sakhalin (Karafuto) are included in the north, and the Loo Choo Islands in the south.

It is to be remembered, too, that Japan has now established a protectorate over Korea. By her acquisition of Formosa, and the annexation by the United States of the Philippines, these two great nations, formerly four thousand miles apart, suddenly became neighbors.

Physical Features. Japan is of volcanic origin and very mountainous. Probably no other region of the world has so many volcanoes to the same area. Twenty active volcanoes are counted, besides numerous extinct ones, while earth-

---

[1] Including Formosa, but not Korea. The exact figures for the entire Japanese Empire are: area, 260,644 sq. mi.; population, 97,697,555 (*Statesman's Year Book*, 1939).

quakes are frequent and destructive. Indeed, the volcano and the earthquake have been the chief makers of Japan and given to it its wondrous beauty. Everywhere wooded mountains, big and little, are in sight, while cascades and waterfalls abound, and valleys of every conceivable shape delight the eye. Peerless Fuji, the highest volcano, rises 12,365 feet above sea level, and has been inactive for 200 years. It is the pride of the nation and the center of its poetry, legend and art. To offset the destruction of life and property wrought by Japan's volcanoes, they have provided her with over one thousand health-giving hot springs, which have proved a priceless boon and been the secret of the cleanliness of the Japanese.

Japan is also subject to another destructive force of nature in the occasional tidal waves which sweep over the coast, killing thousands of people and ruining millions of dollars' worth of property.

Climate. Japan's climate has a wide range. In the north it is cold, and snow falls in great abundance, while in the south it is warm and damp, with trying summer heat. Numerous mountain resorts, however, provide a welcome retreat for foreigners during the hottest season.

Resources and Industries. As a natural consequence of the features just mentioned, there is little level ground in Japan. The soil is not for the most part fertile, and only about one-eighth of the total area is under cultivation, so that considerable food has to be imported, mostly from China. Fertilization and assiduous toil make up for the limited fertility of the soil, and excellent crops of rice are grown, as well as wheat, millet, and a large variety of vegetables and fruits. The Japanese excel in agriculture and are still more famous in horticulture. The country has a good supply of timber and minerals. Fishing, ship-building, silk and tea culture occupy important places, while there are scores of minor industries, and the variety of manufactures is vastly too great to enumerate.

Population. The increase of Japan's population from 33,000,000 in 1872 to 60,000,000 in 1929 reveals the vigorous quality of the race. The density of population in Japan proper is about 469 to the square mile, and the steady increase has led large numbers to move into the Empire's more sparsely peopled islands of Hokkaido and Formosa, and many more to emigrate to foreign lands. In 1936, about 1,000,000 Japanese were reported as residing abroad, mainly in Hawaii, the United States, Canada and China, while over 1,000,000 were in leased territory in Manchuria.

The People. Where the Japanese people originally came from is considerable of a mystery. Their own histories acknowledge this, while stating that undoubtedly some of their ancestors came from Northern Asia, others from Korea, and still others from Malaysia. "They are, at any rate, a mixed race, as any one can see from their different facial types. Some are flat-faced and heavily bearded; others are oval-faced with high brows, more prominent noses, and with scanty beards." [2]

In the northern island of Hokkaido live the Ainu, survivors of an ancient and aboriginal race, now reduced to some 18,000 in number. They are evidently distinct from the Japanese, and are thought by some to be a fragment of the Aryan race. They are said to be the hairiest people in the world, have thick beards, and are of a low physical, mental, and social order. Their religion is a simple nature worship.

Traits of Character. The Japanese possess not a few attractive traits. They are clean and neat in person and habits, æsthetic in their tastes, quick-witted and apt to learn, so polite that they have been dubbed "the French of the Orient," and enterprising and ambitious to a degree. Over against these qualities is a lack of steadfastness in character. They incline to be vacillating and unstable, and in the opinion of Westerners who have spent years in the Far East in business and other lines they compare very unfavorably with the Chinese in point of commercial integrity and general reliability.

Filial piety and national patriotism are the two outstanding characteristics of the Japanese people. The individual is nothing, the family and State are everything. There is no more patriotic people on the face of the earth. Indeed, patriotism often becomes a passion, life is held in light esteem, and no honor is more coveted than to die for "the heaven-descended Emperor" or for country. Unfortu-

[2] "Sunrise in the Sunrise Kingdom," p. 40.

nately, other equally important moral principles and virtues have been all too lightly regarded, and lying and licentiousness must be recognized as national sins. "Where Christianity has not brought reform, truth for truth's sake is a phrase without force or meaning, while concubinage was provided for in the legal and social régime, prostitution was legalized, and without any shock to the moral sense girls were sold by their parents to lives of shame, and accepted their dreadful fate meekly and as a matter of course." [3]

Historical Résumé. Japanese historians claim that the authentic history of their country dates back to 600 B.C., and they furnish unbroken national records from that time to the present. But it is now conceded that all records prior to 461 A.D. are unreliable, and that the genuine history begins only from that date. "For many generations, the islands were divided between various tribes or clans, independent and often at war, but finally all were brought under the sway of a single ruler." [4] "The Buddhist priest brought Chinese civilization, and in the course of two centuries it spread over the country, influencing morality, politics and everything. Sweeping changes were made in the government, which was then organized on the Chinese centralized plan." [5]

While the Mikados were in theory absolute monarchs, they were far from being able rulers, and the affairs of State were administered by powerful vassals. Little by little a military class grew up, and in 1190 the chief of the most powerful clan was raised to the supreme power under the title of "Shogun" (later known in the West as *"tycoon"*), or commander-in-chief. From this time on the Shogun was the real ruler of Japan, the Mikado being little more than a figure-head, and a complete feudal system prevailed for seven centuries, with barons (*daimios*) holding large estates and maintaining about them bodies of armed retainers known as *samurai*, forerunners of the present gentry. Finally, in 1868, the Shogunate was overthrown and the Mikado restored to actual control. Only in 1889 did Japan become a constitutional monarchy.

[3] "A Hundred Years of Missions," p. 341.
[4] *Ibid.*, p. 342.
[5] "The Gist of Japan," p. 40.

Religions. The oldest and indigenous religion of Japan is *Shinto,* "The Way of the Gods," evidence of which is still everywhere to be seen in the shrines and the artistic *torii,* or gateway to the shrine. Shintoism was a system of ancestral and nature worship, which no doubt exercised some moral influence in the early history of the people. But it developed a grotesque pantheon of eight million gods and goddesses and bred all sorts of degrading superstitious and licentious rites. In modern years an effort has been made to revive and cleanse it from these excesses, but while its shrines still attract thousands of worshipers it is doomed to die, and has already begun to lose its religious character and to exist more as a force for the nurture of reverent patriotism. The disestablishment of its great Ise Shrine is a striking indication of the growing influence of Christianity.

Buddhism was introduced from China by way of Korea in 552 A.D. It was several centuries in fighting its way to acceptance, and in doing so it did not scruple to compromise its original moral and ethical standards, and underwent such tremendous evolution of doctrine that Japanese Buddhism has been regarded by Buddhists of Continental Asia as heretical. But it met the longing for light on the great questions of the origin and destiny of life, upon which the national cult was silent, and finally it took complete possession of the field. Buddhism has exerted a powerful influence in Japan, and it still has great life and power. It boasts over 100,000 temples, many of them of imposing style and proportions, and it is to-day naïvely copying Christian methods of work such as schools, Sunday preaching, Young Men's Associations and the like. But the evils of the system, and especially the vicious character of the priests, have drawn the severest criticism from Japanese themselves. Baron Kato Hiroyuki, formerly President of the Imperial University, said in an address: "The priests are indeed a rotten set, and they themselves have the greatest need of reformation. They are absolutely unable to save the masses, and are, moreover, a peril to society."

Confucianism has done much to mold the moral life of the Japanese as well as the Chinese, through the fact that

Chinese is the language of Japanese literature and the Chinese classics have been used in the schools.

II. Missionary Work.

Early Romanist Efforts. The first contact with Japan by Europeans was probably in 1542, when Mendez Pinto, a Portuguese navigator, following in the track of Vasco da Gama, reached the islands. Other adventurers followed and were well received, and with them came the Jesuits and the first introduction of Christianity.

To *Francis Xavier,* the great Jesuit, belongs the honor of being the first missionary to Japan. The story has already been told (*see page* 70) of his meeting with a Japanese refugee named Hanjiro in Malacca, his landing in Japan in 1549, and his subsequent labors there. Xavier himself remained in Japan only two and a half years, and never fully mastered the Japanese or any other foreign tongue. Yet his earnest efforts were wonderfully blessed, and his example inspired scores of other Jesuits to follow him to Japan.

The chaotic political conditions prevailing at the time, together with a decadent Shintoism and a degenerate Buddhism, created a most favorable opportunity for the new propaganda, which bore rapid and abundant fruit. By 1581 there were 200 churches and 150,000 professed Christians. The converts represented all classes, including Buddhist priests, scholars and noblemen as well as the common people. Two Daimios embraced Christianity and ordered their subjects to take the same step or go into exile. Even Nobunaga, the Minister of the Mikado, who hated the Buddhists, gave the new movement his powerful support, though apparently only for political reasons. So loyal to the church were the native converts that they sent an embassy of four young nobles to Rome to pay their respects to the Pope. This embassy was received with high honors, and on its return brought seventeen more Jesuit fathers. The new religion grew apace, its leaders and supporters showing no scruples against the use of coercion and persecution to effect converts. Accessions to the church are said to have reached 600,000 and even a million in number.

Those were palmy days indeed, and high hopes were entertained that Japan would become wholly Christian. But suddenly dark clouds began to gather on the horizon. Nobunaga, the protector of the Christians, was assassinated, and his successors, Hideyoshi and Iyeyasu, two of Japan's greatest men, were turned against Christianity by the fear that the foreign priests had political designs. Nor were their fears entirely groundless, for one of the weaknesses of Roman Catholicism has always been to become entangled in politics, and its emissaries in Japan were no exception to the rule. Added to this, dissensions arose between the Portuguese Jesuits and the Spanish Dominicans and Franciscans, who had come in large numbers from the Philippines, and methods and practices altogether unworthy of true Christianity contributed to bring about disaster to the cause.

Persecution of Christians. Systematic persecutions began, culminating in the famous edicts of 1606 and 1614, which prohibited Christianity and aimed at utterly exterminating it from the realm. Foreign priests and friars were banished and sentence of death was pronounced upon every convert who refused to renounce his faith. The persecutions which followed were of the most horrible kind. Christians were burned, crucified, buried alive, subjected to every form of torture that barbaric cruelty could devise. Their heroic fortitude in bearing suffering and calmly facing martyrdom is said by Dr. Wm. E. Griffis, that eminent authority on Japan and Korea, to have equaled that of the martyrs of bloody Roman arenas in the early Christian centuries.

Finally, in 1638, some 37,000 native Christians, driven to desperation, seized and fortified the old castle of Shimabara and made a brave stand for their lives. A veteran army was sent against them, and after four months the castle was taken and all were slaughtered. Further resistance was futile, and the sword, fire and banishment did their work so completely that it appeared as if every trace of Christianity was swept away. Yet Christians remained, worship was carried on in secret and, when 230 years later the country was reopened, whole villages of professed Christians were found who had retained the faith, albeit in a corrupt form.

Period of Exclusion. Following upon the banishment

and persecution of missionaries and converts came the most drastic measures of exclusion ever put into force by any nation. "The means of communication with the outer world were all cut off; all ships above a certain size were destroyed, and the building of others large enough to visit foreign lands rigidly prohibited; Japanese were forbidden to travel abroad on pain of death; native shipwrecked sailors who had been driven to other lands were not permitted to return lest they should carry the dreadful religion back with them; and all foreigners found on Japanese territory were executed. Over all the Empire the most rigid prohibitions of Christianity were posted. The high sounding text of one of these was as follows: 'So long as the sun shall continue to warm the earth, let no Christian be so bold as to come to Japan; and let all know that the King of Spain, or the Christians' god (thought to mean either Christ or the Pope), or the great god of all, if he dare violate this command, shall pay for it with his head.' These prohibitions could still be seen along the highways as late as 1872." [6]

The only means of communication with the outside world during this long period of exclusion was through a small colony of Dutch traders, who were allowed to remain under strict surveillance on the tiny island of Desima in Nagasaki harbor. Ships were permitted to visit them occasionally, but Bibles or Christian books were rigidly prohibited. Yet it was an object lesson of another civilization which was not without effect upon the Japanese mind and helped to prepare the way for the open door.

The Door Reopened. The steady increase of trade on the Pacific, the cruel treatment of foreign sailors and fishermen from time to time stranded on the Japanese coast, the danger attending well-meaning efforts to return shipwrecked Japanese to their own land—these and other considerations called more and more insistently for the opening of Japan, and it was the United States which took the first definite steps to effect this end.

A fleet of four warships was despatched under *Commodore Perry,* and on July 8, 1853, dropped anchor in Yedo Bay, and an interview with the government was demanded. After a lot of parleying, an official of high rank was sent

[6] "The Gist of Japan," p. 157.

out and received from the Commodore a letter from the President of the United States addressed to the Emperor of Japan. Perry thereupon sailed away, but only to return eight months later with a larger squadron, and to effect under pressure the signing of a treaty on March 31, 1854, by which the two ports of Shimoda and Hakodate were opened to American trade. Other nations were quick to claim similar advantages, but met with strong opposition. In 1858 *Townsend Harris,* representing the United States, negotiated a new and more liberal treaty, as did also Lord Elgin for Great Britain a few weeks later. These treaties secured for the first time the right of citizens of the nations concerned to reside in certain Japanese ports, and thus re-opened the long closed door to missionaries as well as merchants.

It was some time, however, before these rights were enjoyed with safety. Intense anti-foreign feeling prevailed, and a succession of outrages upon foreign residents extended over several years. Severe reprisals were carried out by British and Allied fleets in the form of bombardments of two Japanese ports. These actions not only made a lively impression upon the Japanese, but led to friction among the powerful rival clans and factions, and finally to the overthrow of the Shogunate and the restoration of sovereign power to the Mikado, or Emperor, in 1868. The Emperor himself ratified the foreign treaties, the seclusion of centuries was over, and Japan came forth into a new national day.

The Protestant Vanguard. The church at home had been eagerly watching for the door to open, and was not slow to enter it. Indeed, the advance guard had already been partially prepared for the task by service in the neighboring land of China. The first missionary to arrive was *Rev. J. Liggins* of the *Protestant Episcopal Church* of America, on May 2, 1859, two months before the time stipulated by the treaties. One month later he was joined by *Rev. C. M. Williams* (afterwards Bishop) of the same church. In October, *J. C. Hepburn, M.D.,* and wife, of the *American Presbyterian Board,* landed; in November, *Rev. S. R. Brown* and *D. B. Simmons, M.D.,* of the *Reformed Church of America;* and only a week later *Rev. Guido F.*

Verbeck, also of that church. Early in 1860, *Rev. J. Goble,* who had been with Perry's expedition, arrived under the *American Baptist Free Missionary Society.* Thus, within four months from the opening of the treaty ports to foreign residents, seven American missionaries were on the ground, and within a year four American Societies had begun work.

An interval of nine years elapsed before other organizations added their forces. The *Church Missionary Society* of England and the *American Board* both sent their first missionaries to Japan in 1869, and the *Society for the Propagation of the Gospel* and the *American Methodist Episcopal Church* entered in 1873.

Noble Pioneers. "It was a noble band of men, exceptional even among those whose names have become famous in missionary annals. Not one but has left his stamp upon new Japan. Of great intellectual ability, they were gifted with marvelous tact in dealing with a people that had for half a century been an enigma to the Occidental. Patient, persevering, seeking the best in those with whom they came in contact, they won a personal place such as it has seldom been the fortune of missionaries to win in the first years of their life in a new land." [7] Only meager mention can here be made of the three most outstanding figures of this early group.

Dr. James C. Hepburn was a typical pioneer and medical missionary, who had seen service in Singapore and China before entering Japan in 1859. His medical skill and success, coupled with a gentle and tactful manner, did much to dispel prejudice against Christianity and to win the confidence and esteem of multitudes during his thirty-three years of unremitting labor for Japan. In addition to being a medical missionary he was an educator of the first rank, whose services the Japanese government tried in vain to secure at high prices. But his even greater distinction was as a translator. He prepared a Japanese-English Dictionary and a Bible Dictionary in Japanese, and was the chief translator of the Holy Scriptures among a small group of able men, including Doctors Brown and Verbeck.

"No more sublime hour has been reached in the history of this awakening people than when, after nearly thirty years

7 "The Missionary Enterprise," p. 299.

of patient toil, he (Hepburn) formally presented the Japanese Bible to the nation. Before a great audience, he lifted up the five superb volumes and formally presented to the Sunrise Kingdom the complete Word of God in the tongue of Japan." [8] "Taking in one hand the New Testament and in the other the Old, he said: 'A complete Bible! What more precious gift—more precious than mountains of silver and gold—could the Christian nations of the West offer to this nation! May this sacred Book become to the Japanese what it has come to be for the people of the West —a source of life, a messenger of joy and peace, the foundation of a true civilization, and of social and political prosperity and greatness.' " [9]

Dr. Samuel R. Brown, of the Dutch Reformed Church, left a deep and lasting mark upon the Japanese nation as the pioneer of missionary education. He opened at Yokohama the first English school in Japan, and won great influence by his rare gifts and abilities as well as the deep love which he showed for the people. He insisted upon the Bible as the secret and center of the progress of England and America, aroused enthusiasm in the young men of Japan for western learning and ways, and it was largely due to his influence that the government decided to send the first Japanese students to study in England and America. Dr. Griffis, the biographer of Dr. Brown, calls him "A Maker of the New Orient," and bears testimony that "in this twentieth century Japanese college presidents, editors, pastors, translators, authors, statesmen, men of affairs, and leaders in commerce and literature by the score are 'images of his own life,' while in other countries hundreds gladly acknowledged the inspiration gained under him as their teacher."

Dr. Guido F. Verbeck, the remaining member of this famous triumvirate of early leaders in Japan, became the most distinguished of all, and his influence even outran that of the other two as a molder of New Japan. A rare linguist, he acquired the Japanese vernacular so perfectly that he could not be detected as a foreigner, and charmed his audiences by his fluent speech. In him was combined a great variety of eminent gifts in a degree that is most unusual.

8 "The New Acts of the Apostles," p. 339.
9 "The Modern Missionary Century," p. 116.

He was at once educator and evangelist, orator and translator, brilliant statesman and humble personal worker. In 1868, after the Revolution in Japan, he was invited to take a leading part in organizing the great Imperial University at Tokyo and planning a new system of national education. It was largely under his influence and guidance that in 1871 an Imperial Embassy was sent to visit Western countries, while in 1874 he was called into the service of the Senate to aid in framing a new Constitution for the Empire. "A man without a country," as he styled himself, having actually no rights of citizenship either in Holland, the land of his birth, or in the United States, where he had been educated, he was accorded by the Japanese government a "special passport" never granted to any other foreigner before or since, received the high decoration of "The Rising Sun," and at his death was given a State funeral.

Such are some of the men whom God raised up and used in the mighty task of laying the foundations of missions in this little but wonderful Land of the Rising Sun, a land destined to extend her influence all over the Orient.

Early Difficulties. It was in the face of difficulties neither few nor small that the early Protestant missionaries pursued their work. The political intrigues of the earlier Romanists had left a deep-seated hatred of Christianity. In every town and village the old anti-Christian edicts of the period of exclusion were still posted publicly, and as late as 1868 an edict was issued which read thus: "The wicked sect called Christian is strictly prohibited. Suspected persons are to be reported to the respective officials, and rewards will be given." The missionaries were viewed with suspicion by the government, and with mingled hostility and fear by the people. Spies were constantly sent to watch them, and threatening letters were written them. Their earliest converts, and even some of those merely employed to teach them the language, were secretly arrested and thrown into prison. Only in 1873 were the edicts taken down, and in 1884 new regulations secured larger religious toleration. The Treaties, moreover, permitted foreigners to live only within small "concessions" in a few open ports, and prohibited their traveling in the interior, and it was not until 1899 that such restrictions were wholly abolished.

Then, again, the removal of these restrictions and the influx of more foreigners into Japan brought the fresh obstacle of the baneful influence of the immoral and dissolute lives which many Westerners live in this and every Eastern country, while the ever-increasing intercourse between Japan and the West revealed to the former the flagrant evils of intemperance, murder, gambling, bribery, divorce, dishonesty, greed, and the like, which exist in reputed Christian countries and serve to bring Christianity and missionary work into disfavor and even contempt.

The "Kumamoto Band."   One incident connected with this early period of missions in Japan must here be mentioned, since in the providence of God it was destined to bear vitally upon the whole subsequent spiritual history of the realm.

In 1872 *Captain L. L. Janes,* an American army officer from West Point, was engaged by a feudal prince of the southern island of Kyushu to found a military school in the interior city of Kumamoto.   Although not a missionary, Captain Janes was an earnest Christian, filled with a strong desire to lead to Christ the hundred young men thus placed under his care.   His wife was a daughter of the well-known Dr. Scudder, early missionary to India, and she supported her husband's efforts with much prayer.

Having won the love and loyalty of his pupils by his rare teaching gifts and attractive personality, Captain Janes by and by invited them to Bible readings in his home, and a little later to a preaching service on Sunday mornings.   Before long a deep work of grace began in many hearts, and finally a revival swept through the school, and more than half of the students made a clean-cut decision for Christ. The climax came when one evening, early in 1876, forty students climbed a hill overlooking the city, and after prayer drew up and signed a "declaration" solemnly covenanting to renounce all worldly ambition and dedicate their lives to the high task of preaching the gospel throughout the Empire.

It is not surprising that this action met with loud protest and strong opposition, both in the school and among the relatives of the boys.   Bitter persecution broke out, fathers threatening their sons with the death penalty, mothers threatening to commit suicide in order to atone for the disgrace brought by their offspring upon the family name. Some of the boys were imprisoned, others were banished from their homes, while a plot was laid, fortunately without success, to kill the whole company.

Captain Janes himself was forced out of the school, but not before he had providentially learned through an American newspaper that a Christian school had recently been opened by Neesima in Kyoto. Thereupon thirty members of this "Kumamoto Band," driven from their homes and native province, made their way five hundred miles overland to Kyoto and, together with the handful of students already gathered there, formed the nucleus of the first Christian college in Japan, which was to grow into the great Doshisha University.

Joseph Hardy Neesima. It is fitting to introduce at this point some account of Neesima, that most illustrious of all Christian converts and native apostles of Japan, because of the relation which his career bears to the "Kumamoto Band" just mentioned. One would search far to find a more impressive illustration of the power and providence of God in human life than Neesima's history and its interlinking with that of this memorable Band.

Neesima's life story, as told by at least two biographers in full,[10] and by many other writers in brief, is one of peculiarly fascinating interest. Born in Yedo in 1843, as a mere boy he renounced idolatry. Later, a stray copy of an abridged Chinese Bible falling into his hands, he was struck with the opening words, "In the beginning, God created the heavens and the earth." His youthful mind reached out in a quest for the true God, and he prayed, "Oh, if you have eyes, look upon me; if you have ears, listen for me." He chanced also to catch a glimpse of an atlas of the United States, and filled with a great desire to see the Western world he contrived in 1864 to get to Hakodate and to smuggle himself on board an American schooner for Shanghai. Thence he worked his way to Boston, employing his spare time on the long voyage in studying English and reading a Chinese New Testament bought in Hongkong. It

10 "Joseph Hardy Neesima" (Davis) ; "Life and Letters of Joseph Hardy Neesima" (Hardy).

was without doubt of God's ordering that the ship on which Neesima sailed was owned by the *Hon. Alpheus Hardy,* a prominent Christian man of Boston. Hearing from the ship's captain about the interesting Japanese runaway, Mr. Hardy befriended him, named him "Joseph Hardy," and gave him a good education at Amherst College and Andover Seminary.

In 1871 the Japanese embassy on its visit to America heard of Neesima and engaged him as interpreter. Here was another unmistakable mark of God's guiding hand, for the favor of these distinguished men secured for the young Christian a pardon for the "crime" of having left his own land without permission, enabled him to visit the best educational institutions in America and Europe, and won for him on his return to Japan the friendship and influence and some of the foremost governing leaders. Indeed, every effort was made to persuade Neesima to enter government service, but no attraction of office or wealth could turn him aside from his God-given purpose to devote himself to gospel work. He became at once a bold and earnest witness among his people, and was the pioneer of public gospel preaching in the interior.

Neesima's great life work was the founding of the *Doshisha,* designed as a collegiate and theological school to train Christian workers for Japan. It was a daring scheme for him to choose as a place for such a school the ancient capital and sacred city of Kyoto, with its 3,500 temples and 8,000 Buddhist priests, but, nothing daunted, he opened his school there in a small room in November, 1875, with eight pupils. When, in 1890, death overtook this great man of God in the midst of his active labors, the Doshisha had grown into a great and well-equipped institution of nearly 700 students. It gave the needed impulse to Christian education in Japan, and many among its thousands of graduates have held high places in their country's history.

Growth and Development. We are ever thus being reminded in missions that the gospel is a living seed of irresistible power. The records of missionary labor and results furnish the most glorious Evidences of Christianity in all the world, and Japan has been no exception to the rule.

The first convert was baptized after five years (1864), the next two—one of them, Wakasa by name, being an official of high rank—two years later. The first Japanese church was organized at Yokohama on March 10, 1872, by *Rev. J. H. Ballagh* of the Reformed Church, with eleven members. The years from 1859 to 1872 have been called the *"Period of Preparation."* Next came the *"Period of Popularity,"* from 1873 to 1888, during which Christianity grew steadily in favor. Old customs and ideas were rapidly giving way before the influence of the West, and the missionaries were much sought, not only for spiritual ends but as well because of the useful knowledge they possessed on many lines. It became easy to get large audiences to preach to, and Christian schools became crowded with pupils. There were large accessions to the church, yet among them were undoubtedly not a few in whose hearts no real saving work of grace had been wrought, but who were mere intellectual converts, eager to recognize and embrace the external benefits of the Christian religion.

By 1888 this tide of favor had reached its height, and reaction now began to set in. This was due in part to the strenuous opposition of the Buddhists, who saw their power waning, and realizing the need of new tactics to save their cult from downfall, they began to imitate the methods of their Christian antagonists by opening schools and preaching halls, organizing young men's associations, women's prayer meetings, temperance societies, and the like. But a greater factor than Buddhism in bringing about reaction was the rise of strong nationalistic sentiment, fed by friction with foreign Powers over the revision of treaties and other matters. Conservatives seized the opportunity to stir up antiforeign spirit under the guise of an appeal to national loyalty. This sentiment affected even Christians, causing free criticism of the missionaries, and leading on to the advocacy of a Japanese form of Christianity, a modification of certain doctrinal beliefs, and an "independent" church movement.

These influences, although for a time apparently checking the progress and diminishing the numbers of the Christian Church, were not without their real advantages. A sifting process took place by which nominal converts disappeared but real Christians remained, and with their faith and convictions strengthened. The spiritual life of the church was purified and deepened, and the Lord continued in His own way to "add to the church daily such as were being saved."

Statistics compiled in 1900, after four decades of missionary activity, showed "a total of 42,451 Protestant Christians, 538 churches, of which about 100 were self-supporting, and 348 groups of Christians not yet organized into churches." [11]

Loyalty of Christians. For many years the notion that Christianity was something inherently "foreign" persisted in the Japanese public mind, and the loyalty of the Christians to their own nation was constantly called in question. Opposition to Christianity on this score manifested itself particularly in the schools, and Christian teachers and students were discriminated against in spite of the Constitution's plain declaration of religious liberty and equality.

The war with China in 1894-1895 afforded an excellent opportunity to put such charges and imputations squarely to the test, and it was clearly demonstrated that Christian Japanese could fight no less bravely than their Buddhist compatriots. Later, in 1904-1905, came the more serious war with Russia. "This was Christianity's opportunity. In the camps, at home, on the battlefield, Christian men were in the van. With a Christian admiral to lead her fleets, a Christian American missionary to lead in prayer to the God of battles, Christian women to care for wounded and sorrowing, it became evident that a Christian Japan might not be less Japanese than the old dreams of the *samurai*." [12] As a result, Christianity in Japan vindicated itself, and missionary work won new recognition and influence, has numbered among its converts persons of high standing and even national distinction, and has enjoyed ever-increasing opportunities and returns right up to the present.

Forms of Mission Work. The same methods have been employed in Japan as in other fields, viz., Evangelistic, Educational, Literary, Medical and Philanthropic.

The early missionaries took the leading part in the introduction of the multiplied forms of service for the physical, moral and spiritual welfare of the people, which fall under

---

[11] "Sunrise in the Sunrise Kingdom," p. 116.
[12] "The Missionary Enterprise," p. 311.

these five heads, and missionary work still pursues all of these lines. Yet changing conditions in Japan have greatly modified the need in some directions. The extraordinary progress made by the Japanese themselves in all branches of secular education, and in medical work, has taken the responsibility in these matters largely out of missionary hands. To some extent the same is true of philanthropic work, although the following sentence from Rev. Dr. J. H. Pettee's report of Christian Charities, prepared in 1897, shows how large a part of such work Christians are still doing: "They have fifteen orphanages, eleven homes for discharged prisoners, one blind asylum, five leper hospitals, two homes for the aged, five schools for the Ainu, five free kindergartens, ten industrial schools, ten other schools for the poor, fourteen hospitals, etc. . . . in a word, about one-half of all the regularly organized benevolent institutions of the land."

Among the best known of these institutions are the *Okayama Orphanage* opened by *Mr. Ishii* (the Japanese "George Müller") in 1887, and the *Home for Discharged Prisoners* in Tokyo, founded by *Mr. T. Hara.*

Newspaper Evangelism. This is a new and unique missionary method which has been tried out in recent years, and has proved so successful that it is now adopted as a regular phase of work in more than one Mission. Its plan is to utilize paid space in the daily press for presenting Christian truth through series of short expositions of Scripture texts. An offer to supply Christian literature, or answer questions by interview or by mail, on application to a central office, is appended. The fact that Japan has so many newspapers with a large circulation, and that so large a percentage of the people can read, makes this plan particularly adaptable to this land. The results have been most encouraging. The published articles have brought many personal callers and still more letters asking for literature, and the follow-up work has already led to a considerable number of clear conversions, as well as a wide proclamation of the gospel.

Some Japanese Christian Leaders. Besides Neesima there have been other sons of Japan deserving of mention as valiant apostles in the Christian Church. Some of these received their earliest inspiration from Neesima's example and took their training in the institution which he founded.

A few of the best known and most representative leaders of the present day may here be mentioned.

There is *Paul Kanamori,* who was one of the leaders of that famous "Kumamoto Band" and a member of the first theological class in the Doshisha University. He is known to-day, the world over, for his great "Three-Hour Sermon," which he has preached to multitudes throughout Japan, Formosa and Korea, and which has guided tens of thousands into the Christian faith.

There is *Kimura,* the "Moody of Japan," who in huge evangelistic campaigns conducted in the great cities of Japan, and in tours among his nationals in Manchuria, Korea, Hawaii and the South Sea Islands, has already preached to more than a million people.

There is *Colonel Yamamuro,* the "General Booth of Japan," now the distinguished head of the Salvation Army in the Empire, a speaker of tremendous power, a promoter of many forms of practical effort for the poor, the sick and fallen, and a stirring writer whose "Gospel for the Common People" has gone through 180 editions.

There is *Kagawa,* called the "St. Francis of Japan" because of his sacrificial service to the poor and oppressed classes. He is at once scholar, scientist, mystic, poet, novelist, preacher and social reformer. He is the author of 45 books, several of which have had enormous sales. Having declined the Government's flattering offer of a high official position, he has thrown himself into an aggressive evangelistic campaign known as the "Kingdom of God Movement."

Evangelistic Need. The changed conditions, as noted above, have led one author (Rev. G. H. Moule) to remark: "Does it not seem that God has led the missionary in Japan, by the very force of circumstances, to rely less on the extraneous aid of Western learning and prestige, and to content himself rather with so presenting Christ to the nation's *heart,* that the Japan-spirit being profoundly influenced, changed and strengthened by the Christian faith, may itself be the instrument for giving in due course a Christian tone to the political, intellectual, and social life of the nation?" [14]

Yet it is a sad fact that direct and aggressive evangelism is far from having the prominence it deserves in Japan, but

[14] "The Spirit of Japan," p. 180.

occupies in many Missions a place distinctly secondary to institutional work. A few smaller and more recent agencies, such as the Japan Evangelistic Band and the Oriental Missionary Society, in addition to a few prominent Japanese leaders such as have already been mentioned, are putting their efforts into active evangelistic work, but the combined forces of evangelism in all Missions are painfully insufficient for the task which confronts them.

No greater mistake could be made than to conclude, as many have apparently done from a merely superficial acquaintance with Japan, and from foolishly placing a wrong estimate upon her adoption of so many advanced features of modern civilization, that this fair Sunrise Kingdom no longer needs the same missionary attention as other Eastern lands. Japan is a beautiful land, her people are clever and attractive, her education has been modernized, her commerce has expanded, her army and navy have become strong —in a word, she has been *civilized*. But Japan is still heathen, *grossly* and *persistently* heathen. Missions after sixty years have only touched the fringe of her territory and a fragment of her population.

Over 70 per cent. of the people of Japan live in the rural districts. These country folk constitute not only the bulk, but also the backbone, of the nation. Yet the missionary forces have as yet scarcely penetrated this rural area. Many towns of from 5,000 to 10,000, and thousands of villages of from 500 to 5,000 souls, have not a vestige of Christian work in them.

The foreign and even the Japanese workers are largely in the great cities and provincial capitals. It is here that missionary progress has been greatest. And yet the phenomenal growth of Japan's cities during the last decade has far outstripped the church's advance, so that the crowded industrial and commercial centers and congested slums of the large centers contain millions of souls unreached by the gospel.

Then there are special classes, as well as areas, which lie outside the present bounds of Christian activity. Most of the converts have been from the great middle class. At the top of the social scale, the nobility and wealthy have received little attention. At the bottom of the social scale, besides the industrial masses of the great cities there are 1,500,000 fisher folk, 360,000 miners and 500,000 sailors still waiting for the gospel. Yet another almost totally neglected class are the 1,000,000 outcaste "Eta," who are socially ostracized because of their original occupations as tanners, butchers, grave diggers and beggars, and are compelled to live in segregated quarters in poverty, filth and ignorance.

Conservatively speaking, then, two-thirds of the population of Japan, or over 40,000,000 people, are yet untouched by the gospel. The present Protestant church membership constitutes less than one-third of one per cent. of the whole population.

It is to be remembered, also, that wherein Japan is no longer heathen, she is still predominantly un-Christian. Her new educational system, while weaning her great student body of 600,000 youths away from the old religions of Japan, is leading to atheism and agnosticism rather than to Christ.

A Religious Census of 5,000 students in the Tokyo University, taken a few years ago, told the following shocking tale: Confucianists, 6; Shintoists, 8; Buddhists, 300; Christians, 30; atheists, 1,500; agnostics, 3,000.

The New Industrial Maelstrom. Japan's new industrialism, which has sprung up with such amazing rapidity, constitutes one of her gravest problems of to-day. Twenty years ago there were only 1,400 factories employing 30,000 laborers. To-day there are over 90,000 plants with 2,600,-000 workers, half of them women and girls. This enormously increased demand for industrial labor has caused a steady stream of emigration from the country to the manufacturing centers.

Picture what such a transplantation means to multitudes of women, and of girls and boys in their teens, from the quiet country hamlet, with its pure air and simple living, to the dark recesses of a throbbing metropolis, with its crowded and ill-smelling tenements and its dull drudgery of toil, unrelieved by proper labor laws. The physical results alone are terrible. Thousands of the operatives suffer a steady loss of weight and soon break down utterly, or fall victims to tubercular or nervous trouble or contagious diseases. It is said that 300,000 new recruits are required annually to

repair the losses and keep pace with the development of
these industrial plants.

But the moral results are even worse. Parental control
and other old safeguards withdrawn, and temptations to
coarse pleasures and questionable pursuits alluring them on
every hand, what wonder is it that great numbers of young
girls and boys are soon demoralized and made victims of
vice and crime? "The state of affairs brought on by this
new whirlwind expansion of industrialism," says one author,
"is nothing less than appalling." [15] It is seriously draining
the nation's vital resources and affecting her entire life. The
whole situation cries to high heaven for relief, and presents
a new and peremptory challenge to the Christian forces of
Japan and those who stand behind them in other lands.

Japan's Influence Over Asia. Japan's claims for evangelization are rendered the more urgent by reason of her
leading position among the nations of the East. "What is
done in Japan affects other countries, especially those of
Eastern Asia. The Japanese sometimes compare their country to the rudder of a ship; though the rudder is small, it
directs the course of the whole vessel. The figure is not
wholly unreasonable. The influence of Japan upon the
nations of the Continent is becoming more and more
marked. Unless all the signs are deceptive much of the
world's history during the next century will center about
Eastern Asia." [16]

The end of the World War finds Japan facing what some
believe to be the second great crisis of her history. A
struggle is going on within her between the forces of autoc-
racy and democracy, militarism and freedom. Signs are not
wanting of a new reaction in influential circles against Christianity, as thought to be incompatible with Japanese ideals
and institutions. A new "National Cult" has recently been
formed, which the government proposes to make universal,
and which makes Emperor worship its central dogma.

On the other hand come the most cheering reports of
deepened gospel interest and increased conversions among
the people. Far-reaching issues hang in the balance, and
the situation calls for earnest prayer and redoubled effort,

---

[15] "Creative Forces in Japan," p. 72
[16] "Japan and Its Regeneration," p. 123.

that the tide may be turned in the right direction for Japan and the other countries involved.

America's Responsibility. Let it be remembered that when Japan was a hermit nation, not wishing to have anything to do with the rest of the world, it was America that forced her out of her long seclusion into a new world of mingled benefits and dangers. Upon American Christians, then, most of all, rests the responsibility now of giving to Japan the only message and dynamic which can meet the needs alike of her government and people, and guide their feet into the ways of life and peace.

FORMOSA

I. General Features.

Since this island now belongs to Japan, brief mention of it is in order here. Formosa (called by the Chinese and Japanese *Taiwan*) is 250 miles long and from 50 to 70 miles broad, and is separated from China by the Formosa Channel. Its area approximates 14,000 square miles. Its interior is mountainous, with plains sloping from the mountains to the sea. Its climate is damp and malarial.

The Portuguese settled there in 1590, and were in turn followed by the Spaniards and the Dutch. In 1683 Formosa became a part of the Chinese Empire, and it was ceded to Japan in 1895, at the close of the war between China and Japan. While the present population of 5,200,000 is mainly Chinese, with now a growing number of Japanese, the aborigines are Malay in origin, dwelling in the mountains and retaining their savage habits, including human head hunting.

II. Missionary Work.

Missionary work has been carried on in the south by the *English Presbyterian Church* since 1865, and in the north by the *Canadian Presbyterian Church* since 1872. The career of the Canadian missionary, *Dr. George L. Mackay,* known as "The Black-Bearded Barbarian," constitutes one of the most thrilling narratives in modern missions. With a fearless faith in God he faced all sorts of dangers and difficulties in the early years of his labors, including repeated attempts upon his life. Overcoming hatred and hostility, he gradually won over his worst enemies, endeared himself to the people by his sacrificing devotion to their physical and spiritual needs, and lived to see a large work firmly established in some sixty stations, including schools, hospital, and Oxford College for the training of Christian workers. Dr. Mackay married a Chinese wife, and was among the strongest advocates of a self-supporting and self-propagating church. He showed little desire for reënforcements from home, but attached to himself and trained a large and faithful band of Formosan pastors and evangelists, who have efficiently continued the work after him.

The Remaining Task. Even after more than sixty years of missionary work the evangelistic need still remaining is very great, as the following facts, drawn from *The Christian Movement in Japan, Korea and Formosa* (1926 and 1927) serve to illustrate. Only one person in every 128 in Formosa is reckoned within the Christian community, while the non-Christian community is growing much faster than the Christian community. The aborigines, consisting of nine tribes each speaking its own dialect, live in 719 villages and number 152,350. Yet nothing has yet been done in any definite way to preach the gospel to them.

Statistical Summary. The following figures, covering Japan and Formosa, are from *Interpretative Statistical Survey of the World Mission of the Christian Church* (1938):

Societies at work	54
Foreign missionary staff	871
Residence stations	209
Native workers	6,803
Organized churches and other groups	3,611
Communicants	208,962

QUESTIONS

1. State the location and area of Japan, and how many islands it comprises.

2. Describe its physical features and climate, and cite favorable and unfavorable results of its volcanic tendencies.

3. Give the population, and the probable origin of the Japanese race.

4. Mention their prominent national traits, favorable and unfavorable.

5. Trace briefly the political history of the nation from its beginning to the present.

6. Discuss the character of the three non-Christian religions of Japan, and their respective influence upon the nation.

7. Give a brief account of the origin, character, course and results of early Romanist Missions in Japan.

8. When and how did the so-called Period of Exclusion begin and end? What were the methods employed to effect its objects?

9. Give the names and the years of arrival of the first seven Protestant missionaries to Japan, and give brief accounts of the three most prominent among them.

10. Tell the story of the "Kumamoto Band."

11. Name and describe the career of the best known of Japan's Christian converts.

12. What contributions have Protestant Missions made to the welfare of Japan along philanthropic lines? Give the names of two prominent institutions of this kind and their founders.

13. What new and unique missionary method has been used of late in Japan, and with what results?

14. Name four prominent Japanese Christian leaders of to-day, indicating the special line of each one's ministry.

15. To what extent has Japan not yet been evangelized, and what fact adds emphasis to the importance of her fuller evangelization?

16. Give figures indicating the development of Japan's industrialism, and indicate some of the menaces and problems growing out of these new conditions.

17. State the size and population of Formosa, and the nature of its inhabitants.

18. Mention the main Missionary Societies working in Formosa, and tell something of the work of its most famous missionary.

19. Give latest general statistics of Protestant Missions in Japan and Formosa.

CHAPTER XIII

KOREA

AREA, 85,000 SQUARE MILES.   POPULATION, 23,000,000

The fact that all intercourse between Korea and the Western world is a matter of only a few years, and the further fact of that country's recent absorption by Japan, have led to very brief treatment of Korea by most textbooks on missions, usually in the form of a short postscript to their chapter on Japan. But the phenomenal success which has attended mission work in Korea, as well as certain unique features of missionary policy and methods in that field, which have deeply impressed the entire Christian church, and also the grave situation which has of late developed between the Koreans and their new political masters, all seem amply to justify a fuller and separate consideration of this interesting field.

I. General Features.

Names. The earliest name for Korea, conferred by her Chinese civilizer in the twelfth century before Christ, was *Cho-sen,* or Morning Calm, and this is still the name used by the natives to-day. The word *Korea* comes from *Korai,* the name of the northernmost of three states which were joined into a united Korea a millennium ago. Korea's centuries of deep seclusion have also won for her the name of the Hermit Nation.

Position and Size. Korea lies on the east coast of Asia, between 35 deg. and 43 deg. north latitude. It is a peninsula about 600 miles long and 135 miles broad, with a coastline of 1,750 miles, and an area, including numerous small islands which cluster along its western and southern shores, estimated at nearly 90,000 square miles. Its size is thus almost that of New York and Pennsylvania states combined, or slightly larger than England, Scotland and Wales.

The Yellow Sea on the west and the Japan Sea on the east separate her respectively from China and Japan, while her territory joins that of Russia on the north. She thus occupies a striking position as a "buffer state" between three great political powers, among which she has been a continual bone of contention.

The Country. In the main, Korea is rugged and mountainous, and its coast line presents a bleak and uninviting aspect on the approach from the sea. The interior, however, has many fertile hills and valleys covered chiefly with waving rice fields, although other grains, as well as vegetables and fruits, are grown. Charming scenery is to be found, and Mrs. Isabella Bird Bishop describes Seoul, the capital, as one of the most beautifully situated cities in the world. Despite the crude implements and modes of farming employed, and the fact also that not nearly all the arable land is cultivated, the crops raised are ample for Korea's millions, and in good years leave a substantial balance for export. The land is also rich in minerals, but as in China the prevailing superstitions have prevented much mining until recent years, when Westerners have introduced it.

Foreign residents in Korea boast not a little of its fine climate. The summers are temperate, the winters clear and cold. During the rainy season of six or eight weeks in summer rain falls incessantly and in torrents, reaching a record of five inches in twenty-four hours and twenty-two inches for a single season. The atmosphere at such times is hot and sultry.

The People. Korea seems originally to have been peopled from the mainland, but an admixture at some time is believed to have considerably modified both the physical characteristics and the language of the race. Just as Korea lies geographically between China and Japan, so its people come midway between their two neighbors in physical and intellectual qualities. The Korean resembles the Mongolian in general appearance, is larger in stature than the Japanese, but smaller than the northern Chinese, has good physique and quite average strength and endurance. The woeful absence of all knowledge of hygiene and attention to sanitation and quarantine, however, has caused disease of almost every kind to work dreadful havoc. Ague, smallpox, typhus, and Asiatic cholera especially abound. The mortality among little children is appalling.

In temperament, Dr. Horace G. Underwood describes the Koreans as being "not as phlegmatic as the Chinese nor as volatile as the Japanese," and adds: "They are not as slavishly bound by superstition, not as devoted to their old religions, not as faithful, perhaps, to the traditions of the past, as the Chinese; nor as initiative and ambitious as the Japanese." [1]

Dr. George Heber Jones writes in a leaflet: "Whereas in China the cast of mind is commercial, giving us a nation of merchants, and in Japan it is military, giving us a nation of warriors, in Korea it is literary, giving us a nation of scholars."

By other writers more initiative is claimed for the Koreans than either of these other two races possesses, and they are credited, in common with the Chinese, with real ability, in contrast to the mere genius of imitation and adaptation in which the Japanese excel.

The old prevalent impression about the Koreans, formed by Europeans on their first contact with them, is expressed by the following quotation: "They seemed to be lazy, even for Orientals; generally dishonest, unclean in person, rather the left-overs of Asia, as if Mongols, Chinese and others had successively sought to escape from oppression in their own lands, and going as far as they could, found themselves shut in by the sea in this rocky peninsula." [2] But writers of long residence among the Koreans claim that such low estimates of them are based on unfair and insufficient evidence, and they cite on the contrary the hardy, self-supporting farmer, the busy city merchant and the proficient scholar.

The Language. The Korean language has points of resemblance to both the Chinese and Japanese, and yet is distinct from either. It possesses an alphabet of twenty-five letters. The Chinese ideographs are also used, as in Japan, in addition to the native script, and the Chinese classics have for centuries furnished the basis of literary education.

Religions. It is sometimes said that the Koreans are

1 "The Call of Korea," pp. 45, 46.
2 "The Missionary Enterprise," p. 315.

without any religion. Compared with the peoples of other non-Christian lands they have certainly not been strongly held by any religious system, and certain influences have tended to weaken their faith in their old religions. Temples and shrines are few, and priests are relegated to a very low place in the social scale.

Shamanism is the oldest of Korea's faiths, and to-day still exerts a stronger influence upon the people than any other. It teaches a great array of spirits, good and evil, of which the good ones are to be invoked, and the evil ones, which predominate, propitiated. The system has gathered into itself a mass of grotesque superstitions.

Buddhism entered Korea in the fourth century, and through her was later introduced into Japan. In Korea it gradually gained considerable power, and during a certain dynasty became the national religion. Later on, partly because of its meddling in politics, it came under the ban, and large numbers of its temples were demolished. Stringent laws enacted against Buddhism were not repealed until after the China-Japan war (1895), when the pro-Japanese party came into power. Buddhism has all along maintained large and well-endowed monasteries throughout the country, and among the common people, and especially the women, it still holds its own.

Confucianism came over from China in earliest times, along with her literature, and has done much to mold the thought and life of the nation. But as elsewhere it is to be regarded as a system of ethics rather than a religion. Its adherents are mainly the educated classes, although its chief rite of ancestral worship is universally observed throughout Korea.

Historical Résumé. Reliable records of Korea's past history begin with the coming, in 1122 B.C., of a Chinese noble called Kija, who, having incurred the anger of the wicked Chinese Emperor, migrated with 5,000 retainers, and settling among the aborigines of Korea organized a new state. Comparatively little is known of the centuries which followed, up to within a short time of the Christian era. Thenceforth the history of Korea until recent years, when the first treaties with the foreign Powers were signed, is largely a melancholy record of repeated invasions from

China, Mongolia and Japan. The location of this small and peaceably inclined country made her a ready prey to her stronger and rival neighbors. "The invaders would come on their conquering career, and the people would bend for a time like forest trees before the storm. But, the pressure being removed, they would resume their national life; a nominal tribute would be paid for a term of years; then after a time they would forget they ever had been conquered, when another tidal wave of war would pour over them from without." [3]

During the earlier centuries frequent inter-tribal wars among the states into which the present Korea was then divided led to the calling in on opposite sides of Chinese and Japanese forces to assist, and thus poor Korea became again and again the battleground of opposing armies, foreign as well as native, with terrible resultant destruction of life and property. Gradually the whole country became tributary by turns to China and Japan, and at times to both together. In addition to all this, the fact that the famous Mongol conqueror, Kublai Khan, in 1281 forced the Koreans to assist in an unsuccessful invasion of Japan, as well as the frequent depredations committed by Japanese pirates upon Korean junks and coast towns, engendered bitter hatred between the peninsular kingdom and the island empire—a feature which it is well to bear in mind in considering present-day relations.

Toward the close of the sixteenth century Japan sent a great army of invasion against Korea, with the real aim of making Korea's subjugation a means to the greater end of the conquest of China. For a time they swept on victoriously, taking an awful toll of life. They sent back to Japan enormous quantities of booty, and committed the wanton outrage of cutting off large numbers of the ears and noses of Koreans, pickling and sending them to Japan, where the place of their burial at Kyoto is still shown. But the Koreans rallied bravely, the Chinese came to their help, and eventually the Japanese were defeated and driven back with terrible loss.

Early in the seventeenth century began the struggle between the Manchus and China, ending in the seating of a

[3] "Every-day Life in Korea," p. 26.

Manchu upon the Dragon throne. Korea was invaded by the Manchus, its king captured and the country placed under tribute. This completes the long list of invasions, and brings Korea's chequered history down to recent times.

The First Treaties. In order to have a clear understanding of the present Korean situation and its vital bearing upon missions, it is necessary to trace in outline the main political events which in tragic succession have led up to the completely new régime in which the Hermit Nation of yore finds itself to-day. "Up to 1876 Korea successfully preserved her isolation, and repelled with violence any attempt to encroach upon it. In that year Japan forced a treaty upon her, and in 1882 China followed with 'Trade and Frontier Regulations.' The United States negotiated a treaty in 1882, Great Britain and Germany in 1884, Russia and Italy in 1886, and Austria in 1892, in all which, though under Chinese suzerainty, Korea was treated with as an independent state. By these treaties, Seoul and the ports of Chemulpo, Fusan and Wonsan were opened to foreign commerce." [4]

Japan's Ascendancy. The China-Japan War of 1894-95 was brought on by the sending of Chinese troops into Korea at that country's request, to help quell an insurrection. This the Japanese resented as contrary to an agreement signed by China and Japan in 1885. The Japanese raised the cry of "The Independence of Korea," surprised the world by winning a swift and decisive victory over China, and at once became the dominating power in Korea.

Had Japan's administrative methods been the equal of her military tactics the subsequent course of affairs in Korea might have been very different. But the murder of the Queen, which soon followed, and in which the direct complicity of the Japanese Minister to Korea has been proven beyond a doubt, was no less a grievous tactical blunder than it was a foul crime. This act, and the oppressive measures which followed, drove the King to throw himself into the hands of Russia by fleeing from his palace-prison to the Russian legation, and forthwith began a new chapter consisting of an eight-year diplomatic duel between Japan and Russia for ascendancy in Korea. Both Powers were alike

[4] "Korea and Her Neighbors," p. 11.

selfish in their motives and unscrupulous in the course they pursued of making tools of clever but unprincipled Koreans to promote their ends. Russian intrigue gradually gained the upper hand, and that nation's obvious intention of absorbing Korea not only gave Japan just fears for her own national safety, but also alarmed European nations lest the balance of political power should be seriously disturbed.

The long tension finally broke in 1904 and war ensued, in which the army and navy of the great Russian nation were ignominiously defeated by those of Japan, and the little island empire of the Far East rose into new prominence as one of the first-rate Powers of the world. Korea now agreed to accept Japan's advice in administrative affairs, and Japan renewed her assurances that Korea's independence would be preserved. How vain were such assurances is seen in the prompt assumption of authority which followed. Japan's hand became heavier and heavier upon Korea, and more than one trustworthy Christian writer openly charges the Japanese military régime with extortion, injustice and cruel treatment of the Koreans.

On the other hand, it is pointed out by equally reliable authorities that Korea's obsolete system of patriarchal government, and the persistent failure of her king and his ministers to mend their ways, adjust themselves to a new age, and face seriously the task of effectively administering the country's affairs, inevitably spelled her doom and compelled control by some outside power. Dr. H. N. Allen writes: "The Koreans are reaping the harvest of their own sowing. . . . Instead of heeding good advice and clearing up their premises so no powerful neighbor would have an excuse for doing this for them, they played at all manner of silly pastimes. The government went from bad to worse, until it became an easy prey to any one strong enough to go in and put things to rights. The verdict of war has left that task to Japan." [5]

But to continue the course of events: "As the summer of 1905 drew to a close it became more and more clear that the Japanese government, despite its many promises to the contrary, intended completely to destroy the independence of

5 "Things Korean," p. 245.

Korea." [6]   Marquis Ito was sent to Seoul as Special Envoy
of the Emperor of Japan, to induce the Korean government
to ask Japan to assume a protectorate, but both king and
cabinet held out stoutly, until finally (according to prevailing accounts) military intimidation was resorted to, and
the Foreign Minister was forced to sign the document.[7]

Two years later the final crisis came with the signing of
the Japan-Korea Treaty on July 24, 1907, the old Emperor-
King was forced to abdicate, and Japan, through her Resi-
dent-General, was left in complete control. For two years
Japan maintained a protectorate over Korea and in 1910
formally annexed the country.

II. Missionary Work.

Roman Catholic Missions. Late in the eighteenth century
some members of the Korean Embassy at Peking came in
contact with Roman Catholic missionaries and brought back
that faith to Korea. Supplying, as it did, what the existing
religions lacked, it was well received and grew rapidly. In
1835 two Romanist missionaries secretly entered the country, and others soon followed. Persecution broke out, however, from time to time, incited by the corrupt Buddhist
priests, and many converts suffered martyrdom along with
the missionaries. In 1864, under a new regent who hated
foreigners, and Romanists in particular, a violent storm of
persecution burst, the Roman Catholic Bishop and eight of
his associates were seized and killed, and a veritable inquisition was instituted, under which at least 10,000 converts
were put to death. Roman Catholic Christianity in Korea
was threatened with extermination and has never fully rallied from the blow. The effect of the persecution upon the
Koreans was to create a great dread of all foreign religions,
and this has proved a drawback to subsequent missionary
effort, both Protestant and Romanist.

Protestant Beginnings. The first Protestant efforts in
behalf of Korea were put forth by *Rev. John Ross,* a Scotch
Presbyterian missionary at Mukden, in Manchuria, whose

---

6 "Korea's Fight for Freedom," p. 87.
7 See "The Passing of Korea," Dr. H. B. Hulbert. "The Unveiled East"
and "Korea's Fight for Freedom," F. A. McKenzie. For the pro-Japanese
version of this and associated events see "In Korea with Marquis Ito,"
Professor George T. Ladd.

interest was aroused by his contact with Koreans on the border. He took up the study of their language, translated the entire New Testament into Korean, and sent Korean colporteurs across the border to distribute it. These efforts were so blessed that "when Protestant missionaries came to Korea later they found whole communities in the north professing Christianity, studying the Bible among themselves, and only waiting for some one to come and teach them." [8]

The signing of the treaty between Korea and the United States in 1882 afforded a new "open door" for missionary work which the churches of America promptly prepared to enter. The *Northern Presbyterian Board* in 1884 appointed *Rev. J. W. Heron,* M.D., to Korea, but his departure was delayed, and meanwhile *Dr. H. N. Allen* of the same Society, who was already in China, was transferred to Korea and thus became the first Protestant missionary to the "Hermit Nation." His medical skill, and particularly his success in treating surgically the wounds of a high official who was a cousin of the Queen, were providentially used to win the favor of the court and smooth the way for the missionaries who soon followed, even though Dr. Allen himself did not continue in mission work but entered the diplomatic service.

In 1885 *Rev. Horace G. Underwood* of the Northern Presbyterian Board, and *Rev. H. G. Appenzeller* and *Dr. W. B. Scranton* of the *Methodist Episcopal Board,* arrived on the field. In 1888 the *Y.M.C.A.* of the University of Toronto sent out *Rev. James S. Gale,* who later joined the Presbyterian Mission and has become well known for his interesting books on Korea. Other Societies followed, the *Australian Presbyterian* entering in 1889, the *English Episcopalian* (S.P.G.) in 1890, the *Southern Presbyterian* in 1892, the *Southern Methodist* in 1896, and the *Canadian Presbyterian* in 1898.

Policies and Methods. The consideration of policies and methods of work assumes much more than ordinary interest and importance in the case of Korea by reason of the unusual results which so early attended missionary efforts here. On this point we cannot do better than quote from Dr. H. G. Underwood, one of the earliest pioneers and foremost missionary leaders in Korea for many years. He writes: "Very early in the history of the work, almost at its beginning, God in His Providence led us to adopt methods that have been said by some to have been unique, but in reality are simply those that have been adopted by numbers of missionaries in different parts of the world. The only unique feature has been the almost unanimity with which these have been followed by the whole missionary body in this land." [9]

This writer cites the visit to Korea, in 1890, of *Dr. John L. Nevius,* of Chefoo, China, well known throughout the entire missionary world for his advocacy of methods making for a self-supporting and self-propagating native church, and speaks of the influence exerted upon Korean mission policies by the several conferences held by Dr. Nevius with the Korean missionaries. Continuing, Dr. Underwood writes: "After careful and prayerful consideration, we were led in the main to adopt the 'Nevius method,' and it has been the policy of the Mission—

"*First,* to let each man 'abide in the calling wherein he was found,' teaching that each was to be an individual worker for Christ, and to live Christ in his own neighborhood, supporting himself by his trade;

"*Second,* to develop church methods and machinery only so far as the native church was able to take care of and manage the same;

"*Third,* as far as the church itself was able to provide the men and the means, to set aside those who seemed the better qualified, to do evangelistic work among their neighbors;

"*Fourth,* to let the natives provide their own church buildings, which were to be native in architecture, and of such style as the local church could afford to put up." [10]

Following this line of policy, the first Christians in the place generally became the teachers of others, themselves meeting in classes for Bible study and instruction as to their duties. As one and another evinced special fitness for Bible teaching and Christian service these would be given supervision of districts, their support being undertaken by the

9 "The Call of Korea," p. 5.
10 "The Call of Korea," pp. 109, 110.

groups ministered to. Graded classes for these leaders were formed, which in time developed into schools for systematic theological training.

Bible Classes. Another prominent feature has been the holding of large popular Bible classes in each district, for several weeks during the season of the year most convenient for the Christian community. The attendance at such gatherings has gradually grown, and varies from 200 in the south to 1,300 in the north. Those who thus gather return home to assist in holding local classes under the direction of the missionaries and district leaders, and thus systematic Bible instruction is carried on throughout the entire field occupied. In one year (1907), in the Pyeng Yang station, 191 such classes were held by the Presbyterian Mission, over 10,000 attending. In 1927 there were 541 classes, with an attendance of 7,754 men and 11,325 women.

School Work. The need of educational work has not been lost sight of, although it has been held secondary to evangelism both in proportion and in order. The principle adhered to has been to provide Christian education primarily for the children of the churches rather than to conduct schools for the heathen as an evangelistic agency. Each local church was encouraged to open and support its own primary school under a Christian teacher, and so heartily have the churches responded to their duty on this line that one mission alone, in 1907, reported 337 such primary schools, all but three of which were entirely self-supported.

It became necessary for the missions to take the initiative to some extent in the matter of schools of higher academic instruction, so that in the main they have provided the buildings, equipment, and teaching staff. But even in these the students have been expected to meet their own support and the running expenses of the school, and the native churches have shown a noble spirit in making earnest efforts to share even the cost of these school plants for the education of their sons.

All this stands in striking contrast to the prevailing policies and methods in most other mission fields, and to their results as well. It is impossible to account for the difference by assuming greater material prosperity on the part of the Koreans, for they are certainly as poor as any Eastern race.

These developments are rather an impressive testimony to the splendid results attainable by the adoption and maintenance from the very beginning of true Scriptural principles and methods of missionary work, while at the same time they afford a beautiful example of what the Spirit of grace can accomplish in the hearts of converts but recently saved from heathenism.

Growth and Expansion. Mission work in Korea does not fall into any well-marked periods. Dr. Underwood suggests a possible division into the periods of preparation, expansion, beginning of large harvests, and greater ingatherings, but says: "From the very beginning we have been permitted to see results, and the work has been steadily progressing with an ever-increasing momentum up to the present time." [11]

From the first there were many who gave a willing ear to the missionary's message, and the books he offered were purchased eagerly. The north especially seemed to have been prepared by the wide seed-sowing that had been done earlier from China, and for this reason missionary trips and efforts were at first mainly directed thither. The first three converts were baptized in 1886. In 1890, after only five years, and those necessarily given largely to preliminary itineration, procuring property, language study, translation work, etc., there were over 100 converts.

This receptivity on the part of the Koreans was recognized as a call for reënforcements from home, and the existing Missions steadily enlarged their staffs and expanded their work, while other Societies entered the field. Then, following the China-Japan war of 1894-1895, the period of large harvests began, with ever-increasing numbers of enquirers and converts. But even these great results were in turn completely eclipsed by those of the first few years of the new century, which far exceeded the highest hopes of the most optimistic missionaries, and led to Korea's becoming known as "the missionary marvel of the age." By 1907 there were actually over 1,000 self-supporting churches with some 30,000 members and over 120,000 adherents, and these churches contributed that year nearly $80,000 in U. S. money.

[11] "The Call of Korea," p. 134.

A Sample Station. The name of Pyeng Yang, the most
important city in northern Korea, has become familiar and
famous among Christians the world over, because of its
being identified with one of the most remarkable spiritual
movements in all missionary history. It was a very rich
and very immoral city, commonly called "the worst city in
Korea." The entry and early work of the missionaries there
met with bitter opposition from the local officials. The
first converts and native helpers were sorely persecuted, some
of them thrown into prison and cruelly tortured. Soon
after this, in 1894, the China-Japan war broke out, and
Pyeng Yang was the scene of one of the most decisive battles. The unselfish example and work of the missionaries,
as well as the calm and trustful demeanor of the Christians
during this time of turmoil and anxiety, made a profound
impression upon the people. Moreover, the Christians who
were forced to flee with the other citizens, when the Chinese
troops occupied Pyeng Yang, scattered the good seed of the
gospel throughout the whole district by their personal testimony and the printed page. From that time the attitude of
the populace completely changed, and a spirit of enquiry
began and rapidly spread through the city and the whole
countryside, until the strength of the mission workers was
taxed to the utmost to keep pace with the demands upon
them.

Testimony of a Visitor. Mrs. Isabella Bird Bishop, the
well known traveler and authoress, visited this city in December, 1895, and afterwards wrote: "The Pyeng Yang
work which I saw last winter is the most impressive mission
work I have ever seen in any part of the world. It shows
that the Spirit of God still moves on the earth, and that the
old truths of sin, judgment to come, divine justice and love,
the atonement and the necessity of holiness have the same
power as in the apostolic days to transform the lives of men.
What I saw and heard there has greatly strengthened my
own faith." [12]

The following figures speak eloquently of the growth of
this one station within a period of four short years. In
1895 there were in the city of Pyeng Yang twenty church
members, and in the province adjacent seventy-three bap-

[12] Quoted in "Every-Day Life in Korea," p. 225.

tized persons. In 1899 there were 1,182 church members and 7,433 adherents, meeting in 153 self-supporting churches, and that year the Christian community built thirty-eight new church buildings and gave $1,891 in U. S. money. The latest report of the Presbyterian Mission for Pyeng Yang lists 24 Presbyterian churches within the city and its environs, and there are as many more churches of other connections. In the Pyeng Yang station district there are 400 Presbyterian churches, with 20,000 members and 5,000 catechumens. All of the 70 Korean pastors, as well as 50 other workers, are supported entirely by the Korean Christians.

The Great Revival. This marvelous visitation of the Spirit of God, of which the whole Christian world has heard, centered in Pyeng Yang. Like all other revivals it began with prayer—earnest, united, persevering prayer by missionaries and native Christians alike, born of a deep Spirit-given soul hunger for a richer, fuller experience of divine grace and power. For months, beginning in the late summer of 1906, groups met day after day to pray, and although no manifestation came their prayers knew no cessation.

Then 1907 dawned, and from all points of the north country Christians gathered, 700 strong, for the customary Bible study classes at the central station. It was in the course of those meetings, on January 14, that the Spirit fell upon the whole assembly with deep heart-searching and conviction. It is not easy to describe the wonderful scenes that followed, the intense, conscious presence of God, the pungent conviction, burning tears and agonizing confessions, and the new and marvelous sense of peace and joy and liberty which followed. Old and young, educated and ignorant, missionary, native worker, and young convert—all came under this divine influence and power. Sinners were converted, backsliders reclaimed, Christians got a new vision of God, confessed their sins, failures and short-comings, adjusted their differences, made apologies and restitution, and were filled with new love for Christ and souls and new power for service. For two weeks schoolwork and all other ordinary activities were laid aside and everything gave place to prayer.

The wave of revival soon spread to Seoul and all parts of the land, and here and there similar manifestations occurred. Beyond Korea, too, the movement extended. The churches of Mukden, Manchuria, heard of the revival and sent two elders to investigate. Rev. Jonathan Goforth also came from China. As these messengers carried back reports of what they had seen and heard in Korea the Holy Spirit was poured out in like manner and measure, first in Manchuria and later in center after center in China, with wonderful results which are felt to this day. Thus hath it pleased God to manifest His grace and power through poor, humbled Korea unto the purifying and enriching of the life of the church in the vast empire of China, whence the first rays of gospel light had, a generation before, penetrated the gross darkness of the little Hermit Nation.

Korean Christians. While rightly attributing this wonderful revival and the phenomenal progress of missions as a whole in Korea to the sovereign hand of God, we cannot overlook the fact that certain qualities in the Christian converts of Korea have played an important part in bringing about such results, by providing God with means to work through. We should sadly miss much of the lesson the Lord would teach the entire Christian church through what has taken place in Korea if we failed to observe and ponder some of the traits and graces exhibited in marked degree by the Christians of that land. Among these are to be noted:—

A High Conception of Discipleship. "From the early days of the mission there has prevailed among the Korean converts a very high conception of the privileges and responsibilities of church membership. A Korean Christian is always more than a mere church-member; he is a worker giving his services freely and gladly to extend the knowledge of Christ among his neighbors. It has not been an unusual thing for a pastor of a local church to have not less than one-third of the entire membership of his church on the streets on a Sunday afternoon, engaged in house-to-house visitation and personal work among their unconverted neighbors." [14]

Love for God's Word. This is most marked. Practically all Korean Christians are Bible students. Old as well as young make up the Sunday School enrollment, which is said to aggregate 400,000. Sunday Schools in the large city

[14] "Korea in Transition," pp. 192, 193.

churches vary in attendance from 2,000 to 3,000. Whole chapters of Scripture are commonly memorized even by the illiterate and the aged. An unique feature of mission work in Korea already noted is the system of Bible study classes of all grades, held in the centers for periods ranging from four days to a month. Not only the native workers and more advanced Christians, but the rank and file of the members as well, attend these gatherings, saving and sacrificing to be able to come, and traveling long distances from every part of the district. The Federal Council of Churches in Korea reports many such classes during 1936 with an aggregate attendance of 202,000.

Church prayer meetings, too, are largely attended. The Pyeng Yang church is said to hold a world record on this line, with an average regular attendance of 1,500 at prayer meeting. Nor are Korean Christians as a rule merely hearers of the Word, but doers as well.

Self-propagation and Self-support. It is a question whether any other mission field has furnished an example of zeal and devotion on these lines, or a record of results achieved, to equal those of Korea. It is quite true that striking instances of these traits in individual converts are not wanting in other fields. But the unique feature about Korea is that these features dominate the church as a whole. Let us quote a few testimonies from among many which are at hand.

"From the first the Koreans were made to believe that the spread of the gospel and growth of the church was their work rather than ours. We are here to start them and guide them in their efforts, but it is theirs to do the work." —DR. SHARROCKS.

"The Korean is a preacher of the gospel by a kind of spiritual instinct; he knows and does this one thing only; he provides for his church schools without a cent from the homelands; he gives of his means a tenth or more; sometimes he gives all he has over a bare living."—DR. JAMES S. GALE.

"Not only in prayers, but in works as well, are the rank and file of the Korean Christians instant in season and out. I dare say there is no land in the world where there is so much personal and unpaid—in money—hand to hand, and heart to heart, evangelistic work done as in Korea."—REV. J. Z. MOORE.

"The Koreans themselves established Christianity in distant communities where no white man had ever been."—F. A. MCKENZIE.

"The progress of Christianity is unprecedentedly rapid. Native churches, instead of depending on foreign aid, are becoming self-supporting, self-governing, self-propagating. An astonishing revival spirit and evangelistic zeal prevail, and converts are gathering by scores and hundreds. Self-denying giving is manifested in a unique fashion."—DR. A. T. PIERSON.

Take the Syen Chun (Presbyterian) station as a concrete illustration of what these witnesses attest. Dr. Sharrocks, reporting for 1905, gave the increase in the number of Christians in that one year as from 6,507 to 11,943, an average of 453 conversions per month. Such results could not possibly be attributed to the direct work of the small band of missionaries, nor to the paltry $72 spent on local mission evangelists. The fact is that fifteen evangelists, supported by the native church, were giving their whole time to the work, and in addition the Christians had pledged a total of over 8,000 days of voluntary evangelistic effort. The same report states: "In our station we have fifty-six day schools with 1,192 pupils, receiving not one dollar of foreign money. There are seventy church buildings in our province, into only two of which any foreign money has gone." [15] For the entire support of this station, with all its different phases of work, the Koreans gave $10.62 for every American dollar used.

The continuance of this spirit of evangelistic fervor in the Korean church is evidenced by a report of a week's evangelistic services held in Pyeng Yang in February, 1920, in which 3,000 persons were led to decide for Christ. "These meetings were planned and carried out almost entirely by the Koreans themselves. Men, women and children visited from house to house, and teams of college boys toured the country districts." [16]

Sacrificial Giving. Many touching instances of keen sac-

[15] Quoted in "Korea in Transition," pp. 196-197.
[16] *Missionary Review of the World,* Sept., 1920, p. 824.

rifice in the giving of the Korean Christians "for Christ's sake and the gospel's" could be cited.   Dr. George Heber Jones reports that "Korean men have been known to mortgage their houses that mortgages might be removed from the houses of God; to sell their crops of good rice, intended for family consumption, purchasing inferior millet to live upon through the winter, and giving the difference in cost for the support of the workers to preach among their own countrymen.   Korean women have given their wedding rings, and even cut off their hair that it might be sold and the amount devoted to the spread of the Gospel."

The same missionary tells of the leader of a little village group of Christians, who, when all other resources had been exhausted to meet the cost of a new chapel, sold his only ox, and the next spring he and his brother hitched themselves in place of the ox and dragged the plow through the fields that year.

Subscriptions not only of money, but also of time, to be given to evangelistic work and manual labor in the erection of churches, are quite the order of the day, thousands of Christians contributing from a week to a month of time, and many still longer periods.

Foreign Missionary Efforts.   In addition to all that the Korean churches are doing for the support of the work and spread of the gospel in their own land, they have again set an example to other mission fields by launching missions among their own countrymen in foreign lands, such as Manchuria, Siberia, Hawaii, Mexico, and the Pacific coast of the United States.   In the Shantung province, China, they also have begun missionary work among the Chinese, having accepted responsibility for a section of that province. Four married pastors and one doctor, assisted by fifteen Chinese evangelists, are carrying on fruitful evangelistic, medical and school work.   Regular services are now conducted in upwards of twenty centers, and about 1,000 converts have been baptized.

The Independence Movement.   Japan's administration in Korea since she annexed that country in 1910 has been galling to the Koreans.   It has been a military despotism, a system of arbitrary and drastic measures with the aim of forcing the Koreans to a complete renunciation of their old nationality and an assimilation to Japan. The results of such unfair and short-sighted policy have been the opposite of what the Japanese expected, and the Korean national consciousness has been strengthened rather than weakened. All the material benefits which Japanese rule has introduced, including the improvement of agricultural methods, building of roads and railroads, new public school, banking and postal-saving systems, hygienic regulations and other things, could not atone for the overbearing attitude of the Japanese officers of the law in treating as an inferior and conquered race a people boasting such antiquity and culture. When, therefore, the Great War brought an end to German militarism, and the acceptance by the victorious nations of the principle of "self-determination" of subject peoples, new hopes were born in the breasts of patriotic Koreans of becoming liberated from such intolerable conditions. *A Passive Resistance uprising* was organized, a "Declaration of Independence" was drawn up and signed by thirty-three leaders, and for two months beginning March 1, 1919, demonstrations took place in Seoul and throughout the country, in which the Koreans uniformly refrained from any acts of violence and contented themselves with merely parading and shouting *"Mansei"*—(literally "ten thousand years"), a patriotic expression used much like *"Hurrah"* in English.

The unarmed "demonstrators" were promptly fired on, sabered, bayoneted, arrested, beaten and tortured by the Japanese military police, and a campaign of violent and shocking repression ensued. Pamphlet No. 2 of "The Korean Situation," issued by a Commission of the Federal Council of Christian Churches in America, supplies the following figures among others: Koreans killed, 631; arrested (March 1-July 20, 1919), 28,934; flogged and released (March 1-Oct. 31, 1919), 10,592; sent to prison, 5,156.

Volumes have been written describing the inhuman cruelties and atrocities practised by the police, the horrid tortures resorted to, the shameful indignities to which pure women were subjected, etc.

The missionaries, who were wrongly suspected of complicity in the independence uprising, because of the large number of Korean Christians who took part in it, came in for their share of insult and injury, and a discrimination by the Japanese officials against the Christian movement was plainly noticeable. Seventeen churches were totally destroyed, and twenty-four others partially so. A report of the Presbyterian churches in October, 1919, states that of that denomination alone, 336 pastors, elders and helpers had been arrested, as well as 2,125 male and 531 female members, 41 had been shot and killed, 6 beaten to death, and 1,642 were still in prison. The other denominations suffered proportionately.

The strict Japanese military censorship for a time prevented the facts reaching the outside world, but gradually they filtered through. Then, needless to say, this reign of terror and outrage called forth general and vigorous condemnation and protest. The Federal Council of Churches in America, and later the Federated Missions of Japan, made representations to the Japanese Imperial Government. It took time and pains to convince that government of the existence of such shocking conditions in its Korean administration, but once convinced the Premier and his Cabinet acted with commendable decision and a fair measure of despatch.

Changed Japanese Administration. In August, 1919, the Military Governor General of Korea was recalled and Baron Saito sent in his place. The new Governor held conferences with representative missionaries and Koreans, and addressed himself with evident sincerity to the serious task of correcting abuses and remodeling the government. The military police system has been abolished, an order issued doing away with flogging and torture, promises made of equal treatment of Koreans and Japanese as regards official positions and salaries, of more freedom for the Korean press, of larger liberty and recognition for mission schools, and so on.

As to the merits of what has already been done and of the assurances given for the future, opinions differ. Some things have already occurred which are at variance with the promises given of reform. The Koreans as a whole are not satisfied, and are distrustful of Japan. They feel that the reforms do not go far enough, nor are they disposed to be content with any mere reforms; they want independence. Further occasional uprisings have been reported and fresh arrests made. The *Korean Independence Movement* is still being maintained, with its headquarters in Shanghai, China, and a Bureau of Information in the United States, where it is receiving considerable backing by Americans as well as the Korean student body.

The Missionary Outlook. The ultimate effect of these recent events upon the church and mission work in general in Korea is to some extent problematical. It is too early to speak positively. But it must be evident to every thoughtful person who has followed the course of events closely that the Korean church is being put to a new and severe test, that the missionaries are faced with a task of extreme delicacy in standing firmly against injustice and inhumanity, showing rightful sympathy for those whose individual rights and legitimate national aspirations may be violated, and at the same time maintaining a strictly consistent missionary attitude of non-interference in matters political.

Latest mission reports indicate that the Christian movement is still going on, with a steady growth in the church, numerically at least. Some have feared lest the new zeal for education may mean a letting down in the peculiarly evangelistic efforts of the church. Yet cheering word keeps coming of revival and of ingatherings at various points, and the churches were never so full of young people as at present.

The whole situation calls for sympathetic and believing prayer that through all that has befallen the nation of Korea, or may yet befall her, Korean Christians and missionaries alike may be "more than conquerors," and that the wonderful work of divine grace and power in that afflicted but plucky little nation, which has given her an unique place in missionary annals, may still continue and increase.

Statistical Summary. The following figures are from the *Statistical Survey of the World Mission* (1938):

Societies at work	17
Foreign missionary staff	462
Residence stations	63
Native workers (paid)	6,283
Organized churches and other groups	4,421
Communicants	148,677

NOTE: The total number of Protestant adherents was estimated in 1938 at 400,000.

QUESTIONS

1. Give the boundaries, area and population of Korea.

2. Describe its physical features and resources, and also its climate.

3. Trace the origin of the Korean people, and compare their characteristics with those of the Chinese and Japanese.

4. Briefly describe the various religions which preceded Christianity in Korea.

5. Sketch Korea's history from its authentic beginning until it came under the domination of the Manchu Dynasty of China, giving opening and closing (approximate) dates.

6. Give a list of the first series of treaties between Korea and foreign nations, with dates, and describe the events which led finally to her annexation by Japan.

7. Give an account of the beginnings of Protestant missionary work in Korea, and the names of four of the prominent pioneers and the Societies they represented.

8. What distinctive missionary policies and methods have been followed in Korea? Give illustrations of the results as regards (a) evangelization, (b) schoolwork, (c) support of churches.

9. Give an account of the Great Revival, and some idea of the extent of its results.

10. Cite four outstanding features of Korean Christians as bearing upon the quality and progress of mission work.

11. Describe briefly the foreign missionary efforts of the Korean Church.

12. Give an account of the Korean Independence Movement, suggesting something of its influence upon missionary interests and prospects in Korea.

13. Give latest statistics of Protestant Missions in Korea.

CHAPTER XIV

THE NEAR EAST

The term "Near East," which of late has come into such common use, applies to that group of countries lying around the meeting point of the three great continents of Europe, Asia and Africa. The extent covered by this general term is not precisely defined, but varies with different writers. It is here regarded as comprising Egypt, Asia Minor (including Armenia and Kurdistan), Syria, Palestine, Arabia, Mesopotamia and Persia.

I. General Features.

Area and Population. The swift succession of political changes that have taken place in the Near East during and since the World War has so affected the boundaries and populations of its different countries as to render statistics for the time being very uncertain. The following table is based mainly upon the *Statesman's Year Book* for 1939:—

	Area (sq. mi.)	Population
Republic of Turkey (Istanbul and E. Thrace, Asia Minor and several islands)	294,416	16,158,018
Trans-Caucasia, comprising Georgia, Armenia and Azerbaijan (Republics of Soviet Russia)	71,401	7,110,200
Iraq (Mesopotamia)	116,600	3,560,456
Iran (Persia)	628,000	15,000,000
Arabia	1,000,000	10,000,000
Syria (French Mandate)	57,900	3,630,000
Palestine (British Mandate)	10,429	1,418,618
Trans-Jordan	34,740	300,000
Egypt	383,000	15,904,525

Past and Present Interest. "From whatever standpoint one approaches the Near East, the interest and emotions aroused are more intense and fundamental than those stirred by any other group of countries." [1]

[1] Dr. Jas. L. Barton, quoted in "The Near East: Crossroads of the World," p. 195.

1. *It was the cradle of the human race.* Mt. Ararat, in Armenia, lifting its snow-crowned head 17,000 feet high, stands as a mighty monument to our earliest ancestors, for it is the traditional resting place of the ark, and the site whence Noah and his family replenished the earth. Somewhere in this region to the south, perhaps in the Euphrates valley, the Garden of Eden is thought to have been located. The territory upon which this lofty mountain looks down has throughout all time been the home of the early races of mankind.

2. *It was the site of the world's greatest ancient empires.* Here in the Near East, Egypt, Assyria, Babylon, Medo-Persia and Greece, the mighty kingdoms of the hoary past, all in succession took their rise, flourished and waned. No other region in the world compares with the Near East in its wealth of monuments, ruins and landmarks of ancient civilization, and archeological research has here found its largest field and richest rewards.

3. *It was the land of the Bible and the Saviour.* All the scenes and events of the Old Testament Scriptures lay here, and—what will ever make the Near East of transcendent interest to Christian hearts—the Holy Land is here, the land where our blessed Saviour lived and died and rose again, from which also He ascended to heaven, and to which He will some day return to reign.

4. *It is the present storm center of the world.* Upon this region the eyes of the Great Powers are focused, for here some of the most delicate and difficult problems of the World War have yet to be threshed out. Here, ever since the Armistice was signed more than five years ago, animosity, strife and turmoil have prevailed, Turk and Bolshevist against Greek and Armenian, Frenchman against Arab, Moslem against Jew, Asiatic against European, and even to-day the situation is still one of great uncertainty and the political air is full of disquieting rumblings.

Strategic Importance. But there are still more vital considerations to claim attention for the Near East. A glance at the map reveals at once the strategic position of this area. Constituting as it does a bridge between the three great continents of the Old World—"Asia the continent of the past, Europe the continent of the present, and Africa the continent of the future"—it has well been called the "Crossroads of the World." This term applies with equal force from each of three viewpoints:

1. *Trade.* All trade routes between the East and the West, between the North and the South, lie across this territory, linking together the unlimited raw materials of Asia and Africa with the factories and markets of Europe.

As the writer recently sped by rail across the Syrian desert to Damascus, he saw the Old-World camel trains, laden with rich merchandise, still threading their way across the trackless sands, going to and from Arabia and Mesopotamia.

The opening of the Suez Canal in 1869 revolutionized trade and travel between the Occident and the Orient. Some idea of the volume of traffic through this waterway is given by the fact that in the year 1937 a total of 6,570 vessels aggregating 36,000,000 net tonnage, and carrying 670,000 passengers, passed through the canal.

More recently the iron horse has appeared and begun to effect still greater changes. Aleppo, in northern Syria, bids fair to become one of the leading railroad centers of the world, as it is already in common with Damascus and Cairo a flourishing mart and entrepôt for Eastern and Western wares of every description. Westward from Aleppo stretches a trunk line across Asia Minor to Constantinople, with connections there for the different European capitals. Eastward the line runs through the rich land of Mesopotamia, formerly ending at Baghdad, but now completed to Basra, at the head of the Persian Gulf, where it connects with a weekly line of steamers to India. Southward from Aleppo another trunk line runs through Damascus down to Medina, in the very heart of old exclusive Arabia. From Dera'a, south of Damascus, a line branches off westward across Palestine to Haifa, and thence southward to Jerusalem and Jaffa. And now this route extends on south, over the road built by General Allenby's army, and reaches the Suez Canal and Egypt. Egypt has its splendid Government railway system, comprising 3,500 miles of rails, extending far up the Nile toward the Anglo-Egyptian Sudan, while a "Cape-to-Cairo Railway" through the full length of Africa from north to south, so long the dream of far-visioned British statesmen, is rapidly becoming a reality.

What infinite trade possibilities are to be seen in such a ramification of railroads, added to the older caravan and water highways of travel! And what a future is in store for the Near East as the converging point of such far reaching trade routes, as well as in possessing rich agricultural and mineral resources of its own, waiting to be developed by the introduction of modern methods and machinery!

2. *Religion.* The Near East is the native home of three great religions—*Judaism, Christianity* and *Mohammedanism.* This fact makes it the rendezvous for multitudes of religious visitors from every quarter of the globe.

Every year a stream of English-speaking tourists visit Egypt, Palestine and Syria. Dr. Charles R. Watson estimates the yearly number of such visitors to Egypt alone at 12,000. These include many prominent and representative persons, a large proportion of them actuated by religious motives and interested in mission work. The fact that so many Westerners get in the Near East their first glimpse of missionary work, and their first impressions about it, is an added argument for making the missionary work done and seen here a worthy and convincing sample of what such work should be.

Then there are thousands of pilgrims of the Greek and Latin churches—Russian peasants and religious devotees from Central Europe, South America, Australia and other lands—who annually visit the Christian shrines of the Holy Land.

Moslems, in turn, come from all parts on pilgrimages to Mecca, their Holy City, or to some other celebrated shrine. Dr. Zwemer in his book entitled "Arabia the Cradle of Islam" gives the number of pilgrims arriving by sea at Jidda, the port of Mecca, in 1893, as 92,625. Kerbela, near Baghdad in Mesopotamia, a shrine only less sacred than Mecca, is said to be visited by 200,000 pilgrims each year.

To all these streams of religious pilgrims there must now be added the new influx of Jewish Zionists to Palestine. These are impelled, it is true, by nationalistic rather than religious motives. Yet none the less they contribute along with the rest to create a missionary opportunity of stra-

tegic significance, because of the outreach of its influence to
the very ends of the earth.

3. *Politics.* For centuries these lands have been a crucial
problem in world politics. "Egypt is the gate to Central
Africa, Persia is the bulwark of Southwestern Asia, and
Constantinople is the natural avenue of approach to Eastern
Europe." [2] The Great Powers have therefore vied with
one another in their ambitions and efforts for political ascendancy in the Near East. Great Britain established herself in Egypt with a view to safeguarding the Suez Canal
route to her valued Far Eastern possessions, and gained a
"sphere of influence" in Southern Persia to check possible
Russian designs upon India. Russia, feeling the need of
a secure outlet through the Bosphorus, because her northern ports are ice-bound half the year, has done everything
in her power to obtain possession of Constantinople, which
dominates that waterway. Indeed, Constantinople has been
the coveted prize of all the Great Powers, who recognize its
strategic location for a world capital. France, Italy and
Greece have all staked out colonies and sought special commercial privileges in Syria and Asia Minor. Germany's
ambitious scheme for a mighty empire reaching from the
North Sea to the Persian Gulf led her into shrewd diplomatic
dealings with the Sublime Porte.

The lesson to Christian Missions in all this is not far to
seek. Given a strategic area or center for commerce and
politics and you have the same for missionary work. For
Christianity to become dominant in the Near East would be
for its influence to extend powerfully through the adjacent
continents in every direction. The case of Islam furnishes
a striking proof and illustration of this.

The question may properly be raised as to whether we
have attached to the birthplace of the Founder of Christianity the significance it deserves. We are accustomed to dwell
upon the humble aspect of the Saviour's birth and life on
earth, in the fact of His being identified with so small a
land and nation as that of the Jews. But, on the other hand,
have we rightly appreciated the fact that God planned that
the incarnation and redemptive work of His Son should
be accomplished at the geographical and strategic center of

2 "The Near East," p. 176.

the world? To-day in every large city of the Near East—in Cairo, Jerusalem, Damascus, Aleppo—we find the external features of Pentecost constantly repeated in the mingling together of men "out of every nation under heaven." The variety of faces, costumes and tongues will not soon be forgotten by one who has moved among the crowds in one of those Eastern marts.

The Different Races. To infer that the inhabitants of what has hitherto been known as Turkey in Asia are all Turks, just as those of England are Englishmen and those of China are Chinese, would be very far from the truth. Nowhere within a similar area is there to be found a greater diversity of races—a fact which adds great complexity to the missionary task in the Near East. Hence some mention of these different races is essential to a proper understanding of the situation, from whatever viewpoint it is to be regarded.

Turks. The real Turks are Mongolian in race, and pushed their way westward from the plains of Turkistan, in Central Asia, eight or nine centuries ago. They are thus newcomers as compared with most of the other races. Before the War they numbered about 6,000,000, dwelling mainly in central and western Asia Minor.

The Turks are Mohammedan in religion, grossly ignorant and fanatical in mind, and have earned a world-wide reputation for cruelty and savagery by their brutal treatment of their Christian neighbors. In war they are fierce and courageous fighters. But despite the many bad qualities of the Turk, it is only fair to say that missionaries and travelers testify to kindness and hospitality received at their hands, and that the common peasants are far better than the corrupt and unscrupulous educated and official classes.

Armenians. The Armenians are a very ancient people with a well attested national history of 2,500 years. The kingdom of Armenia once reached from the Mediterranean to the Caspian Sea. When the War broke out the Armenians within the Turkish Empire numbered about 2,000,000. They are a hardy, industrious and intelligent race, decidedly superior to their Turkish over-lords. They have overcome the difficulties of a severe climate and a none too productive soil, and have survived centuries of conflict and repression.

They have set a high value upon education, maintaining their own system of schools and being among the first to embrace the higher educational advantages brought to the Near East. Not a few Armenian young men have made their way to Europe and America for study or commercial purposes, and have accredited themselves well on both lines.

The Armenians have the distinction of having been the first nation to adopt Christianity. This was toward the end of the third century, when their king led the way by receiving baptism from a Christian bishop. Through centuries of persecution and repeated massacres they have held tenaciously to their Christian faith and have displayed the greatest fortitude. If they have made themselves unpopular by a tendency to combativeness and untrustworthiness of character, let it be said that these unpleasant traits are doubtless due in large measure to the many generations of cruelty and injustice which have been their heritage. The wholesale massacres of Armenians in 1895-1896, 1909 and 1915-1917, fiendishly planned and carried out by the Turkish authorities, stand out among the most heinous national crimes in history.

Greeks. Up to a very recent date the coast of Asia Minor was peopled by this race, the direct descendants of the ancient Greeks who lived here. Just south of the Dardanelles lie the ancient plains of Troy (the Troas of St. Paul's day), famous in Grecian history. "Smyrna is practically a Greek city, and at least one-third of the people of Constantinople are Greeks. Before the War there were not less than a million Greeks in this part of the Near East, and many Greek villages are to be found in the interior." [3]

Religiously these people belong to the Greek Orthodox Church, now predominant in Eastern Europe and Western Asia, and of which the seven churches of Asia mentioned in the Book of Revelation were the forerunners. As to occupation, these present-day Greeks are true to the traditions of their ancestors in being largely keen merchants, although many also are farmers and fruit growers. They are intelligent people, a fair proportion are well educated, and, like the Armenians, they maintain a system of good schools, including many of higher grade.

[3] "The Near East," p. 36 (written before the recent sack of Smyrna).

During the War the Greeks suffered only less than the Armenians at the hands of the Turks. It is safe to say that several hundred thousand of them were driven from their homes into the interior, there to perish from exposure and starvation.

Kurds. These hardy, semi-nomadic tribesmen, numbering perhaps 3,000,000, inhabit the region known as Kurdistan, lying in eastern Asia Minor and western Persia, north of Mesopotamia. They dwell mostly in black mohair tents among the mountains, ruled over by feudal chieftains. They are keepers of flocks and herds, but make their living also by plundering their Armenian neighbors and waylaying caravans in transit. Along with their love of booty and other evil propensities, however, they possess some good qualities, for they are home-loving, frugal, as hospitable as the Arab, and for the most part free from polygamy. They are decidedly more moral than the Turks and much less cruel. Instances are recorded of kindness and succor extended by Kurds to bands of Armenians in their helpless plight, as they fled before the brutal fury of the Turk.

The Kurds are of Eastern ancestry, and their language is Aryan at its base, although mixed with Turkish, Arabic and Persian. They are classed as Mohammedans in religion, but are not zealous as such, and their worship is a strange mixture, including elements of paganism and also some rites resembling those of Christianity. They have never been loyal to their Turkish rulers, nor have they ever been brought under complete control. Many Kurds are already favorably disposed toward Christianity, and under better political conditions these people would offer a promising field for missionary effort.

Arabs. The Arabians are an ancient and interesting people, of original Semitic stock. At least the tribes of Northern Arabia are held to be descendants of Ishmael, thus making the Arab a cousin to the Jew. There are said to be from one to one-and-a-half million Arabs of pure Semitic blood. The population of the whole country is a matter of conjecture, since no accurate census has been possible. Published estimates have varied widely. Dr. S. M. Zwemer has considered 8,000,000 a conservative figure. The *States-*

man's Year Book for 1923 suggested four or five million, but its 1939 edition alters the estimate to 10,000,000.

The Arabs have burst the bounds of their original peninsular home and have repeatedly swept over Syria, Mesopotamia and Egypt, leaving a permanent impress of their stock upon these lands. A striking evidence of the influence they have exerted is the fact that Arabic, which is a sister tongue to Hebrew, is the prevailing language all over the Near East, and even beyond. The Arabs, moreover, possess a strong religious instinct, and have with ardent zeal propagated the faith of their prophet Mahomet far and wide in the three continents which meet in the Near East.

Like the Kurds, the Arabs have had no affection for their Turkish masters, and have never been reconciled to the assumption by the Sultan of the Caliphate, or supreme headship of Islam, a title which they claim to belong within the family of the Prophet in Arabia.

The Arabs are fine specimens of physical development, and as a race are above the average in intelligence and mental ability. In appearance and customs they differ widely according to their environment. A more striking contrast could not well be found in any nation than that between the wild, skin-clad Bedouin of the desert and the educated, well-groomed young civil or military officer, with his faultless European speech and manners, whom the writer met in Damascus and other centers. Without doubt the Arab race is an important factor to be reckoned with in the reconstruction of the Near East.

Syrians. This race, dwelling in Syria, Palestine and upper Mesopotamia and numbering about 3,500,000 before the War, is chiefly Semitic in stock, but with Greek, Roman and Crusader blood grafted in. The Syrians are very bright in intellect and keen for education. They are both industrious farmers and shrewd merchants, and have traveled the world over on business enterprises. As to religion, about two-thirds are Moslems, and one-third belong to one or other of the Oriental Christian sects, more especially the Greek Orthodox Church.

Jews. It is a pathetic fact, and a solemn reminder of the certainty of God's judgments, that of the 15,000,000 Jews in the world to-day only 399,800 [4] are to be found in Palestine, the home of their fathers. Some 150,000 more live in Syria, Iraq and Arabia, and 400,000 in Egypt and the other North Africa States, making a total of about three-quarters of a million Jews in the entire Near East. The rest of the Hebrew race are scattered among all nations under heaven.

A place of sad interest to every visitor to the Holy Land is the Wailing Place of the Jews, a narrow alley in Jerusalem adjoining the ancient Temple area. There one sees aged and devout Jews reading the prophets, and mingling their tears with their prayers as they kiss the foundation stones of their former Temple structure. The Mosque of Omar now crowns the site of the Temple, and from this and the other most sacred places God's ancient people have long been rigidly excluded by their Moslem rulers. The Jews one meets in Jerusalem are a poor and unworthy specimen of the race, many of them supported by charity, and as a rule bigoted religiously in proportion to their poverty and ignorance.

But great changes are beginning to appear in the Jewish aspect of Palestine through the efforts of the *Zionist Movement,* organized less than twenty-five years ago with the object of "securing for the Jewish people a publicly and legally assured home in Palestine." Already quite a number of successful agricultural colonies of Zionist Jews are to be seen throughout the land. An expert Zionist commission has made a survey of Palestine, and the claim has been made that with the introduction of modern scientific methods of farming and appropriate industries, and the development of natural resources, the "Promised Land" in its full extent is capable of supporting a population of five or six millions instead of the seven or eight hundred thousand inhabitants in present-day Palestine. A stream of Jewish immigration has begun to flow toward the Holy Land, the largest numbers thus far being refugees from Eastern Europe, and under the powerful patronage and liberal financial support of the Zionist organization this stream promises to increase steadily in volume.

Persians. Whether the name Persia brings to mind the ancient Medo-Persian empire founded by Cyrus and over-

[4] Estimate of June, 1938, in *Statesman's Year Book,* 1939.

thrown by Alexander, or the more modern empire which fell under Arabian domination in the seventh century and has since been swayed by successive Arab, Turk and Mongol rulers, it is one and the same land. The Persians of to-day are of the same old Iranian [5] stock that inhabited the land in the days of Nehemiah and Queen Esther.

The present population, estimated variously up to 15,-000,000, consists of two classes, tent-dwellers and town-dwellers. The former constitute one-fifth of the whole, and like the Bedouin Arabs lead a nomadic life, tending their flocks and herds on the steep mountain sides. The townspeople cultivate the fertile valleys, raising grain and luscious fruits, spinning and weaving wool and mohair, and making vegetable dyes. Others are skilled craftsmen engaged in the manufacture of the world-famous Persian rugs and shawls of beautiful design, the exquisite enamel work on metal, and mosaic work in bone and ivory.

Persia to-day, however, is a pitiable spectacle of deterioration materially, commercially, agriculturally and economically. This condition is fundamentally due to a weak, incompetent and negligent government, but it has been aggravated by the fearful ravages of the late War. The absence of any public school system and the lack of proper roads and communications are a serious handicap. The masses are sunk in poverty and ignorance. The estimated illiteracy is ninety-five per cent. in the towns and cities and ninety-eight per cent. in the villages. The cities and villages are full of idle men, and beggars everywhere abound.

The Arab conquerors of the seventh century forced their Moslem faith upon Persia, and nine-tenths of the present populace is Moslem. The balance is made up of Jews, Oriental Christians (Armenians and Nestorians) and a few remaining Zoroastrians.

It is a cheering fact that the Moslems in Persia are far more tolerant and approachable than in any other Near Eastern land. The influence of the missionaries and their splendid work has told most favorably, the former bitter prejudice has steadily given way, and a large proportion not only of the boys but also of the girls in the Mission schools are now from Moslem homes. The Mission hospitals have

5 *Iran* was the ancient name for Persia.

profoundly influenced public sentiment. The missionaries have come to be treated with friendliness and courtesy, and an unique missionary opportunity exists to-day which is a loud challenge for greatly needed reënforcements.

Egyptians. While the streets of Cairo, Egypt's splendid capital and Africa's greatest city, present a never-ending pageant of Oriental life—Copts, Turks, Syrians, Nubians, Sudanese negroes, Bedouins and many others—for practical purposes the population of Egypt may be said to consist of two classes. *First,* there are the Arab Moslems, originally from Arabia, who have settled in the rich corn lands of the delta of the Nile and now comprise nine-tenths of the entire population. *Second,* there are the Copts, who are the true Egyptians, "the direct descendants of the men who built the pyramids and who, when the rest of the world was asleep, developed a civilization which has been the wonder of the ages." [6]

The Copts are Christians in name, the Coptic Church having seceded from the main body of Christianity as a result of a doctrinal controversy before the time of the Mohammedan invasion. The Copts have suffered much persecution from the Moslems, possibly more than any other Christian sect except the Armenians.

Prior to 1922, when Egypt was given recognition as a sovereign state, a third class was to be reckoned in the population, namely, the ruling class. Up to the War this class was composed chiefly of Turks, and from 1914, when a British Protectorate over Egypt was declared, the high officials were British and the underlings Turkish. The novel spectacle was thus presented of one alien race governing the native race through a second alien race as its intermediary, all three races having their mutual antipathies.

Turkey's Career. By their capture of Constantinople in 1453 the Turks became practical masters of the Near East. Their armies subsequently swept down through Syria, took Jerusalem from the Arabs in 1517, invaded Egypt and brought that land and the other North African states under Turkish sway. From that time the Sultans of Turkey assumed the title and authority of the Moslem Caliphate, wresting it from the Arab line.

6 "The Lure of Africa," p. 45.

The Ottoman rule reached the zenith of its power and glory in the sixteenth century, at which time its dominion extended from the borders of Austria to Persia, and from the Caucasus to the deserts of Africa. "At that time the Sultan of Turkey ruled over an empire 2,000,000 square miles in extent, containing a population of 50,000,000 peoples speaking a score of different languages and dialects. Since then her borders have been constantly contracting: Hungary, the Balkan States, Southern Russia, the Barbary coast, Cyprus and Egypt have one by one slipped from her possession." [7]

On July 24, 1908, the whole world was astounded, and the diverse subjects of the Turkish Empire became delirious with joy at the sudden news of a bloodless revolution in Turkey, by which that most absolute and tyrannical monarchy in the world gave place to a constitutional government. Those responsible for this undreamed-of change styled themselves the *Young Turks Party,* and they at once proceeded to inaugurate a new régime which promised great things for the realm. The bloody tyrant *Abdul Hamid* was dethroned and his harmless brother Mohammed V given the empty title of Sultan in his place. But, alas, all hopes centered in the Young Turks were doomed to disappointment. Plots, counter-plots, intrigues and assassinations followed, but without any substantial change for the better in the government. Finally three men rose to prominence and power, to become one of the famous triumvirates of history. These were *Talaat, Enver* and *Djemal,* all of whom rose from obscurity until, by means of ability coupled with ambition and conceit, they occupied the high offices of Prime Minister, Minister of War and Minister of Marine respectively. They became the "political bosses" of the nation, controlling its policies and shaping its destinies with a ruthless purpose and an iron hand.

It would seem that God sent a deceiving spirit into the counsels of these aspiring and wicked men. Against the wishes of the people and the protests of a number of cabinet ministers, they yielded to the cunning diplomacy of Germany and allowed her to drag Turkey into the War on the side of the Central Powers. In so doing they practically

[7] "The Near East." pp. 21, 22.

signed Turkey's death warrant, and that Power began to move swiftly toward her doom.

The War in the Near East. Early in the War England, having declared a protectorate over Egypt and deposed the pro-Turkish Khedive, proceeded to make Egypt the base of Allied military operations for the Near East. A great training camp and supply station was established at Kantara, on the Suez Canal, and from this point, after the defeat of a daring attempt by the Turks to seize the Canal, *General Allenby* began his hard and memorable advance across the Sinai desert and northward through Palestine.

On the 10*th of December,* 1917—a day never to be forgotten by lovers of Zion—Jerusalem capitulated, and Allenby entered the city at the head of the Allied army. A few more months sufficed to rout the Turkish armies in northern Palestine and Syria, and Turkey's effective part in the War was at end.

Brief mention must also be made of the auxiliary war campaigns in two other sections of the Near East, namely, Arabia and Mesopotamia. In Arabia the Sherif of Mecca at the beginning of the War renounced Turkish allegiance and, with British approval, proclaimed the independent *"Kingdom of Hejaz."* Other Arab tribes rallied to his standard, and under the leadership of his now well-known son, *Emir Feisal,* a strong force of intrepid Bedouins pressed northward along the line of the Damascus-Medina railroad and gave valuable assistance to Allenby.

Mesopotamia and Western Persia were also for a time war sectors of importance. England early despatched a force of her Indian troops to the Persian Gulf, primarily for the protection of her valuable pipe lines from the Persian oil wells. Desperate fighting took place, and eventually the Turkish armies were defeated and driven northward as far as Mosul. Mesopotamia was reclaimed, and with the welcome change from Turkish neglect to British care and enterprise this natural garden spot of the world has revived, so that already the largest harvests in many generations have been gathered.

Turkish War Atrocities. Had the crimes and outrages visited by the Turk upon the non-Moslem peoples of the Near East during the War been committed under some great provocation or in the heat of desperate conflict, even then they would have sufficed to arouse public indignation. But what language can describe the feelings of the whole civilized world in the light of the indisputable fact that those crimes and outrages were the systematic carrying out of a deliberate program, hatched in cold blood by Enver and Talaat and their infernal brood of "Young Turks" for the extermination of all the Christians of the realm! The very details of the barbarous treatment of the detested Christians are known to have been discussed and enthusiastically approved by them. "Every new method of inflicting pain was hailed as a splendid discovery, and the regular attendants were constantly ransacking their brains in the effort to devise some new torment. . . . They even delved into the records of the Spanish Inquisition and other historic institutions of torture and adopted all the suggestions found there." [8]

As early as the spring of 1915 this government policy was determined. "First, the Greeks were driven from the seacoast. Then the Armenians from the interior were deported from their homes; the men and boys were cruelly massacred; the women and children were marched over mountain and plain—barefoot, ragged, hungry, and thirsty —and along the way they were robbed, insulted and outraged. Many fell by the wayside never to rise again; many threw themselves into the streams, unable longer to endure the hardships." [9]

Mr. Henry Morgenthau, American Ambassador at Constantinople during the War, who had better opportunities, perhaps, than any other outsider of knowing fully what transpired within the Turkish Empire, lays bare in his book some of the ghastly details of the official murder of the Armenian nation. One instance is given of a caravan of 18,000 which started from Harpoot. On the seventieth day, after experiences too horrible to relate, an exhausted remnant of 150 reached Aleppo.

At least two-and-a-half millions were victims in one degree or another of this crusade of outrage and massacre, and of these more than half perished. Mr. Morgenthau in

8 "Ambassador Morgenthau's Story," p. 307.
9 "The Near East," pp. 52, 53.

summing up his account writes: "I am confident that the whole history of the human race contains no such horrible episode as this. The great massacres and persecutions of the past seem almost insignificant when compared with the sufferings of the Armenian race in 1915." [10]

And finally, as again attesting the true source and aim of the movement, he quotes verbatim Talaat Pasha's proud boast to his friends: *"I have accomplished more toward solving the Armenian problem in three months than Abdul Hamid accomplished in thirty years."* [11]

II. Missionary Work.

The Vanguard. Protestant Missions in the Near East began with the sending out of two young men—*Pliny Fiske* and *Levi Parsons*—by the *American Board* in 1819. Finding conditions unfavorable for locating at Jerusalem, they made Beirut their base and itinerated extensively throughout Syria, Palestine and the adjacent lands. The missionary career of these two pioneers lasted only five years. Fiske lies buried at Beirut and Parsons at Alexandria in Egypt. But they blazed the way for others who soon followed.

Pioneer Problems. Little did either these earliest missionaries, or yet the home churches which sent them out, realize the magnitude of the task they were undertaking. The Near East was largely an unknown quantity. It was a stunning problem in all its aspects, this vast sweep of territory then known as the Turkish Empire, covering the full extent of Bible lands, and embracing forty or more millions of diverse peoples, thrown together physically and yet separated by irreconcilable differences of race and religion. There were backward material conditions of every kind, prevailing ignorance and illiteracy, outlawry, crime and cruelty—and all under the oppressive hand of a despot at Constantinople, who as Sultan was supreme political ruler and as Caliph was the exalted head of Moslemism the world over.

"The first twenty years of this century of missions was spent largely in spying out the lands. The accounts of the

[10] "Ambassador Morgenthau's Story," pp. 321, 322.
[11] *Ibid.*, p. 342. Significantly enough, Talaat was assassinated in Berlin on March 15, 1921, by an Armenian student bent upon avenging the massacres of his people.

travels, exploits and adventures of these intrepid explorers
are most fascinating and exciting. The story of *Eli Smith*
and of *H. G. O. Dwight* in their journey from Constantinople to Tabriz, Persia, traveling 2,500 miles on horseback
and 1,000 miles by water through a 'wild country beset with
robbers and perils of every kind' rivals any tale of travel
or adventure ever written." [12]

The Religious Situation. Three venerable religions occupied the field then as now, "Judaism, rigid and exclusive;
Islam, arrogantly and persecutingly tenacious; Christianity,
defiantly and degradingly corrupt." [13] All three, having
sprung from the same root, were alike monotheistic and yet
sadly perverted.

It was with a proper sense of the need of evangelizing
both Moslem and Jew that these early missionaries were sent
out, but with an entire misconception of the existing Oriental
Christianity. Taking for granted that the Eastern Christian sects—Greek, Armenian, Copt, Nestorian and others—
were still what they had been in the early centuries, the
church at home had no thought of its missionaries going to
establish a new Protestant sect in these Eastern lands. They
fully expected to coöperate with the historic churches,
stimulating their spiritual life and zeal and making them
the channel for the evangelization of the non-Christian populace. The policy of the missionaries was not to proselyte
nor to interfere in ecclesiastical matters, and those who first
came under evangelical influence were urged to continue in
their churches with the hope of purifying and vitalizing
them.

But the futility of such hopes and efforts soon became apparent. While at first the missionaries received a friendly
welcome in certain quarters, the ecclesiastical leaders of the
Eastern churches soon began to manifest disfavor, and before long open hostility. Finally a storm of persecution
broke out, which Dr. James L. Barton [14] graphically describes. All evangelicals were branded as heretics and ex-
communicated from the church.

This contingency at once created the necessity for a new

---

12 "The Near East," pp. 117, 118.
13 "Modern Missions in the East," p. 113.
14 See his "Daybreak in Turkey," Chapter XV.

organization, inasmuch as according to Turkish law persons
unconnected with some recognized religious sect were denied all civil status, could collect no debts, could be neither
married nor buried—in short, had no longer any part or lot
in their own nation. Accordingly, the first evangelical
church was organized in Constantinople in 1846, and an
official firman was secured from the Sultan in 1847 recognizing the new Protestant sect.

Occupation of the Field. It is impossible to give here any
full or connected account of the actual missionary operations in this vast area, or even to mention by name all of
the Societies which have had part in the work. Speaking
broadly, the *American Board* has been the principal agency
in *European Turkey* and *Asia Minor;* the *Northern Presbyterian Mission* in *Syria* and, together with the *Church Missionary Society,* in *Persia;* the *United Presbyterian, Church
Missionary Society* and *Egypt General Mission* in *Egypt.*

Palestine, as the "Holy Land," has attracted a dispropor-
tionate number of Societies. Over twenty are listed, besides
not a few independent workers, and these represent a great
variety of policies and methods. The *Church Missionary
Society* is the largest. Then come the *Jerusalem and the
East Mission, Edinburgh Medical Missionary Society, Society of Friends, Christian and Missionary Alliance,* and up
to the World War the *German Evangelical Missions.*

With *Arabia* the name of *Ion Keith Falconer* will ever be
associated, as the man whose pioneer efforts were used of
God "to call attention" to that "ignored peninsula." This
young Scotch nobleman, a brilliant Cambridge scholar, gave
up fame and fortune, and with his equally devoted wife set
out in 1885, at his own expense, to reach the destitute Moslems of Arabia and adjacent parts with the gospel. He
made his headquarters at Sheikh-Othman, near the British
port of Aden, and began a survey of the surrounding territory. But repeated fevers sapped his strength, and within
two years he breathed his last. His grave at Aden constitutes at once a challenge and an inspiration for the evangelization of one of the darkest corners of the world. His
work was taken up and is being successfully carried on by
the *United Free Church of Scotland.*

In 1889 another effort in behalf of Arabia was launched

by a small group of students of the (Dutch) Reformed Church in America. The *American Arabian Mission* was formed, with *Rev. James Cantine* as its first missionary. *Rev. Samuel M. Zwemer, D.D.,* who followed in 1890, is its most distinguished worker and one of the foremost figures in the field of Moslem Missions. As yet only four coast points are occupied—*Sheikh-Othman* (Aden), by the United Free Church of Scotland, and *Muscat, Behrein, Koweit* and *Basra,* by the Reformed Church in America. Most of the vast interior is still an unworked area.

Mesopotamia, with nearly 3,000,000 inhabitants, has had only two stations, *Mosul* and *Baghdad,* under the *Church Missionary Society*, and even these had to be given up as a part of that Society's enforced retrenchment after the War. But happily the *Presbyterian and Reformed Churches* of America have arranged together to enter this neglected field. They have respectively occupied Mosul and Baghdad and are planning for at least two other stations.

Advance and Development. A full century of missions in the Near East has just been rounded out. Following the early periods of pioneering and organization the missionary forces have steadily lengthened their cords and strengthened their stakes, until their testimony and influence have spread in some degree to every part of this great area. Mission stations have been planted at strategic points, including almost all important centers in Asia Minor, Armenia, Kurdistan, Syria, Palestine and Egypt, and a limited number in Persia, Mesopotamia and Arabia. Extensive evangelism has been carried on by local and itinerant preaching, by the distribution of literature, and by personal interviews. Schools and hospitals have been opened, Bible translations made, Christian literature published, and a full round of activities carried forward at a tremendous cost of consecrated toil and talent. "A full century of mission work, with the discouragements, persecutions, martyrdoms, achievements, has laid the broad and deep foundations for the building of a Christian civilization in this new day." [15]

Mission Schools and Colleges. Christian education, always an important branch of missionary work in every field, has held a place of prominence and proved singularly effec-

[15] "The Near East," p. 116.

tive in the Near East by reason of the peculiar conditions to
be faced. As one writer puts it: "Superstition and fanaticism are the children of ignorance, hence the proper schooling of the young is the surest means of overcoming these
twin evils." [16]   Moreover, the formidable difficulties and
dangers confronting direct evangelism because of Moslem
rule and religion have heretofore in a measure shut the missionaries up to institutional work.

Primary schools were begun everywhere; schools of
higher grade followed; and finally colleges for men and
women sprang up, reaching twelve in number, with an enrolment of between four and five thousand students. Added
to these, schools were opened for Bible training and a variety of technical subjects, including medicine, dentistry, commerce and engineering. The whole system finds its capstone
in three great institutions which have achieved international
fame. These are *Robert College* at Constantinople, founded
in 1863 by *Dr. Cyrus Hamlin;* the *Syrian Protestant College* at Beirut, founded in 1866 by *Dr. Daniel Bliss;* and the
American College for Girls at Constantinople. All three
of these grew out of the work of the American Board Mission, although the College at Beirut was transferred in 1870
to the American Presbyterian Mission. Each is now independently incorporated and endowed, and the influence they
have exerted upon the entire Near East cannot well be over-
stated.

Let the single case of the Syrian Protestant College at
Beirut serve as an example. It started with sixteen students
in a rented house. It now has its own campus of twenty-
seven acres with twenty-six fine modern buildings. It has
graduated about 3,000 students, who occupy high positions
all over the Near East as preachers, teachers, editors, authors, physicians, lawyers, civil and military officers and
merchants. Its name was changed in 1921 to the *American
University of Beirut* to conform to its larger present scope.
Emir Feisal has borne the following testimony to this institution and its influence upon his country: "Dr. Daniel Bliss,
the founder of the college, was the grandfather of Syria;
his son, Dr. Howard Bliss, the present president,[17] is the

16 "The New East," p. 155.
17 Dr. Howard Bliss has since died (May 2, 1920).

father of Syria. Without the education this college has given the struggle for freedom would never have been won. The Arabs owe everything to these men."

To these outstanding institutions must now be added the new *American University at Cairo,* opened in 1921, with *Dr. Charles R. Watson,* formerly of the United Presbyterian Mission, as its president. This Christian University will head up the large and excellent educational work in Egypt. The United Presbyterians alone have 220 schools with nearly 21,000 pupils.

Mission Presses and Literature. Literary and publication work has also wielded a mighty influence for good in these lands. The wide diversity of races and languages has greatly increased the task of providing translations of the Scriptures and other Christian literature, and such work claimed large attention at the hands of the earlier missionaries.

The first Mission Press was set up at Malta, until conditions permitted its removal to Beirut in 1833. *Dr. Eli Smith,* who established and for thirty years directed this enterprise, and *Dr. C. V. VanDyck,* his successor, rendered monumental service by their translation of the whole Bible into Arabic. This was published by the Beirut Press in 1865, and "its sale extends from Constantinople to Khartum, and from Beirut to Basra, Bombay and even Canton." [18]

The *Beirut Press,* together with the more recently established *Nile Mission Press* at Cairo and another at Constantinople, must be regarded as amongst the potent missionary factors in the Near East, and the streams of evangelical literature constantly flowing from these depots have reached to every corner of the Moslem world.

Peculiar Difficulties. The fact that in the Near East heathenism with its gross idolatry and degrading superstitions has not to be reckoned with, as in most other mission fields, by no means argues an easier task in these parts. Experience has proven, sadly enough, that the religions which possess a partial knowledge of Christian truth, but without its saving message, far from being a stepping-stone to Christ offer a more stubborn resistance to Christianity

[18] "Report of World Missionary Conference," 1910, Vol. I, p. 180.

than even rank paganism. All three of the dominant religions here present formidable difficulties to gospel effort.

Mohammedanism has been notorious for its bitter opposition to Christianity everywhere, and converts from it have been exceeding few. Only during the last sixty years, under strong European pressure, has the law been changed which imposed the death penalty upon any Moslem in Turkish dominions who changed his religion, and even as late as 1919 an official decree was issued which made it clear that it was regarded as no crime to kill a Moslem who became a Christian. Under the old régime, therefore, the only safety for the converted Moslem lay in flight from the country.

The attitude of the *Oriental Churches* to evangelical missions has already been referred to. It needs to be borne in mind that these churches have a national character, so that religion is identified with patriotism. Children do not "join the church"; they are church members from birth. Thus church life becomes national life, and a convert to the evangelical faith cuts himself off from his civil standing no less than from his former religious connection. This fact deters many from a full response to the gospel message.

Judaism, universally exclusive and defiant, is nowhere more so than in the Holy Land. The austere Rabbis of old Jerusalem, with their embroidered robes, and ringlets of hair before their ears, are the true successors of the proud and bigoted Pharisees of Bible days, and use their best efforts to poison Jewish minds against the gospel. *Zionism*, with all its high aims, has already adopted methods aimed deliberately at boycotting mission work in Palestine, as evidenced by repeated utterances in the Palestine Hebrew Press.

Political Events Following the War. The close of the World War marked the passing of the old and the ushering in of a new era in the Near East, but the process to this end has been by a series of events in Turkey which were wholly unforeseen.

The crushing defeat of the Ottoman military power by Allenby's forces put it clearly within the power of the allied nations, had they acted promptly and unitedly, to have imposed upon Turkey such just and drastic peace conditions as would have placed the revival of Turkish rule and Turkish atrocities beyond the bounds of possibility. But delay and vacillation, due to jealousies and rivalries among the Allies, allowed the hard-won victory to slip through their fingers. The wily Turk was emboldened to renew his wicked ways, and fresh massacres took place in Armenia and Cilicia. When finally the Sultan's assent to the *Treaty of Sevres* was exacted, that settlement became a dead letter through the action of the *Turkish Nationalists* under *Mustapha Kemal* in setting up a new government at Angora.

The Nationalists grew steadily stronger and more defiant, and the Allies, divided in policy and without military forces, were helpless to deal with them. Finally *Greece,* backed by British support, took the field against Kemal's forces, only to suffer a crushing defeat. The Nationalists followed up their victory by the bloody *sack of Smyrna* (September, 1922), the destruction of many surrounding towns and villages, and the wholesale deportation of Greeks and Armenians.

At the *Peace Conference* which followed at *Lausanne* they insolently rejected the proposals of the Allies, and dictated humiliating terms to the very Powers before which, only four years previously, they lay defeated and helpless.

The world stood aghast before the spectacle of the unspeakable Turk with all his hideous record of crime, cruelty, perfidy and incompetence, rising suddenly from his prostrate position into a sovereignty even more complete than before. Constantinople, the key to the Bosphorus, became his unconditionally, the allied fleet had to leave Turkish waters, and the "capitulations" safeguarding foreign residents in Turkey were swept away. Worst of all, the whole *Armenian Question* miscarried, and the remnants of that pitiable nation and the other Christian minority groups within Turkey were left to face whatever their cruel over-lords might decree.

One glorious fruit of the defeat of Turkey in 1917 remained, namely, that Syria, Palestine, Arabia, and Mesopotamia continued severed from the Turkish dominions. *Syria* is under a French Mandate; *Palestine* (including *Trans-Jordan*) and *Mesopotamia* were placed under a British Mandate, but Britain later made Mesopotamia an independent state under the name of *Iraq,* with *Emir Feisal* as its king, and entrusted Trans-Jordan to the rule of *Emir Abdullah,* brother of Feisal. *Arabia* now consists of an associated group of independent states and tribes, while *Egypt* is in the experimental stage of self-government.

Drastic Changes in Turkey. When the Turkish Nationalists, after defeating the Greek army in Asia Minor, threw off the Sultan's authority, turned their back upon Constantinople, set up a new capital at Angora, and defied the Western Powers at the *Lausanne Conference,* their gifted young leader, *Mustapha Kemal,* was hailed by the Moslem world as the saviour of Islam, and dreams of Islamic revival under his leadership filled Moslems everywhere with joy.

But these dreams were not to be fulfilled. Mustapha saw that the safety of the new republic of which he was president demanded a break with the old Turkish order. For centuries the political and social life of Turkey had revolved around the Sultan and Caliph. There had grown up a vast, unwieldy structure of mosques, monasteries, priests and dervishes, all controlled by powerful religious orders. Having unthroned and banished the Sultan, Mustapha set out to dispose also of these hierarchal encumbrances. He abolished the Caliphate, confiscated all religious property to the State, drove out the dervish and mendicant orders, closed many mosques and shrines, and prohibited the fez as being a religious headdress. Islam ceased to be the State religion, and Turkey became a secular republic. At the news of all this, cabled round the world, Islam was staggered, and pan-Islamic hopes were dealt a death blow.

Other changes followed rapidly, all aiming at sweeping away every vestige of Orientalism and remodeling Turkey on Western lines. These changes include the adoption of the Latin alphabet and the Western calendar, and the substitution of Sunday for Friday as the weekly day of rest.

The status of women has completely changed. They can now vote and be candidates for municipal office and even for the Grand National Assembly. Two women have been made judges and many are being graduated in medicine and law or given good positions in business, banks and post offices.

Changes in Other Near Eastern Lands. The example of Turkey, and also the new contacts with the West through travel and education, have profoundly influenced the adjacent countries in every way. Railways, motor cars, and now aeroplanes, link together the most widely separated points in the Near East. The education of the sons of better class Moslems in Europe or in institutions in the Near East has revolutionized their thinking and outlook. A new desire for education has also taken hold of the common people, and great numbers are learning to read. Book shops have sprung up everywhere, even in such conservative centers as Mecca and Medina. Arabic newspapers and magazines of every sort are now published in all important cities and circulate widely. Baghdad itself boasts of a dozen varieties. Even newspapers in Persian run up literally into the hundreds. The presses of Egypt are turning out a voluminous literature ranging from scientific works to the sensational novel.

Politically these lands are still having their difficulties of adjustment, whether as between rulers and people in the mandated areas or as between rival racial and religious groups. Particularly tragic has been the bitter feud between Jews and Moslems in Palestine, which the best efforts of Britain as the mandatory power have barely succeeded in holding in check. Other outbursts of rival nationalism in Egypt and Syria have been admittedly dangerous.

Meanwhile Bolshevism from Russia is putting forth its utmost endeavors to undermine all religion, capture the mind of political leaders, and transcend even nationalism as the dominant force in reshaping the life of the Near East.

Bearing upon Missionary Work. The effects upon missions of the profound changes—political, social and religious—that have swept over this area since the War cannot be adequately set forth in any brief statement. They vary widely in different sections and are diverse in any one section.

The area in Asia still belonging to *Turkey* is 284,000 square miles, and its population has been decreased by death and deportation due to the War to less than 12,000,000. The main missionary agency in this field, the *American Board,* suffered a terrific blow through the War and its aftermath. Its missionary force was cut in half by death, and nearly all its pre-War churches, hospitals and educational institutions were closed. Its property loss was estimated at $2,880,000.

Moreover, since the converts were almost all from the non-Moslem subject races, the driving out of these races meant the almost complete extinction of the Christian churches. Missionary work had largely to be begun anew and for the hitherto almost wholly unresponsive Turks. To this task the *American Board* has courageously addressed itself. Fifteen stations are reported occupied by 88 missionaries and 423 native workers. Three colleges, 54 schools and 3 hospitals are in operation.

The attitude of Turkish authorities has improved and is now friendly toward Mission schools, but no Christian teaching is allowed in them. There is a new spirit of general friendliness, however, toward the missionaries, and many points of favorable contact for personal evangelism are presented, so that the Board's latest report says: "The Mission views its task not only with hope but with eager confidence."

In all the mandated countries the opportunity to touch and influence Moslems has immensely improved since the overthrow of Turkish tyranny and the loss of Islam's prestige and power. A marked change is noticeable in the popular attitude toward the missionary and his message as a result of the heroic work of the missionaries, and of the Red Cross and Near East Relief workers, in succoring multitudes from Turkish cruelty and outrage, and from starvation and disease, during and since the War.

In *Persia* larger freedom is accorded mission schools than anywhere else, there has been no interference with medical or evangelistic work, and crowds gather to hear the gospel.

In *Egypt* the day of religious freedom seems to be drawing nearer, although in one or two notable instances of late the liberty of Moslem women to become Christians has been denied. Certain gestures on the part of the authorities in *Iraq* and *Syria* suggest an uncertain attitude toward missionary work. Yet there is in general throughout the Near East a wider open door for the gospel than ever before, with signs of a new spiritual hunger and a growing number of inquirers and converts. An unprecedented demand for Christian literature exists, particularly among Moslems.

Neglected Areas. Despite the faithful labors of a splendid body of missionaries in Near Eastern lands for a full century, large areas are yet wholly unoccupied.

The trans-Caucasian states of *Georgia, Azerbaijan* and *Russian Armenia,* now republics allied to Soviet Russia, with a combined population of 7,000,000, are without evangelical missionaries. So also are the great bulk of 1,000,000 or more *Kurds* directly to the south, and of nearly 3,000,000 people of *Mesopotamia.*

The vast interior of *Arabia,* a territory of 1,500 by 1,100 miles, embracing the provinces of Nejd, Hejaz and Hadramaut, has no missionary among a population estimated at 3,000,000. North of Arabia lies *Trans-Jordan,* with boundaries yet undefined, but with a population of 300,000, mostly Arabs, and as yet only two small mission outposts recently opened from Palestine. Westward toward Egypt is the historic *Sinai Peninsula,* with 50,000 people but no missionary.

Even within *Syria* and *Asia Minor* there are still totally neglected districts, while the whole area must be regarded as far from adequately occupied. For it must be remembered that bitter political opposition and Moslem intolerance limited missionaries to indirect and very meagre contact with the Moslem population under the old Turkish régime.

Coming finally to *Persia,* we find large sections of country that have never seen a missionary. Nomad tribes numbering a million or more are wholly unreached. Dr. Robert E. Speer, writing from Persia on his visit in 1922, dwells upon "the appalling extent of our unaccomplished task," and cites one stretch of country 560 miles east and west, and the same distance north and south, with no resident missionary.

A Momentous Crisis and Its Challenge. The facts already presented, especially those of the new and wonderful open door for the gospel in the Near East, and of large areas and populations still unreached, constitute in themselves a stirring challenge. But there remains one factor of the situation yet to mention which adds tremendous solemnity to its consideration and turns the challenge into a clamant call to action. If the break with the past on the part of the Near Eastern nations meant a turning from false to true religion, from stultifying and degrading superstition to the uplifting and purifying truth of the gospel, from the stagnancy of their ancient civilization to the noblest elements in the civilization of the West, then we might well take heart. But the change is not in such a direction. It is the deliberate casting away of old religion, with its modicum of moral sanctions and safeguards, not for a new faith but for pure secularism and materialism. Herein lies the folly and the peril of it all. As one writer puts it: "In great sweeps Mustapha has destroyed, but he has created nothing to fill the void he has made." Or in the words of another: "A change from

Mohammedanism to materialism does not mean progress. No people can find a permanent home in secularism. Christianity alone can meet the need."

Surely the gravity of such a situation, affecting as it does the temporal and spiritual welfare of at least 70,000,000 people within the Near East and in some real measure the entire Moslem world of four times that number, cannot fail to impress itself upon us. Will these awakened peoples, torn from their old religious moorings, be left to drift into a barren, soul-destroying materialism or, still worse, be sucked into the maelstrom of atheistic Bolshevism which stands ready to engulf and damn them? Or shall they be given in this high day of opportunity "the things that belong unto their peace" and make for their safety and eternal salvation? The answer lies with the Christian churches at home. What is to be done must be done promptly if at all. Who will help evangelize the new Near East?

QUESTIONS

1. Name the countries constituting the Near East, and give the area and population of each.
2. Upon what several grounds does the peculiar interest attaching to the Near East rest?
3. From what different standpoints is the Near East of strategic importance? Give data in support of each point.
4. Name and locate the various races of the Near East, and give a brief sketch of each.
5. Outline the career of Turkey from the beginning of her political ascendancy down to her entry into the War, giving important dates and names of leaders.
6. Describe briefly the course of the War in the Near East.
7. Give some account of the Turkish treatment of the Armenians and other Christian subject races during the War.
8. Outline missionary operations in each section of the Near East from their inception to the present, giving important dates and names of leading missionaries and societies.
9. Mention the most prominent Mission Colleges and Presses in the Near East, and state what part education and literature have played in the work.
10. Discuss the peculiar difficulties attending missionary effort among the three main religious classes of the Near East.
11. Sketch political events in the Near East since the War.
12. Mention some recent drastic changes in Turkey and other N.E. lands, and discuss their bearing upon missionary work.
13. What N.E. areas are still without missionary work?

Chapter XV

AFRICA

AREA, 12,000,000 SQUARE MILES. POPULATION, 150,000,000 [1]

I. General Features.

Names. The word *Africa* is said to have come from *Afarik,* the name of a Berber tribe which dwelt in a corner of Tunis in the days before the greater portion of the continent was known, or its vast extent even suspected.

Stanley called Africa *"The Dark Continent."* The term is fitting from several points of view. Africa is the one continent populated almost wholly by dark-skinned peoples. Then its vast interior lay until recent times in unpenetrated darkness. And finally its native religions are devoid of sacred writings and defined system, are vile and degrading, and have left their followers in the "blackness of darkness" morally and spiritually.

Size. Africa is the second continent in size, Asia alone being larger. Its area is variously given as from 11,500,000 to 12,000,000 square miles. But figures of such dimensions are hard to grasp, and comparisons are better. Africa is three times the size of Europe, about half again as large as either North or South America, and contains nearly one-fourth the total land area of the globe.

Bishop Hartzell ingeniously presents a map of Africa on which the United States is fitted into the narrower southern portion, Europe into the northwest, and India and China (the eighteen provinces) into the northeast, with Scotland, Ireland and Wales filling in the chinks, and Porto Rico and the Philippines easily accommodated on the island of Madagascar.

---

[1] Estimates of native population run from 100,000,000 to 180,000,000, but the latest and most reliable favor the more moderate figures of from 130,000,000 to 150,000,000. The white population, most numerous in South Africa, is probably nearly 2,000,000. There are, besides, some 300,000 Indian and 25,000 Chinese imported laborers in S. and E. Africa.

From north to south Africa measures 5,000 miles, from east to west at its greatest width, 4,500 miles or more.

Physical Features. Africa's configuration has been likened to an inverted saucer, of which the rim is the low-lying coast strip, 50 to 200 miles in width. The raised circle on which the saucer rests is the region of slopes and mountain ranges lying behind the coast strip, with an average height of 2,000 to 3,000 feet, and containing some lofty peaks. The center of the saucer, within the raised circle, is the vast interior plateau, slightly depressed in the middle.

Here in these depressions of the interior section lie the great lakes, out of which flow the mighty rivers that drain the whole continent. The largest lakes are in East Central Africa, Victoria Nyanza, Tanganyika and Nyasa being the most important. Victoria Nyanza is the second fresh water lake in size in the world, only Lake Superior being larger, and Tanganyika while only about forty miles wide is the longest in the world. Lake Tchad, in the Sudan, is the largest of several lakes with no outlet to the sea.

The rivers of Africa may be said to be the dominating feature of its topography. The four giant streams are the Nile, Congo, Niger and Zambesi. By far the longest is the Nile, whose annual overflow gives to lower Egypt its remarkable fertility. With a basin 2,500 miles in length, the Nile is probably next to the Mississippi the longest river in the world, but the Congo, although not so long, drains a still larger basin, and has a volume of water only less than that of the Amazon. Its entire system includes fully 10,000 miles of navigable streams, and the invaluable forests and amazing fertility of the area which it drains make this river the most important one of the continent. On the Zambesi are the famous Victoria Falls, 343 feet high, exceeding Niagara in magnitude and rivaling it in grandeur. There are other large rivers, but of secondary rank compared with the four mentioned. Altogether Africa is said to have 40,000 miles of navigable rivers and lakes.

All the river basins are heavily forested. Stanley has written eloquently of these African forests, telling of growths so dense that the sun's rays never penetrate to the ground, and of luxuriance and beauty unequaled elsewhere. In Rhodesia red and brown mahoganies in great profusion

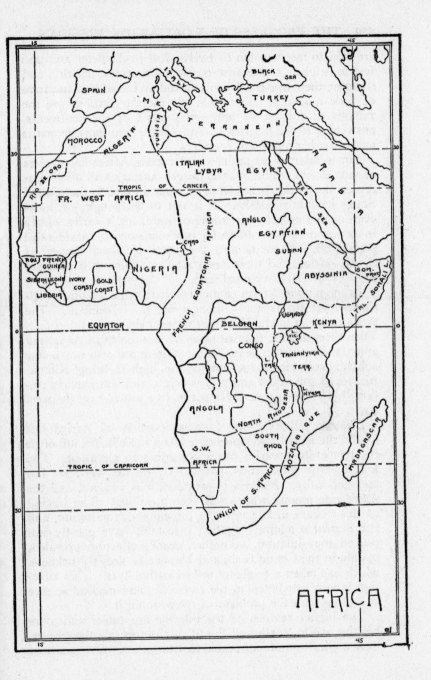

AFRICA

are said to measure ten to twelve feet in diameter and 200 feet in height. Other forests, on the contrary, are thin and scraggy, their tree-trunks so crooked and knotty as to prove of little industrial value. On the central plateaux are the famous savannahs, or long-grass lands of the continents, answering to the prairies of America, where lions, leopards and other big game are found.

But in addition to prairies and forests Africa has deserts of vast extent. The Sahara Desert outranges all other deserts in the world, being actually equal in size to the United States including Alaska. It is not to be thought of, however, as one monotonous waste of sand, for it varies widely in elevation, and has extensive oases supporting considerable population. There is also the great Kalahari Desert of South Africa, and there are stretches of desert land along the Red Sea and in Somaliland.

In mountains Africa cannot compare with the other continents, yet she is not without some fair specimens. The Atlas range in the northwest attains a height of 15,000 feet. Then there are the tangled mass of mountains in Abyssinia and the Drakensbergs in Natal. There are also not a few solitary volcanic peaks, among the highest being Kilimanjaro (19,300 ft.), Kenia (17,000 ft.), and Ruwenzori (16,600 ft.) in the east, and Kamerun (13,300 ft.) on the west coast.

Climate. By far the greatest portion of Africa lies within the torrid zone and hence has a hot climate, although the temperature varies much according to elevation. The low, marshy coast lands, particularly on the west, are hot and unhealthy. Malaria is prevalent and virulent, and the death rate among whites has been appalling. The tracing of this disease in late years to the *anopheles* mosquito, and the measures adopted against infection, have greatly improved the situation. Another deadly affection prevalent mainly in the Congo basin and Uganda is sleeping sickness, which has taken a frightful toll of native lives. This affection is now attributed to the *tsetse* fly, and medical science is dealing with the problem of overcoming it.

The higher regions of the interior are cooler and more healthy, while North and South Africa, outside the tropics, have a climate quite agreeable to Europeans. Over most of the continent dry and rainy seasons alternate. The rainfall is more abundant in the south than in the north, although the tropical forest regions of both parts are profusely watered.

Natural Resources. These are almost incalculable in extent and value, and obviously vary widely according to locality. The Mediterranean States yield grapes, olives and figs. The forests of the Atlas mountains furnish cork-oak, and the oases of the Sahara dates in abundance. The Nile valley grows fine cotton as well as rice, wheat, sugar and vegetables. In South Africa pasture and farm lands predominate, and ostrich-culture is a leading industry. The savannah lands are adapted to grazing and grain-raising, and cattle are the chief product of the Sudan. The rich soil of Equatorial Africa grows in profusion everything suited to a tropical climate, cassava, coffee, sugar, bananas and many other fruits being among the main crops.

Africa's forests produce valuable oil-palm, ebony, mahogany and rubber trees in great abundance. Ivory still remains an important though steadily decreasing product.

Last, but greatest of all, the mineral wealth of this continent is beyond computation. From Kimberley and other South Africa mines come ninety per cent. of the world's diamonds, from Johannesburg one-third of its gold supply. When to these are added rich deposits of copper, silver, iron, coal and tin in various parts, which have only begun to be worked, it can readily be seen what vast possibilities the future holds.

The People. The fact that 523 distinct languages and 320 dialects have been identified in Africa bears impressive testimony to the bewildering array of races and tribes which inhabit the Dark Continent. Authorities pretty well agree in a general classification of the present native population under five heads:

1. *Berbers*—the aborigines of the Mediterranean States and the Sahara, mainly Caucasian in origin and of very fine physical type.

2. *Arabs*—from Western Asia, constituting the great bulk of the population of Egypt and scattered widely over North Africa.

3. *Negroes*—mainly in the great Sudan, from the Nile

to the Atlantic, the purest type being found in the Guinea Coast region. They have receding foreheads, high cheek bones, broad, flat noses, thick lips, woolly hair and coal-black skin. This region furnished a large majority of the slaves taken to America.

4. *Bantu*—comprising almost all the tribes south of the Equator—Kaffirs, Zulus, Basutos, Bechuanas, Matabeles and others. They closely resemble the negroes proper in many respects, but have more regular features, are not generally so black or thick-lipped, and speak an entirely distinct group of languages. It is among these people that missionary work has achieved its greatest results.

5. *Pygmies, Bushmen, Hottentots*—scattered through the Bantu section of the continent, dwarfed in stature, primitive and nomadic in habits, and lowest in the scale of African humanity.

Religions. Reckoning on a basis of 130,000,000 as the total population of Africa, Dr. C. H. Patton [2] estimates that there are 80,000,000 Pagans, 40,000,000 Mohammedans, and 10,000,000 Christians, the last term being used to embrace possibly 3,000,000 Protestants and 7,000,000 members of the Abyssinian, Coptic, and Roman Catholic Churches.

Another author [3] divides Africa, religiously, into three great sections: Mohammedan Africa (north), forty to fifty millions; Pagan Africa (central), one hundred to one hundred and ten millions; Christian Africa (south), three and a half millions.

Mohammedanism as a religion has already received mention in earlier chapters, and as a modern menace to missions in Africa will be dealt with later in the present chapter.

Paganism, or Fetichism, the native religion of Africa, is a species of Animism, or the worship of spirits. It is a religion of gross darkness. Its gods are innumerable malignant demons, which the African conceives of as enveloping him on every side and constantly seeking his injury and death. These demons inhabit every object, animate and inanimate—plants, trees, rocks, rivers, reptiles, birds, animals —and also impersonate deceased relatives. Constantly

[2] "The Lure of Africa," p. 189.
[3] "Christus Liberator," pp. 57, 58.

haunted by fear of such evil spirits, the African resorts to *fetiches,* or charms, consisting usually of a mixture of curious natural objects or carved figures—heads of birds, teeth of a lion, leopard or serpent, pieces of glass, pebbles, human bones, etc.—which he wears upon his body to procure the protection and aid of spirits.

The African's religious philosophy has given rise to various horrible practices. It has led to human sacrifices to supply the needs, avert the vengeance, and win the favor of the gods. It is responsible for the burial alive of the wives of a chief with his dead body, and even for cannibalism, which is said by careful authorities to have originated as a sacrificial feast. It has produced witchcraft, that fiendish system which has taken a toll of countless lives as victims of the witch doctor's poison cup. "It is estimated that 4,000,-000 people are killed annually in the endeavor to discover witches. Whole districts have been depopulated by witch trials." [4]

African Paganism is summed up in the following words of terrible indictment:

"Delicacy permits but the most guarded references to the revolting brutality and nauseating licentiousness which are the legitimate offspring of Pagan gods and religion. To be consistent with his perverted conceptions of religion the African cannot be other than he is. . . . The Pagan African is what he is *because of his religion.*" [5]

"In a word, the religion of the African is a religion of terror and hate. . . . In the things which pertain to God he lives in abysmal darkness. When most religious, he is most fiendish." [6]

Early History. Africa is a paradox in the puzzling contrasts and contradictions its history furnishes. North Africa cradled one of the oldest civilizations of the world. Egypt led the nations in science, art and literature. Her philosophies dominated the thought of the East. Next to Palestine, North Africa was the land most closely connected with Hebrew history. Egypt and Ethiopia figure prominently in both Old and New Testament records. Alexandria

[4] "Daybreak in the Dark Continent," p. 99.
[5] *Ibid.,* p. 101.
[6] "The Lure of Africa," p. 144.

for several centuries was the greatest stronghold of early Christianity, with Carthage as a second center. Within 200 years after Pentecost 900 churches were numbered in North Africa. The first missionary training school was founded in Alexandria in the second century, and from it missionaries carried the gospel to lands near and far. Had the North African Christianity of those early days retained its spiritual life and missionary zeal, the subsequent history of the whole continent might have been very different. Alas, the church fell a victim to theological controversy, became divided into factions, lost its spiritual vitality and missionary vision, and thus enfeebled it was unable to stand before the aggressive Mohammedan invasion of the seventh century. As Roman government in North Africa fell before the Arab conquerors, so Christianity was all but wiped out by the incoming hordes of fanatical Moslems. "For more than 1,500 years Christianity in Africa, except as expressed by the corrupt Coptic and Abyssinian churches, was almost dead, and the 'Dark Continent' throughout its enormous length and breadth remained silent in the shadow of death, waiting for the dawning of a new day." [7]

Discovery and Exploration. With some allowance for the possibility of early Phœnician exploration down the east coast, it is generally conceded that until the fifteenth century little was known of the Dark Continent except along the Mediterranean and Red Seas.

Portugal, in the person of *Prince Henry,* led the way in exploration down the west coast. *Bartholomew Diaz* rounded the Cape of Good Hope in 1487, and ten years later *Vasco da Gama,* pressing farther on, sailed up the east coast and discovered the new route to India.

The English, French and Dutch followed suit in the sixteenth century, and the names Grain Coast, Ivory Coast, Gold Coast and Slave Coast, given to different sections of the Guinea coast, indicate the character of the trade opened up by the early traders of these nations.

Settlements followed the development of trade in the seventeenth century, the Portuguese establishing themselves on the Guinea coast, at the mouth of the Congo and on the east

7 "Outlines of Missionary History," p. 164.

coast, the English along the Gambia River, the French on
the Senegal River, and the Dutch near the Cape.

But it was only the eighteenth and nineteenth centuries
which saw exploration into the yet unknown interior undertaken in earnest. A long line of great explorers laid bare
the secrets of this vast and marvelous continent. Among
those whose names are best known were *James Bruce,
Mungo Park, Speke, Grant, Burton, Baker,* and *Henry M.
Stanley,* besides the missionaries *Krapf, Rebmann, Moffat,*
and—towering above them all—the illustrious *David Livingstone.*

II. Missionary Work.

Early Roman Catholic Efforts. Dominican and Jesuit
missionaries followed closely upon the early Portuguese explorers. Soon after the discovery of the Congo, in 1484,
missions were opened along that river. The beginnings
were promising and thousands were baptized. But the
work was sadly superficial, forms and ceremonies being substituted for vital piety. Moreover, the unscrupulous exploitation of the natives by the traders neutralized the missionary efforts. The Christian communities became degraded and dwindled away, so that when Protestant work
began there was little trace of them left.

Work was also begun by Portuguese missionaries in
Abyssinia with good promise of success, but the proverbial
Roman Catholic policy of meddling in politics brought its
just desert. The missionaries were banished, and Roman
Catholicism has ever since been held in disrepute.

The Protestant Vanguard. To the Moravians belongs
the honor of blazing the Protestant missionary trail in the
Dark Continent. *George Schmidt* was sent out in 1737
from Herrnhut, in response to an appeal in behalf of the
oppressed Hottentots, sent home by Ziegenbalg and Plütschau on their way round the Cape to India (see page 77).
But the Dutch, then in control of South Africa, met with
derision the attempt to Christianize these natives, whom they
regarded and treated almost like animals. Schmidt persisted
bravely, won the confidence of the Hottentots, and within
four years baptized a little company of Christian converts.

This aroused the bitter hostility of the Dutch settlers, and in 1743 Schmidt was ordered home to Holland by the authorities and never permitted to return. Half a century elapsed before his faithful beginning of work could be followed up.

The fact that Africa is not simply a country, but a continent of vast size, presenting a collection of fields totally different one from the other in almost every particular, makes it necessary to divide it into several sections for even the general consideration of its missionary work which the limits of this volume permit. The ordinary division into North, South, East, Central and West, is admittedly somewhat vague, but is perhaps the most convenient for our present purpose.

NORTH AFRICA

Egypt. This country has already been mentioned in the previous chapter, as a part of the Near East. Mission work here has been carried on mainly by the *Church Missionary Society* of England, which entered the field in 1825, the *American Mission* (United Presbyterian), which followed in 1854, and the *Egypt General Mission,* which began work in 1898. The American Mission has developed a strong and extensive work. It has 336 churches and other groups, with over 22,600 members, drawn mostly from the Copts. Reference has already been made to the large and influential educational work of the American Mission, and also to the *Nile Mission Press* as a potent factor, through its output of excellent evangelical literature, in the evangelization not only of Egypt but of the entire Moslem world.

Egyptian Sudan. The efforts of both the *United Presbyterian Mission* and the *Church Missionary Society* have extended more than 2,000 miles up the Nile, and stations have been planted among several of the benighted negroid tribes of the Egyptian Sudan.

A sad and humiliating example of the miscarriage of a missionary project is furnished by *Gordon College* at Khartum. Founded with funds contributed by Christians in England to provide a missionary institution in memory of the noble General Charles Gordon, the College has through the compromising policy of the British authorities been turned into a center of Moslem teaching and influence.

Barbary States. This vast area bordering upon the Mediterranean, and consisting of Tripoli, Tunis, Algeria and Morocco, contains a population of 14,000,000, almost solidly Moslem. Some thirteen missionary agencies are listed, the largest being the *North Africa Mission.* All told there are only some 250 missionaries.

The field has always been a desperately hard one because of the wild nature of the country and its people, and the intolerance of long-entrenched Mohammedanism. Of late years another hindrance has been added through the political control of France and Italy, with their well-known opposition to evangelical missions. Visible results of the faithful labor expended are painfully small, and the vast hinterland must still be regarded as in the main an unoccupied mission field.

Abyssinia. The *Church Missionary Society* attempted an entrance in 1844, but without success. The *Swedish Mission* followed in 1866 and has made determined efforts, against great odds, to reach the heathen tribes. They have stations at Addis Abeba, the capital, and at several points in Eritrea and Italian Somaliland to the north and east of Abyssinia.

In 1919 the *United Presbyterian Mission* entered western Abyssinia and opened two stations. Later, through the favor of the then reigning prince, Ras Tafari, afterwards crowned Emperor, medical work was begun in the capital. In 1929 the *Abyssinian Frontiers Mission* launched pioneer efforts in the south. Later this agency was merged with the *Sudan Interior Mission,* which developed a large and fruitful work. But Italy's invasion in 1935 and subsequent conquest of Ethiopia have disrupted mission work and forced out most of the missionaries.

SOUTH AFRICA

The progress of missions here, subsequent to the earlier pioneer efforts of Schmidt and one or two others, will ever be associated with a few great missionary names well known the world over. Most worthy of mention are the following:

Robert Moffat. Following upon the British occupation

of Cape Colony in 1806, Moffat, sent out by the *London Missionary Society,* arrived in 1817. After some time spent in Capetown, he at length obtained permission to proceed inland and set out for Namaqualand, in the Orange River country. He was warned against Africaner, a native chief whose barbarous crimes had made him a terror to that region. But meanwhile the gospel had reached and influenced Africaner. Moffat spent six months in his town, the chief became a true and humble Christian, and when in 1819 Moffat reappeared in Capetown, bringing with him this converted savage and outlaw, the sensation produced was profound.

In 1820 Moffat, having married Miss Mary Smith, left again for the interior and opened the first station among the Bechuana tribes, at Kuruman. Later he pressed on to the Matabele country as far as the Zambesi River. For many years these brave pioneers labored, preaching and teaching amid great perils and strange adventures, without seeing any converts. But finally their faith was rewarded, and in 1829 the first Bechuana church was formed at Kuruman. There, too, the first Bible in the Bechuana tongue was printed in 1857, the work of translation having been done single-handed by Moffat. In 1870, enfeebled by age and work, the Moffats returned to England, where Mrs. Moffat died the next year and Mr. Moffat in 1883. During their fifty-three years of heroic life and labor in South Africa they succeeded in turning murderous savages into a Christian people cultivating the arts and habits of civilized life, and with a written language of their own.

David Livingstone. This greatest of all Africa's apostles was the direct successor to the Moffats, having joined them at Kuruman in 1840, and later married their daughter, Mary Moffat. His first few years were spent in regular missionary work among various tribes within a limited radius. He then began to push northward, bent upon getting farther into the heart of Africa. After several preliminary trips, during which his family suffered much from illness, he decided to send them to England for two years, while he gave himself to further exploration with a view to opening up the interior to missionary work. Starting out at the end of 1852, Livingstone entered upon his first great journey, which occupied four years. During this time he traced the Zambesi to its source, proceeded thence to the western coast at St. Paul de Loanda, in Angola, and then recrossed the continent to the Indian Ocean, discovering on the way the famous Victoria Falls. This wonderful journey of 11,000 miles, covered entirely on foot, involved untold hardships, dangers and physical sufferings. At its close, in 1856, Livingstone returned to England with a mass of invaluable records, and was there received with great honor by all classes.

Among the many impressions which his journey in Africa had made upon him, the thing that stirred his soul to its depths was the revolting slave trade, ghastly evidences of which he had witnessed everywhere. In all his continued labors to open up the Dark Continent he was fired by a passionate determination to crush this cursed traffic in human lives and heal "the open sore of the world."

While it was under the official appointment of the British Government, and as an agent of the Royal Geographical Society, that Livingstone returned to Africa in 1858, his missionary spirit and motive appear in the following words, uttered in reply to a suggestion that he should relinquish missionary work and give himself solely to discovery. Said he, "I would not consent to go simply as a geographer, but as a missionary, and do geography by the way. The opening of the country is a matter for congratulation only so far as it opens up a prospect for the elevation of the inhabitants. I view the geographical exploration as only the beginning of the missionary enterprise."

The remaining fifteen years of his life, except for a second brief visit home in 1864-65, were spent in persistent exploration, during which he discovered the sources of the Nile, located the great lakes of East Central Africa and verified the upper courses of the mighty Congo. For long periods of time he was cut off in the far interior from communication with the outside world. What his mission cost him few if any will ever fully know. Racked by disease, attacked by wild beasts, threatened by savages, robbed and betrayed by carriers, tortured in spirit by the horrors of the slave hunters, "not one man in a million would have pushed forward as he did in the heart of Africa." It was in 1871 that Henry M. Stanley, at the head of a relief expedition sent out by the *New York Herald,* found Livingstone in an exhausted condition at Ujiji, on Lake Tanganyika. But all Stanley's efforts to persuade Livingstone to accompany him home proved in vain, and so the two men parted, Stanley bearing home Livingstone's precious journals of six years, while Livingstone, renewed in health and spirits by his few months' companionship, set out on a fresh journey of exploration, impelled by a firm conviction that his task was not completed. The remainder of the story until that morning of May 1, 1873, when he was found dead upon his knees in a rude hut in Chitambo's village of Ilala, on Lake Bangueolo, has been rehearsed the world around.

Livingstone's remains were embalmed and carried, together with all his papers and instruments, a year's journey to Zanzibar, by Susi and Chuma, his faithful African servants. Thence they were conveyed to England and buried with the nation's noble dead in Westminster Abbey. But his heart lies buried in the remote heart of the great Continent whose darkness he lived and died to lighten. The names Africa and David Livingstone will always suggest each the other.

John Mackenzie, of the *London Missionary Society,* was a missionary statesman. While his immediate field lay among the Bechuanas, he "multiplied the significance of his life by promoting the expansion of British empire over the regions Livingstone explored. He thus saved native states from annihilation by the Boers and ensured the best colonial rule in the world to vast stretches of Africa." [8]

Barnabas Shaw arrived in 1816 as the pioneer of *Wesleyan Missions,* which have since spread widely over South Africa with large results. He was divinely guided to the Namaquas at a time when they were feeling after God, and a great work of grace began among them.

François Coillard was the most famous missionary of the *Paris Evangelical Society,* which began work in 1829. He and his colleagues witnessed God's wonderful working first among the Basutos and later among the incorrigible Barotsi of the upper Zambesi.

James Stewart, better known as "Stewart of Lovedale" after the title of his biography, stands out as the distin-

[8] "Daybreak in the Dark Continent," pp. 229, 230.

guished missionary of the *United Free Church of Scotland,* which entered this field in 1824. *Lovedale Institute,* founded by Stewart, is called the Hampton of South Africa, to indicate its commanding importance as an educational and industrial mission center.

The American Board began work in Natal in Zululand in 1835. *"Forty Years Among the Zulus"* tells the thrilling story of the saintly *Josiah Tyler* and his comrades in that field.

The South Africa General Mission was established in 1889, with the well known and godly Andrew Murray as president of its South Africa Council and *Spencer Walton* as its director. This is a Faith Mission whose work covers a wide area, reaching from Cape Town to Nyasaland on the northeast and the borders of Congo Belge on the northwest. Its latest advances have been into Portuguese East Africa, and a section of Angola (Portuguese West Africa) containing 2,500,000 people, which field has been designated as the "Andrew Murray Memorial."

Other Societies, including several of *German* and *Scandinavian* origin, cannot be mentioned by name. In all, forty or more mission agencies divide the South Africa field. Mission work is also carried on by the *English and Dutch colonial churches.* The mission churches of a number of the British and American Societies already mentioned have attained their majority and been set free from the control and support of their parent organizations.

EAST AND CENTRAL AFRICA

So closely are these two sections connected in the record of missionary advance that it seems best to consider them together. In this great region missions have achieved some of their most splendid results, but not without much heroic suffering and the sacrifice of many noble lives.

Krapf and Rebmann. These brave men were the Protestant pioneers of the east coast. John Ludwig Krapf, after sharing in the unsuccessful attempts of the Church Missionary Society in Abyssinia, landed in Mombasa in 1844. Two months later his wife and only child died. "Himself sick to death with fever the deeply stricken man wrote to the directorate of the Society the prophetic words: 'Tell our friends that in a lonely grave on the African coast there rests a member of the Mission. That is a sign that they have begun the struggle with this part of the world; and since the victories of the church lead over the graves of many of her members, they may be the more convinced that the hour is approaching when you will be called to convert Africa, beginning from the east coast.' " [9]

Krapf projected bold plans for a chain of mission stations across Africa from east to west and north to south, in the form of a cross, each station being named after an Apostle. People at first smiled at his idea as a mere idealistic dream. But although long delayed the fulfilment of his vision is now well on its way, with but a short gap existing between the Nile Missions and those of South Africa, and between the Congo Missions and those of the east coast.

John Rebmann joined Krapf in 1846, and together they added to their missionary achievements the geographical distinction of discovering Mounts Kilima-njaro and Kenia. The news of their discovery, along with their announcement of the existence of a great lake in Central Africa, aroused European geographers and set in motion a whole series of exploring expeditions.

The Advance Inland. An even stronger impulse to the opening up of Central East Africa to missionary occupation than that of Krapf and Rebmann was imparted by the discoveries of the great Livingstone, and even more by his untiring agitation against the slave trade. Britain, at length aroused, wrung from the Sultan of Zanzibar a treaty abolishing this cursed traffic. British warships liberated a large number of slaves, and the problem of caring for these led the *Church Missionary Society* to establish a refuge for them at *Frere Town,* opposite Mombasa. This colony thus became the center and point of departure of missionary activity in East Africa. Another impulse was soon added by Stanley, who was so profoundly influenced by his intercourse with Livingstone that he resolved to consecrate his life to the continuation of the latter's work. Entering upon his famous journey through the Dark Continent, Stanley sent back to England from Uganda in 1875 his stirring

[9] "History of Protestant Missions," Warneck, p. 258.

"Challenge to Christendom." *King Mtesa* had asked for missionaries for his people. Would Christians respond to this cry from the heart of Africa? The effect was like magic. Men and means for the projected mission were soon forthcoming, and the next year (1876) saw the first contingent of eight missionaries on their way to Africa under the *Church Missionary Society*.

Mackay of Uganda. The leading one of these eight, who was to become a famous figure in missionary history, was Alexander Mackay, a highly educated and gifted young Scotch engineer. "My heart burns for the deliverance of Africa," he wrote the Church Missionary Society, "and if you can send me to any of those regions which Livingstone and Stanley have found to be groaning under the curse of the slave hunter I shall be very glad."

"Mackay's farewell speech to the Board of Directors is characteristic: 'I want to remind the committee that within six months they will probably hear that one of us is dead. Yes, is it at all likely that eight Englishmen should start for Central Africa and all be alive six months after? One of us at least—it may be I—will surely fall before that. When the news comes, do not be cast down, but send some one else immediately to take the vacant place.' " [10]

How sadly prophetic were these words! Within three months one was dead, within a year five, and in two years Mackay himself was the only survivor. For twelve years he fought on against terrible odds—fever, persecution, the intrigues of Moslem Arab and Roman Catholic priest, and repeated attempts upon his life. The story of his career—his early struggles and later successes, the use of his engineering skill, his keen diplomacy, his tireless energy, his supreme sacrifice for an ungrateful people—reads like a romance. He was finally driven from his field through the subtle influence of Arabs upon *King Mwanga,* and took refuge at the southern end of Victoria Nyanza. There, undaunted, he pursued his labors for three years longer, and then, attacked with fever, he died on February 8, 1890. He had received urgent appeals to give up and come home, but turned a deaf ear and wrote in his last letter: "It is not a time for any one to desert his post. Send us our first

[10] "Daybreak in the Dark Continent," p. 234.

twenty men, and I may be tempted to come and help you find the second twenty."

A Wonderful Mission. Mackay died facing the foe and without being permitted to see the fruit of his labor. But he and his comrades had laid the foundations of one of the most wonderful missions of modern times.

The transformation wrought by the gospel in Uganda has few parallels in any land. Stanley accurately described these Baganda people, despite their strong physique, expressive features, cleanly habits and superiority in many points to the surrounding tribes, as "crafty, deceiving, lying, thieving knaves, taken as a whole." Polygamy, witchcraft, vice and violence were rife. Human life was held of little account. King Mtesa himself sacrificed 2,000 captives to his dead father's spirit. Yet in barely twenty years from the advent of the first missionaries, *Pilkington,* one of Mackay's worthiest co-workers, whose name also shines with luster, could write (in 1896) the following remarkable summary: "A hundred thousand souls brought into close contact with the gospel—half of them able to read for themselves; 200 buildings raised by native Christians in which to worship God and read His Word; 200 native evangelists and teachers entirely supported by the native church; 10,000 copies of the New Testament in circulation; 6,000 souls eagerly seeking daily instruction; statistics of baptism, of confirmation, of adherents, of teachers, more than doubling yearly for the last six or seven years, ever since the return of the Christians from exile; the power of God shown by changed lives—and all this in the center of the thickest spiritual darkness in the world! Does it not make the heart reel with mingled emotions of joy and fear, of hope and apprehension?" [11]

The history of the Uganda church is not without its baptism of fire and blood. Under Mtesa's successor a terrible persecution broke out. The missionaries were driven from the country, and many of the native Christians suffered inhuman torture and martyrdom. Their sublime faith shone brightly amidst these fierce testings. Some of the Christian boys actually went to the flames singing the hymns they had been taught. Such testimony could not fail to bear fruit;

[11] "Pilkington of Uganda," pp. 272, 273.

before long the missionaries were back again, the tide turned and the church entered upon a period of rapid growth which has continued to the present.

The cathedral at Kampala, dedicated in 1919, is probably the largest Christian church in Africa. At the opening services the vast building was quickly filled and the throng outside was estimated at 20,000. The following Sunday 864 communicants partook of the Lord's Supper.

In 1937 there were 3,500 church groups with 77,000 communicants, and a Christian community of 329,000.

Schools now also flourish, there is material prosperity on every side, and recently the native leaders in Uganda inaugurated a missionary movement in behalf of neighboring tribes. Thus the "zone of Pagan darkness" has become the "zone of Christian advance," and Uganda has been called the "brightest spot on the map of Africa."

Bishop Hannington. Another missionary whose name, like the names of Mackay and Pilkington, has become a household word, was this young martyr bishop. Cruelly murdered on his arrival in 1885, by order of the wicked King Mwanga, he said to his executioners: "Go tell Mwanga that I die for Baganda, and that I have purchased the road to Uganda with my life."

A Group of Great Missions. The inspiration imparted by Livingstone's life and labors found expression not only in the C.M.S. Mission in Uganda, but through other channels in other localities as well. At least four other missionary enterprises in this section of Africa are traceable to the same origin.

The *Universities Mission* grew out of the interest kindled by the great missionary explorer's visit to Oxford and Cambridge in 1857. Its earliest attempts in the Shiré Highlands cost the lives of Bishop Mackenzie and others. Later it extended its work beyond Nyasaland into Northern Rhodesia, Portuguese East Africa, Tanganyika and Zanzibar.

The *London Missionary Society,* which with pride counts Livingstone among its missionaries, sent out its first party in 1860. Its present fields lie in the Union of South Africa, Bechuanaland, Northern and Southern Rhodesia.

The *Blantyre Mission,* named after Livingstone's birthplace, was established at the southern end of Lake Nyasa in 1875, by the *Established Church of Scotland*. The site chosen proved an unusually healthy one and is now crowned with a flourishing town wearing a decidedly Scotch air, a kind of miniature "Edinburgh" in Africa. The work of this Mission—evangelistic, medical and industrial—has been much blessed and its influence extends far afield.

The *Livingstonia Mission* is the most distinguished of all these memorials of Livingstone. Begun by the *Free Church of Scotland* in 1874, it now occupies the whole western shore of Lake Nyasa. *Dr. Robert Laws*, the leader of its pioneer party and still in active service, has all along been the outstanding figure of this remarkable work. The story of the Mission, including the early struggles and dangers attending the opening up of the field, the subsequent trials and vicissitudes heroically met and overcome, and the ultimate progress and spiritual victories achieved, is one which has seldom been equaled in missionary literature. All the lake peoples, whom Dr. Laws found indulging gross superstitions and hideously cruel customs, have been profoundly influenced.

Perhaps the greatest victory was won among the wild and wicked Ngoni tribe. After eight years there were only two converts. Ten years later the regular church attendance was 10,000. At the opening of a lofty new church among them on a Sunday morning in 1904, 3,130 sat on mats on the floor, 300 carefully selected adult candidates were baptized, and 904 of those one-time nude savages sat reverently at the Lord's table.

Among the results to date of the Livingstonia Mission which can be tabulated may be mentioned the reduction of eight languages to writing, 700 schools with 41,000 pupils, a church membership of 22,400 and a Christian community of 66,000. A central training school known as *Overtoun Institution* is in the scope and character of its work a second "Lovedale." Such is the fruitage of only fifty years.

German Missions. The occupation by Germany of territory on the east coast led to the initiation of six German Missions. The earliest of these efforts began in 1886. The World War brought German activities to an end, German East Africa became British, under the name of Tanganyika

Territory, and the mission work was taken over by other agencies. Four German Societies have since reoccupied the field and Christian converts have greatly increased.

The *Africa Inland Mission* was organized in 1895 as an interdenominational society on the faith principle of support, with the object of carrying the gospel to unoccupied parts of the interior. Its founder and first General Director was *Peter Cameron Scott* and he was followed by *Charles E. Hurlburt,* who served until 1925. It has a present staff of 275 missionaries and 1,800 native workers, occupying 50 stations and 1,400 outstations among 25 tribes in Kenia, Tanganyika, West Nile District (Uganda), Belgian Congo and French Equatorial Africa.

West Africa

Next to South Africa this coast constitutes the oldest field of evangelical missionary effort on the continent. But its past and present conditions have made it one of the hardest fields.

More than any other part of Africa the West Coast was the slaver's hunting ground. Indeed, it was the interest aroused by African slaves imported by that wicked trade into so-called Christian lands which gave the strongest impulse to the early missionary efforts on this coast. Alas! along with the missionary came also the curse of foreign rum and "civilized" vices to counteract the gospeler's influence. In no part of Africa, moreover, have tribal customs been more atrocious, or has heathen religion sunk to lower depths of vileness.

Added to all this is the barrier of a most unhealthy climate, which has made the heaviest drafts upon missionary life. To give but one illustration, between 1804 and 1824, 53 missionaries of a single Society laid down their lives in Sierra Leone. Fortunately the death rate in later years has been greatly reduced by improved living conditions and the discovery of the true mode of malarial infection—the *Anopheles* mosquito—and the adoption of protective measures.

Christian Colonizing Experiments. Two early philanthropic enterprises took the form of Colonies for African freedmen. The first of these was *Sierra Leone,* begun by Englishmen in 1788 and handed over to the British crown in 1808. The second was *Liberia,* originated in 1816 by the *American Colonization Society* under the influence of Samuel J. Mills and others. In 1847 this Colony developed into the Republic of Liberia.

While the success of both these experiments was very limited as to their design of promoting Africa's evangelization through colonies of her emancipated and civilized sons, yet they served a good purpose in pointing the way and providing starting points for more direct missionary effort.

Distribution of Missions. Seventy or more agencies— British, American, and European—are at work, about half of them being old and well established, the others comparatively recent and small. Only a few of the larger and better known can be mentioned here.

In *French Sudan* is the *Christian and Missionary Alliance.* In *Sierra Leone* are the *Church Missionary Society* and *Methodist Missionary Society of England,* and the *United Brethren of America.* In the *Gold Coast* are the *Methodist of England* and the *Presbyterian of Scotland.* In *Nigeria* are the *Church Missionary Society, Methodist, Church of Scotland, Qua Iboe* and *Sudan United Missions of Great Britain, Sudan Interior Mission* and *Southern Baptist of America,* and *Basel Mission of Germany.* In *Kamerun* are the *Northern Presbyterian of America* and *Paris Evangelical Society.* In *French Equatorial Africa* are the *Swedish Missionary* and *Paris Evangelical Societies.* In *Angola* are the *American Board, Methodist Episcopal, United Church of Canada,* and *South Africa General Mission.*

In *Belgian Congo,* among some 40 Societies listed, are the *Baptist and Regions Beyond Missionary Union of England, United Christian* (*Disciples*), *Northern Baptist, Southern Presbyterian, Methodist Episcopal,* and *Christian and Missionary Alliance of America, Africa Inland Mission, Swedish Missionary Society,* and several large *Congo Societies.*

Some Worthy Pioneers. The record of suffering and sacrifice, of heroism and endurance, by a long succession of missionaries on the west coast, constitutes a glorious bequest to the Church universal. "Nowhere is death such a King of Terrors as in Equatorial Africa. Nowhere is weakness more liable to overmaster or character to be sapped than on the equator. But the men and women who held this coast for Christ knew their God and did exploits. They drank more deeply than others of the Saviour's cup of sacrifice, and out of a fuller experience than the first disciples had, they could say, *We are able.*" [12]

Only a few names, among many deserving ones, can be mentioned here:

Melville Cox, the first foreign missionary of the *Methodist Episcopal Church of America,* landed in Liberia in 1833, only to die within four months. But his noble example stirred the church, and his dying appeal, "Let a thousand fall before Africa be given up," was heeded and obeyed.

Thomas Comber reached the Congo from England in 1876, at the age of 24, and after ten years of eager toil filled one of those lonely graves which have been the stepping-stone of Christianity into the interior of dark Africa. Stanley wrote of him: "Again and again, as I looked at him, he reminded me of the young man with the banner on which was the word 'Excelsior.'"

George Grenfell, one of the early heroes of the *English Baptist Mission,* stands high in the honor list of African explorers as well as missionary pioneers. Reaching Africa in 1873, he contributed thirty-three years of splendid service. It was he who in his little Steamer *Peace* discovered the Ubangi, the largest tributary of the Congo, and the story of his journeys through cannibal tribes and his escapes from showers of spears and poisoned arrows is unsurpassed for exciting interest.

Henry Richards planted the gospel seed at Banza Manteke, on the lower Congo, in 1879, and after watering it with prayers and tears for seven years reaped the first ripe sheaf. Thereupon broke out the *"Pentecost on the Congo,"* which swept a thousand souls into the kingdom. "All the people around Banza Manteke abandoned their heathenism. They brought their idols, and at the first baptism had a bonfire of images, destroying every vestige of idolatry." [13]

Adolphus C. Good, the talented and dauntless pioneer of

12 "Christus Liberator," pp. 157, 158.
13 "New Acts of the Apostles," p. 279.

the *American Presbyterian* work in the Gabun, labored un-
tiringly for twelve years (1882-94), and saw the first beginnings of those marvelous changes which the gospel has
wrought in that fruitful field. "He carried the standard
of the Cross a step farther towards the heart of the continent and left the path open to others. 'May good men never
be wanting for this Interior,' was his dying prayer." [14]

Mary Slessor of Calabar is probably best known of all
to present readers. Her life-story rivals in many particu-
lars that of David Livingstone. She served in Africa under
the *United Free Church of Scotland* from 1876 to 1915.
From an unlettered factory girl in the homeland she advanced into the foremost rank of missionary pathfinders.
Her work was that of a pioneer among the most savage
tribes of the Calabar hinterland. Practically single-handed
she tamed and transformed three pagan communities in succession. It is a question if the career of any other woman
missionary has been marked by so many strange adventures,
daring feats, signal providences and wonderful achievements.

Having thus touched separately upon the missionary work
of the various sections of the continent, it remains to mention a few features relating to the field and work as a whole.

Adaptive Methods of Work. The missionary task is
different in Africa from what it is in most other fields, because of different conditions to be faced. India, Persia,
China and Japan have a civilization, a literature, a culture of
their own upon which to build. Africa has nothing of this
kind, and society has to be built from the ground up. The
missionary has had to reduce languages to writing, establish
social customs and institutions, formulate moral codes and
introduce the first rudiments of education. The problems
involved in such a program are many and great, and they
challenge the brightest mind and highest statesmanship.

In addition to direct evangelism, always the preëminent
method, there is a great field for *industrial education,* and
the contribution to missionary success made by such institutions as *Lovedale* in Cape Colony, *Kondowe* in Nyasaland
and *Elat* in Kamerun is beyond computation.

[14] "Christus Liberator," pp. 159, 160.

Medical missions have a sphere of need in Africa hardly equaled elsewhere, because of the unhealthy climate, the prevalence of malaria, blackwater fever and other deadly diseases, the fearful ravages of sleeping sickness and imported diseases of civilization, and the prevailing ignorance of the first laws of sanitation and health.

The fact that so many regions are unfit for white residence enhances the responsibility of the native church for Africa's evangelization, and thus the importance of *Training Schools* for native workers.

African Christian Converts. The African is of a deeply religious nature, and gives abundant evidence of ability to apprehend lofty spiritual truth. That some converts backslide, yield to temptation, and fail at some point in their Christian walk is not to be wondered at when one considers the terrible heathen heredity and abysmal depths of degradation from which they have emerged. Yet many African Christians have come into a spiritual experience of a very high order. Their openness of mind and simplicity of faith have led some of them to a knowledge of Christ and a likeness to Him in character and walk beyond the generality of believers in Western lands. A few out of many examples may be cited.

Samuel Crowther is one of the most conspicuous trophies of African missions. Belonging to the inferior Yoruba tribe on the Niger, he was as a boy carried off by Portuguese slave raiders, rescued by a British war vessel and sent to school in Sierra Leone. He early accepted the Saviour, and showed such ability and devotion in his studies that he was sent to England to complete his education.

In 1864 he became Bishop of the Niger, and his missionary career up to his death in 1891 was one of rare consecration and high distinction. The story of how he found and baptized his own mother, for whom he had long searched, is full of tender pathos.

Paul, "The Apostle of Banza Manteke," is another wonderful convert. The son of a chief, his wickedness won for him the nickname of "the curse." He did everything in his power to obstruct the local missionary work until, like Paul the Jew, he was suddenly arrested by Jesus and changed from a child of the devil to a saint of the Lord. Thereafter he was filled with a holy passion for Christ and souls, cheerfully endured ostracism and opposition, laid gospel siege to the stoutest pagan stronghold, and at his death left behind him a church of 600 converts, all won through his personal ministry.

King Khama of Bechuanaland is a fine witness to the miracle-working power of the gospel. Yielding his heart and life to Christ, he firmly withstood his father's persuasions to have the son succeed him as sorcerer as well as chief, and became a veritable "Alfred the Great," waging war alike upon heathen customs and the white man's rum and other vices. He was at once a devout and humble Christian and a firm and sagacious state builder, who turned a whole savage tribe into a peaceful and industrious Christian people. "To pass from Bechuanaland before Khama to Bechuanaland with Khama is like passing from Dante's Inferno to his Paradiso." [15] The news of the death of this fine old Christian king on February 21, 1923, in his ninety-fourth year, has just been cabled the world around.

And the time would fail to tell of *Moolu,* the humble attendant of Prof. Henry Drummond in his journey through Central Africa, whose godly life so impressed his master that he wrote: "I believe in missions, for one thing because I believe in Moolu"; of *Susi* and *Chuma,* Livingstone's heroic "bodyguard"; of *"Old Nana,"* the Christlike "firstfruits of the gospel" in Bululand (Kamerun); of *Kanjundu,* the Angola Chief, wonderful in his forgiving spirit toward his persecutors—all of them lustrous gems from the spiritual diamond fields of the Dark Continent.

Neglected Areas. The impression might be gathered from the account given of existing missionary operations that the evangelization of Africa has now been fairly well provided for. Such an impression would be very wide of the mark. It must be remembered that in this chapter, as in no previous chapter, we are dealing with a whole continent, and that continent the largest but one in the whole world. When all that missions in Africa have accomplished has been summed up at full value, it still remains true that the proportions of the territory yet unoccupied and the populations yet unreached are staggering.

15 "Daybreak in the Dark Continent," p. 261.

The vast integral region lying at the heart of the continent, known under the general name of the Sudan, is reserved for the chapter on Unoccupied Fields. But aside from that there are many other areas, larger and smaller, in all the political divisions where mission work has been begun which are still wholly neglected.

Reference has already been made to the unreached interior of all the Barbary States, and to the spiritual destitution of Abyssinia. French Equatorial Africa and French Sudan are still largely unoccupied. In the former the *French and Swedish Missions,* in the latter the *Christian and Missionary Alliance,* have established work. Despite a number of stations in the various Colonies of the Guinea coast, manned by *English Wesleyans* and others, the hinterland of all that region, including Liberia also, contains an unreached population of several millions. Large sections of Nigeria and Kamerun are still beyond missionary effort. In Belgian Congo, with a population of 12,000,000, "4,000,000 are being reached by existing agencies, 4,000,000 more are within the radius of present influence, while the remaining 4,000,000 are still to be provided for." [16] Two millions or more in Portuguese West Africa (Angola), and almost or quite as many in Portuguese East Africa, have no missionaries among them. Even in Uganda, the best occupied field, nearly one-half of the people are reported not to have been reached. Italian, British and French Somali lands together contain about a million people, mostly nomads, as yet practically untouched.

The above is given not as a complete list of unworked areas, but only as an illustration of the dimensions of the unfinished task of missions in Africa. Under existing conditions no figures in this connection can lay claim to accuracy, but the estimates of those who have given the greatest attention to the subject put the number of Africa's people who are still beyond the reach of present missionary forces somewhere between 50,000,000 and 70,000,000. Well does the Report of the Edinburgh Conference say in closing its review of the situation: "The question can be seriously raised, Has the Church more than made a beginning in the evangelization of the Dark Continent?" [17]

16 "Rock Breakers," pp. 47, 48.   17 Vol. I, p. 282.

Roman Catholic Opposition. Those who know this religion only as practised in free countries will hardly be prepared to appreciate the situation which Protestant Missions face in those large sections of Africa controlled by Roman Catholic States, where Roman Catholicism is actively supported by the government. The whole training of the priests leads them to hate Protestant missionaries and to oppose them in every way. "At the beginning of Congo Missions the College of Propaganda at Rome issued this Encyclical, 'The heretics are to be followed up and their efforts harassed and destroyed.'"[18]

The early Protestant Missions to Abyssinia were expelled through Jesuit intrigue. Mackay and his colleagues in Uganda were maligned, persecuted and plotted against by Roman Catholic missionaries. Any amount of evidence is forthcoming from missionaries laboring in Belgian, Portuguese and Spanish territory as to the systematic and determined efforts of the priests, often by foul means, to obstruct and destroy Protestant work.

Added to this are the hampering legal restrictions imposed by Roman Catholic governments upon Protestant Missions, and the serious hindrance of the compromising policies and corrupt practices of Roman Catholic propagandists.

Opposing Forces from Without. As if paganism, witchcraft, superstition, ignorance, deadly climate and other formidable enemies already present in Africa were not a sufficient challenge to missionary work, two gigantic evil forces from without have come to add their powerful opposition:

(a) *The Moslem Menace.* Dr. Cornelius H. Patton in his "Lure of Africa" devotes a chapter to Islam on the March. He reveals in startling fashion the magnitude of the Moslem menace throughout the northern half of the continent. And he is only one of many writers who have sounded a loud alarm. Both the World Missionary Conference at Edinburgh in 1910, and the Conference on Moslem Missions held in Lucknow in 1911, characterized the Moslem advance in Africa as perhaps the largest world missionary problem confronting the whole church at the beginning of the twentieth century.

18 "Triumphs of the Gospel in the Belgian Congo," p. 176.

The facts in brief are these. The Arab slaver of yesterday has become the Arab trader of to-day. His attitude
toward the African has changed from one of arrogance to
one of condescension. Closer akin than the European to
the black man, he has more readily adapted himself to
native conditions, and with shrewd diplomacy and patient
persistence has succeeded not only in capturing trade, but
also in making converts by the wholesale to the Moslem
faith. The easy-going morals of Mohammedanism make
it far simpler to win "converts" to that religion than to
Christianity.

Tribe after tribe has been annexed by these Moslem
"missionaries," until now by far the larger portion of the
great Sudan has been preëmpted for the false prophet, and
the Moslem advance is sweeping southward into the Congo
region and down the two coasts. Nigeria is two-thirds
Mohammedan, and Kamerun is said to have 500,000 adherents to Islam. The important Swahili tribe of British
East Africa is being rapidly won over, and Moslem influence
is being powerfully felt as far south as Uganda, Tanganyika Territory and Nyasaland.

An important factor in this Moslem advance, too little
realized at home, is the attitude of the European governments concerned. Great Britain and France, the controlling
Powers in the Sudan, have not merely tolerated Mohammedanism, but have actually become its patrons for reasons
of political expediency. They have found that Moslem
ascendancy over pagan chiefs has tended to diminish tribal
wars and make European control more secure. The amazing spectacle has thus been presented of so-called Christian
governments restricting activities of Christian missionaries
and in some instances positively prohibiting them, lest they
offend the sensibilities and arouse the fanaticism of the
Moslem chiefs.

(b) *The White Peril.* The aggression of the white man
has resulted in the partition of almost the entire continent
among the Powers of Europe. Only little Abyssinia and
Liberia have continued to be the black man's countries.
Egypt has just recently been given self-government, with
results yet to be seen.

As a general principle it may be granted that it is for the

good of the world that barbarism be displaced by civilization. But a no less important principle requires that the civilized nations assuming control should respect native rights, and rule in such a way that the natives may share the benefits of the new order and not be victims of exploitation for selfish ends.

What, then, must be our appraisal of the case for civilization in Africa in the light of these principles? It must be acknowledged that European government has brought some great material benefits to the African. Tribal wars have been suppressed, law and order established, cruel and revolting native customs put down, better agriculture, industries, sanitation and business enterprise introduced.

Railway development is rapidly revolutionizing the continent. The dream of that British statesman of South Africa, Cecil Rhodes, of a "Cape-to-Cairo" railroad is rapidly being fulfilled, for already 2,000 miles are completed and in operation from the Capetown end and 1,300 miles from the Cairo end. Britain alone built 1,500 miles of railroad in the Sudan in fifteen years, besides constructing 5,000 miles of telegraph wires and inaugurating 2,000 miles of steamboat service on the great lakes and rivers. France has also built some railroad lines and projected others in her Sudan territory, while still other roads have been built in Belgian, Portuguese and German colonies. Altogether eight lines penetrate the interior from the east coast and sixteen from the west.

Due credit must also be given for some instances of beneficent colonial administration, resulting in greater security of life and property and other advantages to the natives.

But secular civilization in Africa has its debit as well as its credit side, and in the mind of the African native, strange as this may seem to the European, the debit side far outweighs the other.

There is, first of all, the indelible record of the horrible slave trade of past generations, and the hardly less iniquitous record of brutal repression and wholesale massacre openly tolerated, and in some cases deliberately instigated, by certain European governments. The notorious Congo rubber atrocities are perhaps the best known illustration.

But there are present scores as well. The African smarts under the contemptuous attitude of the white man. He resents being cuffed and kicked as if he were a dog. He chafes under the burden of taxation—poll tax, head tax, cattle tax, etc.—imposed by his civilized overlords, and also under the galling restriction upon his freedom of leaving his immediate locality without a permit which is difficult to secure. Moreover, he blames the white man for the fact that the railways and steamers, while improving travel facilities, are the means of spreading cattle pests and such deadly human diseases as smallpox, tuberculosis and syphilis.

But there is still much more to be said. As one writer puts it: "Christian civilization without Christ is worse than Paganism. The state of morals among some Europeans is scarcely whisperable. It is awful, the amount of corruption and filth introduced by them."

Take the liquor question, for example. How often has attention been called to the deplorable fact that almost invariably the same ship which carries one or two missionaries to convert the African, carries also thousands of gallons of rum to damn him! The proportions of this foreign rum trade and the demoralization wrought by it are appalling. Dr. Patton states that during the year ending in April, 1916, 3,815,000 gallons of spirits were imported into British West Africa, and during 1914-15 there were shipped from Boston alone to the west coast of Africa, 1,571,353 gallons of rum.[19]

Another fearful moral menace has sprung from the rapid transformation of the South African *veldt* into a great industrial district. The rich gold mines of Johannesburg and the diamond fields of Kimberley have drawn together a multitude of native laborers from all the tribes south of the Zambesi. The mining region known as "The Rand" has a population of nearly or quite 500,000. The natives who compose this conglomerate mass have been removed from all family and tribal restraints and thrown under conditions of life which make for unbridled moral license along every line. Low-down whites, including some of the worst crooks and criminals, have gravitated here from all parts of Europe and America. What the resultant situation is may be con-

[19] See "The Lure of Africa," p. 123.

jectured from the fact that Johannesburg has been named "the university of crime." The vices and crimes of civilization have been added to those of heathenism, and thousands have become the victims of drunkenness, gambling, robbery, murder, sodomy and prostitution. Nor are these terrible conditions restricted to this one center; they prevail also in such cities as Kimberley, Pretoria, Durban and Capetown.

After discussing candidly both sides of the case for secular civilization, Dr. Patton proceeds to "strike the balance" and concludes as follows: "Clearly civilization finds itself on the wrong side of the account: *It has brought more evil than good to the African.* The plain and ugly fact is that in many parts of Africa the natives would be better off, physically and morally, if European enterprise had never come." [20]

As to the bearing of all this upon missions, the following quotation speaks for itself: "It is comparatively easy to convert primitive Africans to Christianity, and to establish them against the later introduction of the vices of civilization. It is supremely difficult to Christianize them after they have become viciously civilized." [21]

Challenge to Christianity. We have seen Africa's plight, sunk in the filthy mire of paganism, deceived and misled by crafty Mohammedanism, cruelly wronged and oppressed in the past by the stronger nations of Christendom, and now threatened with physical and moral ruin before the colossal vices of godless civilization. What hope remains for her? Verily, the power of pure Christianity alone! And what a superb challenge to the Christian church does Africa present with her vast size and her vaster potentialities! The work of Christian Missions in the Dark Continent has been prosecuted at a costly sacrifice of lives, but the trophies already won have been a glorious evidence alike of the sufficiency of the gospel to meet the African's need and of the susceptibility of the African to the gospel's deepest influences and highest demands. In other words, the results to date are an inspiring sample of infinitely greater possible results. But such greater results can only follow a vastly greater invest-

20 "The Lure of Africa," p. 127.
21 "Daybreak in the Dark Continent," p. 120.

ment of life and prayer and treasure than has yet been made available.* Missions have little more than begun the work of Africa's complete evangelization. The doors are wider open than ever before, the possibilities are infinitely larger. Will the church see, and heed, and act in terms of the actual completion of the task?

MADAGASCAR

AREA, 241,000 SQUARE MILES. POPULATION, 3,800,000

Location and Size. It seems most natural that any mention of this island should be made in connection with Africa, because of its close proximity to that continent. Madagascar, now a French possession, lies about 250 miles off the east coast of Africa. It is the third largest island of the globe, in area slightly larger than France and Belgium combined.

The People. Its inhabitants are called Malagasy and are of Malay origin. They are divided into numerous tribes, of which the Hova is much the largest.

Madagascar first attracted notice by its terrible traffic in slaves. The island was given over to idolatry of the most degraded kind and was the scene of perpetual war, lust and superstition. Vices were exalted as virtues. So hopelessly depraved were the people that the French Governor of a neighboring island told the first missionaries that they might as well attempt to convert sheep, oxen and asses. Yet through the wondrous working of divine grace this island has later been made famous by the heroic faith of its Christian martyrs.

Early Missions. In 1818, during the reign of the beneficent *King Radama,* the *London Missionary Society* opened work. The Bible was translated, schools and industries were begun, and the work met with such favor and success that by 1833 the native church numbered 2,000 members, and 30,000 Malagasy were able to read.

Persecution. Upon the death of King Radama one of his twelve wives, known as *Ranavalona I,* seized the throne, murdering all rivals, and began a reign of terror that won for her the name of the "Bloody Mary" of Madagascar.

* Latest Protestant figures for all Africa, including Madagascar and outlying islands, are: Foreign missionaries, 8,447; Native workers, 81,625; Communicants, 2,163,000.

She was a veritable monster of cruelty, and it is said that "from twenty to thirty thousand victims fell annually a prey to her atrocious crimes."

This wicked queen turned her malicious eye of death upon the Christians, and from 1835 to 1861 a terrific storm of persecution raged, with only short intervals of respite. Every conceivable torture was employed with the object of stamping out the Christian faith, yet none of the native Christians turned back to heathenism. They bore the severest suffering, and even death itself, with quiet heroism and unfaltering trust in God. "To the amazement of the queen, for every one she put to death a score accepted the new faith. . . . And wonder of wonders—the little company of believing men and women, left by their English pastors and teachers in 1836 as sheep without a shepherd, had multiplied at least twentyfold in 1861, the year of the queen's death." [22]

Turning of the Tide. The son of Ranavalona I, who succeeded her on the throne, proclaimed religious freedom and protection for all Christians. In 1868 a wonderful change took place when *Ranavalona II* became queen, for soon after her coronation she openly confessed herself a Christian and was baptized. As her predecessor, Ranavalona I, became notorious for her infamous cruelty, so Ranavalona II became renowned as a wise and gentle Christian queen. Under her rule idolatry with its corrupt rites and practices received its death blow, and Christianity became the recognized faith of the realm. Large accessions to the church followed, reaching within a short time to several hundred thousand, and the sifting of professed converts and the instruction and discipline of the churches imposed upon the missionaries a task far beyond their ability adequately to cope with.

Missionary Reënforcements. Other Societies thereupon came to the help of the London Missionary Society and entered the Madagascar field. These were the *Society for the Propagation of the Gospel* (1864), the *Norwegian Missionary Society* (1867) and the *British Friends,* or Quakers (1867). The work of all these agencies grew and prospered up to the occupation of the island by the French.

22 "Wonders of Missions," pp. 277, 278.

More recently two American Societies began work in this field, namely, the *Norwegian Lutheran Church of America* (1892), and the *Lutheran Free Church* (1895).

The London Missionary Society in 1938 reported a staff of 23 missionaries and 3,190 Malagasy workers, and a church membership of over 40,000. At Amparibè its Sunday morning congregations range from 1,000 to 2,000 in attendance.

Results of French Subjugation. A very sad postscript has to be added to the story of missionary progress just sketched. In 1885 France established a protectorate over Madagascar, and in 1896 formally annexed the island. From the first the French authorities, incited by the Jesuits, were hostile to the English missionaries and did everything to oppose and hamper the evangelical churches. Native Christians and workers were imprisoned as suspects, some were even put to death, practically all the mission schools and many of the churches were closed, and for a time it looked as if the missionaries would all be obliged to withdraw. The situation was partly relieved by the action of the *Paris Evangelical Society* in coming to the aid of the hard-pressed Protestants, sending out French pastors and taking under its care much of the work of the English Societies. But the promising aggressive movement of the mid-nineteenth century has been suppressed with a heavy hand, and "it yet remains to be seen if the martyr spirit of their ancestors is in the present Malagasy, and if they will remain as faithful under the persecution of a Christian nation as did their forefathers under that of a heathen queen." [23]

Present Day Moral Problems. A missionary writes of blatant heathen worship going on round an enclosed ancestral tomb right in the midst of the church area, and expresses the fear that many professing Christians still follow ancestral customs. He laments the fact that marriage vows are broken with ease, and loose morality exists among the young. The European non-Christian environment is saturated with the lowest moral practices, and strong drink is becoming a growing evil.

QUESTIONS

1. Give the size and population of Africa, and the name by which it is commonly known.

[23] "The Missionary Enterprise," p. 219.

2. Describe its main physical features, and name its prominent rivers, lakes and mountains.

3. Describe the climate and natural resources of its different parts.

4. Give the names and distribution of its main racial groups, and state the number of languages and dialects spoken.

5. Divide its population on a religious basis, and name and describe its native religion.

6. Explain how early Christianity in North Africa became almost extinct.

7. Sketch the course of discovery and exploration in Africa down to the present century, and name six prominent explorers.

8. Describe early Roman Catholic missionary efforts, their character and results.

9. Who blazed the Protestant missionary trail in Africa, in what year, and with what success?

10. Name the chief missionary agencies at work in Egypt, Egyptian Sudan, and the Barbary States, and state the nature of the last mentioned field.

11. Sketch missionary efforts in Abyssinia.

12. Give accounts of Robert Moffat and his illustrious son-in-law.

13. Mention four other prominent missionaries in South Africa, and the Societies which they represent.

14. Name and describe the work of the first two Protestant pioneers in East Africa.

15. Tell the missionary story of Uganda, and of the great missionary whose name is identified with it.

16. Name and locate four Missions in East Africa whose beginnings were inspired by Livingstone's career.

17. (a) What state of things led to the first missionary efforts on the West Coast? (b) What form did those efforts take, and with what success?

18. Give the general distribution of Missions down the entire West Coast.

19. Write brief notes on six worthy pioneer missionaries on this Coast.

20. What methods of work have been found specially well adapted to conditions in Africa?

21. Give brief accounts of three noted African converts.

22. Indicate the areas in Africa at present most neglected.

23. Discuss (a) the Roman Catholic attitude toward Protestant work; (b) the influence of Mohammedanism; (c) the pros and cons of civilization in its various aspects.

24. Give size and population of Madagascar, and describe conditions when missions entered.

25. What Society began missionary work on the island, and when?

26. Sketch the course of missionary work there through its successive stages down to the present.

CHAPTER XVI

LATIN AMERICA

AREA, 8,000,000 SQUARE MILES.[1]   POPULATION, 125,000,000[1]

The Americas. We are accustomed to speak of two Americas—North and South. Geographically there are in reality four—North, South, Central and Oceanic. Racially there are two—Anglo-Saxon America and Latin America. The Rio Grande is the dividing line, and Latin America stretches south from that line to Cape Horn and the Antarctic Ocean. It comprises about four-sevenths of the entire Western Hemisphere, Anglo-Saxon America's area being 7,225,000 square miles against Latin America's 8,000,-000 square miles. In population, however, the ratio is reversed, since Anglo-Saxon America has 130,000,000 inhabitants against Latin America's 125,000,000.

"Latin Americans." While the inhabitants of Latin America are commonly designated Latin Americans, the truth is that from the racial point of view only a small proportion—one-fourth at most—can be properly so called. The foreign blood that is in them is mainly Latin, and the comparatively small upper class is dominantly of Latin blood; but the racial basis of the Latin American peoples as a whole is Indian, not Latin.

This fact, standing in striking contrast as it does to the case of Anglo-Saxon Americans, is readily explained by the totally different nature of European colonization in these two sections of the Western Hemisphere. The early Anglo-Saxon colonists in North America were actuated largely by religious motives. They came seeking freedom of conscience to worship God, came with their wives and little ones, came to establish new homes and communities and

---

1 *Statesman's Year Book* (1939) figures give total of 124,725,093, but this is based upon census returns for some countries and estimates for others.

to settle down to till the ground and develop the country. They encountered the Indians, fought and drove them back, but disdained any idea of intermingling or intermarrying with them.

Not so the Portuguese and Spaniards who first touched the shores of the Southern Continent. These were daring adventurers, lured to the New World by the tales they heard about its fabulous treasures of gold and silver. They came as single men or without their families. Moreover, the first Indians they found were very different from those of North America, for the Incas were civilized, docile and skilled in agriculture. So while the *Conquistadores* from overseas shamefully mistreated the native races, decimated their numbers and reduced them to slavery, they did not wipe them out, but mixed freely with them, and thus the surviving Indians furnished the stock upon which the Latin blood from Europe was grafted.

To this day, as the traveler passes from republic to republic of Latin America, he readily observes the varying degree in which Indian blood has been affected by European strain. In Bolivia, Peru and Ecuador he finds great masses of mixed population in which Indian features and character are dominant; while in Chile and Colombia the mixed populace, although retaining many Indian qualities, is more strongly Spanish in character. The people of Argentina and Uruguay are almost purely European, and constitute nearly one-half of the all-white population of Latin America. In the case of Brazil, and to a much more limited extent Venezuela also, the admixture of blood has become still greater because of the importation by the early colonists of large numbers of African slaves.

Racial Classification. Latin America's population, based on the old total of 85,000,000, is roughly classified as follows:

Whites	18,000,000
Indians	20,000,000
Negroes	6,000,000
Mixed White and Indian................	32,000,000
Mixed White and Negro.................	8,000,000
Mixed Negro and Indian................	700,000
East Indian, Japanese and Chinese........	300,000
	85,000,000

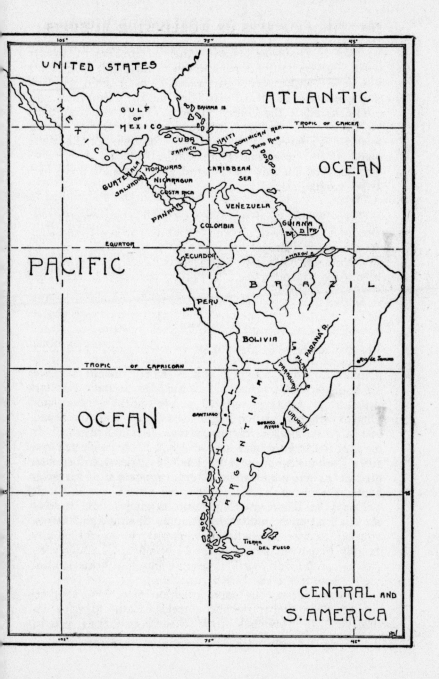

Political Divisions.　Latin America consists of twenty republics—ten to the north and ten to the south of Panama—together with colonies of France, Great Britain, Holland and Denmark, and also Porto Rico and the Canal Zone now administered by the United States.　These twenty republics together form the largest group of democracies in the world.　Eighteen of them speak Spanish, Brazil alone speaks Portuguese, and Haiti speaks French.　About 15,-000,000 Indians can be reached only through their own tribal languages.

Since South America comprises by far the greater portion of Latin America, being a continent in itself, and since its dominant features are common to the whole, our main attention will be given to it, leaving only such additional mention of the other sections as their particular interests call for.

SOUTH AMERICA

AREA, 7,000,000 SQUARE MILES.[2]　POPULATION, 87,000,000 [2]

Names.　Miss Lucy Guinness named South America *"The Neglected Continent."*　Later, Dr. Francis E. Clark called it *"The Continent of Opportunity."*　Still later, Bishop Stuntz styled it *"The Continent of To-morrow."* All three authors are correct in their designations.

That it has been, and still largely is, "the neglected continent" admits no argument.　The rest of the world has been strangely content to remain in gross ignorance of the geography, the resources, the commercial, educational and social progress of these growing Latin countries, and to class them all together indiscriminately as illiterate and lawless tropical states—a negligible quantity in world affairs. Highly humorous stories are told of absurd errors on the part of prominent North American business firms in dealing with orders from South America.

Commenting on the scant attention paid these southern countries, one writer remarks tersely: "Latin America was discovered by Columbus in the fifteenth century; it was re-

2 *Statesman's Year Book* (1939) figures give total of 87,003,220.

discovered by North Americans in the twentieth century." [3]

But Miss Guinness had chiefly in mind the spiritual neglect of South America, and this is by far the saddest and most serious aspect of the matter. No satisfactory reason can be offered for the aloofness and inaction of centuries on the part of the churches of Protestant lands, and especially North America, toward a continent of 87,-000,000 people lying so close at hand, united to North America by physical bonds and by many common features and interests as well, yet sunken in moral and spiritual degradation of the deepest sort.

Even when a century ago the church at home was awakened by Carey and Mills to new vision and zeal, and the modern missionary movement set in, it was to the distant lands of India, China and Africa that missionaries were sent, and several decades elapsed before any serious attention was directed to South America, despite its being so much nearer and more accessible. To plead as an excuse the unfavorable attitude of Roman Catholic governments and the bitter hostility of the degenerate priests toward Protestant effort is weak, in the light of the even greater perils faced and obstacles surmounted in carrying the gospel into remoter heathen and Moslem lands. To argue that Latin America has no need of Protestant missionaries because of the pretentious claims of the Church of Rome in that region is, in the light of plain facts, the hollowest evasion. The truth is that Christianity's long neglect of this great and needy land was a *guilty* neglect, due to the lack of spiritual concern for the souls of men.

In recent years a gradually rising tide of interest in our South American neighbors has set in. This is evidenced by more books and magazine articles upon this region, by a new stream of tourist travel in this direction, by strengthened diplomatic relations, and by new and heavy investment of capital in South American enterprises. All this, along with quickened spiritual interest and increased missionary effort, goes to prove that the world has at last discovered in South America "the continent of opportunity," and desires a share in it as "the continent of to-morrow."

Size. Comparisons, not figures, convey the best idea of

[3] "The Living Christ for Latin America," p. 17.

size. South America is seven-eighths as large as North America, or nearly twice the size of Europe. It has a coast line of 18,000 miles. Its largest country, Brazil, would hold the entire United States and still leave room for Germany and Portugal. Argentina is equal to all of the United States east of the Mississippi plus the first tier of states to the west. Bolivia and Venezuela are each more than twice the size of Texas. Chile, nicknamed "the shoe-string republic," because of its long narrow shape, stretches from north to south as far as from New York to San Francisco, and would make two Californias or four Nebraskas. Ecuador, so tiny on the map, is equal to New England, New York and Pennsylvania combined.

Physical Features. But South America's claims do not rest merely upon her size. She can boast the largest rivers, the densest forests, and, with the single exception of the Himalayas, the highest mountains of the world. She also has the greatest stretch of undeveloped fertile territory. "There is more undiscovered territory in Brazil than there is in the whole continent of Africa." [4]

The Amazon, largest of all rivers, offers 2,200 miles of waterway to ocean-going vessels and 25,000 miles to steamers of lighter draught. The La Plata, comprising in its system the Paraná and its affluents, is 150 miles broad at its mouth, and pours into the ocean a volume of water seven times that of the St. Lawrence. It is navigable by sea-going vessels for 1,200 miles beyond Buenos Aires. Of lesser magnitude than these, but yet great in size and importance, are the Orinoco, 1,500 miles in length, the Magdalena, San Francisco and many other streams.

The majestic Andes range extends the whole length of the continent, forming a massive bulwark along the Pacific. In Ecuador alone fifteen mountain peaks rise to a height of over 15,000 feet, including the famous Chimborazo (20,697 feet) and Cotopaxi (19,493 feet), while farther south towers the peerless Aconcagua (22,868 feet), the crowning peak of the Western Hemisphere.

As illustrations of engineering skill may be mentioned the scenic Trans-Andean Railroad, which pierces the Andes on the Argentina-Chile boundary line by a two-mile tunnel

[4] "Problems in Pan-Americanism," p. 16.

at an altitude of 10,000 feet, and the Central Railroad of
Peru, which climbs to a height of 15,865 feet—the highest point reached by any railroad in the world.

Climate. The great bulk of the continent lies within the
tropics, although most of Chile, half of Paraguay, all of
Uruguay, and practically all of Argentina are in the south
temperate zone. The tip of Patagonia is not far from the
antarctic circle. The normal effect of latitude, however, is
greatly influenced by such factors as altitude, moisture,
prevailing winds and ocean currents, so that South America
presents great variations and some very unique phases of
climate. An elevation of a mile near the equator gives the
mean temperature of a point a thousand miles north or south
at sea level. The Humboldt current from the south polar
sea lowers the temperature of the southwest coast by twenty
degrees. Higher up the same coast is a large rainless area.
The great interior offers every variety, from dry and barren
deserts to regions of excessive rainfall. Brazil has a hot
tropical climate, and its vast Amazon basin is feverish and
unhealthy. Uruguay, Argentina and Chile have a climate
much like that of the United States. The southern extremity
of the continent consists of a bleak, wind-swept, fog-covered
area which provides pasture for millions of sheep.

Resources and Industries. No part of the world is more
richly endowed with natural resources than South America.
Her wealth of mine, forest and soil is almost beyond esti-
mation.

Of minerals practically all the useful ones are found,
many of them in abundance. Rich seams of gold exist in
almost every State, and some of the very mines worked successively by pre-Inca, Inca and Spanish miners centuries
ago are to-day being worked by modern machinery, with
no signs of their output diminishing. Fifteen million
ounces of silver are produced annually. The mountains
of Peru, Bolivia and Chile contain such enormous deposits
of copper, tin and iron as to have led wealthy American
and British capitalists and manufacturing firms to invest
money by the tens of millions in plant, machinery and other
equipment for mining and exporting these ores on a gigantic
scale.

Chile's nitrate fields largely supply the world with fertilizer. The total export in 1937-38 was $1,544,000. Great coal fields in the Andes lie as yet almost untouched, and mining engineers have barely begun their task.

The forest wealth of the continent is likewise incalculably great. Brazil abounds in virgin forests of mahogany, rose-wood, ebony and other rare and expensive hardwoods, and the rubber district of the upper Amazon is one of the richest known.

The agricultural and pastoral resources even eclipse in extent and value those already mentioned. While there are certain large areas of desert, swamp and jungle land, there are other enormous sections, particularly in Brazil, Uruguay, Argentina, Chile and Colombia, unsurpassed in fertility anywhere. The grain-growing pampas of these countries aggregate hundreds of millions of acres and yield huge crops of grain, cereals, sugar and other products.

In the Argentine stock raising surpasses farming. In 1914 that nation owned 123,612,000 cattle, horses, sheep, goats, mules, pigs, etc., of which 80,000,000 were sheep. The world's greatest packers have established bases here, and the export trade in grain, wool and frozen meats has taken on huge proportions.

Brazil furnishes three-fourths of the world's coffee, ex-porting in 1938 over two billion pounds. Ecuador from her ivory nuts supplies one-third of the world's buttons, besides cacao beans and the finest panama hats. Luscious tropical fruits are sent north by shiploads from the Caribbean coast.

The rapidity of development in every line of this great continent's production, industries and export trade is almost without a parallel elsewhere, and has a large significance for the whole world.

The Early Races. The origin of South America's earliest people is wrapped in mystery. Fragments of earthen pots and crude implements found on the coast of Peru seem to point to a primitive people in the remote past. Following these came a race much more advanced, massive stone relics of whose remarkable civilization are still to be seen near Lake Titicaca in the highlands of Peru and Bolivia. Certain resemblances between these people and the Chinese, Japanese and Malays have led to theories of their Oriental origin, but where they came from is an unsolved problem.

Of the next succeeding Indian races, most prominent among whom were the *Incas* of Peru, the *Caras* of Ecuador and the *Aztecs* of Mexico, we have fuller and more reliable knowledge. The Cara kingdom reached its zenith at the end of the fourteenth century, when it was overthrown and partly absorbed by the Incas.

The wonderful civilization of the Incas has been the fascinating theme of many authors.[5] The Inca Empire attained its height of power and prosperity in the generation just before the coming of the Spaniards. It stretched along the Pacific for nearly 3,000 miles and embraced perhaps 10,000,000 people. Agriculture was developed to a remarkable degree by schemes of irrigation, terraced fields and vast aqueducts. Great cities, splendid roads and bridges and magnificent temples were built. The government was paternalistic and socialistic, controlling everything. The king lived in a gorgeous palace of stone, his subjects in huts of sun-dried brick, and an impassable gulf lay between the ruler and the ruled. It would appear that the swift and sudden overthrow of so great a nation by a mere handful of Spanish adventurers was mainly due to the inherent frailty of this socialistic order. It developed weak dependence rather than virility of character, so that when a blow was struck the central government the whole civilization at once collapsed.

Beyond the domains of the Incas and Caras other Indian tribes of varying social order down to the rude savage peopled the continent. Inter-tribal wars were common and contributed to the ultimate conquest of the country by the white man.

European Discovery and Conquest. *Columbus* himself began the Spanish exploration of South America. On his third voyage, in 1498, he sighted the Venezuelan coast, and in his fourth and last voyage, in 1502, he sailed along the Colombian shore to the Isthmus of Panama.

In 1513 *Balboa* crossed the Isthmus and discovered the Pacific Ocean. The several colonies planted in that region became centers of further exploration north and south. *Cortez* invaded Mexico in 1519, overthrew the Aztec Em-

---

[5] Prescott's "The Conquest of Peru" and Dawson's "South American Republics" are among the best authorities.

pire in 1521, and in 1525 extended his conquest for Spain
to the territory now comprising Central America. Meanwhile Portuguese navigators had discovered Brazil. The
earliest landing there was effected by *Cabral* in 1500, at
Bahia. He was succeeded by *Amerigo Vespucci,* whose
name was given to the new world, and *de Souza,* who in
1532 founded the first colony at São Vincento, near the
present great coffee port of Santos. From this beginning
Portuguese colonization spread along the Brazilian coast
and to the mountain site of the present city of São Paulo,
colonial government was established and the sugar industry
begun.

It was the startling tales that reached the Spanish colonists on the Isthmus of the wealth of the Incas that prompted
a party of some three hundred daring freebooters to undertake, in 1531, a hazardous voyage from Panama down the
west coast. Their captain was *Francisco Pizarro,* a man of
low birth and no education, utterly without principle, but
equally without fear, and full of reckless daring. The
thrilling story of this expedition and its momentous results
is too well known to need recounting here in detail. After
a series of fierce assaults Pizarro in 1532 stormed the Inca
capital of Cuzco, seized the sacred *King Atahualpa,* and
after demanding and receiving an unheard-of ransom of
gold to the value of $22,000,000, foully betrayed his pledge
and slew his captive. By a succession of vigorous campaigns the whole vast Inca Empire was subdued by 1540,
and twenty years later almost the entire western and southern sections of the continent had been overrun and brought
under Spanish control.

Three Centuries of Iberian Rule. The story of the three
centuries which followed the subjugation of the continent
to Spain and Portugal cannot be fully told here. It is no
easy task justly to appraise the varied factors of the new
régime. It cannot be denied that Iberian occupation brought
many material benefits to South America, such as civilized
laws and letters, the introduction of new and valuable animals, grains and fruits which raised the level of the well-
being of such inhabitants as survived. But its wrongs and
injustices so far outweigh these benefits as to make possible
only one verdict. It brought untold suffering to the Indians,

and such sweeping destruction to their civilization that Peru to-day is vastly worse off in many important respects than it was under the Incas. "The masterful whites simply climbed upon the backs of the natives and exploited them." [6] The Indians were driven, under the cruel lash of the task-masters, to impressed labor in mines and plantations. Of 10,000,000 Incas only 2,000,000 lived through the first century of serfdom. Well does Dawson call the colonial period "the devil's dance of Spanish carnage." Nor was it alone the native people who suffered. An intolerable burden was laid upon the colonists themselves, by reason of the outrageous colonial policy of arbitrary exactions and restrictions in regard to immigration, trade and everything else. To this day the republics of the western seaboard bear the blighting mark of those dark centuries. Finally, as one writer expresses it, "oppressive rigor and shameful abuse of privilege brought their own corrective and finally ousted the last henchman of Spain." [7] The fires of revolution, long smoldering beneath the surface, burst into flame, and the desperate struggle for freedom began.

Mexico was the first to declare her independence, in 1810, and by 1826 eight sovereign states had been set up. The names of *Francisco Mirando,* the able pamphleteer who first spread the doctrines of freedom, and *Bolivar, San Martin, O'Higgins, Juarez,* and *Sucre,* the military leaders in various parts of the continent, are immortally enshrined in the hearts of all Latin Americans.

The Republics. The history of the present ten South American republics, now about a century old, has been a checkered one. The previous régime was devoid of all training or preparation for self-government. This fact, as well as the racial complications, partly explains the slow progress of the majority of the republics and the frequency of revolutions. Paraguay has become notorious for her revolutions, which cost her so many men that at one period the female population outnumbered the male five to one. Venezuela has had fifty-two uprisings within a century. Others of the republics, however, have a much better record.

The republics recognized as progressive are Argentina,

---

[6] "South of Panama" (E. A. Ross), Preface.
[7] "The Living Christ for Latin America," p. 39.

Brazil, Chile and Uruguay. The remaining six are classed as backward, with Ecuador and Colombia footing the list. While each of the ten has to-day all the machinery of republican administration, politics and patronage play a serious rôle in government affairs, and corruption at elections is general.

The Roman Catholic Church, which exerted such strong influence in colonial times, is no less a political force in the republics. The church party constitutes the conservative wing, against which are arrayed the radicals and liberals. The aggressions and political pretensions of the church are increasingly resented and opposed, not only by the other political parties, but by the public in general.

Social Features. A striking characteristic of Latin civilization in South America has been its development of a few great cities to the neglect of the country. Think of one-fifth of the entire population of Argentina being in its capital, Buenos Aires, which is the largest city not only in South America, but in the whole Southern hemisphere. Two cities in Chile together contain almost one-fifth of her whole population. "The small population of each land gives to its one or two largest cities a predominant influence. Almost everything centers in the capital. Such a condition is not wholesome. These cities suck in the wealth of the nation, beautifying themselves with revenues needed for the development of the nation's wider interests, and they absorb the energy of government which should be national and not urban." [8]

Nothing strikes a visitor to South America more than the wide contrasts between urban and rural conditions. We found the main cities, Buenos Aires and Rio de Janeiro in particular, wonderfully developed and attractive. Buenos Aires, with a population of 2,300,000, combines the commercial features of London with the beauty and pleasures of Paris. Rio de Janeiro, with a population of 1,700,000, is said to be the cleanest and loveliest city in the world. Its finest *avenida* rivals Fifth Avenue, New York. Montevideo, Santiago, Lima, Quito and São Paulo are among the other best cities. But one has only to go a short distance into the country from any of these centers of com-

8 "South American Republics," p. 66.

merce and culture to meet with conditions of life as crude as
in the interior of Asia.

A most serious feature of South America's social order is
the almost entire absence of the middle class, which constitutes the backbone of other countries. The population is
divided into the rich aristocracy, who although comprising
less than ten per cent. of the whole, are the landlords of the
country and exercise almost complete control, and the common people who are their tenants and for the most part
extremely poor. There are scarcely any small farmers.
Five per cent. of the Latin Americans own ninety-five per
cent. of the land and make it well-nigh impossible for others
to secure any of it.

With the exception of a few more advanced cities, such as
those already mentioned, there is everywhere an appalling
ignorance of modern sanitation and hygiene. Open sewers
run through the streets, meats are exposed to swarms of
flies in the public markets, and other filthy conditions prevail
which promote diseases of every sort. Even in a progressive
republic like Chile, with an almost ideal climate, seventy-five
to eighty per cent. of the children die under two years of
age, and the general rate of mortality is nearly twice as high
as that of Europe. Epidemics of smallpox, typhoid and
other infectious diseases rage on unchecked. Guayaquil,
the flourishing port of Ecuador, was in 1918 altogether the
filthiest city of its size we had ever seen. It had become
notorious as a hotbed of malaria, yellow fever and bubonic
plague, with Callao, the main port of Peru, a close second.
Reports indicate that there has been some improvement
since then. The sacrifice of so many lives as victims of
diseases which might be prevented or cured by better knowledge and simple means is deplorable.

Illiteracy is one of the fundamental problems. Until
recently it was about forty per cent. in such progressive republics as Uruguay and Argentina, and ran to eighty per
cent. in such backward ones as Venezuela and Peru. The
average for the entire continent is estimated at about seventy-
five per cent., or three illiterates out of every four persons.
An up-to-date authority states that New York City's present
budget for education equals the national budget for education
of all the twenty republics of Latin America.

Moral Conditions. Dr. Speer says: "The fundamental trouble in South America is ethical. . . . Speaking generally, the people are warm-hearted, courteous, friendly, kindly to children, respectful to religious things, patriotic to the very soul; but the tone, the vigor, the moral bottom, the hard veracity, the indomitable purpose, the energy, the directness, the integrity of the Teutonic peoples are lacking in them." [9] Another writer mentions the prevalency of untruthfulness, often cleverly hidden beneath evasive words, in which the Spanish language is rich. The inordinate love of pleasure of the Latin Americans finds vent in gambling, card-playing, horse-racing, cock-fighting and bull-fighting, social evils which have grown to large proportions, and which are not frowned upon by the Church of Rome.

Drunkenness is another terrible evil. Large sections in Argentina and Chile are devoted to grape-growing, and in Chile ordinary wine is cheaper than milk. More Latin Americans are drunkards than total abstainers. "With few exceptions the Chilean laborer gambles away or drinks up most of his wages." [10] It is said that in Valparaiso, a city of 193,000, there is one saloon for every twenty-four men. Drink has nearly wiped out the Indians of Chile and is undermining the strong constitution of the whites.

But the crowning evil is moral unchastity. Conditions on this line are too shocking to permit the plainest speaking, but too well known by all who have given any attention to South America to require it. The blame rests most heavily upon the men. Male chastity is almost unknown, and the idea that a man should be morally pure is commonly ridiculed. Nor is the evil even mainly confined to unmarried men, for marital infidelity is deplorably common. Estimates by reliable writers as to the proportion of illegitimate births for all South America vary from one-fourth to one-half of the population. Even when due allowance is made for cases where couples are faithful to each other, but have dispensed with the formal marriage ceremony because of the extortionate fees demanded by the clergy, the record is a truly appalling one. The lack of any popular conscience in

9 "South American Problems," pp. 73, 74.
10 Quoted in "South of Panama," p. 219.

the matter makes it that much worse. These illegitimate births are duly registered, the names of father and mother appearing in the public record, and yet no shame attaches to it. What an awful blot is such a state of affairs upon any people, not only condemning them before God, but also effectually barring all true and lasting progress and prosperity, which can be the heritage only of nations built upon individual morality and the sanctity of the home!

Romanism on Trial. To turn to the consideration of spiritual conditions is to confront squarely the issue of the Roman Catholic Church in South America. For four centuries she has had an absolutely free hand, without a competitor, and in the main with the substantial backing of the State. Under such conditions she has had the best possible opportunity of showing what she can do to uplift the people. What use has she made of this opportunity, and what results has she to show? Applying the Master's own test, "By their fruits ye shall know them," the following facts speak for themselves:

Romanism has systematically and bitterly opposed every movement toward civil, political or religious freedom. She has herself been a political rather than a religious power, and her unscrupulous methods have won for her contempt and antagonism in politics.

She set up the infamous Spanish Inquisition in South America, at the hands of which 120,000 people were tortured and 189 were burned at the stake in Lima, and its overthrow was effected only in the teeth of her strenuous resistance.

She has not scrupled to employ the boycott and every form of persecution to intimidate those who have sought peace outside her fold, nor to use violence, imprisonment and even the assassin's dagger and bomb to dispatch heretics.

She has been the inveterate foe of popular education, thereby contributing to the prevailing illiteracy. Her leaders in Argentina persistently fought the Morris Schools, which befriended and educated thousands of homeless waifs in and around Buenos Aires.

She has opposed the translation of the Bible into the vernacular, and its distribution, has forbidden her people to buy or read it, and has publicly burned the Book. Bible colporteurs have been stoned, flogged, imprisoned and murdered at the instigation of her clergy.

She has defiled herself by becoming a partner in the lottery and other iniquitous practices.[11]   She has encouraged Sabbath desecration through the sanction of the use of that day for public games, excursions, feasting and social merriment, if only early mass has been attended.

She has promoted irreverence to the point of sacrilege, in allowing sacred terms to be applied to common objects and commercial affairs in a way that profoundly shocks all true religious sentiment.   We personally came upon such business signs as "Butcher Shop of the Holy Spirit," "Furniture Shop of the Saviour," "Tailor Shop of Jesus on the Cross," "Fishmonger of Holy Mary."   A bottled mineral water in Peru was labeled "Jesus Water."   But the most blasphemous instance which came under our notice was that of a magazine which on Good Friday featured as an advertisement a picture of Christ upon the Cross, with Judas and others standing in the background, and the words put into Judas' mouth: "If I had had such cigarettes to smoke I wouldn't have betrayed Him."

But the case against Rome in South America is even yet stronger when her doctrines and morals are examined. Her teaching deserves to be called Mariolatry rather than Christianity, for a godhead of four persons, not three, is recognized, and with Mary the first person. The Jesuits taught their converts to say: "We confess that the Holy Virgin Mary should be held in greater esteem by men and angels than Christ Himself the Son of God."[12]

"On a tablet beside the door of the Jesuit Church in Cuzco, Peru, there is an inscription in Spanish: 'Come to Mary, all ye who are laden with works, and weary beneath the weight of your sins, and she will succor you.'"[13]

Except in the larger coast cities, where foreign influence is strong, few sermons are ever preached and no prayers offered in any of the churches, in the language of the people.

[11] The author of "The Living Christ for Latin America" testifies to having seen over a moving picture show managed by Franciscan monks the sign "Recreation Hall of the Child Jesus," and more than one wine cellar directly beneath the altar of a church.

[12] "The Evangelical Invasion of Brazil" (S. R. Gammon), p. 99.

[13] "The Living Christ for Latin America," p. 95.

The observance of ritualistic forms and sacraments is made
the hollow substitute for repentance and regeneration, as a
perusal of the authorized Roman Catholic catechism of
Christian doctrine in use will show. And along with these
empty ceremonies a whole stock of grossly sacrilegious
superstitions are foisted on an ignorant and credulous people.

The priests are largely responsible for the shockingly
low moral standards, not only by their extortionate marriage
fees, but even more by their own abominable immoralities,
which have called forth loud protests from an outraged
public, from high dignitaries in the Church, and even from
the Pope himself.

A certain bishop in Bolivia wrote concerning the priests
of his district: "I have done all in my power to pull them
out of the cesspool of ignorance and vice. . . . They are
always the same—brutal, drunken, seducers of innocence,
without religion and without conscience. Better would be
the people without them. . . . You cannot imagine the pain
these things give me. I am sick and tired of it all. There
are exceptions, but so very few that they are not enough to
mitigate the pain." [14]

Little wonder is it that a great proportion of the people,
particularly the educated and intelligent classes, have turned
in disgust from such a travesty of religion to absolute unbelief, so that the chief task of evangelical missions is not to
proselytize from the Roman Church, but to call to a rational
faith and a pure and upright life those who have already
thrown off this false religion and are drifting toward
atheism and moral ruin.

Said an intelligent man in Argentina to a missionary who
was endeavoring to awaken in him a concern about spiritual things: "Sir, we have been so miserably deceived and
defrauded by this damnable religion, that it will be a long
while before we can be expected to take any interest again
in anything that bears the name of religion." He spoke
with evident heat, and who will blame him? Yet there are
people who resent the idea that South America is a legitimate
field for evangelical missions, because it is a "Christian"
country under the care of a "sister" church! Let the facts
cited speak for themselves. While gratefully recognizing

[14] "The Continent of Opportunity," p. 317.

the true Christian faith and character of certain individuals within the Church of Rome, and the heroism and self-sacrifice of some of her early pioneers in this continent, we must solemnly affirm that Romanism in South America stands condemned on its own record, at the bar of God and humanity alike, and is hopelessly impotent to meet the social, moral and spiritual needs of 87,000,000 needy souls. After personal contact with South America and most of the great mission fields of Asia and Africa, we share the deep conviction of many other observers that *South America to-day stands in need of the gospel not one whit less than China, India, Africa and the Moslem world.*

II. Missionary Work.

Early Roman Catholic Missions. In the discovery and settlement of Latin America the religious motive was not lacking along with the political and commercial, and the very earliest expeditions were accompanied by monks or priests. The first of these were of the Franciscan and Dominican Orders, but the Jesuits who followed were here, as elsewhere, the great missionary agency of Rome.

Some of these were worthy disciples of Loyola and Xavier, and faced hardship, danger, disease and persecution in a heroic spirit deserving of all praise. They penetrated the continent at many points, and "there was no tropical wilderness too intricate or far-stretching for them to traverse, no water too wide for them to cross, no rock or cave too dangerous for them to climb or enter, no Indian tribe too dull or refractory for them to teach." Yet they were a part of the militant, ecclesiastical and political system of the times, so that their ardent evangelism and humanitarian service were strangely mingled with cruel slaughter and subjection of the natives, and extortion of their land and wealth. Conversions were often by a wholesale process, and the Church ingeniously adapted its doctrines, rites and symbols to suit the religious traditions and notions of its pagan "converts."

For the above reasons it is not unfair to say, nor is it surprising, that Roman Catholic Missions in Latin America have proved an almost complete failure. The greatest temporary triumphs of the Jesuits were in the interior of southern Brazil and in Uruguay and Paraguay, but later they fell under the suspicion and disfavor of both Portuguese and Spanish governments because of their great accumulation of wealth and assumption of power. In the eighteenth century the Jesuits were expelled, their possessions confiscated and their work shattered, never to be restored.

First Protestant Efforts. The first Protestants to land in South America were a company of French Huguenots sent to Brazil in 1555 by Calvin and Coligny, with the hope of founding a colony for persecuted Protestants. They landed on an island in the Bay of Rio de Janeiro and were reënforced by a second company a year later. But their leader, Villegagnon, turned traitor and abandoned the colony, which was later destroyed by the Portuguese. A few survivors escaped into the interior and attempted work among the Indians, but these were hounded down and put to death by the Jesuits.

In 1624 the Dutch captured Bahia and attempted to plant colonies there and at Pernambuco, with alleged religious as well as commercial ends in view. Religious liberty was decreed and work begun among the Indians, but the Dutch West India Company later decided to withdraw, and so this second missionary attempt was aborted.

Modern evangelical effort may be said to have really begun in 1735, when the Moravians opened work in British Guiana. In 1738 this work was extended to Dutch Guiana.

The Lancasterian Schools. The dawn of the era of independence among the South American republics, early in the nineteenth century, coincided with the awakening of the church in Europe and America to new missionary endeavor, and the formation of societies for the translation and distribution of the Bible. In England a project had been begun by one named Joseph Lancaster for a system of popular schools for children, with the distinctive features that the Bible was the main textbook and that the older scholars were made pupil-teachers of the younger ones. The success of the project at home led to plans for extending its benefits to other lands, and so "The English and Foreign School Society" was organized. The British and Foreign Bible Society had just begun its great work abroad, and these two societies united in sending *Mr. James Thomson* to South America.

Thomson began his work in Buenos Aires in 1820, only four years after Argentina's declaration of independence. He preached the first Protestant sermon ever preached there. His plans met with immediate success, over one hundred schools were opened in Buenos Aires, and he won the favor and support of the leading statesmen. Uruguay and Chile soon called for his services and initiated his school system under government patronage. Thus he passed from one republic to another, his good work enjoying a temporary triumph which was most gratifying. In Peru, General San Martin turned out the friars of the Convent of St. Thomas and handed the place over for a Lancasterian school. Bibles were everywhere sold in large numbers, and auxiliary Bible Societies were formed in several republics, with the endorsement and support of prominent officials.

But stern reaction soon set in through the secret and powerful tactics of the jealous priesthood. Parents were forced to take their children from the schools, and those who had purchased Bibles were ordered to surrender them to the priests. "Gradually the coils tightened about the evangelical institution and it was strangled by political and clerical pressure. It received a warm welcome because it purported to be educational; it met with a violent death by priestly suffocation because it was evangelical." [15]

Mr. Thomson returned to England in 1826, and the few who followed him grew discouraged under the difficulties which beset them and were compelled to abandon their efforts on these lines.

Captain Allen Gardiner. "The first enduring Protestant Mission to South America began with the sacrifice of Captain Allen Gardiner, who perished of starvation in September, 1851, in Spanish Harbor, Tierra del Fuego." [16]

This noble British naval officer had seen service in many parts of the world, was converted during one of his voyages, and became filled with a passion for Christ and lost souls. He was deeply impressed with the pitiable condition of the

15 "The Living Christ for Latin America," p. 115.
16 "South American Problems," p. 219.

aborigines of South America, and made earnest efforts to open work among the Indians of Chile and the region in northern Argentina and western Paraguay known as the *Chaco*. Being persistently balked by the opposition of the priests he turned his attention to Patagonia.

The Indians of that extreme southern tip of the continent and the adjacent Island of Tierra del Fuego were among the most degraded people in the world. The eminent naturalist, Charles Darwin, dubbed them "the missing link" between man and monkey, and declared them incapable of moral discernment. Gardiner accepted this challenge and was permitted to labor long enough to convince Darwin of his error.

After some preliminary work among the Patagonians he returned to England in 1843, and effected the formation of the *South American Missionary Society* in 1844. His remaining six or seven years were full of adventure and hardship in his dauntless efforts to plant mission stations in that remote and inclement region and to win the debased Indians to Christ. Driven from their center at Banner Cove by the truculence and pilfering of the unregenerate Indians, Gardiner and six companions, who had recently joined him from England, put to sea in their little vessel and took refuge in Spanish Harbor, where they waited and prayed for the coming of the promised supply ship from home. Before it arrived starvation had slowly overtaken every member of the heroic little band, Gardiner himself being the last to succumb. Their bodies and diaries were found to tell the pathetic tale. " 'Poor and weak as we are,' wrote Gardiner, 'our boat is a very Bethel to our souls, for we feel and know that God is here. Asleep or awake, I am, beyond the power of expression, happy.' Instead of repining or lamenting, he left behind only earnest entreaty that the mission should not be abandoned, and left a brief plan outlining further operations." [17]

The news stirred the Church of England to its depth and gave new impulse to the work among the Indians. The transformation wrought among the Fuegians as a result of the work begun by Gardiner drew from Darwin a frank

[17] "The New Acts of the Apostles," pp. 111-112.

testimony of astonishment and appreciation, accompanied by a donation to the Society's funds and a request to be made an honorary member.

Some Early Trail Blazers. There were hardy pioneer missionaries among the Latin population as well as the Indians.

Rev. D. P. Kidder of the *M.E. Church* of the U.S.A. made the first attempt to plant the gospel in Brazil. Landing in 1836, he traveled overland and up the great Amazon, braving hardships, perils and bitter opposition in his work of distributing the Scriptures for the first time in that vast republic, till circumstances compelled his leaving the field in 1841.

The first agency in Brazil which has continued its service to the present was launched in 1855 by *Dr. R. R. Kalley,* a Scotch physician whose work, begun independently, is now carried on by an interdenominational society known as "Help for Brazil."

The first permanent denominational work in this State was the *Presbyterian Mission* founded in 1859 by *Rev. A. G. Simonton.*

Worthy pioneers in other parts included *Rev. David Trumbull, D.D.,* of the *Foreign Evangelical Society,* who entered Chile in 1845, and *Rev. H. B. Pratt,* who began the work of the *Presbyterian Board* in Colombia in 1856.

The Bible Societies. The contribution of the Bible Societies to the evangelization of South America can hardly be overestimated. Reference has already been made to the early efforts of the *British and Foreign Bible Society* through its first agent, Mr. James Thomson. The *American Bible Society* later entered the field, and these two great Societies shared the enormous task of sowing this Scripture-less continent with the Word of God.

Their representatives did largely the preliminary scouting which opened the way for local missionary work. The full record of their heroism as they toiled across desert sands, through fever-laden swamps and over mountain trails, and as they exposed themselves to insult and injury by their bitter enemies, the Roman Catholic priests, will never be known this side of heaven.

A colporteur of the American Bible Society, *José Mon-*

giardino by name, dared to penetrate Bolivia in the face of the declaration of a high Roman Catholic functionary that he would never get out alive. He sold all his books, but in a lonely spot on the road he was beset by two cut-throats hired by the priests, and foully murdered. In 1883 two distinguished agents of the same Society, standing by this martyr's grave, bared their heads and consecrated their lives anew to the service of Christ. These were *Dr. Andrew M. Milne,* General Agent of the Society, who on account of his long journey among Indian tribes in unexplored territory has been called the Livingstone of South America, and *Rev. Francisco Penzotti,* the worthy head of the La Plata Agency, who through a period of forty years of valiant service has repeatedly suffered stripes and imprisonment for the Master's sake.

These are outstanding names, but hundreds of colporteurs of humbler rank, but similar courage and devotion, have followed in their train in this invaluable department of missionary work. It is estimated that within the last half century over 2,000,000 copies of the Word have been circulated in Spanish and Portuguese America. To these must be added thousands upon thousands of tracts, books and periodicals to make up the great sum total of evangelical literature, the use of which has been one of the most potent factors in South America's evangelization.

Statistical Summary. The figures for the continent given by *Statistical Survey of the World Mission* (1938):

Foreign missionary staff 1,786
Residence stations 482
Native workers 4,735
Organized churches and other groups 7,504
Communicants 343,351

Brazil (41,500,000), the first republic to be entered, still leads all other Latin American countries in Protestantism. *The Southern Baptist and Methodist, Northern and Southern Presbyterian, Evangelical Lutheran, Protestant Episcopal churches,* and the *Evangelical Union of South America* and *Inland South America Missionary Union,* are here.

The work was begun on sound lines and has yielded larger and better results than in any other republic. Several of the denominations have quite a number of self-supporting churches. The Independent Presbyterian Church has over 13,000 members. Much earnest gospel witnessing is done by volunteer workers. One church of 1,059 members in Rio de Janeiro carries on 16 missions and 100 Sunday-schools in its city and suburbs.

The missionary educational work heads up in a number of high grade colleges, of which the best known is *Mackenzie College* at São Paulo.

All the missionary work in Brazil, however, is yet confined to the fringe of coast line and a few adjacent interior states. The greater portion of the vast interior has scarcely been touched, and northern Brazil is one of the most neglected fields on earth.

Argentina (12,700,000) is worked by the *Methodist Episcopal, Southern Baptist, Evangelical Lutheran, and Mennonite churches,* and also the *South American Missionary Society, Christian and Missionary Alliance,* and a group of *Brethren.*

This republic is a great melting pot for European immigration, and the forces of agnostic socialism and materialism are strong. The attitude of the people toward the gospel is one of indifference rather than opposition. It is said that there is no other great city in the world with so few places of worship as Buenos Aires. Brooklyn alone has as many churches as the whole of Argentina, Protestant and Roman Catholic combined. Great areas, including hundreds of towns, are yet untouched by evangelical missionaries.

Chile (4,600,000) has several strong Missions—the *Northern Presbyterian, Methodist Episcopal, Christian and Missionary Alliance* and *Southern Baptist.* The first two have a *Union Training School* and magazine at Santiago, where there are also mission colleges for boys and girls. The Alliance Mission has a number of stations with vigorous churches in central Chile, and is pressing its evangelistic efforts southward into a hitherto totally neglected area. The Chileans are a strong, virile nation, and the Missions are developing a fine type of native worker.

Uruguay (2,000,000) is the smallest, but most progressive of all the republics, with a high percentage of literacy and some advanced educational institutions. The *Methodist Episcopal* and *Brethren* are the main agencies in this field. Work has been confined largely to Montevideo, the capital, and the rural districts have hardly been touched. In all there are only 25 church groups, with 1,600 members.

An unique feature in Uruguay is the existence of a strong colony of *Italian Waldensians,* whose pioneers came over in 1858. They have survived many early hardships, as well as persecutions by the Roman Catholic Church, and to-day are a prosperous colony of about 6,000. With their Latin and Protestant inheritance they offer fine material for evangelical missions, if brought under the right spiritual influence and properly trained.

Paraguay (940,000), in its diminished population, poverty and general backwardness, still bears the scars of a long succession of wars and revolutions. Formerly it was the seat of aggressive Jesuit Missions, but religion is to-day at a low ebb. Evangelical work is as yet limited to a few centers, aside from that carried on among the Indians. The main agencies are the *South American Missionary Society,* the *Brethren,* and *New Testament Missionary Union.* The *United Christian Missionary Society (Disciples Church)* has a Christian school at Asuncion with an enrollment of 300 students.

Bolivia (3,200,000) is 50 per cent. Indian and 25 per cent. half-breed. The population is confined to fertile spots, with vast stretches of poor and unsettled country between, illiteracy amounts to 85 per cent., conditions are terribly backward, and the problem of adequate missionary occupation is staggering.

The *Methodist Episcopal, Canadian Baptist, Bolivian Indian, Brethren, Society of Friends,* and *San Pedro Missions* have each a small staff. Church groups number over 60, with 3,700 members, and there are four mission hospitals, and three schools with a total of 500 pupils.

Peru (6,500,000) is 50 per cent. Indian, 15 per cent. white, and the remainder half-breed, Negro and Chinese. The racial and language differences, the extreme illiteracy, and the geographical divisions with deserts and mountains intervening are features of difficulty here.

The *Methodist Episcopal, Nazarene* and *Scotch Church*

Missions, Evangelical Union of South America, Christian and Missionary Alliance, and *Inland South America Missionary Union* all have limited forces, utterly inadequate to the need. Most of northern Peru is still unoccupied.

Ecuador (2,700,000), one of the most backward countries on earth, was formerly more intolerant religiously than any other republic. Now, however, it is wide open to missionary work, of which it stands in desperate need. The only agency at work, apart from a few independent units, is the *Christian and Missionary Alliance,* which has a force of thirty missionaries engaged in evangelistic work. There are as yet no mission schools, and missionary plans for Ecuador greatly need strengthening and enlarging.

Colombia (8,700,000) has been worked for 80 years by the *Northern Presbyterian Mission,* which can even yet count only 600 church members in 50 groups. The *Christian and Missionary Alliance* and *Gospel Missionary Union* have also had work for some years, while the *World-wide Evangelization Crusade, Inland South America Missionary Union,* and *Scandinavian Alliance Mission* have recently entered the field. There are still regions which have never yet heard the first sound of the gospel.

Venezuela (3,300,000) has work under the *Northern Presbyterian, Scandinavian Alliance, Orinoco River, Brethren,* and *Evangelical Free Church Missions.* A great portion of the widely scattered population lies beyond the reach of the present missionary forces and in a condition of illiteracy and moral and spiritual degradation.

The Guianas (540,000) have a mixed population, mostly East Indian, Negro and half-caste. A number of *British and American Societies* are laboring in British Guiana, and the *Moravians* pretty well occupy Dutch Guiana. No information is at hand regarding evangelical work in French Guiana, and it is safe to conclude that little exists.

The Indians. No positive figures can be given for the purely Indian population of South America to-day. Most estimates have lain between 5,000,000 and 6,000,000. A fairly recent estimate by Dr. W. E. Browning, formerly Educational Secretary of the Committee of Coöperation in Latin America, is considerably higher. His figures are:—

Colombia	2,000,000
Venezuela	300,000
Ecuador	1,600,000
Peru	3,000,000
Bolivia	1,000,000
Guianas	40,000
Brazil	1,500,000
Paraguay	50,000
Argentina	50,000
Chile	102,000
	9,642,000

The Indians are divided into a number of main groups, and these subdivided into about 350 tribes. The South American governments have done little for them, while the rubber trade and other "civilized" enterprises have shamefully despoiled them and made them victims of drunkenness and other vices. The Roman Catholic Church for the most part has totally neglected them, and the little work it has done has left them still pagans at heart, with a thin veneer of medieval Catholicism.

Protestant work has been begun in several regions. The *South American Missionary Society,* which grew out of the heroic Allen Gardiner's efforts, stands first in the field of Indian work. *Rev. W. Barbrooke Grubb* in 1888 led a party into the interior of Paraguay, and began a work among the *Lengua Indians* which has been replete with thrilling experiences. It has now extended to other tribes in what is known as the *Gran-Chaco,* including adjacent territory in Paraguay, Argentina and Bolivia. Mr. Grubb is an accredited authority on conditions there.

The same Society carries on a good work among the *Araucanian* or *Mapuche Indians* of Chile, with evangelistic, industrial, school and medical features, and the *Christian and Missionary Alliance* has a station in the same tribe.

In Bolivia the *Bolivian Indian and San Pedro Missions* have a few centers among the *Quichuas.* The *Seventh Day Adventists* maintain a fairly well equipped and aggressive work among the *Aymaras* in the Lake Titicaca region of Peru. Near Cuzco, in Peru, the *Evangelical Union* has a good farm work for the *Quichuas.*

The *Christian and Missionary Alliance* has worked for some years among the *Quichuas* of Ecuador and has more recently entered other tribes in Colombia and Peru.

The *Inland South America Missionary Union* is at work among the Terena, Nhambiquara, Bacairi, and Xinguano Indian tribes of Brazil, the Campas and Chamas in Peru, and the Goajiras in Colombia, and has contacted ten tribes far up the Xingu River in Brazil.

These are the main points of contact to date. They have involved real sacrifice and danger for the brave, devoted pioneers, but they have barely touched the outer fringe of the Indian problem. In addition to these hordes of semi-civilized Indians, who have not in any adequate sense been evangelized, there are still unknown numbers of savage Indians on the eastern slopes of the Bolivian and Ecuadorian Andes, in northern Peru, in southeastern Colombia, along the Orinoco in Venezuela, and above all in the vast, unexplored interior of Brazil, who have yet to be touched by the first missionary. Many of them are utterly wild, nude savages, hidden away in the forests, never having seen a white man. The difficulties of access, climate and language, as well as the gross moral and spiritual darkness of these tribes, make the task of reaching them one of the mightiest challenges ever presented to Christian heroism and faith. Who will dare to accept this challenge, and when?

CENTRAL AMERICA

Divisions. This area, lying between Mexico and South America, comprises *British Honduras* and the six small republics of *Guatemala, Salvador, Honduras, Nicaragua, Costa Rica* and *Panama.*

Area and Population. Its area, about 227,000 square miles, is the same as that of the combined Atlantic seaboard States from Maine to North Carolina inclusive. Its population approximates 7,000,000, one-and-a-half to two millions of whom are Indians.

Spiritual Neglect and Need. Rich in resources, densely populated, capable of magnificent development, and lying so close to the United States, Central America is still one of the most neglected mission fields in all the world. "The

Roman Catholic Church is here as inefficient, bigoted and corrupt as in the worst South American countries." It employs the lottery for raising its funds, has repressed popular education and left the people steeped in ignorance of mind and darkness of soul.

Inadequate Missionary Forces. The *Central American Mission* has work in all the republics except Panama, with a total of 66 missionaries. In addition, there are the *Presbyterians, Nazarenes* and *Friends* in Guatemala; *Evangelical Synod, Friends* and *Brethren* in Honduras; *Baptists* in Salvador; *Moravians* and *Baptists* in Nicaragua; *Methodist Episcopals* in Costa Rica; *Methodists* and *Episcopalians* in Panama. But some of these agencies have only recently begun work, and their forces and equipment are small and altogether inadequate. While considerable seed has been sown through the distribution of Bibles and itinerant preaching, there are as yet only a very few well-organized centers of work. Until quite recently there were only two small training schools for native workers and one mission hospital in the six republics. Latest reports list eight Bible schools and four hospitals.

In 1921 the *Latin America Evangelization Campaign* was organized to conduct special gospel campaigns throughout Latin America in coöperation with existing Missions. Its center is in Costa Rica, where it has training schools for men and women and a hospital, with a staff of 26 missionaries.

For many years the *Moravians* have done most worthy work among the Indians of Nicaragua, and their converts number nearly 15,000. In the other republics the Indians have until recently been sadly neglected. Now 4 Missions are at work among 5 of the 23 tribes of Guatemala, which number 1,300,000. There is also aggressive work among the San Blas Indians in Panama.

Statistical Summary. The figures for Central America from *Statistical Survey of the World Mission* (1938) are:

Foreign missionary staff 299
Residence stations 79
Native workers 917
Organized churches and other groups 1,105
Communicants 32,215

MEXICO

Area and Population. Mexico has an area of 764,000 square miles—almost the size of the United States east of the Mississippi—and a population of 19,200,000.

Resources and Main Features. Mexico is enormously rich in resources, leading the world in silver and ranking second in petroleum, copper and dye-woods. In 1937 it produced 47,000,000 barrels of petroleum. But in social and educational conditions it is only emerging out of the sixteenth century, while it suffers the blight of corrupt and lifeless religion and chronic political revolution.

No other country presents more striking contrasts than Mexico. With a university founded before Harvard or Yale was ever dreamed of, its masses are distressingly illiterate. With a hospital established before the American Colonies were formed, its people in general are ignorant of the simplest laws of sanitation and hygiene. While a few landowners possess unlimited wealth and live in palaces, the bulk of the populace are poverty stricken and live in hovels.

The "Mexican Problem"—by which is meant the perennial state of revolution and the evils attendant thereupon—has become a hackneyed phrase. But as to this condition the Mexican people deserve sympathy rather than blame, for their problem can be solved only as they are brought into vital touch with Christ and His teachings. As one writer remarks: "There would be no Mexican problem to-day if the United States and other Christian countries had displayed the same interest in the development of Mexico's soul that they have in the exploitation of her natural resources."

Evangelistic Opportunity. Mexico presents at this time a strategic opportunity for missions. To the former legal religious liberty has now been added actual religious equality. Evangelical Christianity is favored in official circles, and the product of the Christian schools is receiving full recognition. Better still, a spiritual hunger has been awakened, and the response to direct evangelistic efforts among all classes is such as has never before been known in Mexico and is equaled in few other Latin countries. This is the more gratifying in the light of the unsettled political and social conditions, and also the bitter opposition of the Roman Catholic Church, amounting in some places to open persecution and acts of violence.

Inadequate Missionary Occupation. The principal mission work has been carried on by the *Northern and Southern Presbyterian and Methodist, Southern Baptist, Congregational* and *Episcopal Churches* of the United States. Unfortunately there has been until very recently no united plan of work, or agreement as to division of territory among the missionary forces. The distribution of effort has been so unequal that fourteen of the twenty-eight states, comprising 5,000,000 people, or one-third of Mexico's total population, are said even yet to have no resident missionary. There are cities of 20,000 which are totally neglected. With only 300 ordained ministers, both foreign and native, to preach the gospel to 19,200,000, each minister has 64,000 people dependent upon him.

The Neglected Indians. The Indian population has been variously estimated from 3,000,000 to 10,000,000. Rev. L. L. Legters of the *Pioneer Mission Agency,* who has made a special study of this field, reports 41 tribes which speak their own Indian tongue almost exclusively. One of these tribes numbers 517,000, while 17 others range from 22,000 to 300,000 each. Until recently there was no direct missionary work for Indians, but now 17 American workers are among 13 tribes, in one of which there are after seven years 100 Christian groups, and in another 70. But the Indian problem has been barely touched and the need is a desperate one which calls imperatively for attention. Indeed, the whole array of facts concerning the Mexican field is tremendously shocking, and the humiliating truth is that the nearest of all foreign mission fields to the Christian churches of North America, lying at their very door, is to-day one of the most neglected and needy fields in the world.

Statistical Summary. The following are the latest figures for Mexico as given by *Interpretative Statistical Survey of the World Mission of the Christian Church* (1938):

Foreign missionary staff 205
Residence stations 48
Native workers 859

Organized churches and other groups 1,037
Communicants 45,976

Latin West Indies

Extent and Population. These islands are three in number, *Porto Rico, Santo Domingo-Haiti* and *Cuba.* Their
combined area is over 77,000 square miles, or about the size
of Ohio and Indiana together, and their total population
about 10,500,000. All but Haiti are Spanish in race and
language, except as English is coming more and more into
use under the present dominating influence of the United
States. Haiti, formerly a French colony, is almost purely
negro, and is French-speaking.

Resources. The islands are all extremely fertile, producing and exporting large crops of sugar, tobacco and coffee,
besides all varieties of tropical fruits and vegetables. The
forests of Cuba and Santo Domingo are rich in valuable
cabinet and dye woods.

General Conditions. Social, moral and religious conditions in all these islands, excepting Porto Rico, are largely
those of the less advanced states of the Caribbean seaboard.
The control of land, industries and political power is in the
hands of a few individuals, and the masses are cut off from
opportunities of culture and advancement and live in poverty
and ignorance.

In Cuba a striking contrast is now presented between the
low material order of things in general and the new and
up-to-date aspect of the leading centers. Havana, the capital, and the largest and wealthiest city of the West Indies,
has magnificent driveways and elegant buildings, and is both
a great commercial metropolis and a gay pleasure resort
which attracts visitors at all seasons.

American intervention in Cuba and Santo Domingo has
brought about decided improvement in government, education, and conditions in general, particularly in the case of
Santo Domingo, which was formerly the most backward
of all the Spanish islands. Political graft in Cuba stands
seriously in the way of good government and education.
Haiti has been influenced least of all, and has ranked lowest
in civilization of all the republics in the world. It has been

controlled by unscrupulous rulers, and only three per cent.
of its people can read or write. Voodooism, a relic of
African fetichism, is said to be widely practised.

Since Porto Rico became a part of the United States, in
1898, general conditions in that island have undergone great
changes for the better. Road building and sanitation have
been promoted, an excellent system of English schools has
been established, and the whole social and moral order improved. On the other hand, industrial opportunities are
limited and there is much poverty among the people.

Missionary Work. Roman Catholicism has been the
prevailing religion of all the islands, but to the majority of
the people it has been little more than a name. The formalism, corruption and political activities of the Church
have developed a strong antagonism toward it, and many
have discarded all religion and gone over to spiritualism.

Although some missionary work has been carried on in
the islands for many years, it was of a disjointed character
and with utterly inadequate forces. Only recently, following American intervention, have the American churches
given serious attention to the spiritual needs of the islands.
Under the guiding hand of the Committee on Coöperation
in Latin America a united program of occupation has been
launched by the various Home Mission Boards.

In Porto Rico the field was from the start divided among
the denominations, and a high degree of coöperation has
been realized. Perhaps the most rapid and solid expansion
of the evangelical movement anywhere in Latin America
is taking place here, and the steady growth of the churches
and of native Christian leadership promises not only the
speedy evangelization of Porto Rico itself, but also a contribution of no small value toward the work in other Latin
American countries.

In Cuba the work is also progressing encouragingly.
More is being done by the Missions in an educational way
than in Porto Rico, because of the marked insufficiency and
inefficiency of the public schools.

In Santo Domingo the *Presbyterian, Methodist* and
United Brethren Boards have agreed to establish a *United
Protestant Church* without denominational distinctions,
while in Haiti the *Baptists* have been asked to assume the

primary responsibility for occupation of the field. Actual operations in both these republics are still in the initial stages.

The efficient part played by the *American Bible Society* in carrying the Bible into every part of the Latin West Indies should not go unmentioned.

OTHER WEST INDIES

Passing mention may appropriately be made here of the other islands of the West Indies, which do not belong to the Latin group. These consist of (a) *French Islands—Guadeloupe* and *Martinique,* and (b) *British Islands—Bahamas, Jamaica, Leeward Islands, Windward Islands, Barbados* and *Trinidad.* The population of all these islands consists mainly of negroes and mulattos. In the French Islands the population of half a million is nominally Roman Catholic. There is no Protestant community, and the islands have been entirely neglected by all Protestant agencies except the *American Bible Society.* As a result of Bible circulation there are a few evangelical believers.

In the British West Indies, which have a population of about 2,200,000, the long-continued labors of several leading Societies, chiefly British, have been richly rewarded, and strong indigenous churches have developed, some of which have not only become self-supporting, but are now assisting in the extension of gospel work to less favored islands and to parts of Central America—whither some of their members have migrated. At the same time the shockingly low social, intellectual and moral conditions yet prevailing among many communities, even in the most advanced islands, are an evidence of the need still existing for missionary effort.

QUESTIONS

1. How many Americas are there (a) geographically, (b) racially?

2. Compare Latin America with Anglo-Saxon America (a) in area and population, (b) in the nature of their early colonization.

3. Classify the population of Latin America racially, and give its divisions politically.

4. Give the area and population of South America, and the names by which it has been called, with the reasons for them.

5. Describe its physical features, naming its chief rivers and mountain peaks.

6. Describe the climate, resources and industries of its different parts.

7. Tell what is known about the early races of South America.

8. Trace the steps of European discovery and conquest in South America, giving dates.

9. Describe Iberian rule in South America, and the rise of the republics.

10. Describe the prevailing social and moral features of South America.

11. Cite the charges against Romanism on the ground of her record in this continent.

12. Discuss the course and character of early Roman Catholic Missions here.

13. Give a brief account of the first Protestant missionary efforts.

14. What were the Lancasterian Schools, when and by whom were they introduced, and what success did they achieve?

15. Outline the career of the great pioneer missionary to the South American Indians.

16. Name five other noted early missionaries in South America.

17. Describe the part played by the Bible Societies in South America's evangelization, giving the names of leading workers.

18. Name the chief Societies working in each South American country, and mention any important missionary institutions or other features.

19. Give the population and distribution of Indians in South America, and indicate the present points of missionary contact with them.

20. Name the countries comprising Central America, and the islands comprising the Latin, French and British West Indies.

21. Give the areas and populations of Central America, Mexico, and Latin, French and British West Indies, describe their social, moral and spiritual condition, and indicate what missionary work is being done within them.

CHAPTER XVII

OCEANIA, OR THE PACIFIC ISLANDS

I. General Features.

Divisions. The Island World is usually regarded as comprising the following groups of islands lying in the Pacific Ocean :—

Malaysia, or East Indies—including Sumatra, Java, Borneo, Celebes, the Moluccas and many smaller islands. The Philippines, while usually classed as a separate group by themselves, are closely adjacent and a part of the Malay Archipelago.

Melanesia (the Black Islands)—lying west of 180° E., east of Malaysia and south of the Equator, the principal groups being Fiji, Loyalty, New Caledonia, New Hebrides, Banks, Santa Cruz, Solomon, Bismarck and Papua or New Guinea.

Micronesia (the Little Islands)—lying north of the Equator and west of 180° E., including the Gilbert, Marshall, Caroline, Ladrone (or Mariana) and Pelew groups.

Polynesia (the Many Islands)—lying east of 180° E., including the Hawaiian, Marquesas, Paumotu (or Low Archipelago), Society, Austral, Hervey (or Cook), Tonga (or Friendly), Samoa, Ellice, Phœnix and other groups, besides almost innumerable isolated islands.

Wide Distribution. The Pacific Ocean is the largest body of water in the world, its area being more than a quarter of the earth's surface. Over this vast expanse are scattered some 30 main groups of islands, and many lesser groups and separate units. The total number of islands is estimated at 1,500, exclusive of Malaysia and the Philippines, with an area of 383,000 square miles.

To illustrate the isolation of the separate members of this great family of islands, the Carolines may be cited. This group consists of 49 islands, with a total area of only 600 square miles (one-half the size of Rhode Island), and yet

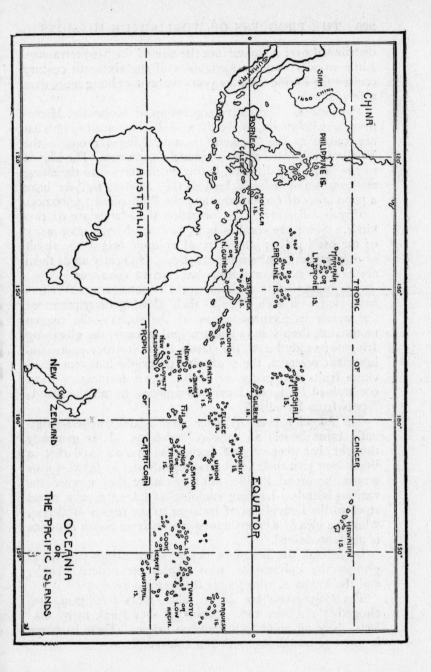

distributed over a sea-surface the size of the Mediterranean. Little wonder that the navigators of the sixteenth century cruised the Pacific for fifty years without sighting more than a few islands.

Population. The native population of Melanesia, Micronesia and Polynesia, or the three divisions constituting what are known as the "oceanic" islands, lying far out in the Pacific, is estimated at approximately 2,000,000. The islands of the Malaysian division, known in distinction to the above as "continental" islands, because they lie close to Asia, have a population of 60,700,000, and the Philippines 13,300,000.

Physical Features. In formation the islands are of two kinds. Some are coral islands, built up by the slow work of the coral polyp; others are of volcanic origin, the result of upheaval during volcanic eruption. On nearly all of them are extinct craters, and some have active volcanoes.

The beauty of this island world is entrancing. Writers have vied with each other in their glowing descriptions of the wondrous picturesqueness of the scenery, the rugged mountains, deep valleys and tranquil lagoons, the glistening fringe of sandy beach, the stately trees, feathery palms and luxuriant creepers, the profusion of bright blossoms, delicious fruits and gorgeous birds. Such features as these constrained Professor Henry Drummond to call the islands "spots from Paradise."

The Island Races. Whence these island dwellers originally came is still an unsolved problem. It is generally thought that their original home was in Asia, and that in the distant past their forebears were driven by fierce storms across the broad Pacific, until gradually they peopled the various islands. Leading ethnologists trace the main racial stock to the Dravidians of India or to the region of Persia, while the idea of a contributory stream from South America is also entertained.

In general, the Islanders may be divided into two racial groups, the Polynesians, who inhabit the eastern islands, and the Papuans, who people the western groups.

The *Polynesians* are fairer, taller, more intelligent, and altogether the finer race. Although they speak many dialects, these all point to a common origin. Their language is soft and melodious, with few consonants.

The *Papuans* are short in stature, black, frizzly-haired, with flat noses, and physically and mentally inferior to the Polynesians. They speak a multiplicity of languages which abound in consonants.

The *Fijians* stand on the border line between these two races, having strong characteristics of both.

The *Micronesians* are also a mixed race, having a Polynesian basis, but with admixtures of Japanese and Papuan blood which produce quite different types on the various islands. They are small of stature, with light brown skin, dark eyes and straight black hair.

Social Conditions. Allowing for certain racial and local differences, the customs and habits of all the Islanders are strikingly similar. For many centuries they have been completely isolated from the rest of mankind, uninfluenced by the great currents of thought and life that have so changed other parts of the world. The warmth of the climate, the ease with which they can obtain varied products from a rich soil—yam, taro, sugar cane and bananas—and an ample supply of fish from the sea, tend to develop an indolence which is one of their chief dangers. In their primitive condition they wore little or no clothing, and their homes were slight mat structures raised on posts or perched high in trees. They knew nothing of modern tools or weapons, yet with their crude stone axes and adzes they constructed wonderful canoes out of the trunks of trees. The women were clever at weaving mats from grasses and the pandanus leaf, and beating out cloth from the bark of the paper-mulberry or the breadfruit tree.

It is sad, yet true, that where nature has achieved her best, man is often found at his worst. And so these islands of enchanting beauty have been the haunts of the lowest savagery.

"Wars almost exterminated the populations of some of the islands; the immorality was appalling; from one-fourth to two-thirds of the children were buried alive; cannibalism was frequent; the sick and aged were usually killed rather than left to die a natural death." [1]

Religion. "In religion they were polytheists almost to the extent of pantheism, for nearly every object in nature was

[1] "The Pacific Islands, from Savages to Saints," p. 5.

in their eyes a god of good or evil portent. Their religious ceremonies were accompanied with sorcery, human sacrifices, and bestial orgies such as might characterize the infernal regions." [2]

"The spirits of ancestors also were worshiped and their aid sought in battle and in witchcraft. Their crowning superstition was the *tabu*. By this certain articles of food, certain localities or occupations, were forbidden under pain of death. The *tabu* forbade women to eat with men, or to eat pork, fowls, bananas or fish—in fact, most of the choice articles of food." [3]

Yet amidst all this paganism some remnant of man's nobler nature remained and at times asserted itself, and it would be an injustice not to make mention of these better traits to offset in some degree the darkness of the picture.

"In spite of all the cruelty and horror of their lives, these people maintained a sunny brightness of disposition, shared their goods with one another, practised unlimited hospitality, and in their best moments reached out toward something higher and better. Through offerings, sacrifices, charms, and ceremonies beyond number, they sought to bridge the gulf that separated them from God, but because their knowledge of God was so mistaken their lives were lived under shadows that were often black as a starless night." [4]

Contact with Civilization. The first European to look upon the broad waters of the Pacific seems to have been Balboa, who reached its eastern shores across Panama in 1513. Seven years later Magellan sailed the first European ships through the Strait which is called after him, and into what he himself named the Pacific Ocean. Other navigators and explorers followed, the most famous being Captain Cook, who was sent out by the British government, and the account of whose voyages between 1768 and 1778 did so much to awaken the interest of the West in this new part of the world.

In the wake of the navigators came whalers, traders in sandalwood, copra, pearl shells and tropical fruits, and in

---

2 "The Pacific Islands, from Savages to Saints," p. 5.
3 "Christus Redemptor," pp. 7, 8.
4 "The Kingdom in the Pacific," pp. 15, 16.

gators, there seem to have been few, in contrast to other lands, so that when the modern missionary movement began hardly any traces of them were to be found. The record begins, therefore, with Protestant effort. We shall deal here with the outstanding facts connected with a few of the main island groups.

SOCIETY ISLANDS

London Missionary Society Pioneers. The accounts of Captain Cook's voyages, which, as we saw in an earlier chapter, were an important factor in shaping Carey's missionary purpose, aroused extraordinary interest in the South Seas, so that when in 1796 the *London Missionary Society* was formed, it was decided to make these islands its first field of operation. A party of thirty missionaries sailed in September, 1796, in the *Duff,* under Captain Wilson, and in March, 1797, reached *Tahiti,* the largest of some thirteen islands comprising the Society Islands, named in honor of the Royal Geographical Society. Eighteen of the party remained here, ten went on to the Tonga (or Friendly) Islands, and two to the Marquesas. Only one of the latter remained, while those on Tonga suffered severe privations and perils, three of them were martyred and the rest finally escaped.

Early Hardships. The missionaries at Tahiti were at first well received by King Pomare, and glowing reports carried back to England by Captain Wilson called forth fresh enthusiasm and recruits. But the *Duff* on her second voyage was captured by the French, and it was five long years before supplies or communications reached the lonely workers. Meanwhile they had been reduced to sort straits, three were killed, others fled, so that when the nineteenth century dawned but five men and two women were left, the only missionaries in all the vast Pacific.

Opposing Forces. Moral and religious conditions on the island were fearful, and cruel wars were well-nigh incessant. Pomare's treatment of the missionaries fluctuated between courtesy and threats. He was a fickle and brutal king, who during his career offered 2,000 human sacrifices to his gods. He died in 1804, and his son, Pomare II, who succeeded him, at first walked in his footsteps, until the missionary outlook became as dark as possible.

Turning of the Tide. Prompted by the grave reports received from the field, a special meeting was called in London in July, 1812, to pray for Pomare's conversion, and in that very month he gave up his idols and asked for baptism. This was the turning point of the work in Tahiti. Idolatry was completely overthrown, the king sent for a printing press to prepare Bibles and hymn books for his people, and at his own expense he built a huge church, where in the presence of 4,000 of his subjects he was baptized. The light spread not only over all Tahiti, but also from island to island of this and other groups, through the efforts of the Tahitian Christians as well as the missionaries, and Tahiti will ever be known as the seed-plot from which the gospel was scattered far and wide over Oceania.

French Occupation. Unspeakably sad to relate, this new and happy state of affairs in the Society Islands was ruthlessly broken up by the greed of a so-called Christian nation. A long succession of intrigues and oppressions began with the violent intrusion of Roman Catholic propagandists in 1836, under the protection of French warships. In 1842 a French protectorate was forced upon the islands, and full annexation followed in 1880. Liquor and vice were introduced, mission schools closed, and all the work of the missionaries obstructed, until finally the London Missionary Society had to withdraw and turn over its operations to the care of the *Evangelical Society of France.*

FIJI ISLANDS

Population. This group lies on the border line between Polynesia and Melanesia, and about 1,000 miles north of New Zealand. "When first visited, more than a century ago, the population numbered about 200,000, but it has been reduced since then to 117,000 or less, largely through the ravages of certain infectious diseases." [6]

The People. Of the Fijians, Dr. D. L. Leonard says in part: "Physically and intelligently they rank among the foremost in the South Seas; but before Christianity wrought its

---

[6] "The Pacific Islanders" (1906), p. 143. But *Statesman's Year Book* for 1939 gives 198,379 as the latest estimate.

astounding miracles of transformation they had no equals
for brutality, licentiousness and utter disregard of human
life. The world over their name was a synonym for all that
is atrocious, inhuman and demoniacal." [7]

Another author writes: "In character they occupied a
preëminence of degradation unrivaled by that of any other
islanders. . . . Cannibalism, occasional on many of the
island groups, or reserved for the treatment of conquered
foes, was here elevated into a national cult and custom. The
man who had eaten the greatest number of human beings
was highest in social order. They used to mark these pleasant little achievements by memorial stones. The great chief,
Ra Undreundre, had 872 of these set up to mark his
prowess." [8]

Missionary Beginnings. The story of how the gospel was
introduced into this "annex ante-chamber to the bottomless
pit" is a novel one. It came about by means of a curious
combination of circumstances which man might regard as
pure accident, but which was unmistakably of God's design-
ing. The first ray of light came through converts from the
Tonga Islands, 300 miles east, where the *English Wesleyans*
had begun work in 1823 and had reaped a rich reward in
the conversion of several thousands. Among the Tongans
who crossed in their canoes to Lakemba, an eastern island of
the Fiji group, for purposes of trade, were some recent
Christian converts whose testimony made a deep impression upon the Fijians. This led to the sending of *Revs.
Wm. Cross* and *David Cargill* in 1835. They met with a
rough reception, several of their native Christian teachers
were killed, and their own lives were in danger. But before
long their kindness broke down the hatred and won the
good will of the savages. In five months 31 were baptized,
and 280 within one year.

But meanwhile by a stranger providence the gospel was
finding entrance into Ono, a small island 150 miles south
of Lakemba. In 1835 a terrible epidemic raged on this
island, and all the efforts of the pagan priests to overcome
it by devices to appease the angry gods utterly failed. In
this emergency one of the chiefs, crossing to Lakemba,

7 Rev. D. L. Leonard in "The Pacific Islanders," pp. 143, 144.
8 "Christus Redemptor," pp. 139, 140.

learned from another Fiji chief who had visited Tahiti that the only true God was Jehovah, and that one day in seven should be set apart for His worship. Laying hold of this fragment of truth he and his people set aside the seventh day and, dressing in their festive attire, attempted to worship this unknown God. While they were thus groping their way toward the light, a Christian Tongan teacher visited Ono and told them all he knew of the new faith. Later, other teachers were sent to them from Tonga, and a deep work of grace began. The entire population of this and a neighboring island renounced idolatrous practices. In 1839 *Rev. James Calvert,* who had the previous year reached Lakemba, was sent over to Ono, and within a few months it was given to him to baptize 200 converts.

Strongholds of Satan. As yet, however, only the outskirts of the awful realm of darkness in Fiji had been touched. The worst islands lay to the west, whither the missionaries proceeded. A fierce battle lay before them, for they seemed to be attacking the very seat of Satan. Some of the horrors which they were forced to witness— at one time the strangling of the sixteen wives of the king's son who had been drowned, at another the cooking and eating of the bodies of eleven war captives—were almost beyond endurance. For a full decade their faith continued to be sorely tested.

Wonderful Transformation. Finally, in 1845, a sweeping revival began. Several influential chiefs—one of them a monster of iniquity—came under pungent conviction of sin and were regenerated by the Spirit, and their people followed in large numbers. From these beginnings such a marvelous work of grace swept the entire islands that sixty years later there were 826 churches and 1,000 points where the gospel was regularly preached. Church members numbered 36,000, additional inquirers 17,000, and 80 per cent. of the whole population were attendants upon public worship. The baptismal font of one fine church, made out of a stone upon which formerly human victims for cannibal feasts were slaughtered, speaks eloquently of what the gospel has done in the Fiji Islands.

New Hebrides Islands

Extent and Population. This group, lying to the west of the Fiji Islands, comprises about 70 islands, some 30 of which are inhabited. The estimated population is 60,000, but among that number 20 different languages are spoken.

Three Great Missionaries. In connection with the marvelous work of transformation which has taken place among these Islanders, once ferocious savages degraded by horrid customs and steeped in gross superstition, three names will ever shine with peculiar luster. These names are John Williams, John Geddie and John G. Paton—"the three epistles of John," as they are sometimes called.

John Williams, the first of the trio and deservedly called "the Apostle of the South Seas," was identified with the New Hebrides in death rather than in life. Born in England in 1796, he was sent out by the *London Missionary Society* in 1817 to its work in the Society Islands. He was a born leader and a man of unusual resource and action, whose vision for the work reached out far beyond that of the missionaries who preceded him. Declaring that he could not content himself "within the narrow limits of a single reef," he launched a campaign of expansion and began the training of a native agency to augment the missionary force for carrying the gospel to other islands. The result was the extension of missionary effort within a few years to the Austral, Hervey, Samoan, Fiji and other groups. From first to last five mission ships, purchased or built by himself, were pressed into service by this dauntless apostle, and with such effect that by 1834 "no group of islands, nor single island of importance within 2,000 miles of Tahiti had been left unvisited." [9]

The inception of the work upon each new island involved dangers and hardships not a few, but the native workers no less than the English missionaries rose nobly to the task, and they were as nobly backed by the prayers and gifts of the native churches.

The blessing and power of God attended the efforts of Williams and his co-laborers, particularly in the case of *Raratonga* in the Hervey group, and also *Samoa,* in a degree

[9] "The New Acts of the Apostles," p. 119.

seldom paralleled elsewhere.   Says Dr. A. T. Pierson: "The changes which the Apostle to the South Seas saw defied description, and when described seem fables for the credulous.   He himself was overawed by the proofs of the hand of God.   At Tahiti over 14 years had gone by before one convert was made.   Yet Williams witnessed changes nothing short of a radical revolution, within 20, 18, 12 months, and sometimes within as many days.   He went to islands where all were heathens; he visited them later to find chapels with thousands of worshipers; he found them without a written language, and left them reading in their own tongue the wonderful words of God." [10]

Williams spent four years in England (1834-38) publishing his "Missionary Enterprises," the sale of which ran to 40,000 copies, seeing through the press the Raratongan New Testament, raising money for a new ship, securing new recruits and perfecting other plans.   His visit awakened immense new interest in South Sea Missions.

Soon after his return to the scenes of his previous triumphs in Raratonga and Samoa, he set his heart on a visit to the New Hebrides, and sailed for that group in his new ship *Camden,* taking with him 12 native teachers as pioneers. On November 20, 1839, he landed on the Island of *Erromanga* with Mr. Harris, a young man sailing in the *Camden.* All seemed pleasant at first, but suddenly a shout was heard, the natives turned upon them, and before they could make the shore both men were felled by the clubs of savages and then speared to death.   Their bodies were dragged into the bush for a horrid cannibal feast.

As the tidings of Williams' martyrdom reached Samoa a wail of profound grief rose from the hearts of thousands of converts.   But at once 25 volunteered to take his place, and in six months the *Camden* was again at Erromanga, where two were landed, but after a year of suffering were forced to withdraw.   Continued attempts were made at the cost of a number of lives and much suffering, and by 1852, through the agency of these Samoan teachers and their Erromangan converts, 100 had been won from heathenism and two chapels built.   But even after that Erromanga was stained by the blood of many another missionary martyr.

10 "The New Acts of the Apostles," pp. 118, 119.

By arrangement during Williams' visit to England, the
London Missionary Society was to open the New Hebrides
work with native workers from other islands, and the field
was then to be manned by the Presbyterians of Scotland
and Nova Scotia.

John Geddie, "the father of Presbyterian Missions in the
South Seas," reached the most southerly island of *Aneityum*
in 1848. As a boy in Nova Scotia "little Johnnie Geddie"
had pored over the stories of the heroes of the South Seas
and longed to become a missionary. Finally his persevering
efforts were rewarded and the Nova Scotian churches sent
him as their missionary.

It was through many trials and vicissitudes, and by dint
of infinite patience and perseverance, that Mr. and Mrs.
Geddie won the confidence of the natives and eventually
saw the gospel triumph over vile heathen practices and immorality. Mr. Geddie reduced the language of Aneityum
to writing, and his translation of the Gospel of Mark was
the first completed book published in any language of the
Western Pacific. He established a printing press and a
training school for native workers, and 50 evangelists have
gone forth from Aneityum to other islands, supported by the
gifts of the native church.

"On a tablet in the large church, seating 1,000 people,
this inscription was placed in memory of John Geddie:—
'When he landed in 1848 there were no Christians here;
when he left in 1872 there were no heathen.' " [11]

John G. Paton became perhaps the best known of all the
missionaries of the last generation, because of the world-
wide circulation of his wonderful autobiography. "No narrative of missionary toils and triumphs is either more read-
able or more romantic, more graphic or pathetic, or more
abundant in proofs of supernatural power." [12]

Born in a Scotch highland home, with its plain living
and high thinking, Dr. Paton was sent out in 1858 by the
Presbyterian churches of Scotland, Canada, Australia and
New Zealand, and with two associates and their wives
settled on the Island of *Tanna,* where Messrs. Turner and
Nesbit and their wives, missionaries from Samoa, had

11 "Christus Redemptor," p. 160.
12 "The New Acts of the Apostles," p. 347.

landed in 1842 and after terrible experiences had been rescued by a passing ship. For four years these new missionaries battled against all the powers of darkness. Their lives constantly threatened by dark foes and in danger of treachery from professed friends, they went steadily on, teaching, healing, and befriending all whom they could reach. But after they had displayed superhuman courage and overcome tremendous difficulties, the situation grew so grave that nothing remained but flight from the island.

Dr. Paton's subsequent labors were upon the small Island of *Aniwa,* where, after a series of experiences as thrilling as ever fell to the lot of any missionary, he finally witnessed a marvelous work of grace which changed the whole population from murderers and cannibals into the "most openly and reverently Christian community that he had ever visited." The story of this heroic man "records perhaps fifty cases in which his life was threatened, or death by violence overhung him; yet in marvelous ways deliverance came, so that his preservation seemed like a perpetual miracle." [13]

The work of evangelizing the several islands which still remain heathen, as well as caring for the churches already established, is now in the hands of the *John G. Paton Memorial Mission,* with a staff of five missionary couples and some 120 native teachers. The work includes a native teachers' training institute and three small mission hospitals.

MELANESIA

In addition to the New Hebrides and Fiji groups, the former always classed as belonging to Melanesia, the latter usually so classed, brief mention must be made of two other islands—*Santa Cruz* and *New Guinea*—because of their connection with two great missionary martyrs, Patteson and Chalmers.

Bishop Patteson. In 1849 Bishop Selwyn, the missionary bishop of New Zealand, began the work of the *Melanesian Society* of the Anglican Church of New Zealand. He cruised extensively among the islands, and established a center first at Auckland and later on Norfolk Island, where promising young men from the different islands were trained to become native teachers and evangelists among their own people.

In 1855 Selwyn was joined by John Coleridge Patteson, an Oxford graduate of rare gifts and rarer consecration. In 1861 Patteson was made missionary bishop of Melanesia, and thereafter for ten years he directed the work of island evangelization far and near with singular devotion and success. The greatest difficulty he encountered was the wicked work of white traders in carrying off Islanders for enforced labor in the plantations of Fiji and Queensland. He fought this fiendish traffic with all his power.

It was in 1871 that with a group of his beloved island workers in the *Southern Cross* he headed for Nikapu, one of the Santa Cruz Islands. Landing alone and without suspecting any harm, he was cruelly murdered and his body placed in a canoe to drift back to the ship. Upon his breast had been inflicted five wounds covered over with a palm branch tied in five mysterious knots. It was learned later that this signified that the deed was done in revenge for the kidnaping and death of five natives at the hands of white traders some time before. It is reported that work is being carried on vigorously in over 30 islands by Bishop Patteson's Society. Young people from all these islands are being trained on Norfolk Island, and in 1905 there were already 550 natives teaching in 250 schools and churches with more than 16,000 scholars, while there were over 12,000 baptized members in the native church of Melanesia.

James Chalmers. The name of this other great missionary will ever be associated with Papua or *New Guinea,* the land for which he laid down his life as a martyr.

New Guinea has the distinction of being the largest island in the world. Its area is 312,000 square miles, or more than the combined area of all the other Pacific islands to the east of it, comprising Melanesia, Polynesia and Micronesia. "If you were to place the map of New Guinea upon the map of America it would stretch from New York to Omaha, and from Canada to St. Louis." [14] It is thus a vast country of high mountains, forest-clad valleys, broad plains, great rivers and rich resources still largely undeveloped. Indeed,

[14] Rev. C. W. Abel in *The Missionary Review of the World,* March, 1923, p. 187.

although the island was discovered by the Portuguese in 1511, a great portion remains yet unexplored, owing to the trying climate and the ferocity of the natives.

The northwest section now belongs to the Dutch, the southeast (and since the War the northeast, which was formerly German) to the British. The whole native population is estimated at 1,000,000.

James Chalmers, called by Robert Louis Stevenson the "Great Heart of New Guinea," was born in Scotland, and as a boy received the missionary vision through hearing an address on the Fiji Islands. He and his wife were sent out by the *London Missionary Society,* in 1867, to Raratonga, where they spent ten years.

When Chalmers went to New Guinea in 1877 the work there, already begun by such noble men as *Dr. MacFarlane* and *Dr. Lawes,* was in its early pioneer stage. Chalmers with his physical strength, superb courage, quick intuition, tact and resourcefulness, was eminently fitted for pioneering. He pursued a policy of broad exploration and the planting of a chain of stations at intervals along the coast. His career was marked by many thrilling adventures and hairbreadth escapes. His heroic character and splendid achievements were among the foremost influences that changed Stevenson from a prejudiced critic to an enthusiastic friend of missions.

Chalmers twice revisited England, and threw himself with tremendous energy into presenting missions in great meetings throughout the country. His simplicity, fervor and contagious enthusiasm stirred thousands to new missionary interest.

His thirty-three years of lofty service ended in martyrdom in 1901. Together with a young missionary named Tomkins and several native helpers Chalmers landed on Goaribari Island to make some explorations. Without warning they were set upon by the savages, clubbed to death and their bodies eaten. The news of Chalmers' death was received with passionate sorrow by the thousands of natives to whom he had been friend and father. Later, a monument to the martyrs was erected on the spot, and a church now stands near the ground where their red blood stained the sands.

The *London Missionary Society* now has 11 stations
along the southern coast of New Guinea, at an average of
50 miles apart, while the *Anglican, Wesleyan* and *Lutheran
churches* of Australia occupy some 40 points on the east
coast. The *Kwato Mission of Papua* was founded in 1890
by *Rev. Charles W. Abel*, at that time a missionary of the
London Missionary Society and for eleven years associated
with *James Chalmers*. Mr. Abel died in 1930. The work
is being carried on by the *New Guinea Evangelization Society* of America, organized in 1923, and the *Kwato Extension Association*, an interdenominational society founded in
1918. There are 20 missionaries in eastern Papua, with six
stations, 27 outstations, and 4,000 baptized converts. Unworked territory to the west has been entered.

HAWAIIAN ISLANDS

Special interest attaches to this group because of the complete transformation wrought by the gospel within an incredibly short time.

Discovery. The islands were discovered in 1778 by the
famous English navigator, Captain Cook, who named them
the Sandwich Islands. Cook was killed by the natives in
an unfortunate affray. Hawaii lies at the "cross-roads of
the Pacific," over 2,000 miles from San Francisco, and is
the central point of a great network of ocean highways between all parts of America and Asia, as well as the other
Pacific Islands groups.

Size and Population. The islands have an area of 6,435
square miles, slightly smaller than New Jersey, and a population of 411,485, according to the latest reliable estimate.[15]
An analysis of this population is significant as showing how
the bulk of the inhabitants are no longer Hawaiians, but belong to other races, the Japanese largely predominating.
The exact figures are: Hawaiians, 21,268; part Hawaiians,
40,867; Chinese, 28,380; Japanese, 153,539; Portuguese,
30,406; Filipinos, 52,810; Porto Ricans, 7,639; Spanish,
1,248; Koreans, 6,707; Americans, British, Germans and
Russians, 62,798; others, 915. The serious bearing of such
a diversified population upon missionary work is obvious.

Physical Features. The islands are largely of volcanic

15 Estimate of June 30, 1938. See *Statesman's Year Book* (1939).

origin and contain a number of noted active volcanoes. Their exquisite natural beauty and fertility, together with their delightful climate, have won for them the name "Paradise of the Pacific."

Early Conditions. Like the other Islanders, the Hawaiians were sunk in the lowest social degradation and moral pollution, and given over to spirit-worship and all sorts of debasing superstition. The *tabu* had here reached a highly developed system which held the people in its tyrannous grip.

These terrible conditions were further aggravated by the visits of white traders, who violated every law of God and man, dealt treacherously and brutally with the natives, indulged in shameless debauchery, and introduced rum and venereal diseases which wrought fearful havoc and decimated the population.

How the Gospel Entered. The story of how the gospel first entered Hawaii is one of unusual interest. A Hawaiian lad named Obookiah escaping from a tribal war was brought to America by a kind-hearted ship captain. He was found one morning weeping upon the steps of Yale College, in despair of getting an education for which he longed. Some Christian students, Samuel J. Mills among them, befriended him, and his education was provided for. He became a Christian, and was zealously preparing to go back as a missionary to his people when he sickened and died. But his example had stirred the hearts of others. *Hiram Bingham,* a student of Andover, volunteered to go in his stead, others joined him, and on October 17, 1819, a company of seventeen set sail from Boston and reached the islands in March, 1820. Thus began the famous Mission of the *American Board* to the Hawaiian Islands.

Idolatry Banished. These first missionaries on their arrival found a situation altogether unique. A strong and able chieftain, *Kamehameha I,* had succeeded in uniting the islands in one powerful state, and thus putting an end to the constant and bloody wars. Moreover, a reaction had set in against idolatry, mainly because of tidings which had come concerning the wonderful changes wrought by the gospel in Tahiti and other southern islands. The Hawaiians had turned against their idols, destroyed their temples and

made a beginning at abolishing the *tabu*. The missionaries
were astonished to find a people actually without a religion.

Yet there were difficulties enough still to face, one of the
most formidable being the vicious influence of unprincipled
white traders. These wickedly sought to turn the king and
people against the missionaries by subtle lies about their
aims, and persistently opposed every effort for reform.
Nevertheless the work took root, the language was reduced
to writing, a printing press established and stations opened
on several islands.

Royal Converts. Among the first converts were the
queen, the queen-mother and other members of the royal
family, who became devout Christians and took an active
interest in the work of the gospel. The most famous of all
Hawaiian converts was the high chiefess *Kapiolani,* in whom
the grace of God wrought a marvelous change. The story
is a thrilling one of how she resolved to break the lingering
hold of superstition upon her people by defying the much-
feared goddess Pele, who had her abode in the depths of the
fiery volcano Kilauea. Against the pleadings of her ter-
rorized subjects she made the terrible journey of a hundred
miles on foot over rough lava beds, ate freely of the berries
sacred to Pele, and fearlessly ascending to the very brink
of the crater hurled stone after stone into the great lake of
fire, challenging the reputed fire-goddess to avenge herself.
"It was a brave and heroic deed that has been likened to that
of Elijah on Mt. Carmel, challenging the priests of Baal,
and to Boniface in Germany, cutting down the sacred oak
of Thor," [16] and it had its similar effect upon the people.

The Great Awakening. For some years the numerical
growth of the church was small, the missionaries being extremely careful not to admit any who might wish to adopt
the new faith merely in imitation of their rulers. By 1825
there were only 10 baptized members, and by 1832 only
577 in all the islands. Then, in 1837, came "The Great
Awakening," largely the result under God of the evangelistic tours of *Rev. Titus Coan.* A wave of spiritual revival
swept the island, congregations increased to thousands, and
the missionaries labored day and night with throngs of
anxious inquirers. On one memorable Sabbath day at Hilo,

[16] "The Transformation of Hawaii," p. 100.

1,705 were baptized by Mr. Coan, and 2,400 sat down at the Lord's table.

Under the heading *"The Pentecost at Hilo"* Dr. Pierson has graphically described the wonderful scenes witnessed as a result of the Holy Spirit's work. The revival continued in full force until 1843, and during those six years about 27,000 converts were received into the church. Ultimately this awakening brought about the transformation of the social, political and industrial life of the island.

Growth and Extension. The robust character of the Christian churches of Hawaii early showed itself in their efforts to spread the gospel to other island groups. In 1852 they joined enthusiastically with the American Board in launching the first mission in *Micronesia,* and have ever since continued to send and support their own representatives there. The work in these islands has passed through the same successive stages and accomplished the same cheering results as in those already mentioned, until the foreign missionary agencies have been able gradually to withdraw and to entrust the spiritual interests of the now largely evangelized islands to the well-developed native churches.

So great was the advance towards a Christian civilization in the Hawaiian Islands that the American Board in 1870, on its fiftieth anniversary of the founding of the Mission, announced its decision to withdraw from the field, leaving the work entirely under native leadership.

Annexation to U. S. A. In 1894 Hawaii became a republic, in 1898 it was annexed to the United States, and in 1900 it was organized as a Territory. Missionary problems have since been greatly complicated by the influx in such large numbers of other races, chiefly Japanese and Chinese, bringing with them their heathen religions and customs.

PHILIPPINE ISLANDS

Location, Area and Population. These islands, called by some writers "The Land of the Palm and the Pine," lie about 500 miles east of Indo-China, and are separated from Borneo, of the Malaysian group, by the Sulu Sea. There are some 7,000 islands and islets, more than a thousand of

which are named. Eleven are large and important, the
largest being *Luzon* in the north, and the next *Mindanao*
in the south. The total land area is 114,000 square miles,
or about equal to New England and New York, and nearly
as large as Great Britain and Ireland. The population, according to the latest estimate, approximates 13,300,000.

Physical Features and Resources. The islands are volcanic in origin, with a number of volcanoes still active,
mountainous and well wooded, and they possess a wealth of
verdure and a rich soil yielding heavy crops of rice, hemp,
sugar cane and tobacco. The cocoanut industry is one of
the largest, and rubber plantations are now assuming importance. Mineral resources are also great, but as yet undeveloped.

The climate is tropical, with wet and dry seasons, but
varies considerably in different parts according to elevation.
Though hot, it is not unhealthy, and with present improved
facilities Americans can live here comfortably.

The People. The great variety of tribal divisions and
languages to be found on the islands has led many writers
to erroneous statements about the diverse character of the
people. More careful study has shown a high degree of
solidarity of race among the native population.

The Negritos are regarded as being the aborigines of the
islands, driven back into the interior by the invading race.
They are diminutive blacks, living in a semi-savage state,
and are slowly dying out.

Apart from these, the Philippine Islanders give evidence
of being Malay in origin, the differences among them being
accounted for by earlier and later migrations. Of these
there are three main divisions, known as Igorrotes, Moros
and Filipinos.

The *Igorrotes,* lowest in social order, consist of a number
of more or less fierce tribes living mainly in the mountains.
They probably represent an earlier migration of more primitive Malay stock, and are strong, energetic people—fine material in the rough. They still retain their primitive pagan
religions.

The *Moros* are "Mohammedan Malays who were rapidly
pushing their conquest of the Archipelago when the Span
iards conquered the islands. Their advance was checked by

the Spaniards and they were driven off the northern islands and confined for the most part to the Sulu Archipelago and the island of Mindanao." [17]   They are divided into several tribes, and hold fanatically to a degraded form of Moslem faith.

Neither the Igorrotes nor the Moros were ever brought under control during the Spanish occupation, but they have begun to yield encouragingly to the fairer and more tactful dealings of the American administration.

The *Filipinos,* traced to a later migration of Malay stock, constitute nine-tenths of the native population.   They are the highest type of the Islanders, have been more or less nominally converted by the Spaniards to the Roman Catholic faith, and are known as *Christian Filipinos.*

In addition to these native races there is a large foreign population, representing many nationalities—Spanish, Portuguese, Chinese, Korean, Siamese, etc.   Of these the Spanish and Chinese have all along been the most numerous and have exerted the deepest influence upon the Philippines. Both have intermarried with the Filipinos, giving rise to an influential *mestizo,* or half-caste population.   The Spanish *mestizos* became the aristocrats of the Philippines.   The Chinese, who began to trade with the islands even before their discovery by Magellan, have by their keen business ability and industry easily captured the bulk of trade from the easy-going and none-too-industrious Filipino, and are to-day everywhere the leading merchants.

Historical Résumé.   The Philippines were discovered in 1521 by Magellan, the Portuguese navigator, and later were named in honor of Philip of Spain.   The first serious attempt to colonize and Christianize them was made by Legaspi in 1564.   Spain kept possession until 1898, when by the swift victory of Admiral Dewey over the Spanish fleet in Manila Bay her supremacy was broken and the Philippines passed into the hands of the United States.

The Old and New Régimes.   Spain is to be credited with some accomplishments in the islands.   She introduced the beginnings of civilization, reduced the principal dialects to writing, gave some education to the upper classes, and supplanted heathen religion by at least the form of Christianity,

17 "Christus Redemptor," p. 221.

with its truer viewpoint and higher ideals. But what she failed to do stands out far more prominently than what she did, and the record of her stewardship is one of superficiality and inefficiency.

American occupation found the islands at a low level materially, intellectually, morally, religiously. It is safe to say that the first twenty years of the new régime have seen more accomplished for the advancement and welfare of the Islanders than four centuries of the old.

Particularly noteworthy has been the new educational system introduced by the United States government. Within three years of the transfer of the islands the first shipload of 500 American teachers had landed in Manila, and five years later the enrolment of pupils in the secular schools had reached 500,000. With practical ends in view, stress has been laid upon industrial and normal training, until the work of American teachers is now largely supervisory and the bulk of the teaching is in the hands of trained Filipinos. In 1937 there were 7,938 public schools, with 99 American and 28,385 Filipino teachers.

The Roman Catholic Friars. Under the Spanish régime the political power passed to the ecclesiastical leaders. The Report of the Taft Commission says: "The friars, priests and bishops constituted a solid, powerful, permanent, well-organized, political force which dominated policies." [18] They acquired property to an enormous value, all free of taxation. They enriched themselves by exorbitant fees for religious rites, stifled all freedom of thought, and imposed a galling yoke of oppression upon the people. Besides all this, their foul sensuality has made their profession of celibacy a stench, and has been a prime factor in bringing about a general condition of shocking sexual immorality.

Moreover, the Roman Catholic Church has not censured, but has rather tolerated, the social evils of cock-fighting and gambling, so prevalent and ruinous in Filipino life. The record of Roman Catholicism in the Philippines, therefore, is practically the same as in Latin America. It has been largely a hollow farce of external rites and priestly trappery, devoid of reality and saving power.

Evangelical Missions. In the light of what has just been

18 Quoted in "The New Era in the Philippines," p. 126.

said, no apology need be offered for the prompt entry of Protestant missionary agencies into the field when control passed from Spain to America, and religious liberty was established. A conference of American Mission Boards was called and an agreement made for the division of the field, with Manila as a common center.

The first permanent missionaries to enter were *Rev. and Mrs. J. B. Rodgers,* of the *Presbyterian* Board, who arrived in April, 1899. The *Methodist Episcopal* and *Baptist* Boards began work in 1900, followed very soon by the *United Brethren, Disciples* and *Protestant Episcopal* and later the *American Board* and *Christian and Missionary Alliance.* Two great *Bible Societies*—the British and Foreign and the American—were also early on the ground to contribute their invaluable aid.

Rapidity of Results. From the very first the evangelistic work met with a warm response from the people. In the Presbyterian work in Manila alone there were 9 converts the first year, 27 the second, 200 the third, and 410 the fourth. In other stations and societies there were similar results. Within five years after the first missionary landed there were over 2,000 adult Protestant Christians in the islands; now there are at least 194,000.

Accessory Methods. Educational and medical work have been added to evangelism. The first Mission hospital was opened by the Presbyterians at Iloilo in 1901, and the first Mission boarding school was the now prominent *Silliman Institute* at Dumaguete, on the island of Negros.

A fruitful agency has been the Christian hostels for Filipino students attending the Government schools of higher learning in the large centers. These hostels surround the students with moral safeguards and pure spiritual influences in the midst of strong temptations, and they have been the means of winning many of these bright young people to Christ and leading some of them to dedicate their lives to His service.

Unreached Sections. It must be remembered that missionary work thus far has been almost wholly confined to the so-called "Christian" Filipino population. The Mohammedan Moros and the pagan tribes, together numbering nearly a million, have scarcely been touched. These present a field of pressing need and no little difficulty, and there should be no further delay in entering that field.

America's Stewardship. In the providence of God the privilege and responsibility of ministering to the spiritual need of these 13,300,000 bright, responsive, but hitherto neglected Islanders has been entrusted to the Christians of America. It is not enough to give the Philippine Islanders liberty and education, and to train them for ultimate self-government, high and worthy as these objects are. They need to know the only true God and Jesus Christ whom He hath sent to be their Saviour. Will the true followers of Christ in America see to it that this knowledge is given them, given *all* of them, and without delay?

MALAYSIA

Location. Malaysia consists of a vast Archipelago of large and small islands lying between southeastern Asia and New Guinea and Australia. These islands are otherwise known as the *Dutch East Indies,* with the exception of *North Borneo,* which is British, and *North Timor,* which is Portuguese.

Population and Races. This division of the Island World covers a vast expanse of 873,000 square miles, and has a population of over 61,000,000.

This population presents one of the greatest mixtures of racial elements to be found anywhere in the world. There are the indigenous races such as the *Malays, Javanese, Sundanese, Bataks* of Sumatra, *Dyaks* of Borneo and a host of others. Then come the *Chinese,* both Straits-born and from China, numbering a million or more and speaking five different dialects, *Tamils* and *Telugus* from India, *Arabs, Eurasians* of all varieties, a large number of *Europeans* of different nationalities, and finally quite a few *Americans.* Singapore, on the tip of the adjoining Malay Peninsula, which serves as a great rendezvous and distributing point for the island races, is perhaps the most cosmopolitan city in the world, and throughout Malaysia 150 languages are said to be spoken.

The Missionary Problem. Missions face the task of reaching three main classes:

(1) *Mohammedans.* These form the bulk of the population, numbering perhaps 40,000,000. Islam began its penetration of this region as early as 1200 A.D. To-day it holds religious sway over most of the indigenous tribes, and is advancing rapidly with the hope of absorbing the remaining heathen. Fortunately Mohammedans here are more approachable and more easily influenced by the gospel than elsewhere, so that the fruits of missionary work among them are many times larger than in the Near East. But the situation calls for prompt and energetic action, for no less than 20,000 Arabs are here zealously carrying on Moslem propaganda, and the ever-increasing pilgrimages to Mecca are binding Malaysia more and more closely to Islam.

(2) *Chinese.* These are already numerous and are said to be increasing by immigration at the rate of 250,000 a year. They are the most industrious and progressive element and have become the commercial masters of the Archipelago. With their keenness for Western education and enlightenment they show a disposition to support liberally Christian schools. They constitute a strategic base, both for Malaysia and for China itself, and their thorough evangelization is imperative.

(3) *Native Heathen Tribes.* Perhaps eight or nine million aborigines remain who have not yet been laid hold of by Islam. These belong mostly to inland tribes difficult of access. They are very low in the social scale, some of them still wild cannibals. But missionary effort among them, notably on Sumatra and Celebes, has already been blessed with abundant harvests, and they are becoming more and more open to the gospel.

Missionary Occupation. Christianity was introduced into the Archipelago in the sevententh century by the ministers of the Dutch East India Company, but it was of a very low order, and the early missionaries of the *Netherlands Missionary Society,* which in 1812 began work in the islands, found the professed Christians so degenerate as to be scarcely distinguishable from the heathen. They labored faithfully among them, however, with good results. Other *Dutch Societies* followed, as well as the *Rhenish Mission* from Germany, and to-day eight or more continental agencies are still at work. The pioneer missionaries suffered severe hardships and dangers and some were martyred. The records contain some noble names, albeit little known in English-speaking countries.

The *American Methodist Episcopal Mission* also opened work in 1905, while in 1929 the *Christian and Missionary Alliance,* in conjunction with the *Chinese Foreign Missionary Union* of South China, entered this field. This last combined agency, with headquarters at Makassar in Celebes, has been greatly blessed of God. It has pressed on aggressively into hitherto unreached territory, and after only 10 years has work in different parts of Celebes and Borneo, in Sumatra and several adjacent islands, and has recently blazed a new trail into Dutch New Guinea. It reports a staff of 31 American and 23 Chinese missionaries, 131 native workers, and nearly 11,000 baptized Christians in 94 organized groups.

Altogether the missionaries in this broad Archipelago number close to 600, and the native Christian membership is about 600,000, including 50,000 converted Moslems.

Unevangelized Territory. Recent surveys of Malaysia call attention to large portions of Sumatra, Borneo, Celebes, and even Java, together with such islands as Banka, Madura, Flores, Timor, Bali, Lombok, and several of the Molucca and Sulu groups, as yet being without any missionary work. Areas peopled with 12,000,000 are definitely closed to Missions, while at least an equal number in parts open to the Gospel have not been reached. In all the islands except Bali and Lombok, where Hinduism prevails, Islam is either dominant or is rapidly displacing paganism. This fact makes their evangelization the more urgent.

Conclusion

Nowhere has the gospel won more glorious triumphs or wrought more wonderful transformations than in the Island World. But nowhere have spiritual victories cost more dearly. They are sealed with the blood of many a martyr and bear the scars of heroic sacrifice and suffering.

In some parts of Oceania the work of evangelization is complete, in others it is only partially done, while there are parts which still await the beginning of work. "Nearly a million-and-a-half of the total population [mainly in New Caledonia, Papua, New Hebrides, Santa Cruz, the Solomon and Bismarck Islands] are still unreached by the Christian Church, even in a region which has been popularly considered as a most successful mission field." [19]

The years that have passed since this ocean field was entered have increased, rather than diminished, the missionary problems. The influence of trade and "civilized" vices is penetrating more and more deeply. Practically every one of the island groups has now come under the political control of one or other of the Great Powers, and the sad fact is that this has proven with few exceptions to be to the moral and spiritual detriment of the Islanders. Under French rule, which now extends over a population of about 80,000 in the South Seas, Protestant Missions find themselves thwarted and hindered.

Commercial expansion has led to the introduction of Asiatic labor into the Pacific. In the Fijis alone there are now 40,000 Indian coolies. This means for the imported Asiatics a life little different from absolute slavery. It means for the Islanders fresh exposure to the influences of false religion. "The Moslems among the coolies are strenuously seeking to win not only the Hindus, but also the Christian Fijians, to Islam. Whether they succeed or not, the coolie element is increasing so rapidly that Fiji will soon be heathen again. The islands that were won so gloriously, and at such a cost of blood and treasure, are passing under the sway of Islam before the very eyes of the Church, and she does practically nothing till Islam has obtained a tremendous advantage; and what is happening in Fiji is just what is bound to happen all over the Pacific." [20]

Must it ever be that the "children of this world are wiser . . . than the children of light?" Will the churches of Christendom awaken to see the dangers that threaten to reverse the victories already won, and will they bestir themselves to worthier efforts to check the challenging forces, and strengthen and complete the good work so well begun? The future of the Pacific Islands hangs upon the answer to this question.

[19] "Missionary Survey of the Pacific Islands," 1930, p. iii.
[20] "The Kingdom in the Pacific," pp. 121, 122.

QUESTIONS

1. Give the great divisions of the Island World, and the main islands or groups in each.

2. Give some idea of the number, extent of distribution and population of the Pacific Islands, and describe their physical features.

3. Divide the Islanders into racial groups, and describe briefly each one.

4. Describe the social and religious life of the Islanders before Christianity reached them.

5. Tell how civilization first touched the islands, and what its prevailing effect has been.

6. Give some account of the aggressions of European Governments in the Pacific.

7. Sketch the story of Missions in each of the following island groups, giving dates, names of prominent Societies, missionaries and converts: (a) Society, (b) Fiji, (c) New Hebrides, (d) Hawaii.

8. Give an account of the martyr missionary of (a) Santa Cruz, (b) New Guinea, and the subsequent development of the work in those islands.

9. Give the location, size, population, physical features and resources of the Philippines.

10. Name and describe the main divisions of the people of the Philippines.

11. Outline the history of the Philippines, and contrast the old and new governmental régimes.

12. Describe the character of the Roman Catholic Friars and their work.

13. Sketch Protestant missionary work in the Philippines, giving date of first missionary arrival, names of main Societies, and some idea of the results.

14. Give the area and population of Malaysia, and some idea of the variety of races and languages.

15. Name the chief Societies working in Malaysia, and describe the three distinctive classes to be reached.

16. What proportion of the Island World is still unevangelized, and what detrimental influences are at work where the gospel has already gone?

Chapter XVIII

THE JEWS

The only reference thus far made to the Jews in this volume is in connection with Palestine and the Near East, but the great bulk of the Hebrew race lives no longer in the Holy Land, but in Europe and North America. While these two continents do not fall within the geographical scope of our present missionary survey, yet that survey would be seriously incomplete without some further mention of the race which, although it gave the world its Redeemer and its first Christian missionaries, is now scattered far and wide, a fugitive among all nations, and is as needy of missionary effort as any heathen or Moslem people.

Number and Distribution. According to the *American Jewish Year Book* for 1938-39, the total Jewish population of the world is slightly under 15,300,000. The distribution by continents is:—

Europe	9,137,051	or 59.75%
North and South America	4,740,048	or 31.00%
Asia	785,133	or 5.13%
Africa	601,797	or 3.94%
Australasia	26,954	or 0.18%
	15,290,983	100.00%

The above figures show that nearly two-thirds of the Jews live in Europe, and nearly one-third in North and South America. The other three continents combined have only between 7 and 8 per cent. of the total population.

The countries having the largest Jewish population are: United States, 4,228,000; Poland, 3,029,000; Ukrania, 1,-574,000; remainder of European Russia, 733,000; Roumania, 728,000; Germany, 500,000; Hungary, 445,000; Czecho-Slovakia, 357,000; Austria, 191,000; British Isles, 300,000; France, 240,000; Argentina, 260,000.

The vast majority of Jews in every country live in the larger cities in separate communities, closely packed together, and distinct in social life from the surrounding Gentiles. Greater New York has 1,765,000 Jews, the largest Jewish population of any city in the world. Chicago has 300,000, Philadelphia 247,000, and eight other U. S. A. cities have each between 50,000 and 100,000.

Language. Most Jews speak the language of the country in which they dwell. In addition, however, *Yiddish* is spoken by perhaps nine-tenths of all the Jews, including the majority of those in continental Europe, the British Empire and the United States. Yiddish has been well called the international tongue of the Jews throughout the world. It is not based upon any Eastern language, but is a corrupt German of the Middle Ages with a sprinkling of Polish and Hebrew words, written with Hebrew characters. A very extensive literature has sprung up in this exclusively Jewish tongue, and at least twenty-five newspapers are published in it. In the case of many of the poorer classes it is the only language known, making it necessary for the Jewish missionary to learn it in order to reach his hearers.

Progress and Prominence. The Jews are in many ways the most remarkable race in the world. Next to the Chinese and the Egyptians they are the oldest race, with a history that stretches back over 3,800 years. Threatened with national destruction at least five times in the course of their history, they have been divinely preserved, and to-day they are more in number, probably, than at any previous time. Always and everywhere an object of dislike and prejudice, and many times of plunder and massacre, they have not merely survived. not merely increased in number, but have made for themselves a worthy record of progress and achievement along every line, intellectual, social, political and commercial. The Jew has become a factor of prime importance in every civilized nation, and the Jewish question holds the attention of the entire world to-day.

The names of Jews stand high in the list of distinguished men of letters, historians, poets, novelists, journalists, scientists, musicians, artists, scholars, educationalists, physicians, lawyers, bankers and capitalists down through history.

As to the prominence and influence of the Jews in America the following facts relating to New York City speak for themselves. A trifle under 30 per cent. of the population of that greatest American metropolis is Jewish. Yet the Jews have their grip tightly upon the chief wholesale and retail business, own and control all theaters and comprise the bulk of industrial workers. They own at least two of the English daily newspapers, six English weeklies, and 50 other periodicals in English, Yiddish or Hebrew. Of the public school children 38 per cent. are Jewish, while a survey of nine of the leading colleges and universities in 1918-19 showed 38½ per cent. of their entire student body to be Jewish.

In a striking article entitled, "Is there Room for the Jew?" in the *Missionary Review of the World* for December, 1915, Rev. S. B. Rohold sets forth a striking array of facts and figures to show the vital place of the Jew in the affairs of the great nations, and particularly his contribution in men, money and brains to the World War. At that early stage of the War 550,000 Hebrew soldiers were already in the ranks—*double* the proportion of Gentiles engaged—and many of them won distinction and were awarded decorations for deeds of heroism. In Great Britain five Hebrews were holding positions in the Cabinet, five were in the House of Lords, six were Privy Councilors, sixteen were Baronets, fourteen were Knights, and eighteen were members of Parliament. It was *Lord Reading,* Britain's Lord Chief Justice—a Jew—who at a crisis moment secured for Britain and her Allies a loan of $500,000,000 in the United States, in the face of strong opposition. It was *Henry Morgenthau*—a Jew—who as Ambassador for the United States at Constantinople during the War bore a superhuman strain of responsibility for the lives, property and interests in Turkey of the citizens of ten other nations besides America, and won the praise and gratitude of all alike for his devoted and splendid service. It was *Herr Arthur Ballin*—a Jew—who organized and directed that wonderful railway transportation system of Germany by which the Kaiser's troops were skilfully transferred time after time, and with tremendous effect, from one fighting front to another. These are but a few instances among many which the article in question cites. Summing up, Mr. Rohold says: "The Jew, imperishable as ever, has been strenuously leading in all the episodes of the War, in its politics, in its economy, in its finances, in its organizations, in its supplies, in its armies and in its horrors. The Jew is not wanted, yet at the same time he is being sought after, especially by the warring nations."

Religious Conditions. As to religion the Jews are divided into two main classes or sects—Orthodox and Reformed.

The *Orthodox Jews* are found principally in Eastern Europe and the Near East, and also in America and London. They accept the Old Testament and also the traditions of their fathers as contained in the Talmud, and they look and long for the coming of the Messiah and for restoration to their own land. They answer to the Pharisees of old.

Reformed Jews are found mostly in Germany, France, Italy, the British Empire and America. The sect was founded in Germany less than a century ago, and has had its fullest development in America through the late Rabbi Wise and others. Reformed Jews belong mostly to the well-to-do, educated classes. They reject the Talmud and the inspiration of the Old Testament, have given up the hope of a personal Messiah and of a return to Palestine, and have practically become Judaistic Unitarians. They answer to the Sadducees of old. To some extent they imitate Christian methods in worship and church work, in many cases even to the holding of their religious services on Sunday.

"In a general way it can well be said that the Jews the world over are religiously disintegrating, and that the younger generation is drifting away from the religion of the fathers." [1]

Jewish Missions. We cannot here attempt any account of Jewish Missions through the first eighteen centuries of the Christian era, with their ebb and flow of enthusiasm, early successes and medieval persecutions, revived interest after the Reformation, and subsequent decline and disappearance before the wave of German rationalism.

Modern Missions to Jews began in 1809 with the founding of the London Society for Promoting Christianity among the Jews, more commonly known as the *London Jews' Society.* Its scope, originally confined to London,

[1] "Report of World Missionary Conference," Edinburgh, Vol. I, p. 272.

gradually extended, as doors opened, until it has Missions in almost all parts of the world—Europe, Asia, Africa and America. This Society in 1930 reported a staff of 215 missionaries, some 45 of whom were Christian Jews.

From time to time other Societies entered the field— British, Continental, American, Canadian, Asiatic, Austral- asian and African. Accurate figures as to the present num- ber of missionary agencies and workers among the Jews throughout the world are difficult to secure. A good deal of the work in Europe was disrupted by the War, and is only now beginning to be resumed. On the other hand, the forces in the United States and in Palestine have increased since the War. It is probably pretty near the mark to say that there are about 150 Jewish missionary agencies, with 800 workers. Many of these agencies, however, carry on work in only one center, with one or two workers and very limited equipment.

Methods of Work. The equipment of the larger centers of work among Jews is varied and extensive. The staff usually consists of one or more missionaries, Gentile or Jewish, who can speak Hebrew or Yiddish and also the local language of the community, assistants for house-to-house visitation, colporteurs, Bible women, school teachers, doctors and nurses.

The departments of work embrace preaching in halls and on the street, distribution of literature by colporteurs and in Bible depots, day, boarding and Sunday schools, mother's meetings, classes for sewing, cooking, etc., hospital and dis- pensary. Comparatively few centers combine all of these features. Direct preaching has nearly always held the fore- most place, and the distribution of the Word has gone hand in hand with it. In some countries, where laws restrict pub- lic preaching, colportage work and Bible depots have been the most important methods.

Medical work has been a fruitful means of overcoming prejudice and winning open doors among the Jewish masses, while schoolwork has attracted great numbers of children, in spite of the bitter opposition of the Jewish leaders.

Missionary effort, however, has been largely confined to the common classes of Orthodox Jews, and the mission methods ordinarily employed are not well adapted to reaching and influencing the more educated and cultured Jews.

Results Achieved. The results of Jewish Missions are much greater than they are generally thought to be. Their success can never be measured by statistical tables. For example, a number of missions do not baptize converts or receive them into church membership, but confine themselves to evangelization. Many converted Jews remain secret disciples because of the ostracism, persecution, and in not a few cases danger to their very lives, which open confession of Christ would involve. Still others change their abode and later on are baptized in some Christian church or another mission. And yet it is stated on good authority that during the nineteenth century 224,000 Jews were baptized, of which number about one-third entered the Protestant Church and the remainder the Greek and Roman Catholic Churches. Protestant converts were one to 156 of the Jewish population, while the converts from heathen and Moslem nations were only one to 525. Since the War it is estimated that 100,000 Jews have been baptized.

In quality and worth Jewish converts stand very high. Thousands among them have heroically endured fierce persecution for Christ's sake, while a large percentage have become preachers of the gospel. Hebrew Christians constitute a large majority of the missionaries among the Jews to-day.

In the list of converted Jews stand such honored names as *Saphir, Edersheim, Neander, Schereschewsky, Rabinowitz,* and many more.

But the indirect results of Jewish missionary work are noteworthy, as well as the direct. The bitter prejudice of Jews against Christ and Christianity has been greatly modified. The no less bitter spirit among Gentiles toward the Jews, which goes under the name of anti-Semitism, has been lessened. The manifestation of Christian love by the missionaries, and especially such practical forms of Christian service as medical and relief work, have proven a happy and effective antidote to the shameful and un-Christian persecution of Jewish communities in Europe and the insulting treatment of Jews in other parts.

One need but scan a current issue of any one of the several excellent Jewish missionary magazines to be impressed with the fruitfulness and hopefulness of work among Hebrews everywhere, despite all attendant difficulties and handicaps.

The Task Remaining. With a very few possible exceptions, no part of the Jewish mission field is yet adequately occupied. New York City, for example, with 1,765,000 Jews, or nearly half the entire number in the United States, has half-a-dozen Missions, each with a mere handful of workers and very inadequate equipment. There are 21 other American cities each with 20,000 or more Jews, and 193 cities each with over 1,000, in many of which there is not a single worker among the Jewish residents.

The Christian forces at work among the millions of Jews in Eastern Europe are hopelessly insufficient, while practically no effort is being made to reach the Orthodox Jews in Central Asia, and little or none the Reform Jews in Germany and the United States.

The Call to Advance. The evangelization of the Jew rests upon a threefold claim—what the Jew has been, what he is to-day, and what he is yet to become in the future.

Can we ever forget what we owe to the race which has given us the Bible, the Saviour, the first missionaries who took the gospel to our pagan ancestors in Europe? Can we fail to appreciate the leading rôle played by this race in every department of the life of civilized nations to-day, and the tremendous force they are bound to exert, for good or for evil, according to the influences brought to bear upon them?

An investigation of present conditions in Greater New York as regards such matters as social vice, crime, organized labor and radicalism, and the relation of the Jews to all of these things, would be a revelation to many complacent Christians.

And lastly, are we ignorant of the wonderful place reserved for this chosen race in the divine program of the future, as clearly foretold in the Scriptures, when no longer rebellious and rejected as now, but repentant and restored to God's favor, they shall be His willing and effective witnesses to the whole world? Let us remember that "blindness in part is happened to Israel until the fullness of the

Gentiles be come in." But "if the casting away of them be the reconciling of the world, what shall the receiving of them be but life from the dead?" (Rom. 11:15, 25). "Whatever the future may unfold, this much at least is evident from Scripture, that God purposes using the Jews in a large way in bringing the world to Christ. . . . 'To the Jew first' reveals the divine strategy of Missions, not only in the first century, but in all centuries. If the Jew is the center of the divine purposes, then his evangelization ought to be the supreme object of Christian effort. The Jew is the key of the world's missionary campaign." [2]

But however Christians may differ in their interpretation of prophecy in relation to the future, there should be no two opinions as to the need and duty of giving the gospel to every Jew in the world to-day. On this point we cannot do better than close with a quotation from one of the most recent books on this subject:

"What is the Christian's present-day duty in behalf of the evangelization of Israel? On the very face of it the answer to the question must be measurably affected by the fact that 15,000,000 souls of men in blindness and hardness of sin are in the presence of Christian people, whose field is encompassed by nothing less than the word 'whosoever' . . . How a person with a Bible in his hands can advocate missions to Mexicans, missions to South Americans, missions to Alaskans, and to Asiatics, Africans, and the benighted among the islands of the sea, and neglect or oppose missions to Jews challenges reasonable consideration." [3]

QUESTIONS

1. Give the present number and distribution of Jews throughout the world.

2. What languages are most spoken by the Jews to-day?

3. Give illustrations of the progress and prominence of the Hebrew race in past and current history.

4. Name and describe the main religious sects among present-day Jews.

5. (a) When did Modern Missions to Jews begin? (b) Name the first Society to open work, and state the present extent of its field.

[2] "A Century of Jewish Missions," p. 275.
[3] "The Jew and His Mission," p. 143.

6. Describe the activities of a typical Jewish mission center.

7. Indicate something of the results, both direct and indirect, of Jewish mission work, and name several highly honored converts.

8. Mention some of the most neglected fields among the Jews to-day.

9. On what threefold claim can the evangelization of the Jew be said to rest?

CHAPTER XIX

UNOCCUPIED FIELDS[1]

There are two ways of considering missions. One is to dwell upon the work already accomplished; the other is to contemplate what yet remains to be done. For the most part, consideration of the subject has been wholly from the former standpoint. It is quite legitimate, and it is highly gratifying and inspiring, to reflect upon missionary progress to date, to recount obstacles overcome, fields entered, stations opened, converts won, churches established, and all the splendid and varied achievements of missions, both direct and indirect.

But in the joy and satisfaction of contemplating the unparalleled progress of missionary work in recent years, the Christian Church must guard against the serious danger of a self-complacency which takes pride in what is after all only a partial accomplishment of her allotted task. She needs to remember, and to apply to the missionary situation to-day, the words of God to Israel, long after they had entered Canaan and begun the conquest of the Promised Land: *"There remaineth yet very much land to be possessed."*

The "Regions Beyond." When we turn our eyes from what has already been done, and view the vast proportions of the yet unfinished task of missions, all ground for easy complacency and congratulation is at once swept from under us. Says Dr. Zwemer: "We must not be blind to the fact that there is still work which remains to be *begun,* as well as

1 Available data upon which to draw for this chapter are necessarily meager and liable to inaccuracy for want of more complete surveys, census, and general knowledge of many regions involved. The main sources of information have been Dr. Zwemer's "The Unoccupied Mission Fields of Africa and Asia" (1911), the pamphlet entitled "The Unfinished Evangelistic Task" prepared by Mr. C. H. Fahs for the Jerusalem Meeting of the I.M.C. in 1928, "Unoccupied Fields" and other articles in "Statistical Survey of the World Mission" (1938), successive field surveys by the World Dominion Movement, and magazine articles, reports and personal letters from pioneer missionaries in various fields.

work which remains to be finished, if the plan of campaign is to be all-inclusive in its scope. There are still many portions of the world and great areas of population without organized missionary effort; where the forces of evil hold their own as securely as if the Saviour had never conquered; where the famine-stricken have never heard of the Bread that came down from Heaven for the heart-hunger of the world; where the darkness of superstition and error has never been illumined by the torch of civilization and the light of the Gospel." [2]

A Moral Obligation. Frank and serious attention to the problem of the unoccupied sections of the missionary world is "justified and demanded both by the claims which Christianity makes and by the command of our Lord. Christianity claims to be, for all ages and peoples, the all sufficient and the only sufficient religion. A moral obligation attaches itself to such a claim. If Christianity be the only sufficient religion for all the world, it should be given to all the world. Christ's command also lays upon the Church an obligation for nothing less than a world-wide promulgation of the Gospel." [3]

Twofold Division. We may perhaps best consider unoccupied fields under the following twofold classification: (1) Large integral areas practically untouched and outside the plans of existing missionary operations; (2) Unreached areas and constituencies within countries already entered.

I. INTEGRAL AREAS PRACTICALLY UNTOUCHED AND OUTSIDE THE PLANS OF EXISTING MISSIONARY OPERATIONS.

It is a most solemnizing fact that at this late date, and after more than a century of the modern missionary era, vast areas lying at the heart of each of the three great missionary continents—Asia, Africa and South America—remain almost wholly untouched.

1. *The Heart of Asia.*

A survey of this immense region includes the following countries:

Mongolia. Lying to the west of Manchuria, and divided into Inner and Outer Mongolia, this vast plateau equals

---

2 "The Unoccupied Mission Fields of Africa and Asia," p. 3.
3 "Report of World Missionary Conference," Edinburgh, 1910, Vol. I, p. 279.

in area China's original 18 provinces. Estimates of its population vary all the way from 1,800,000 to over 8,000,-000, but the later ones lie between two and three million. All existing missionary work is confined to the southeastern part of Inner Mongolia, where several small groups of workers are engaged, but almost wholly among the Chinese population. In all Outer Mongolia, which constitutes three-fourths of the area, there is no mission station, the one which existed for a time at Urga having been closed by the Soviet authorities. Here, then, are several million nomadic people wholly unreached with the gospel.

Chinese Turkistan. This region, lying still westward, is now known as Sinkiang, or the New Dominion. Like Mongolia, it is a Chinese dependency, and it consists of a series of sandy basins surrounded by lofty mountains. Its inhabitants are of various races and number over 4,300,000. "The highest trade route in the world leads from India over the Karakoram Pass, 18,300 feet, into Chinese Turkistan. Caravans loaded with 'tea, spices, cloth and Korans' make the dangerous journey. Skeletons of horses and camels strew the pathway, and yet 1,500 Chinese Moslem pilgrims chose this path over the roof of the world to Mecca in a single year." [4] Except for a few scattered points of light this whole region lies in utter spiritual darkness. Only two Societies are represented. The *Swedish Missionary Society* began work in 1892, and has had stations at Kashgar and three other points in the far west, while the *China Inland Mission* has occupied Urumtsi and two other towns in the east. But Moslem opposition and Soviet influence have combined to obstruct missionary efforts, and the door for the Gospel appears to be fast closing.

Tibet. A lofty tableland ranging from 10,000 to 17,600 feet in altitude, and with mountains reaching 28,000 feet, Tibet, which lies between the Himalayan and Kwenlun mountains, has been called "The Roof of the World." Because of the extreme difficulty of access and the fierce hostility of its people, it long remained a land of complete mystery, despite repeated attempts of explorers and missionaries to enter. Within recent years the country has been penetrated as far as Lhasa, its proud capital, although no

4 "Report of World Missionary Conference," Edinburgh, Vol. I, p. 194.

foreigner has been allowed to remain there, or anywhere within Inner Tibet. The country is bleak and rugged, and large regions still remain unexplored.

The Tibetans belong to the Mongolian family, although differing considerably in type from the Chinese. Formerly the country was under the sovereign authority of China, but while Chinese suzerainty is still recognized in name Tibet is virtually self-governing, under a ruler known as the Dalai Lama. The population has ever been a matter of speculation. Successive editions of the *Statesman's Year Book* have given estimates ranging from one-and-a-half to six million, but its latest issue (1939) suggests a little over 3,700,000.

The prevailing religion is Lamaism, a corrupt form of Buddhism with strongly Animistic features. The country is completely in the hands of the priests or lamas, who dwell in highly decorated monasteries, lead abominably dissolute lives, and lay the common people under a crushing burden of taxation. Polyandry is commonly practised, in some sections at least, and moral conditions in general are shocking.

Missionary attempts to enter Tibet have repeatedly been made ever since the Roman Catholic Fathers Huc and Gabet penetrated to Lhasa in 1845, only to be arrested and sent as prisoners to Canton. The story of these prolonged efforts to enter this great closed land is full of heart-stirring heroism. A cordon of missionary outposts is being drawn around Tibet, and although the walls of this defiant "citadel of Satan" have not yet fallen, much faithful labor has been bestowed upon Tibetans on both the India and China borders, and the wedge of missionary occupation is being driven slowly but firmly into the forbidden territory.

The oldest effort is that of the *Moravian Mission* laboring in the remote and isolated region of Lesser Tibet, adjoining Kashmir, India. Entering in 1856, this heroic little band has exhibited the highest courage and consecration in the midst of severe hardship and danger. Seven missionaries now occupy 4 stations, and there are 149 Christian converts.

The *Church of Scotland and Free Church of Finland Missions,* and a few independent workers, are laboring at points along the India frontier. On the China side are the *China Inland Mission, Christian and Missionary Alliance,*

United Christian Mission and *Pentecostal Bands of the World,* each occupying one or more strategic points within, or close to, the border of Tibet, and itinerating over considerable areas.

The names of two missionary martyrs—*Petrus Rijnhart,* a Hollander, who lost his life in 1898 while making the attempt with his wife, Dr. Susie Rijnhart, to reach Lhasa, and *Dr. A. L. Shelton,* the intrepid pioneer and devoted doctor of the United Christian Mission, who was shot by brigands in 1922, will ever be treasured in the memory of those who have longed and prayed for the conquest of Tibet. There is to-day no land that stands in sorer need of missionary effort and intercession than this one.

Nepal and Bhutan. South of Tibet, and high up within the Himalayan range, are these two independent kingdoms, with a combined population of 6,000,000. The people vary in race and religion. Some are Mongolian in origin and Buddhists; the majority are Hindu in descent and faith. Both the Gurkhas, who dominate Nepal, and the Bhutanese are fine robust people and fairly progressive, but the countries are still closed to Europeans and without a Christian missionary. A few frontier stations in India lie near the border.

Afghanistan. Westward still, and lying between N.W. India on the east and Persia on the west, is Afghanistan, with a population of some 10,000,000, according to latest estimates. Afghans comprise the dominating race, and Persian and Pushtu are the main languages spoken. The government is an absolute despotism under the Amir, with Kabul as his official seat.

The country is largely mountainous, yet there are fertile parts with considerable agriculture. The government's rigid policy of excluding foreigners has restricted trade with other nations and stood in the way of development and progress of every kind. "Afghanistan is morally one of the darkest places of the earth, 'full of the habitations of cruelty.' Judicial corruption and bribery are universal, and the criminal law, based on the Koran and tradition, is barbarous in the extreme. Torture in every conceivable form is common, and the prisons of Kabul are horribly inhuman." [5]

[5] "Report of World Missionary Conference," Edinburgh, Vol. I, p. 193.

In religion Afghanistan is fanatically Moslem. There is no such thing as personal freedom, and a rigorous law makes the profession of Christianity punishable with death. Even more than Tibet, therefore, Afghanistan stands out as a Gibraltar of stubborn resistance to missionary effort. It is regarded as the most absolutely unoccupied and closed mission field in the world to-day. And yet there are indications that at last the impact of the West is beginning to be felt in this isolated land. Afghan traders have penetrated into the remote bazaars of India, Moslem pilgrims pass through Persia to the shrines of distant Mecca and Kerbela, and the Afghan government has recently made a move toward establishing trade relations with America. These are cheering signs that the long and unnatural insularity of Afghanistan is breaking down. Whatever the process employed, these changes unquestionably find their efficient cause in God, and are being wrought through the fervent prayers of those who jealously long for the opening of this last land to the message of the Cross.

For years a thin line of missionary outposts has been forming on the various sides of this stronghold of the enemy. The earliest gospel effort for Afghans is to be traced to Bannu, on the Indian frontier, where the *Church Missionary Society* opened a station in 1865. There the gallant *Dr. Pennell* gave his life by contracting blood poisoning from an Afghan patient, and died a martyr to the cause. This Society has stations at Peshawar and two other points in the Northwest Frontier Province close to the several passes into Afghanistan, and through its hospitals and circulation of Scriptures its 14 missionaries are seeking to evangelize the wild border tribes. The only other Societies now in this field are the *Central Asian Mission* and *Worldwide Evangelization Crusade,* which entered in 1902 and 1920 respectively, each occupying a single station.

On the Persian side the *American Presbyterian* station at Meshed, quite near the border, offers one of the most strategic points for advance. Meshed is closely connected with Afghanistan by one of the main caravan trade routes. During 1917 Afghan merchants here purchased 1,791 copies of the Scriptures, while many Afghans have been treated in the Mission hospital. In 1924 four missionaries, including a doctor, were officially permitted to visit the city of Herat, where for three weeks medical aid was dispensed. A good impression was made, and it is hoped that this may prove the entering wedge into this dark domain.

Baluchistan. South of Afghanistan and on the extreme west of India lies Baluchistan. A small portion of this country is directly under British administration, and the remainder under native government with British supervision. It is a bleak and arid country, almost unknown to most people, and has been named by one traveler "the rubbish heap of the world." The latest figure given for its population is about 800,000. Its social, moral and religious conditions are those of Afghanistan. The only mission station is that of the *Church Missionary Society* at Quetta, which now has a church of 40 members.

Russian Central Asia. Under this head is included all that region of the late Russian Empire lying between Kashmir, Afghanistan and Persia on the south and Siberia on the north, and between Chinese Turkistan on the east and the Caspian Sea on the west. This vast area of over 1,600,000 square miles was formerly known under the names Turkistan, Bokhara, Khiva, the Trans-Caspian province and the Steppes. Since 1919 the Soviet Government has gradually extended its authority over the whole region. The native dynasties of Khiva and Bokhara have been expelled and the territory divided to form six Soviet Socialist Republics. The region embraces lofty mountains, ghastly deserts, grassy plains and fertile valleys, and has wide extremes of climate and other features. Its population reaches 15,000,000, and comprises "a conglomeration of different races, tribes and peoples, struggling for existence rather than for mastery." Despite railway connections with the Siberian line and the steamers on the Caspian Sea, making Central Asia accessible to Europe and bringing a touch of Western civilization, life still preserves much of its primeval simplicity.

Islam for many centuries has held almost undisputed sway, and its usual fruits of social and moral putrefaction are in full evidence. Eighty-five per cent. of the population is illiterate. Almost the only education is the study of the Koran in Arabic by groups at the mosques. The city of Bokhara, with 10,000 students and 364 mosques, has been called the "Cairo of Asia," as being the center of Moslem learning and influence for all the Middle East.

The evangelization of this great area, with its diversified population living in sin and superstition and under the blight of Islam, constitutes a task unsurpassed anywhere in its attendant difficulties and hardships. A few brave pioneers have battled against the well-nigh insuperable barriers presented by the combined forces of man and nature in seeking to penetrate this isolated region. And now, to such opposing forces has been added still another in the bitter anti-Christian attitude of the Soviet Government.

Only a few missionaries have ever lived in Russian Central Asia. At one time a little group of *German Mennonites* began work among the tent-dwelling Kirghiz, but the War put an end to their efforts. The *British and Foreign Bible Society* has scattered Scriptures in Russian, Arabic, Turkish and one or more tribal languages. An educated and heroic lady of Russian birth, *Miss Jenny de Mayer,* labored with singular devotion for years among Moslems over a wide area. She suffered great hardships and met with bitter opposition from the Soviet authorities and has finally been exiled and imprisoned. But in spite of these worthy individual efforts this field is yet virtually unoccupied territory.

To sum up the foregoing, we find at the heart of Asia a solid block of territory, stretching 1,000 miles due north from the Indian frontier, and 3,000 miles from the border of Persia on the west to that of Manchuria on the east, 4,200,-000 square miles in area, or larger than either the United States or Europe, and containing a population of at least 34,000,000. Apart from a few tiny points of light, this vast expanse still lies in unrelieved spiritual darkness.

2. *The Heart of Africa.*

To an even greater degree than in the case of Asia, the heart of Africa constitutes an unoccupied field, a vast area of unrelieved gloom. Dr. Karl Kumm in particular has called attention to this region, which is geographically known as the Central African Ironstone Plateau. It embraces six or eight large states directly south of the great Sahara, of which the best known are Wadai, Darfur and Kordofan, with a dense population of Hamitic and Negro peoples. In none of these states is there a Christian missionary. From the easternmost mission station in Nigeria to the nearest station on the Nile the distance is 1,500 miles. "It is as if the United States had one missionary in Maine and one in Texas, and not a ray of gospel light between." [6]

South of these states, again, is a conglomerate of pagan tribes, of which Dr. Kumm names forty-seven as the most important ones. Nor is there a missionary among any of them. "The nearest station to the south lies beyond 500 miles of virgin forest on the Congo; the nearest to the north, beyond the Sahara, is Tripoli on the Mediterranean, 2,000 miles away." [7]

Much fresh information about this great region has recently been furnished by the extensive travels of Mr. W. J. Roome, of the British and Foreign Bible Society, and also by World Dominion surveys. The Anglo-Egyptian Sudan is still largely unoccupied and seven of its provinces, with a population of over 1,500,000, are practically untouched. Mr. Roome presents a mass of facts and figures pertaining to French West Africa, Liberia, Kamerun and French Equatorial Africa, setting forth the appalling spiritual destitution of the twenty to thirty millions inhabiting those vast regions. He puts the total number of tribes at over 600, the majority pagan, though some have become Moslem, and the great mass of them still wholly unreached by the gospel.

Surely facts like these give tremendous force to the trenchant words of the Committee on Survey in its Report to the Edinburgh Conference in 1910:

"Africa has suffered many wrongs in the past at the hands of the stronger nations of Christendom, and she is suffering wrongs at their hands to-day; but the greatest wrong, and that from which she is suffering most, is being inflicted by the Church of Christ. It consists in withholding from so many of her children the knowledge of Christ. The flags of Christian nations float over nearly the whole of Africa, but there are large domains in which not a missionary station has been planted. The untouched regions of Africa are a clamant call to the Church."

3. *The Heart of South America.*

As in Asia and Africa, so also in the Western Hemis-

<hr>

[6] "Daybreak in the Dark Continent," p. 275.
[7] *The Missionary Review of the World,* June, 1921, p. 435.

phere, so near to the land whence have gone forth the larger part of the missionary forces into all the world, the humiliating fact of untouched territory confronts us, for a vast area in the heart of South America has still to be written down as wholly unoccupied by missions.

"The greatest stretch of unevangelized territory in the world lies in the center of South America, including the interior of Brazil, Venezuela, Colombia, Ecuador, Peru, Bolivia and Paraguay. An irregular territory some 2,000 miles long and from 500 to 1,500 miles in width would only include two or three missionaries. In northern Brazil there are seven states, with populations ranging from that of Maine to that of New Jersey, with no foreign missionary."

"Northern Brazil is one of the most neglected fields on earth. North and west of the San Francisco River lies about two-thirds of Brazil, half the area of South America. . . . Two-thirds of this region is covered with virgin forests, through which wander native tribes which have never heard the name of Christ. The Amazon and its tributaries furnish 10,000 miles of navigable water by which to reach the 8,000,000 people who live there."

"In the northern half of Peru, a stretch of territory larger than our own thirteen original states, there is not one evangelical missionary." [8]

Putting together these great geographical stretches which have been brought into view, we find at the heart of the three great missionary continents solid areas gigantic in extent, and containing an aggregate population, according to the most conservative estimates, of from one hundred to one hundred and twenty million human beings who are yet completely outside the range of present missionary work.

II. UNREACHED AREAS AND CONSTITUENCIES WITHIN COUNTRIES ALREADY ENTERED.

The distinction between the larger integral unoccupied areas above considered and the smaller areas and constituencies lying within countries already entered is, after all, more or less arbitrary. Impressive and well-nigh overwhelming as is the survey of the one class, the other is of equal im-

[8] Extracts from "Survey of Interchurch World Movement," 1920.

portance and to be regarded no less seriously. Indeed, there is a sense in which the fields classified under the second heading call for even greater emphasis, since the fact that they lie within, or adjacent to, areas where some missionary operations exist tends to create the impression that they are provided for, whereas in reality they are no less destitute than the larger and remoter sections where no missionary agencies have entered.

Attention has already been called to most of these smaller unoccupied areas in the preceding chapters, so that further reference to them here is unnecessary.

One field, *Siberia,* calls for a word, since the fact that it is related to European Russia and is nominally occupied by the Greek Church and its Missions places it as a whole beyond the scope of our present study. A great proportion, however, of the 17,000,000 people inhabiting this vast northern land are utterly destitute of vital Christianity, and there are many actual pagans, such as the Buriats of southern Siberia, whose horse-sacrifice and other ceremonies, as described by a reliable traveler,[9] are gruesome to a degree. No one after reading such an account of superstitious rites can question their need of the gospel, or the duty of the Church to carry it to them.

Far from our being justified in regarding the unoccupied areas within lands already entered as of secondary importance, the investigations of the Committee on Survey for the Edinburgh Conference of 1910 made it clear that the combined population of these areas greatly exceeds the totals for the large integral regions still wholly untouched.

Causes of Non-Occupation. We cannot be aware of such great stretches of unoccupied territory, and of so many millions of souls still hopelessly beyond the reach of the saving gospel, without being aroused to an earnest inquiry into the causes for such an awful situation, with a view to their correction. Among the causes are the following:

1. *Lack of Exploration and Difficulty of Access.* While the missionary objective has in many instances supplied the strongest incentive for geographical exploration, and not a few of the world's most famous explorers have been missionaries, yet it remains true that in some parts of the world

9 J. Curtin, "A Journey in Southern Siberia," pp. 44-46.

to-day the further advance of missions has been checked by the absence of exploration and consequently of means of transportation.

This factor applies to all three of the great unoccupied regions at the hearts of the continents of Asia, Africa and South America, and in some measure also to Arabia and a few of the larger islands, like New Guinea and Borneo. It is a fact, too, that the shifting of the great highways of travel in recent times from overland to ocean routes has led to the abandonment of many once popular caravan roads, and this likewise bears upon some of the above regions.

2. *Political and Religious Prohibition.* The strong arm of the state, sometimes backed by religious fanaticism, has debarred missionaries from some lands. Afghanistan, Arabia and Tibet are the most notable present day examples of this hindrance, as the Latin American Republics once were. In Nepal, Bhutan and certain native states of India missionary work is also excluded or restricted.

But unfortunately political hindrance has not been confined to Moslem, Buddhist and Hindu governments. France and Portugal have been guilty of prohibiting Protestant missionary work in their extensive colonial possessions in East Asia, Africa and the Pacific Islands, and even to-day hampering restrictions are imposed in some of them.

3. *Hostility of Savage and Uncivilized Tribes.* Opposition of this sort is happily for the most part a thing of the past, yet it is still in evidence in parts of the interior of Latin America, Africa and Asia, and in some of the Pacific Island groups.

4. *Lack of Missionary Coöperation and Strategy.* While missionary operations have been marked increasingly by a fine spirit of unity and comity, as well as the display of able statesmanship, yet the neglect both of great integral areas and of sections of existing fields of labor is unquestionably due in part to a lack of sufficiently comprehensive vision. Too many missionaries and societies have been content to view the success of the work merely from the standpoint of a measure of progress achieved, and have never begun to think and plan and act in terms of the actual completion of the task. The thought of carrying the gospel to *all* the world has not largely dominated missionary operations.

Consequently unoccupied areas, small and great, have not compelled the attention and effort which they deserve, whereas activities which, although legitimate and worthy in their proper order and proportion, are in the light of the church's marching orders distinctly secondary to the main business of a speedy world-wide proclamation of the gospel, are being unduly stressed, and are absorbing altogether too large a proportion of the missionary forces. A readjustment of the work in hand and a redistribution of the existing forces could be made so as materially to modify the extent of unoccupied fields.

5. *Inadequacy of Missionary Forces and Resources.* When due weight has been given to the last mentioned cause this more must be said, than which nothing is clearer, that the present forces and resources made available for the missionary task render practically impossible the completion of that task. In multiplied instances these forces and resources are strained to the breaking points in their attempt to keep pace with the work already in hand, so that without reënforcement any project of entering new fields or launching new efforts must be indefinitely postponed.

6. *Absence of a World-wide Missionary Vision.* The causes already mentioned are contributory; this one is fundamental. When all else has been said, is it not true that the supreme reason why so large a proportion of the world remains at this late date unoccupied by missionary forces is that the Christian Church as a whole has never caught the true vision of God's world-wide purpose and her own vital relation to its accomplishment? Lack of vision has resulted in lack of concern, and lack of concern in lack of adequate effort. A true vision, sincere concern and serious effort on the part of the whole church to reach the whole world with the gospel would, under God, have resulted long ago in the accomplishment of the task, all the above mentioned hindrances notwithstanding. Let us recognize the facts and make this frank confession.

Facing the Problem. There ought to be no remaining unoccupied field in the world to-day. The existence of even one such field, not to say many fields, is a reproach upon the Christian Church which should with all possible speed be removed. How shall this be done? If the suggested causes of non-occupation are the right ones, then the solution of the problem lies directly along the line of their correction.

1. The facts should be marshaled and laid before the united missionary administrative bodies at home, in their annual conferences, and through the constituent societies be brought to the attention of the entire church. Since obviously there are no missionaries in unoccupied areas to make known their spiritual destitution, some special agency should be charged with making thorough investigations and reporting.

2. There should be strategic planning, including any necessary readjustment of present work and redistribution of present forces and resources, and the apportioning of the unfinished tasks among the various missionary agencies as they are willing to accept fresh responsibilities.

3. Where unoccupied fields lie within areas already claimed as the sphere of established missions, or adjacent to them, these missions should if possible be reënforced so as to enable them fully to occupy the territory. Where such additional responsibility cannot be accepted by the existing missions, arrangements should be sought for some other agency to occupy the neglected field.

4. Where the unoccupied fields are so far removed from the territory of established missions as to preclude the prospect of their being overtaken by a process of extension, new missions are called for. It is especially desirable that such new missions be inaugurated, as far as possible, by existing societies, preferably those having work nearest these fields, so as to utilize the wisdom, experience and resources of a well-established organization in meeting the peculiar difficulties which attend the opening of a new field. But it would be unwise policy for existing societies whose forces and resources are already taxed by the demands of their present work to attempt to establish new missions to the weakening of the existing work. New societies, or new missions of existing societies, should rely upon the enlistment of additional recruits and enlarged giving for their support.

5. The duty and ideal of carrying the gospel to the whole world must be brought home to the conscience and heart of the church. It should be made a test of the church's loyalty to Jesus Christ. There is no question as to the church pos-

sessing the requisite resources for the unfinished task. It is simply a question of her heart and will being enlisted, the task being clearly shown her, and her resources of prayer and men and money being called forth and directed to the desired end.

The Crowning Challenge of this Age. Two quotations fitly sum up the theme of this chapter, lifting it to the loftiest plane and appealing to the highest sentiment of every true and loyal Christian.

The first quotation is from a pioneer missionary on the borders of Tibet: "The eyes of the Christian world turn as instinctively toward the lands closed to the gospel in this missionary age as do the eyes of a conquering army toward the few remaining outposts of the enemy which withstand the victors and hinder complete victory, without which the commander-in-chief is unable to close the campaign." [10]

The second is from a well-known missionary statesman who has belonged both to the circle of missionary administration at home and to that of missionary leadership on the field: "The occupation of all the unoccupied fields is the distinctive and crowning challenge of this missionary age. Upon the church's acceptance of that challenge great issues seem to depend: issues affecting the vitality of the Christian Church, issues determining the welfare and happiness of millions of our fellow creatures, issues conditioning the lives of nations, issues upon which God Himself has been pleased to hang the unfolding of His eternal purposes in Christ. The unoccupied fields must be occupied, and what is the price of their occupation? The pathway which leads to their occupation lies across other unoccupied fields—great areas these—in our own lives and hearts, not yet surrendered to the will of Christ, not yet fully occupied by His Spirit, not yet touched by the flame of a perfect love and consecration. Only as He is permitted to fully occupy these nearer areas in our own lives will He be able to gain entrance into those more distant fields of the unoccupied world." [11]

[10] John R. Muir, missionary of the China Inland Mission.
[11] Rev. Chas. R. Watson, D.D., President, American University at Cairo.

QUESTIONS

1. (a) From what two standpoints may the work of Missions be considered? (b) What moral obligation is implied by the claims made for Christianity and the fact of unoccupied mission fields still existing?

2. Give a twofold classification of unoccupied mission fields.

3. Where do the greatest wholly unoccupied areas lie?

4. Give the main facts about each of the following countries of Asia, as bearing particularly upon their missionary need and supply, and including names of related Societies or missionaries: (a) Mongolia, (b) Chinese Turkistan, (c) Tibet, (d) Nepal and Bhutan, (e) Afghanistan, (f) Baluchistan, (g) Russian Central Asia.

5. Describe the location, extent, population and other features of the great unoccupied sections of (a) Africa, (b) South America, (c) Siberia.

6. Discuss six causes of non-occupation, giving concrete illustrations where such apply.

7. Suggest five practical measures looking toward the speedy occupation of neglected fields.

8. What unoccupied fields in a spiritual sense are suggested by the existence of these material unoccupied fields at this late date?

CHAPTER XX

THE PRESENT MISSIONARY OUTLOOK

Having traced the outlines of Christian Missions from their inception in apostolic times down to our own day, and having also looked at the proportions of the unfinished missionary task, it remains to sum up briefly the present situation and outlook and, in so doing to discover, if we may, some practical lessons which the situation holds for the Church and individual Christian to-day.

I. Salient Features at the Field End.

1. *Favorable Features.* These include the following:

A World-Wide Open Door. Time was, and not so very long ago, when the burden of nearly every missionary address was an appeal for prayer that doors of entrance might be opened into closed lands. But with a very few exceptions that appeal is no longer heard, for God has answered prayer, and doors have been flung wide open throughout the world.

Nothing is more remarkable than the completely changed aspect of the missionary world in this respect within the short span of a single generation. The writer recalls that when he first set foot in China, only thirty odd years ago, two entire provinces of that great land, with 30,000,000 people, were still tightly closed against the gospel, and large sections of practically every other province were in a like condition. As a member of a band of pioneer missionaries who battled their way into those last two provinces he can testify how every step of advance, right up to the Boxer year of 1900, was in the teeth of the most stubborn resistance, marked by frequent insult and rioting, and occasional loss of life. Twenty years later it was his privilege to make a journey through eleven provinces, right across China to the Tibetan border, and in all those thousands of miles of inland travel he cannot recall a single instance of insult or injury, but only uniformly courteous treatment and unrestricted freedom for missionary testimony.

It needs to be borne in mind that Japan, which has made such phenomenal strides forward into the very forefront of nations, was only two short generations ago emerging from medieval seclusion, before American insistence in the shape of Commodore Perry's cruiser squadron. It is but forty odd years since missionaries first gained entrance into the "Hermit Kingdom" of Korea. But to-day the 500,000,000 inhabitants of China, Japan and Korea, constituting one-third of the whole human race, have become wholly accessible.

In the providence of God, India, with another one-fifth of the human family, has become a part of the British Empire—a fact which no one who has visited India can fail to recognize as a potent factor in making possible the evangelization of that great land.

Similarly, God has seen fit to wrest from decadent Spain and corrupt Romanism the fair Philippines, Cuba and Porto Rico, and to entrust them to the tutelage of the United States, with the result that more than 16,000,000 islanders have been brought for the first time within the range of evangelical effort. The fact is patent to all who know these islands, that some thirty years of American occupancy have done infinitely more for the advancement of their promising peoples than the whole four centuries of the previous régime.

For years every Protestant missionary effort to enter French Indo-China was repulsed under the influence of the entrenched Jesuits there. But prayer was made and answered, and through the rupture of State-Church relations in France the long-closed door swung open twenty years ago, thereby bringing 20,000,000 benighted Annamese within missionary reach.

When many readers of this book studied geography the vast interior of Africa was still largely a blank upon the map, for it was only in 1873 that Livingstone, prince of African explorers, laid down the uncompleted task, which Stanley in turn took up, of discovering the inner secrets of the Dark Continent. But now Africa's vast interior has been explored and opened up, so that, from the standpoint it least of an open door of access, the prophecy that

"Ethiopia shall stretch out her hands unto God" stands fulfilled.

Turning to the other great continent of the southern hemisphere, South America, which until recent years was closed to Protestant Missions, it may be said that the very excesses of that corrupt and spiritless religion which for centuries held unrivaled sway provoked such widespread revulsion against itself as to fling open the door of welcome and opportunity to evangelical forces.

Thus, by a series of wonderful providences, the present generation has witnessed a breaking down of barriers and a thrusting open to world-wide missions of age-long closed doors, such as whole centuries heretofore could not record.

When the World War broke out the one notable exception in the matter of an open door was the Near East, which constitutes the bulk of the Moslem World. In that region missionary work still faced a wall of adamant, progress was at a snail's pace and results were painfully small. But over against many sad results of the War one result, at least, caused all true Christian hearts to rejoice, and that was the blow struck at Turkish dominion in the Near East. The driving out of this tyrannical Power from most of his Asiatic domains—notwithstanding the subsequent humiliating compromise which that victory was allowed to suffer has ushered in a new day of liberty for millions of shackled souls in Syria, Palestine, Arabia, Mesopotamia and Egypt, and has opened a great new door of missionary opportunity throughout Near Eastern lands.

Behold, then, the inspiration, and the challenge as well, of a world-wide open door.

Improved Material Facilities. No less providential than the opening of closed doors has been the rapid improvement in the means of world-wide travel, communication and other facilities bearing upon missionary life and labor. Steam and electricity have belted the globe by land and sea, bringing almost every part within safe and easy reach. The post and telegraph, and later the wireless also, have placed themselves at the service of the Kingdom of God. In many lands automobiles have cut not in *two,* but actually in *ten,* the time consumed in country tours, and have immensely extended the radius of the missionary's field of operations.

Where formerly the outgoing missionary had to take with him supplies for a whole term of service, and had often to subsist upon the slender and ill-suited food supply of some far inland native market, to-day in many instances he can start for his field with no more baggage than he would require for an ordinary trip at home, assured of ample provision for his every need through improved local markets, mail and freight orders from home, and rapid transportation. Better houses, better sanitary conditions, better food, better means of travel, and a hundred and one modern conveniences and advantages contribute to making missionary life safer and more comfortable, and missionary work easier and more effective, than ever before.

Changed Attitude of Eastern Peoples. An open door is essential, and to have secured it is a great achievement for the missionary cause; but an open mind is no less essential, and yet much more difficult, and to have secured that is an even greater achievement. Many a missionary having gained physical access to a heathen community has found that a thick wall of prejudice and hatred still intervened between him and the people about him.

Nothing in modern missions is more impressive than the remarkable way in which the peoples of mission lands have changed within a few years from an attitude of hostility and exclusion to one of friendliness and open-mindedness toward the missionary and his message. The complete change of this kind that has taken place in China, the greatest and most conservative of all nations, within an incredibly short space of time, furnishes a notable example, and it is nothing less than a miracle of God's own working. But other notable examples of the same kind are to be found in every part of the missionary world.

Nothing struck the writer more forcibly on his several extended journeys in mission lands within the last few years than the sharp contrast everywhere apparent between disturbed political conditions and the favorable attitude toward missions. The Near East was at the time seething with political unrest, racial frictions were everywhere in evidence, British soldiers were patrolling the streets of Cairo and other Egyptian centers to forestall threatened uprisings; and yet the missionaries at center after center testified to newly awakened interest in the gospel. In old Jerusalem a steady stream of Jews, and others, kept coming to the Mission House to read and discuss the Scriptures, while there were a number of open confessions of Christ in the chapel services. On several other stations in Palestine gospel meetings were having a marked increase in attendance, and a number of Arab sheikhs showed a friendliness which was in striking contrast to their former cold demeanor. In Egypt an ever-increasing number of individuals and groups were seriously inquiring into Christian truth, while the demand for Christian literature for Moslems was almost beyond the power of the presses to supply.

In India, just at the time when feeling against the British Government and Europeans in general was strong, as a result of the agitation of the Indian Nationalists for home rule, the writer witnessed the progress of a genuine spiritual revival in a section of the field theretofore notorious for its stubborn resistance to all missionary approach. And during the years which have followed, filled as they have been with political anxiety as to what might occur at any moment, missionaries have reported larger sales of Scriptures and more response on their preaching tours among the villages than ever before.

The writer will never forget his royal reception as an invited guest in the home of a Tibetan chieftain, in whose village only three years earlier the first two missionaries to venture into that part of the forbidden land of Tibet barely escaped with their lives. Through persistent and tactful missionary effort this one-time bitter foe had been turned into a warm friend and protector.

In short, the impression gained by wide personal contacts and from published reports and also direct correspondence with nearly every part of the field is that throughout the missionary world to-day more minds are open, more hearts susceptible to the message of the gospel, than ever before. It is a situation big with the promise of an unprecedented harvest if only the opportunity is promptly and fully taken advantage of.

Cumulative Effect of Work Done. The imagery of husbandry, or the tilling of the soil, is commonly employed in Scripture in connection with the ministry of the gospel, with the result that we have come to use such terms as sowing and reaping, harvest-time and the like, in a spiritual sense as familiarly as in a material sense. And when we come to consider it, the analogy between the processes of material and spiritual husbandry is a very close one indeed. In both we have the successive stages of the preparation of the soil, seed sowing, cultivating and harvesting.

In missionary work these stages are very clearly marked. The early pioneers in every field had the task of blazing the trail and doing a lot of hard, slow, preliminary work to make ready the ground for the seed of the gospel. Then came the period of seed sowing, with its patient, plodding, persevering toil. Little by little, line upon line, by varied means and methods, the seed was scattered and watered with prayers and tears. Often long years ensued with little or no visible sign of fruit to cheer the toilers. In course of time the first fruit appeared, converts began to come by ones and twos, then in gradually increasing numbers, and the first infant churches were formed.

But it has remained for the present generation to witness the harvest of missions in full force. The cumulative effect of long years of faithful labor is now showing itself in large and ever-increasing ingatherings of souls, and in substantial progress along every line of missionary effort. The seed has germinated and taken root, the seedlings have been transplanted far and wide, the assiduous cultivation of the growing grain has told effectively, and now the fields are waving with golden grain ready for the reaper's sickle. To-day is the harvest-time in world-wide missions in a sense that no previous day has been, and the returns for a single day eclipse those of a whole year in any earlier generation. If only the ranks of the reapers could be doubled or trebled at once, with the strength of the *whole* Church behind them, the immediate results would be beyond estimate on any basis of reckoning hitherto employed.

Development of Native Churches and Leaders. True missionary vision looks beyond the work of the foreign missionary force to a firmly planted indigenous church, aiming at and eventually reaching the ideal of supporting and governing itself and assuming the responsibility for the evangelization of its own land. Progress toward this goal was

never before as encouraging as it is to-day. It has taken a
long time for the policy and aim of a self-supporting, self-
propagating native church really to grip the missionary body
and control its methods, but this policy seems at last to have
laid hold effectively upon the missionary body and the native churches of nearly every field.

No feature in the present situation is more inspiring, or
fraught with greater promise, than the fine growth, in character as well as in number, of the native churches, and the
development of a corps of native Christian leaders of firm
faith, sterling character and fine ability, who are advancing
steadily into the leadership of the Christian movement in the
greater mission fields. The display of sound judgment and
long-visioned statesmanship by the Chinese delegates who
constituted a majority in the great Chinese National Christian Conference of 1922 was a revelation to the whole Christian world, and that Conference undoubtedly marked the
passing of the high leadership of the Christian enterprise
in China from foreign to native hands. A place of similar
prominence has been accorded to native leaders in Japan,
while in India, Korea, Latin America and parts of Africa
and the Island World native leaders are rapidly coming to
the front.

It is a cause for no little rejoicing that from the churches
of Oriental lands God has thus early raised up such great
evangelists as Kanamori of Japan, Kim of Korea, Ting-
li-mei of China, Sadhu Sundar Singh of India, Juan Varetto
of Argentina, and many others almost as well known.

Strong local evangelistic campaigns and Home Mission
movements at longer range have been successfully launched.
Notable among these are the National Missionary Society
of India, organized in 1905 to evangelize parts of India
unoccupied by Foreign Missions, and the National Chinese
Home Missionary Society, started in 1920, which has opened
work in the remote provinces of Yunnan and Manchuria.
More recently, in 1921, the General Assembly of the Indian
Presbyterian Church took the initial steps toward beginning
foreign missionary work, with Tibet and Mesopotamia the
probable fields, and appointed a committee to formulate a
society for this purpose. Korea, itself among the youngest
of mission fields, has set a noble example to all others, for

in addition to taking the leading part in home evangelism its churches have sent missionaries to Korean communities in Manchuria, Siberia, Hawaii, Mexico and the United States, and also to labor among the natives of China and Siberia. In such movements as these, more than in anything else, lies the hope of the completion of the task of evangelizing the world.

2. *Unfavorable Features.*

Conditions Following the World War.   Serious as were the effects of the World War upon missions while it lasted, its baneful influences did not cease with the signing of the peace treaty.   The truth is that real peace has never yet been restored, and all the nations are still suffering severe results of those horrible years of conflict.   Among other features noticeable are the universal higher cost of living, greatly increased rates of travel, the financial bankruptcy of certain European countries with resultant damage to international trade, a seriously lowered standard of morals, an increase of outlawry and crime, and a general atmosphere of unrest and uncertainty the world over.   All these conditions have their obvious bearings upon missionary interests.

In particular is to be noted a widening breach of distrust on the part of the weaker nations of Asia and Africa toward the stronger nations of Europe.   The old feelings of reverential awe and slavish fear with which the Asiatic and African regarded the wonderful European have worn away. The War brought the East and the West into closer touch than ever before, but unfortunately under anything but ideal conditions.   They met in the trenches and under the stress of war, and the East saw the West not at its best, but at its worst, beheld its vices rather than its virtues.   The consequence was that familiarity bred contempt, and European prestige went down in the Orient, never probably to rise again to its old level.

The War gave distinct impetus to the ambitions of the backward races of the world for political autonomy.   It quickened their hopes of throwing off completely the hated yoke of Western domination.   In every Eastern country the clever leaders of nationalistic organizations seized upon the popular watchwords "democracy" and "self-determination," coined for them in the West, and from country to country, as one journeyed through the Orient, were to be heard the slogans: "Egypt for the Egyptians," "Arabia for the Arabians," "India for the Indians," "The Philippines for the Filipinos," and so on *ad libitum*. While it is easy for Westerners to regard such an attitude on the part of these other races as uncalled for and foolish, there is much to be said on the other side. All the larger nations of Europe have against them an unenviable record of aggression in their dealings with these backward races, greed and cruelty have figured with ugly prominence, and might has repeatedly been substituted for right. Little wonder that the peoples of Africa, Asia and the Pacific Isands chafed to be free, and that their experiences at the hands of so-called Christian nations have been, and still are, a serious stumbling-block in the way of the missionaries in seeking to gain the confidence of the natives and to present to them the gospel.

Influence of Godless Civilization. Not only does the aggression of Western nations as such react unfavorably upon the cause of missions, but the base character and shameful conduct of many representatives of those nations who come in contact with the Eastern and Island races as traders, travelers and at times even as officials of Western governments, constitute one of the most vexatious trials to missionaries and their work.

It must be kept in mind that the ever-widening "open door" which we rejoice in for missionary effort is no less an open door for the devil's forces, and he is taking fullest advantage of his opportunity, and is importing into these lands in a steady stream all the moral vices of a godless civilization, all the deadly poison of perverted religions, and all the subtle fallacies of modern cults. These features have already been noted in previous chapters as bearing upon missionary work in the past, and reference is here made to them again only as a reminder that they are matters still to be reckoned with to-day, some of them possibly in even more aggravated form or measure than heretofore.

Effect of Liberalistic Doctrine. In addition to these opposing forces from without must be mentioned, not without deep pain of heart, a force within the missionary ranks which is working grievous injury to many members of the body of Christ in mission fields and weakening the whole cause of missions. We refer to what is commonly known as "modernism" or "liberalism" in theological belief and teaching, which rejects the historic interpretation of the Bible, in favor of a rationalistic interpretation based upon modern scientific theories along evolutionary lines. These views have long existed and been made the ground of attacks upon Christianity by skeptics outside the Church. In recent years, however, they have gained currency among many within the Church, until destructive Biblical criticism and new theology have spread to an appalling extent in pulpits and theological seminaries. And now, through the product of these liberalistic seminaries at home, such false teaching has reached the mission fields and brought sharp division in the missionary ranks. So serious has the issue already become that the Bible Union of China and the Bible League of India, Ceylon and Burma have been formed, for the purpose of withstanding the influence of modernism upon the mission churches by strong and united testimony and teaching on the fundamental truths of Christianity.

Nothing more deplorable could well be imagined than this rending of the missionary forces by those who are repudiating the very foundations of the Christian faith and substituting a new gospel of ethical teaching and human improvement for the old gospel of divine grace and regenerating power, which has wrought such mighty transformation in the lives of multitudes in every mission field.

Nor are the injurious effects of this modernistic trend upon the missionary enterprise confined to the field end. They are equally in evidence at the home end, where the discarding of vital Christian doctrine in the pulpit is producing spiritual declension in the pew, and this in turn is cooling missionary zeal and curtailing missionary support by prayer and gift. It is a solemn and significant fact that in America, where money is poured out unstintingly along every other line, there is a marked falling off in missionary contributions and the Mission Boards are hard pressed financially. In some cases retrenchment on the field has become necessary, in others much needed reënforcements have to be held back, while not a few Boards are facing large deficits for the current year.

II. Vital Factors at the Home Base.

The relation between the success of the missionary enterprise abroad and the condition of the Church at home has been mentioned, and its importance can hardly be too strongly emphasized. The enterprise is one. Missions abroad are the projection of the Church at home into other lands, and their welfare and progress depend vitally upon sympathy and coöperation at the home base. The missionaries at the front can "lengthen the cords" of the gospel tent only in proportion as those who stand back of them at home "strengthen the stakes." To attempt the one without the other would spell·collapse and disaster. We have already seen how the situation in the mission fields to-day is one of readiness for a strong advance, with the promise of unprecedented harvests. But whether that advance can be made, and those harvests realized, depends on the Church at home rather than on the missionaries afield. The latter are working to the limit of their strength, and utilizing to the utmost the resources at their disposal. Anything more cannot fairly be expected of them under existing conditions; the next move must be made by the Church at home. What, then, are some of the stakes which must be strengthened at the home base to permit the lengthening of the missionary cords abroad?

Renewed Conviction as to the World's Need of Christ. Time was when the lost condition of the heathen constituted one of the strongest grounds of missionary appeal. But times have changed, and we hear much less said on that line to-day. Men seem to like to dwell upon the benefits of faith rather than to face the consequences of unbelief. It is to be feared that there is very prevalent doubt, amounting in many quarters to positive unbelief, regarding the hopeless condition of those who are without the gospel.

Yet Scripture is clear and emphatic in statements as to the·sin and guilt of the heathen, and missionary experience everywhere confirms the testimony of Scripture on this point. The plea so often made for the heathen that they are living up to the light they have is meant to be charitable, but it rests on ignorance of plain fact. The heathen themselves as a rule make no such claim, for they well know the opposite to be true. Without entering here upon the question of possible exceptions to the rule, the undeniable fact is that the great mass of heathen to-day are living in the wilful indulgence of gross sins of every sort. Unless, therefore, divine law is to be abrogated, they must be visited with the penalty of sin. The Word declares that "the wages of sin is death," with no hint that such statement applies less in one part of the world than another. God's only remedy for sin is salvation through Jesus Christ. John 3: 16 declares the glorious news of this salvation, but no less plainly does this verse declare the doom of all men outside of Christ, when it says, "that whosoever believeth in Him *should not perish, but have everlasting life."* We do well to remember that it was for a world *already lost,* and not merely in danger of being lost, that God gave His Son. To question the necessity of the gospel for the people of heathen lands is to question its necessity for the people of our own land.

After all, perhaps the most convincing argument for the heathen's need of Christ is found within our own hearts. If I can get along without Christ here, then I may conclude that the heathen can likewise get along without Him there. But if only Christ can cleanse *my* sin, and give peace to *my* guilty conscience, who else than Christ can do the same for *them?* By our own confessed need of Christ, and our own conscious salvation in Him, do we establish the need of every other man for Christ as his only Saviour.

Without a question, this current unbelief or half-belief regarding the absolute need of the heathen world for the gospel is cutting the nerve of missionary zeal and effort. It is a logical conclusion that the cost entailed in carrying the gospel to the heathen is too great unless the heathen are in the gravest spiritual peril. Only where desperate need exists is unlimited sacrifice demanded or even justified. Hudson Taylor, when near the end of his life, testified that he would never have thought of becoming a missionary but for the deep conviction of the lost condition of the heathen and their utter need of Christ. Brainerd, Martyn, Carey and Judson all held the same conviction, and the heroic and effective missionary careers of these men must be interpreted in the light of that conviction.

When Christians get back to the Book on this point, as well as every other, and accept its plain and solemn verdict regarding the heathen, a new day of missionary concern and effort will follow.

A Stronger Sense of Christian Responsibility. It is positively distressing to discover how few, comparatively, appear to have any clear, scriptural conception of missionary responsibility. The great majority of professing Christians give the matter little or no thought at all. Statistics tell the shocking tale that only one-third of the Protestant churches and only one-fourth of the Protestant church members of America make any contribution to missions. Many others conceive of missions at most as a philanthropy, a charity extended to people for whom they bear no responsibility, so that anything they may give or do for the heathen is just so much to the good, and quite beyond that which constitutes their duty.

How different is the Scriptural conception as expressed by the great missionary apostle Paul! Even after his missionary labors had already covered the extensive territory of Asia Minor, Macedonia and Greece, he writes to the distant Romans: "I am *debtor* both to Greeks and to Barbarians . . . so, as much as in me is, I am ready to preach the gospel to you also that are in Rome." No claim of merit here! No sense of conferring a favor upon those to whom he would carry the gospel! It was his duty, his *debt,* and he was only seeking as an honest man to discharge it. He even adds: "Woe is unto me if I preach not the gospel." Elsewhere he uses such terms as steward, trustee, witness, ambassador—all conveying the same idea of responsibility and obligation to give the gospel to all who had it not.

Each of the above terms applies to every Christian to-day not a whit less than to Paul in his day. We *owe* all men the gospel; we are their *debtors*—out of loyalty to Christ, out of gratitude for our own salvation, out of compassion for human need and helplessness, out of the realization that the gospel is the only remedy for their sin, the only panacea for their many ills, the only hope for their souls' eternal salvation. To be a true child of God, and to confess Jesus Christ as Saviour and Lord, is to be essentially related to this supreme divine enterprise, and to be committed to some definite share in carrying it out.

It was the general acceptance of this responsibility by the

rank and file of apostolic Christians which gave to that first generation of missionary effort its marvelous character and success. It has been that same high conception of missionary obligation permeating the whole Korean Church which has made the results of the work in that field the marvel of this missionary age. If only that same conviction and spirit were to take hold of all the churches of Christendom to-day, such would be the resultant blessing and power of God upon their efforts that the end of the task of world-wide witnessing would very soon be in sight.

A Clearer Understanding of God's Missionary Program. It is vital to the success of any enterprise that the end in view be clearly defined by the one who initiates it, and be as clearly understood by those who engage in it. Of no enterprise is this more true or more important than of missions, since that enterprise is the greatest in all the world. But although the divine program of missions for this age has been made unmistakably clear in the Word, it seems to be far from clearly understood by the whole Church.

Two widely different conceptions are in evidence. One of these makes the objective of present-day missions to be the conversion of the whole world to Christ. Those who hold this view conceive of gospel effort and influence proceeding onward and outward with ever-increasing momentum, until by a steadily progressive, evolutionary process not only will individuals be converted, but all social and moral evil will be overthrown, society regenerated, politics purged, nations lifted to pure Christian ideals and conduct, and thus, by the gradual Christianization of the present entire social and political order, a millennium of peace and righteousness under the universal reign of Christ will be ushered in.

As regards this view, not only is it difficult to see its justification by the teaching of the Scriptures concerning the course and culmination of the present age, but it is equally difficult to harmonize its hopes with the actual condition and trend of affairs to-day. One thing, at least, is certain, that if the goal of present-day missions is as above stated we are as yet a very long way from that goal. For despite the encouraging progress and blessed fruits of missionary work in every field, it cannot be said with any semblance of truth that any one of the great mission lands has been brought to a state even remotely approximating national conversion.   On the contrary, it is an actual fact that heathen and Moslems are increasing far faster by natural propagation than are Christian converts by regeneration. There are actually more heathen in the world to-day than when Carey launched the modern missionary movement. Accordingly, this view necessitates the postponement of the full fruition of missionary hopes to the distant future, and makes present missionary operations merely a preliminary stage in an indefinite process.   It is this very thing, in our opinion, that is largely responsible for the indifference and apathy as to missions which have settled over so large a section of the Church, since it is only natural to feel that it matters little whether one does much or little to aid an enterprise which looks ahead to future generations for its completion.

The other conception of the missionary program is quite different.   It regards the present age of missions as a preparatory and not a final one, and its goal not world conversion but world-wide evangelization, or gospel witnessing. Indeed the word "witness," used so prominently in this connection in the New Testament (e.g., Acts 1:8; Matt. 24:14), furnishes the keynote for the present missionary program, according to this view.   The task enjoined is seen to be not that of bringing the whole world to Christ, but bringing Christ to the whole world; not converting all nations as such, but calling out of all nations a people for His name, who shall constitute the true Church or Bride of Christ made ready for His return.

Perhaps the central passage of Scripture, among many others, upon which this view is based, is Acts 15:12-18, which gives an account of the first apostolic, or missionary, council at Jerusalem.   The whole program of Gentile missions and ingathering is here explicitly set forth, consisting of (1) *a present elective stage,* following Israel's rejection after Christ's first coming, and (2) *a future universal stage,* following Israel's restoration after Christ's second coming. It is important to note, as concerning this view of the Church's present missionary task, not only its comprehensiveness in reaching out to the uttermost part of the earth, but also its delimitation, in that it finds the goal not in a final and complete harvest of world conversion, but in a firstfruits harvest of souls called out from among all nations.

It is at once obvious that the outlook of this kind of a program is radically different from that of the program previously outlined. For while we saw in the one case the necessity for an indefinite postponement of the result aimed at, tending to discouragement and loss of zeal, we see in this case the practical possibility of the completion of the task within the present generation, and this tending to inspire hope, kindle zeal and stimulate effort. Could anything be more inspiring to a missionary society than the hope that it might have the high privilege of penetrating the last unoccupied region and thus completing the world-wide witness for Christ? Could anything be sweeter to the lonely pioneer, far away on some distant outpost of the mission field, than the thought that in the gracious providence of God it might be his high honor to bring in the last soul to complete the "people for His name" and thus prepare the way for his Lord's return?

God's children, even His missionaries, do not see alike regarding the nature of the divine program and the Church's appointed task in this dispensation, nor need their differences of view stand in the way of true Christian fellowship and mutual appreciation. But the sincere conviction is here expressed, in all generosity of spirit, that nothing contributes more to stimulating missionary zeal in the home churches, and enheartening and sustaining the toilers on the fields yonder, than the cherishing of the blessed hope of the personal return of Christ, and seeing the relation between the task of giving the gospel to the whole world and the realization of that blessed hope.

A Mighty Revival of Spiritual Life. There are other things which might well be given a place in our consideration of vital missionary factors at the home end. Intercessory prayer comes particularly to mind as fundamental and vital. But when we mention the need of a mighty revival of spiritual life we strike at the deepest root of all, one which really underlies prayer, sacrificial giving and the other things which might be spoken of.

The late Dr. Andrew Murray followed with close scrutiny the deliberations of the great Ecumenical Missionary Conference in 1900, and then with keen spiritual discernment wrote "The Key to the Missionary Problem." He showed that the root of the whole matter lay far below all considerations of strategy, coöperation, method and the like; that it lay in *the spiritual state of the Church*. He reminded his readers that the Great Commission was given in connection with Pentecost, and that its fulfillment was made entirely dependent upon the reality of a pentecostal experience. "The pentecostal commission can only be carried out by a pentecostal church, in pentecostal power." Then, in successive chapters, he went on to show the intimate relation of Moravian Missions to the spiritual revival under Zinzendorf, of the China Inland Mission to the faith and power which emanated from the holy life of Hudson Taylor, and of the great forward movement of the Church Missionary Society, a generation ago, to the mighty spiritual quickening which attended the visit of Moody to Cambridge, and also the early years of the Keswick Convention.

Dr. A. J. Gordon, in his illuminating book, "The Holy Spirit in Missions," expressed the same truth in strikingly similar terms. Starting with Acts 1 : 8 as laying down the relation between Pentecost and Missions, he proceeded to trace the succeeding spiritual and missionary histories of the Church in their bearing one upon the other. The following sentences are illustrative of his impressive line of thought: "The history of later missions has been, in this respect, the repeated facsimile of this history of apostolical missions. . . . Whenever, in any century, whether in a single heart or in a company of believers, there has been a fresh effusion of the Spirit, there has followed inevitably a fresh endeavor in the work of evangelizing the world. . . . I think it would be no exaggeration to affirm that, just as distinctly as we can trace the missionary movement of the first century to the little company who were baptized with the Holy Ghost on the Day of Pentecost, so clearly can we find the spring and inspiration of the missionary movement of the eighteenth century in the heart of that little band of German Pietists of whom Spener and Franke were the most conspicuous leaders. . . . Life begets activity, and

there could not fail to be a missionary revival as the out-
come of this evangelical revival."

Then follows, in his book, the citation of instance after
instance down through the years of how new missionary
impulse has owed its origin to a revival of spiritual life.
The evangelical revival of Wesley and Whitefield quickened
the pulse of foreign missions in England. Moravianism
was born out of Pietism in Germany. A fresh vision of
God which brought a rich new experience to the hearts of
Jonathan Edwards and David Brainerd caused them, like
Isaiah of old, to cry, "Here am I, send me," and sent them
forth to the North American Indians. A powerful revival
in Bavaria brought to Gossner a wonderful anointing of the
Holy Spirit, and thereupon he became "the father of faith
missions."

Illustrations of this sort could be multiplied were there
further need. But surely enough has been said to prove that
true missionary zeal can spring only from real spiritual life,
and that a genuine spiritual revival invariably leads to quickened missionary concern and endeavor. Just as Pentecost
had to precede Missions in the apostolic days, as constituting
the essential preparation for the work, so the pentecostal
experience of the Holy Spirit's infilling has been the fore-
runner of every fresh missionary inspiration and advance
in the centuries that have followed. And further, it is the
only thing which can bring that new missionary vision, conviction and passion, so manifestly needed to-day, to enable
the Church to hearken to the world's cry of need and to
see and seize the golden opportunities of the present missionary situation.

A mighty spiritual revival in the Church of Christ is the
fundamental need of the hour; it is the only thing that will
avail. In view of the tremendous issues involved, both to
an embarrassed Church and to a dying world, unceasing
prayer should ascend to God day and night, from every loyal
and discerning heart, for such a revival. When it comes the
problems of missionary recruits and missionary support will
be solved. When it comes a new volume of missionary
intercession will release the omnipotence of God, before
which every obstacle will give way, every opposing force
will be rendered impotent, the whole enterprise of world

evangelization will move onward to its consummation, and "the ends of the earth shall see the salvation of our God."

QUESTIONS

1. Discuss five favorable features, and three unfavorable features, of large bearing upon the missionary enterprise to-day at its field end, giving concrete facts by way of illustration.

2. Applying to the enterprise the imagery of Isaiah 54:2, 3:

(a) To which ends of the enterprise respectively would the expressions "lengthen thy cords" and "strengthen thy stakes" appropriately belong?

(b) Upon which end would the hope of further advance seem primarily to depend to-day?

(c) Suggest four vital "stakes" which need to be "strengthened" at home, expanding the lesson under each heading.

SUMMARY OF PROTESTANT WORLD MISSIONS

(BASED UPON "STATISTICAL SURVEY OF THE WORLD MISSION," 1938)

Foreign missionaries	27,577
Residence stations	6,172
Native workers	203,468
Organized churches	55,395
Communicant members	6,045,726
Christian community (Communicants, baptized non-communicants and others under Christian instruction)	13,036,354
Contributions of native churches	8,305,495
Income on field for Educational, Medical, and other work	20,433,295
Contributions from home through Societies	30,938,450
World contributions for Foreign Missions	59,677,240

RATIO OF PROTESTANT MISSIONARIES TO POPULATION

	missionaries per million
Asia	13
Japan	*12*
Korea	*20*
China	*13*
India	*14*
Arabia	*6*
Palestine	*172*
South America	21
Central America, Mexico and West Indies	30
Africa	56
Oceania	421

Total for world field—19 missionaries per million.

"He is waiting with long patience
    For His crowning day,
For that kingdom which shall never
    Pass away.

And till every tribe and nation
    Bow before His throne,
He expecteth loyal service
    From His own.

He expecteth—but He heareth
    Still the bitter cry
From earth's millions, 'Come and help us,
    For we die.'

He expecteth—doth He see us
    Busy here and there,
Heedless of those pleading accents
    Of despair?

Shall we, dare we disappoint Him?
    Brethren, let us rise!
He who died for us is watching
    From the skies.

Watching till His royal banner
    Floateth far and wide,
Till He seeth of His travail,
    Satisfied!"

—*Selected.*

BIBLIOGRAPHY

Missionary literature has grown to comprise an immense number of books dealing with the various fields and phases of the missionary enterprise. Limitation of space makes possible the mention here of only a very few, and those have been selected which the author thinks may prove most helpful to the student or general reader in amplifying the necessarily brief record of missions contained in the present volume. The selection purposely includes some old standard volumes giving the records of the past as well as more recent books dealing with present-day missions.

The Student Volunteer Movement and Missionary Education Movement, both of New York City, periodically issue selected lists of new books, but the Missionary Research Library, 3041 Broadway, New York City, has the most complete collection of missionary books and magazines on file anywhere in North America, if not in the world, and is prepared to furnish accurate information upon any field or aspect of missions.

HISTORICAL AND GENERAL

BARNES, L. C. *Two Thousand Years of Missions before Carey.* 1900. Christian Culture Club.

BLISS, E. M. *The Missionary Enterprise.* 1908. Revell.

CARVER, WM. O. *The Course of Christian Missions.* 1932. Revell.

CAVERT, SAMUEL McC. *The Church Faces the World.* 1939. Round Table Press.

DENNIS, JAS. S. *Christian Missions and Social Progress.* 3 vols. 1897. Revell.

Directory of World Missions. J. I. Parker (Ed.). 1938. International Missionary Council.

Foreign Missions Conference of North America, Report of. (Annual.) Foreign Missions Conference.

HODGKINS, L. M. *Via Christi.* 1903. Macmillan.

International Missionary Council, The Jerusalem Meeting of. 8 vols. 1928. International Missionary Council.

Interpretative Statistical Survey of the World Mission of the Christian Church. J. I. Parker (Ed.). 1938. International Missionary Council.

LATOURETTE, K. S. *A History of the Expansion of Christianity:* vol. I (First Five Centuries). 1937; vol. II (A.D. 500-1500). 1938. Harper.

LATOURETTE, K. S. *Missions Tomorrow.* 1936. Harper.

Laymen's Foreign Missions Inquiry; Supplementary Series. (Fact Finders' vols.) O. A. Petty (Ed.). 1933. Harper.

MATHEWS, BASIL. *Through Tragedy to Triumph* (The World Church in the World Crisis). 1939. Friendship Press.

McAFEE, CLELAND B. *Changing Foreign Missions.* 1927. Revell.

373

MOTT, JOHN R. *Present-day Challenge to the World Missions of Christianity.* 1931. Cokesbury.

PHILLIPS, G. E. *The Gospel in the World.* 1939. Duckworth.

SMITH, GEORGE. *A Short History of Christian Missions.* 1913. T. and T. Clark.

SPEER, R. E. *Missions and Modern History.* 2 vols. 1904. Revell.

Task of the Christian Church: A World Survey. 1926. World Dominion Press.

The World Mission of the Church. 1939. International Missionary Council.

WARK, HOMER E. *A New Era of Missions.* 1929. Revell.

WARNECK, G. *History of Protestant Missions.* 1904. Revell.

World Missionary Atlas (1925). Institute on Social and Religious Surveys.

World Missionary Conference. 9 vols. 1910. Revell.

World Survey (1920). Interchurch World Movement of N. A.

BIBLE BASIS OF MISSIONS

ALLEN, ROLAND. *Missionary Methods: St. Paul's or Ours.* 1912. Robert Scott.

CARVER, WM. O. *Missions in the Plan of the Ages.* 1909. Revell.

CARVER, WM. O. *The Bible a Missionary Message.* 1921. Revell.

COOK, EDMUND F. *The Missionary Message of the Bible.* 1924. Lamar & Barton.

MARTIN, C. *Apostolic and Modern Missions.* 1898. Revell.

McLEAN, ARCHIBALD. *The Primacy of the Missionary.* 1920. Christian Board of Publication, St. Louis.

McLEAN, ARCHIBALD. *Where the Book Speaks.* 1907. Revell.

MISSIONARY APOLOGETIC AND APPEAL

BROWN, ARTHUR J. *The Foreign Missionary.* 1907. Revell.

BROWN, ARTHUR J. *The Why and How of Foreign Missions.* 1921. Missionary Education Movement.

CABLE and FRENCH. *Ambassadors for Christ.* 1935. Hodder & Stoughton.

GORDON, A. J. *The Holy Spirit in Missions.* 1893. Revell.

KRAEMER, HENDRIK. *The Christian Message in a Non-Christian World.* 1938. Harper.

MACNICOL, N. *Is Christianity Unique?* 1936. Student Volunteer Movement.

MONTGOMERY, HELEN B. *Prayer and Missions.* 1924. Central Committee on United Study of Missions.

MOTT, JOHN R. *The Pastor and Modern Missions.* 1904. Student Volunteer Movement.

MURRAY, ANDREW. *The Key to the Missionary Problem.* 1901. American Tract Society.

PATTON, C. H. *The Business of Missions.* 1924. Macmillan.

PIERSON, ARTHUR T. *The New Acts of the Apostles.* 1894. Revell.

SMITH, E. W. *The Desire of All Nations.* 1928. Harper.

SPEER, R. E. *Missionary Principles and Practice.* 1902. Revell.

SPEER, R. E. *The Church and Missions.* 1926. Doran.

SPEER, R. E. *The Gospel and the New World.* 1919. Revell.

WARBURTON, STACY R. *Making a Missionary Church.* 1924. Judson Press.

ZWEMER, S. M. *Thinking Missions with Christ.* 1934. Zondervan.

COMPARATIVE RELIGIONS

CASH, W. W. *Christendom and Islam: Their Contacts and Cultures Down the Centuries.* 1937. Student Christian Movement.

KELLOGG, S. H. *A Handbook of Comparative Religion.* 1905. Student Volunteer Movement.

MARSHALL, E. A. *Christianity and Non-Christian Religions Compared.* 1910. Bible Institute Colportage Association.

McLEISH, A. *Jesus Christ and World Evangelization.* 1934. J. C. Winston.

RICHARDS, E. H. and others, editors. *Religions of Mission Fields as Viewed by Protestant Missionaries.* 1905. Student Volunteer Movement.

SMITH, E. W. *The Religion of Lower Races.* 1923. Macmillan.

SOOTHILL, W. E. *The Three Religions of China.* 1913. Doran.

SPEER, R. E. *The Finality of Jesus Christ.* 1933. Revell.

SPEER, R. E. *The Light of the World.* 1911. Macmillan.

TISDALL, W. ST. C. *Christianity and Other Faiths.* 1912. Revell.

ZWEMER, S. M. *Christianity the Final Religion.* 1920. Eerdmans-Sevensma Co.

MEDICAL MISSIONS

BALME, HAROLD. *China and Modern Medicine.* 1921. Union Committee for Missionary Education, London.

DODD, E. M. *How Far to the Nearest Doctor?* 1933. Friendship Press.

HAMILTON, F. E. and COCHRANE, T. *Basic Principles in Education and Medical Mission Work.* 1928. World Dominion Press.

LAMBUTH, W. R. *Medical Missions: The Two-fold Task.* 1920. Student Volunteer Movement.

MOORSHEAD, R. F. *Heal the Sick.* 1929. Carey Press.

SCHWEITZER, A. *On the Edge of the Primeval Forest.* 1929. A. and C. Black.

SCHWEITZER, A. *The Forest Hospital at Lambarene.* 1931. Henry Holt.

TAYLOR, MRS. F. HOWARD. *Guinness of Honan.* 1930. China Inland Mission.

WANLESS, W. *An American Doctor at Work in India.* 1932. Revell.

MISSION FIELDS AND BIOGRAPHIES

INDIA

AZARIAH, V. S., and WHITEHEAD, H. *Christ in the Indian Villages.* 1930. Student Christian Movement.

CARMICHAEL, AMY W. *Things As They Are.* 1906. Revell.

CARMICHAEL, AMY W. *Overweights of Joy.* 1906. Revell.

CAREY, S. P. *Wm. Carey.* 1923. Doran.

CHIROL, SIR VALENTINE. *India, Old and New.* 1921. Macmillan.

CLARK, A. H. *India on the March* (rev. ed.). 1930. Missionary Education Movement.

DYER, HELEN S. *Pandita Ramabai.* 1923. Pickering & Inglis.

EMERSON, G. *Voiceless India.* 1930. Doubleday Doran.

EWING, J. C. R. *A Prince of the Church in India.* 1918. Revell.

HIGGINBOTTOM, S. *The Gospel and the Plow.* 1921. Macmillan.

HOLCOMB, H. H. *Men of Might in India Missions.* 1901. Revell.

JUDSON, EDWARD. *The Life of Adoniram Judson.* 1883. Randolph.

MACNICOL, N. *India in the Dark Wood.* 1930. Edinburgh House.

MAYO, KATHERINE. *Mother India.* 1927. Harcourt, Brace.

MAYO, KATHERINE. *The Face of Mother India.* 1935. Harper.

MCKENZIE, J. (Ed.). *The Christian Task in India.* 1929. Macmillan.

MCLEISH, A. *Christian Progress in Burma.* 1929. World Dominion Press.

PADWICK, C. E. *Henry Martyn: Confessor of the Faith.* 1923. Doran.

PATON, WM. *Alexander Duff, Pioneer of Missionary Education.* 1923. Doran.

PICKETT, J. W. *Christ's Way to India's Heart.* 1937. Lucknow Publishing House.

READ, MARGARET. *The Land and Life of India.* 1934. Edinburgh House.

RICHTER, J. *History of Protestant Missions in India.* 1908. Revell.

SORABJI, C. *India Calling.* 1934. Nisbet.

STREETER, CANON. *The Message of Sadhu Sundar Singh.* 1923. Macmillan.

WARNER, G. L. et al. *Moving Millions; a Pageant of Modern India.* 1938. Missionary Education Movement.

WISER, MRS. C. E. *Behind Mud Walls.* 1930. Harper.

YOUNGHUSBAND, F. *Dawn in India.* 1930. Murray.

SOUTHEASTERN ASIA

BROWN, A. J., and ZWEMER, S. M. *The Nearer and Farther East* (*Moslem Lands, Siam, Burma, Korea*). 1909. Macmillan.

BROWN, A. J. *The Expectation of Siam.* 1925. Woman's Board, Presbyterian Church.

DODD, WM. C. *The Tai Race.* 1923. Torch Press.

IRWIN, E. F. *With Christ in Indo-China.* 1937. Christian Publications.

MCFARLAND, G. B. (Ed.). *Historical Sketch of Protestant Missions in Siam.* 1928. Bangkok Times Press.

ROBBINS, J. C. *Following the Pioneers: A Story of American Baptist Work in India and Burma.* 1922. Judson Press.

CHINA

ANDREW, G. F. *The Crescent in North-West China.* 1921. China Inland Mission.

BASHFORD, JAS. W. *China: An Interpretation.* 1919. Abingdon Press.

BROOMHALL, M. *Hudson Taylor: The Man Who Believed God.* 1929. China Inland Mission.

BROOMHALL, M. *Islam in China.* 1910. China Inland Mission.

BROOMHALL, M. *Robert Morrison: A Master Builder.* 1924. Doran.

BROOMHALL, M. *The Bible in China.* 1934. China Inland Mission.

China Christian Year Book. 1936-37. Missionary Education Movement.

GLOVER, A. E. *A Thousand Miles of Miracle in China.* 1904. Hodder & Stoughton.

HODGKIN, H. T. *China in the Family of Nations.* 1923. Doran.

HOUGHTON, F. *China Calling.* 1936. Inter-Varsity Fellowship.

KUHN, ISOBEL. *Precious Things of the Lasting Hills.* 1938. China Inland Mission.

LATOURETTE, K. S. *A History of Christian Missions in China.* 1929. Macmillan.

LATOURETTE, K. S. *The Development of China.* 1929. Houghton Mifflin.

MACKENZIE, A. R. *Church and Missions in Manchuria.* 1928. World Dominion Press.

MONROE, PAUL. *China a Nation in Evolution.* 1928. Macmillan.

MORTON, T. R. *Today in Manchuria: The Young Church in Crisis.* 1939. Student Christian Movement.

SCOTT, C. E. *China from Within.* 1917. Revell.

STAUFFER, M. T. (Ed.). *The Christian Occupation of China.* 1922. China Continuation Committee, Shanghai.

STIMSON, HENRY L. *The Far Eastern Crisis.* 1936. Harper.

TAYLOR, DR. and MRS. F. HOWARD. *By Faith.* 1938. China Inland Mission.

TAYLOR, DR. and MRS. F. HOWARD. *Hudson Taylor in Early Years. Hudson Taylor and the China Inland Mission.* 2 vols. 1920. Morgan & Scott.

TAYLOR, MRS. F. HOWARD. *Pastor Hsi: Confucian Scholar and Christian.* 1907. China Inland Mission.

TAYLOR, MRS. F. HOWARD. *The Call of China's Great North West.* 1923. China Inland Mission.

TAYLOR, MRS. HOWARD. *The Triumph of John and Betty Stam.* 1935. China Inland Mission.

WILLIAMS, S. WELLS. *The Middle Kingdom.* 1883. Scribner.

JAPAN, KOREA, FORMOSA

AXLING, WM. *Japan on the Upward Trail.* 1923. Missionary Education Movement.

Bishop, Isabella B. *Korea and Her Neighbors.* 1897. Revell.

Brown, Arthur J. *Japan in the World of Today.* 1928. Revell.

Christian Movement in Japan, Korea and Formosa, The. (Annual.) Foreign Missions Conference of N. A.

Clark, C. A. *The Nevius Plan for Mission Work, Illustrated in Korea.* 1937. Christian Literary Society, Seoul.

Fisher, G. M. *Creative Forces in Japan.* 1923. Missionary Education Movement.

Gale, Jas. S. *Korea in Transition.* 1909. Missionary Education Movement.

Griffis, Wm. E. *Verbeck of Japan.* 1900. Revell.

Griffis, Wm. E. *The Mikado's Empire.* 2 vols. 1913. Harper.

Hardy, A. S. *Life and Letters of Joseph Hardy Neesima.* 1891. Houghton Mifflin.

Hulbert, H. *The Passing of Korea.* 1906. Doubleday, Page.

Kagawa, T. *Christ and Japan.* 1934. Friendship Press.

Kanamori, Paul. *Kanamori's Life Story.* 1921. S. S. Times.

Mackay, George L. *From Far Formosa.* 1895. Revell.

McKenzie, F. A. *Korea's Fight for Freedom.* 1919. Revell.

Soltau, T. S. *Korea: The Hermit Nation and Its Response to Christianity.* 1932. World Dominion Press.

Wildes, H. E. *Japan in Crisis.* 1934. Macmillan.

THE NEAR EAST AND MOSLEM WORLD

A Century of Mission Work in Iran (1834-1934). Board of Foreign Missions Presbyterian Church.

Allen, H. E. *The Turkish Transformation.* 1935. University of Chicago Press.

Armstrong, H. *Turkey and Syria Reborn.* 1930. Lane.

Cash, W. Wilson. *The Moslem World in Revolution.* 1926. Edinburgh House.

Coan, F. G. *Yesterdays in Persia and Kurdistan.* 1939. Saunders Studio Press.

Conferences of Christian Work Among Moslems. 1924. International Missionary Committee.

Davis, W. S. *A Short History of the Near East.* 1922. Macmillan.

Dodd, E. M. *Mecca and Beyond.* 1937. Central Committee on Study of Foreign Missions.

Elliott, Mabel E. *Beginning Again at Ararat.* 1924. Revell.

Halidé, Edib. *Turkey Faces West.* 1930. Yale University Press.

Hall, Wm. H. *The Near East Crossroads of the World.* 1920. Interchurch World Movement.

Harrison, Paul W. *The Arab at Home.* 1924. Crowell.

Jenkins, H. D. *An Educational Ambassador to the Near East.* 1925. Revell.

Kohn, Hans. *Nationalism and Imperialism in the Hither East.* 1932. Harcourt, Brace.

McGillivray, M. *The Dawn of a New Era in Syria.* 1920. Revell.

Morgenthau, Henry M. *Ambassador Morgenthau's Story.* 1918. Doubleday, Page.

MOTT, J. R. (Ed.). *The Moslem World To-day.* 1925. Doran.
PHILBY, H. ST. J. B. *Arabia.* 1930. Benn.
PIGOTT, B. A. F. *I. Lilias Trotter.* 1930. Marshall.
RICHTER, J. *History of Protestant Missions in the Near East.* 1910. Revell.
ROBSON, JAS. *Ian Keith Falconer of Arabia.* 1924. Doran.
SHEDD, MARY L. *The Measure of a Man, Wm. A. Shedd of Persia.* 1922. Doran.
SHIELDS, R. F. *Behind the Garden of Allah.* 1937. U. P. Board of Missions.
STORM, HAROLD. *Whither Arabia?* 1938. World Dominion Press.
WATSON, CHARLES R. *In the Valley of the Nile.* 1908. Revell.
WATSON, CHARLES R. *What Is This Moslem World?* 1937. Friendship Press.
WIGRAM, W. A. and E. T. A. *The Cradle of Mankind.* 1922. A. and C. Black.
WILSON, S. G. *Modern Movements Among Moslems.* 1916. Revell.
WOODSMALL, R. F. *Moslem Women Enter a New World.* 1936. Round Table Press.
WYON, O. *An Eastern Palimpsest: A Survey of Turkey, Syria, Palestine and Egypt.* 1927. World Dominion Press.
ZWEMER, S. M. *Across the World of Islam.* 1929. Revell.
ZWEMER, S. M. *The Disintegration of Islam.* 1916. Revell.
ZWEMER, S. M. *The Law of Apostasy in Islam.* 1924. Marshall Bros.

CENTRAL ASIA

BELL, CHARLES. *Tibet, Past and Present.* 1924. Clarendon Press.
CABLE and FRENCH. *A Desert Journal.* 1934. Constable.
CABLE and FRENCH. *Through Jade Gate and Central Asia.* 1927. Hodder & Stoughton.
CABLE, MILDRED, et al. *The Challenge of Central Asia.* 1929. World Dominion Press.
EKVALL, R. B. *Gateway to Tibet.* 1938. Christian Publications.
ETHERTON, P. T. *In the Heart of Asia.* 1926. Houghton Mifflin.
HEDIN, SVEN. *Through Asia.* 2 vols. 1898. Harper.
HUTTON, J. E. *A Story of Moravian Missions* (Section on Western Tibet). 1922. Moravian Publication Office.
LEARNER, F. D. *Rusty Hinges.* 1933. China Inland Mission.
MACMUNN, G. *Afghanistan, from Darius to Amanullah.* 1929. Bell.
PENNELL, T. L. *Among the Wild Tribes of the Afghan Frontier.* 1909. Lippincott.
SHELTON, FLORA B. *Shelton of Tibet.* 1923. Doran.

AFRICA

BAKER, ERNEST. *Life and Explorations of Frederick S. Arnot.* 1923. Seeley Service.
BLAIKIE, W. G. *The Personal Life of David Livingstone.* 1880. Revell.

CASH, W. WILSON. *The Changing Sudan.* 1930. Church Missionary Society.

COOKSEY, J. J. *The Land of the Vanished Church: Survey of North Africa.* 1929. World Dominion Press.

CRAWFORD, DAN. *Thinking Black.* 1912. Doran.

CRAWFORD, DAN. *Back to the Long Grass.* 1923. Doran.

DAVIS, J. M. *Modern Industry and the African.* 1933. Macmillan.

DU PLESSIS, J. *The Life of Andrew Murray of South Africa.* 1919. Marshall Bros.

DU PLESSIS, J. *The Evangelization of Pagan Africa.* 1930. Juta, Capetown.

FRASER, AGNES R. *Donald Fraser of Livingstonia.* 1934. Hodder & Stoughton.

GALE, W. K. *Church Planting in Madagascar.* 1937. World Dominion Press.

LIVINGSTONE, W. P. *Mary Slessor of Calabar.* 1916. Harper.

LIVINGSTONE, W. P. *Robert Laws of Livingstonia.* 1922. Doran.

Mackay of Uganda, The Story of the Life of. By his Sister. 1891. Doran.

MACKENZIE, JEAN. *Black Sheep.* 1916. Houghton Mifflin.

MATHEWS, BASIL. *Consider Africa.* 1936. Friendship Press.

MAXWELL, J. L. *Nigeria.* 1929. World Dominion Press.

MCLEISH, A. *Light and Darkness in East Africa.* 1927. World Dominion Press.

MILLER, W. R. *Yesterday and Tomorrow in Northern Nigeria.* 1938. Student Christian Movement.

MOREL, E. D. *The Black Man's Burden.* 1920. Huebsch.

OLDHAM, J. H. *White and Black in Africa.* 1930. Longmans.

PADWICK, C. E. *Temple Gairdner of Cairo.* 1929. Macmillan.

PHILLIPS, R. E. *The Bantu Are Coming.* 1930. Student Volunteer Movement.

RICHTER, J. *Tanganyika and Its Future.* 1934. World Dominion Press.

ROOME, W. J. W. *Can Africa Be Won?* 1927. Black.

ROOME, W. J. W. *Through Central Africa.* 1930. Revell.

ROOME, W. J. W. *A Great Emancipation: A Survey of Nyasaland.* 1926. World Dominion Press.

ROOME, W. J. W. *Through the Lands of Nyanza.* 1930. Marshall.

ROSEBERRY, R. S. *The Niger Vision.* 1935. Christian Publications.

SCHWEITZER, A. *Out of My Life and Thought.* 1933. Henry Holt.

SHAW, MABEL. *God's Candlelights.* 1933. Edinburgh House.

SIBREE, J. *Fifty Years in Madagascar.* 1924. Houghton Mifflin.

SMITH, EDWIN W. *Aggrey of Africa.* 1929. Student Christian Movement.

SOUTHON, A. E. *Khama the Conqueror.* 1930. Atlantis Press.

TILSEY, G. E. *Dan Crawford, Missionary and Pioneer.* 1929. Oliphants.

WELLS, JAS. *Stewart of Lovedale.* 1909. Revell.

WESTERMANN, DIEDRICH. *The African Today and Tomorrow.* (Revised edition.) 1934. Oxford University Press.

LATIN AMERICA

BROWNING, W. E. *The River Plate Republics.* 1928. World Dominion Press.

BROWNING, W. E. *New Days in Latin America.* 1925. Missionary Education Movement.

BROWNING, W. E. *Roman Christianity in Latin America.* 1924. Revell.

BROWNING, W. E., et al. *The West Coast Republics of South America: Chile, Peru, Bolivia.* 1930. World Dominion Press.

DAWSON, THOS. C. *South American Republics.* 2 vols. 1910. Putnam.

ENOCK, C. R. *The Republics of Central and South America.* 1913. Scribner.

GRUBB, K. G. *An Advancing Church in Latin America.* 1936. World Dominion Press.

GRUBB, K. G. *Lowland Indians of Amazonia.* 1927. World Dominion Press.

HAY, ALEX. R. *The Indians of South America and the Gospel.* 1928. Revell.

INMAN, S. G. *Latin America, Its Place in World Life.* 1937. Willett, Clark.

JORDAN, W. F. *Central American Indians and the Bible.* 1926. Revell.

JORDAN, W. F. *Crusading in the West Indies.* 1922. Revell.

JORDAN, W. F. *Glimpses of Indian America.* 1923. Revell.

MACKAY, J. A. *That Other America.* 1935. Friendship Press.

Panama Congress on Christian Work in Latin America. 3 vols. 1916. Missionary Education Movement.

PARKES, H. B. *A History of Mexico.* 1938. Houghton Mifflin.

Report of Congress on Christian Work in South America. 1925. Revell.

ROSS, E. A. *South of Panama.* 1915. Century Company.

SPEER, R. E. *South American Problems.* 1914. Holt.

STOWELL, J. S. *Between the Americas.* 1930. Missionary Education Movement.

WHEELER, W. R. and BROWNING, W. E. *Modern Missions on the Spanish Main.* 1925. Westminster Press.

WHEELER, W. R., et al. *Modern Missions in Mexico.* 1925. Westminster Press.

WHEELER, W. R., et al. *Modern Missions in Chile and Brazil.* 1926. Westminster Press.

OCEANIA

BEAVER, W. W. *Unexplored New Guinea.* 1919. Seeley Service.

BRAIN, BELLE M. *The Transformation of Hawaii.* 1898. Revell.

BROWN, ARTHUR J. *The New Era in the Philippines.* 1903. Revell.

BURTON, J. W. *Missionary Survey of the Pacific Islands.* 1930. World Dominion Press.

COLWELL, JAMES. *A Century in the Pacific.* 1915. Kelly.

ELLIS, JAS. J. *John Williams: The Martyr Missionary of Polynesia.* 1889. Revell.

HURST, H. L. *Papuan Journey.* 1938. Angus & Robertson.

LAUBACH, F. C. *The People of the Philippines.* 1925. Doran.

LAUBACH, F. C. *Toward a Literate World.* 1938. Columbia University Press.

OSIAS, CAMILO and LORENZANA AVELINA. *Evangelical Christianity in the Philippines.* 1931. U. B. Publishing House.

PALMER, A. W. *The Human Side of Hawaii.* 1924. Pilgrim Press.

PATON, FRANK L. *The Triumph of the Gospel in the New Hebrides.* 1908. Doran.

PATON, FRANK L. *The Kingdom in the Pacific.* 1913. United Council for Missionary Education.

PATON, F. H. L. *Patteson of Melanesia.* 1930. Society for Promoting Christian Knowledge.

PATON, JAS. *John G. Paton, an Autobiography.* 1907. Doran.

RAUWS, J. *Netherlands India.* 1935. World Dominion Press.

SMALL, ALEX. *Chalmers of New Guinea.* 1924. Doran.

WARNECK, JOH. *The Living Christ and Dying Heathenism* (On Sumatra). 1910. Revell.

WORCESTER, DEAN C. *The Philippine Islands and Their People.* (New ed.) 1930. Macmillan.

YOUNG, F. S. H. *Pearls from the Pacific.* 1930. Marshall.

THE JEWS

Christians and Jews: A Report of the Atlantic City Conference. 1931. International Missionary Council.

GIDNEY, W. T. *The Jews and Their Evangelization.* 1907. Student Volunteer Movement.

MATHEWS, B. *The Jew and the World Ferment.* 1935. Friendship Press.

OSTROM, HENRY. *The Jew and His Mission.* 1923. Bible Institute Colportage Association.

PARKES, J. W. *The Jew and His Neighbor.* 1930. Student Christian Movement.

The Christian Approach to the Jew: A Report of Conferences Held at Budapest and Warsaw. 1927. Edinburgh House.

THOMPSON, A. E. *A Century of Jewish Missions.* 1902. Revell.

UNOCCUPIED FIELDS

FAHS, C. H. *The Unfinished Evangelistic Task.* 1928. International Missionary Council.

GRAHAM, J. A. *On the Threshold of Three Closed Lands.* 1897. R. & R. Clark.

SPEER, R. E. *The Unfinished Task of Foreign Missions.* 1926. Revell.

ZWEMER, S. M. *The Unoccupied Mission Fields of Africa and Asia.* 1911. Student Volunteer Movement.

INDEX

Abdul Hamid, 211; massacre of Armenians by, 214.

Abeel, Rev. David, 137.

Abel, Rev. Charles W., work at Kwato, 315.

Abgar, accepts Christianity, 42.

Aboriginal Hill Tribes, in India: Bhils, 98; Karens, 98; Khonds, 98; Khols, 98; Santals, 98.

Aborigines, in Formosa, 174; of Korea, 180.

Abraham, as a missionary, 27.

Abyssinia, 237; first entry of Gospel into, 42; mountains in, 230; Portuguese missionaries in, 235; Roman Catholic missions in, 235; unoccupied fields of, 237.

Abyssinian churches, 234.

Abyssinia Frontiers Mission, 237.

Abyssinia, new emperor of, 237.

Access, difficulty of, 347.

Accessions during Apostolic Period, 39.

Aconcagua, peak in Ecuador, 268.

Acts, The, a missionary textbook, 30.

Addis Abeba, 237.

Aden, 216.

Afghan border, missionary outposts on, 342.

Afghanistan, 341, 343, 344, 348; move to establish trade with America, 342; Persian, language in, 341; Pushtu, language in, 341; recent changes in, 342.

Afghans, at Meshed, Persia, 342.

Africa, 227-262, 348, 361; adaptive methods of work in, 250; aggression of the white man in, 255; area of, 227; black man's country in, 255; Christian converts in, 251; climate of, 230; colonial administration in, 256; deserts of, 230; discovery and exploration of, 234; diseases in, 251, 257; early history of, 233; early Roman Catholic efforts in, 235; European governments in, 256; forests of, 228, 231; indus-

trial education in, 250; Jews in, 328; laid open to missions, 354; lakes of: Nyasa, 228; Tanganyika, 228; Tchad, 228; Victoria Nyanza, 228; liquor question in, 257; medical missions in, 251; mineral wealth of, 231; Inland Mission, missionary stations of, 247; missionary work in, 235; Mohammedan invasion of, 234; mountains of, 230; names of, Afarik, 227; The Dark Continent, 227; native leadership in, 359; natural resources of, 231; neglected areas in, 252; opposing forces from without, 254; the people of, 231; physical features, 228; policy of European Governments in, 255; population of: Chinese imported laborers, 227; Indian, 227; native, 227; white, 227; power of Islam in, 255; railways in, 256; religions of, 232; rivers of: Congo, 228; Niger, 228; Nile, 228; Zambesi, 228; Roman Catholic governments in, 254; opposition to missions in, 254; size of, 227; South, 237-241; steamboat service in, 256; taxation in, 257; telegraph in, 256; unevangelical heart of, 344; unoccupied fields in, 252, 253, 344; volcanic peaks in, 230; Western vice and crime in, 257; Inland Mission, 247, 248.

African slave trade, the open sore of the world, 239.

Africaner, barbarous crimes of, 238.

Agnostics, in Tokyo University, 172.

Aggression of Western nations resented, 361.

Ainu, ancient race in Hokkaido, 154; schools at, 169.

Akbar, founded Mogul Empire, 99.

Alaska, Moravian missions to, 83.

Albigenses, persecution of, 66.

Aleppo, 204; caravan of Armenians

Animism, in Africa, 232; in India, 98.

Aniwa, Paton on Island of, 312.

Annam, protectorate of French Indo-China, 127; Tourane on coast of, 128.

Annamese, in Siam, 123; made accessible, 354; people of French Indo-China, 127.

Annus mirabilis, 95.

Anopheles mosquito, carries malaria, 230.

Ansgar, apostle to Denmark and Sweden, 58; apostle of the North, 59.

Anthony, West Indian negro, 83.

Antioch, a missionary center, 43; captured by Crusaders, 62.

Anti-Christian propaganda in China, 141.

Anti-Semitism, 333.

Apocalypse, seven churches of, 42.

"Apostle of the South Seas," 309.

Apostolic Missions, period of, 30-40.

Appeal, India's, 118.

Appenzeller, Rev. H. G., in Korea, 185.

Arab rulers of Persia, 209.

Arabs, 206; in Africa, 231; in Malaysia, 323.

Arabia, 199, 217, 222, 301, 348; early churches in, 42; extension during apostolic period, 38; extension during early church period, 41; missions in, 216; new open door in, 355; territory of, unevangelized, 225; the war in, 212.

"Arabia for the Arabians," 361.

"Arabia, the Cradle of Islam," book by Dr. Zwemer, 202.

Arabic, Bible in, 344.

Araucanian Indians, 289.

Areas, neglected, in Near East, 220.

Argentina, 274; climate of, 269; European characteristics of people of, 264; immigration into, 286; missions in, 286; progressive republic, 273; size of, 268; unoccupied fields in, 286.

Armenia, 199, 217; cradle of the human race, 200; massacres in, 221; Russian, unevangelized, 224.

Armenian Church, 215.

Armenian Question, miscarries, 221.

Armenians, accept Christianity, 42; first Christian nation, 205; history of, 204; persecutions and massacres of, 205.

Armistice, 200.

"Arrow War," 138, 140.

Aryans, in India, 98.

Ashmore, Dr. William, 139.

Asia, 348, 361; Japan's influence over, 173; Jews in, 328; heart of, unevangelized, 338; savage tribes in, 348; southeastern, 120; unoccupied fields in, 338.

Asia Minor, 199, 217, 365; control of, by Mustapha Kemal, 222; early spread of Mohammedanism in, 55; extension during early church period, 41; missionary tour of Paul in, 38; neglected districts of, 225.

Assam, in India, 98; missionary work of, 120; people of, 120; population of, 120; religion of, 120.

Assisi, Francis of, 65; in Morocco, 65.

Atahualpa, King of Incas, 272.

Atheists, in Tokyo University, 172.

Atrocities, rubber, in Congo, 256; Turkish war, 212.

Attitude, changed, of Eastern Peoples toward Missionaries, 356.

Auckland, 312.

August Francke, 76.

Austral Islands, 298.

Australasia, Jews in, 328.

Australia, Moravian missions to, 83.

Australian Anglicans, in New Guinea, 315.

Australian Presbyterian Society, in Korea, 185.

Austria, first treaty with Korea, 182; Jews in, 328.

Aymaras, tribe in Bolivia, 289.

Azerbaijan, 199; unevangelized, 224.

Aztec Empire, overthrown by Cortez, 272.

Aztecs, 271.

Babylon to Spain, covered by missionary work, 39.

Baghdad, 201, 217, 223.